Applied Business

A2

Charlotte Davies Peggy McGregor Chris Nuttall Mark Shorey

Collins

William Collins' dream of knowledge for all began with the publication of his first book in 1819. A self-educated mill worker, he not only enriched millions of lives, but also founded a flourishing publishing house. Today, staying true to this spirit, Collins books are packed with inspiration, innovation and practical expertise. They place you at the centre of a world of possibility and give you exactly what you need to explore it.

Collins. Do more.

Published by Collins
An imprint of HarperCollinsPublishers
77–85 Fulham Palace Road
Hammersmith
London
W6 8JB

Browse the complete Collins catalogue at
www.collinseducation.com

© HarperCollinsPublishers Limited 2006

10 9 8 7 6 5 4 3 2 1

ISBN-13 978 0 00 720041 2

ISBN-10 0 00 720041 2

British Library Cataloguing in Publication Data

A Catalogue record for this publication is available from the British Library

Commissioned by Graham Bradbury

Cover design by Blue Pig Design Limited

Cover picture courtesy of Corbis

Series design by Patricia Briggs

Book design and project management by DSM Partnership

Additional material by Christine Swales and Paul Stirner

Indexed by Marie Lorimer

Picture research by Thelma Gilbert

Production by Sarah Robinson

Printed and bound by Butler and Tanner Ltd, Frome

This high quality material is endorsed by Edexcel and has been through a rigorous quality assurance programme to ensure that it is a suitable companion to the specification for both learners and teachers.

This does not mean that its contents will be used verbatim when setting examinations nor is it to be read as being the official specification – a copy of which is available at www.edexcel.org.uk.

Acknowledgements

The authors and publisher would like to thank the following for permission to reproduce photographs and other material:

Advertising Archives: p90–1, p114, p117, p196, p285.

Alamy: p14, p41, p48–9, p50, p77, p83, p84, p203, p216, p221, p232–3, p278, p297, p300.

Avia: p86–8.

Anthony Blake Picture Library: p196.

Ecological Services Ltd: p148-9, p169.

Empics: p69, p94, p174, p188–9, p212, p231, p270–1, p277.

FireAngel: p12.

Sally & Richard Greenhill: p38, p242, p247, p260.

Eric Hands: p46.

Lush Products: p150.

Steve Moulds: p146–147

M&S: p55, p201.

Nike: p229.

Oxfam: p234.

Photofusion: p236.

Photos.com: p15, p24, p58, p70.

Red Raven: p10.

Rex Features: p8–9, p17, p107, p190, p192, p194, p219, p210, p212, p275, p291, p299.

Science & Society Picture Library: p100, p301.

Roger Scruton: p13, p27, p37, p57, p113, p118, p124, p129, p198, p284, p287.

Tesco: p34, p75, p108, p197, p303.

Thames Water: p272.

Michael Upchurch: p245.

Every effort has been made to contact copyright holders, but if any have been inadvertantley overlooked, the publishers will be pleased to make the necessary arrangements at the first opportunity.

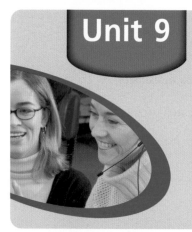

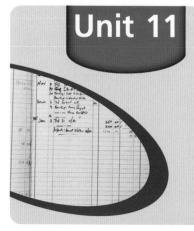

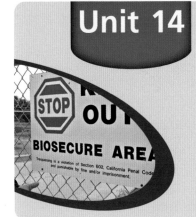

About this book

Welcome to A2 Applied Business. This textbook is written specifically for students taking the Edexcel Applied Business awards and covers everything you will need to know to complete either the single or double award (see table below).

Single award	
AS-level units	**A2-level units**
■ All units are compulsory	■ Unit 8 (compulsory)
Unit 1 Investigating People at Work (External test)	**plus** two more units from 9 to 14
Unit 2 Investigating Business (Internal assessment)	
Unit 3 Investigating Marketing (Internal assessment)	
Double award	
AS-level units	**A2-level units**
■ Units 1, 2 and 3	■ Units 8 and 10 (compulsory)
■ **plus** Unit 6 (compulsory)	■ plus five more from the remaining units
■ **plus** two units from 4, 5 or 7	Unit 8 Business Development (External test)
Unit 4 Investigating Electronic Business (Internal assessment)	Unit 9 Managing and Developing People (Internal assessment)
Unit 5 Investigating Customer Service (Internal assessment)	Unit 10 Marketing Decisions (External test)
Unit 6 Investigating Promotion (External test)	Unit 11 Impact of Finances on Business Decisions (Internal assessment)
Unit 7 Investigating Enterprise (Internal assessment)	Unit 12 Internal Dimensions of Business (Internal assessment)
	Unit 13 Organising an Event (Internal assessment)
	Unit 14 External Influences on Business (Internal assessment)

■ To gain a single award you must successfully complete three AS-level units plus three A2-level units, which must include the compulsory units.

■ To gain a double award you must successfully complete six AS-level units plus six A2-level units, which must include the compulsory units.

Your teacher will explain the combination of units you require to complete the award for which you are studying.

The assessment of your knowledge and understanding of the different units will be follow the same pattern as your AS-level award:

■ an assignment that is written and marked by your teacher (internal assessment)

■ a written examination lasting one and half hours, which is written and marked by Edexcel, your awarding body (external test)

Collins Applied Business A2 for Edexcel is divided into seven units and each unit in this book corresponds to a unit of the Edexcel A2 Applied Business award. The units in this book are divided into topics and each topic provides a manageable chunk of learning covering the subject content of an Edexcel A2-level unit. The contents list at the beginning of this book and at the start of each unit will show you how the topics correspond to the Edexcel Applied Business A2-level specification.

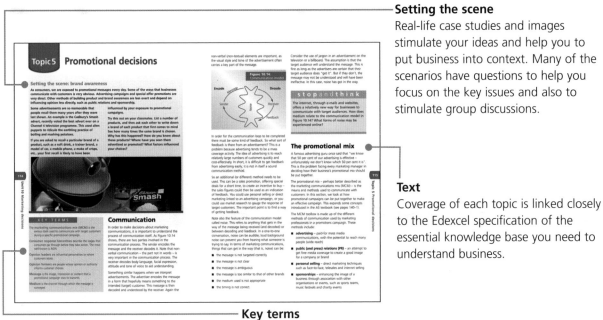

Setting the scene
Real-life case studies and images stimulate your ideas and help you to put business into context. Many of the scenarios have questions to help you focus on the key issues and also to stimulate group discussions.

Text
Coverage of each topic is linked closely to the Edexcel specification of the essential knowledge base you need to understand business.

Key terms
The specialist terminology used in business is explained in simple terms.

Business practice
A variety of case studies based on real-life business, followed by questions on the key issues, allow you to apply your newly acquired knowledge.

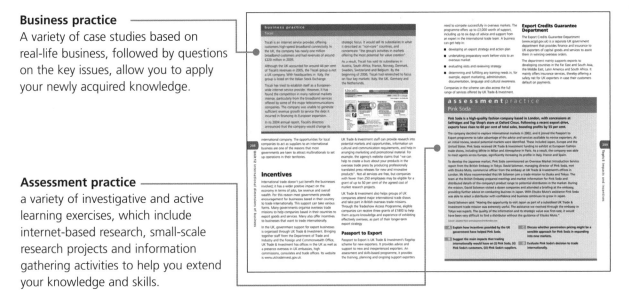

Assessment practice
a variety of investigative and active learning exercises, which include internet-based research, small-scale research projects and information gathering activities to help you extend your knowledge and skills.

Good luck with your GCE A2-level studies. This book provides you with interesting, supportive and motivating learning materials that we hope will help you to succeed in your applied business course.

BUSINESSES OPERATE IN A COMPETITIVE ENVIRONMENT. TO SUCCEED, business owners and managers need to be innovative and resourceful. They need to be able to respond to a variety of internal and external pressures.

This unit considers business development. The focus is on the processes and planning involved in establishing a new business, taking you from the initial ideas through to a fully operational business. In investigating business development, the unit considers:

- the business idea
- resource and quality issues
- financial resources
- feasibility and evaluation.

Throughout the unit, the concepts are illustrated using real business examples. The featured examples are not household names, but small enterprises (many recently established) that are developing their businesses for real. The names of the owners and the businesses have sometimes been changed to protect confidentiality.

Business development

Introducing business development

Setting the scene: Red Raven Industries

Red Raven is an extreme sports component company. Based in Northern Ireland, the company is the brainchild of Jonathan Knight. With a passion for cycling and an eye for good business planning, he has taken his business idea all the way to develop a successful company.

Knight is a former Northern Ireland downhill racing champion. He reckons he knows how performance in his sport can be raised through better design of bike components.

Red Raven's mission is "to innovate and push the sport (cycling) to new levels, while pushing riders and technology beyond current limits". By making extreme bike racing products to a higher specification, the company also hopes to make the sport safer.

The company's main target for its products are high-performance cyclists. It distributes its goods by mail order and has an online ordering service. Its products are also available through several highly specialised retail outlets.

Red Raven uses a range of media to promote the business, including sponsorship of events, use of the internet and e-commerce, and involvement in business competitions.

Through using his expertise and contacts in the cycling industry, Jonathan Knight has built up a successful niche business for himself. In 2005, Jonathan Knight was named Northern Ireland's Shell LiveWIRE young entrepreneur of the year.

For more information, visit Red Raven's website at www.redravenindustries.com

KEY TERMS

SMEs is an abbreviation for small and medium-sized enterprises. The EU classifies SMEs into three types: micro enterprises, with fewer than 10 employees; small businesses with fewer than 50 employees; and medium-sized businesses with fewer than 250 employees.

Unincorporated businesses are businesses operating as either sole traders or partnerships. The owners of unincorporated businesses trade in their own right and have unlimited liability for the debts of the business.

Enterprise culture describes a society that has a positive attitude towards business, and in which a significant proportion of the population are willing to set up their own businesses. (See pages 288–9 of your AS textbook.)

The importance of business development

The business sections of the media tend to focus on large established companies. By definition, these are high-profile businesses – the companies that are quoted in the leading share price indices. However, most economists agree that smaller businesses, particularly new and developing businesses, are crucial to the long-term success of any economy. They argue that the industries of the future will emerge from the small business sector. That is why the United Nations Economic Commission for Europe describes SMEs as "the engine of economic development".

In the UK, the Department of Trade and Industry (DTI) reported that the total number of businesses, including small companies, partnerships and sole traders, rose by 260,000 in 2004 to 4.3 million (source: www.dti.gov.uk). This is up from the previous year – 220,000 new businesses were created in 2003 – and represents the strongest net creation figures for new businesses since the DTI began collating this data in 1995.

This is success for government policy. Successive UK governments have sought to encourage small business start-ups. Behind the policy is a belief that small businesses are the lifeblood of a healthy economy, that they contribute to a stronger economic base, and that they have the ability to prosper in a competitive global business environment.

The government also encourages small businesses because they are:

■ a source of employment

■ flexible and innovative

■ responsive to gaps in the market

■ able to accommodate mavericks, people with a passion for a product who might not flourish in a large corporation.

Business planning

Policy-makers recognise that it is not sufficient to simply encourage an enterprise culture. If new entrepreneurs are to succeed, if new businesses are to thrive, then it is critical that they appreciate the central role of planning. As you saw in Unit 2 of the AS course, a business plan is the bedrock of new business development, and it encourages an entrepreneur to think ahead and plan, as far as possible, for the business to be successful.

Writing a business plan will not in itself ensure that a business survives. However, it is an invaluable exercise, forcing entrepreneurs go through planning steps to make sure their business propositions are viable. A business plan draws on concepts, skills and knowledge that have been presented throughout the Applied Business course. These include:

■ doing market research to make sure that planned products and services meet customer needs (covered in Unit 3 of your AS textbook)

■ understanding the market by analysing competitors' products, services and prices (see Unit 3 in your AS textbook)

■ setting clear business aims and objectives (see Unit 1 in your AS textbook)

■ finding sufficient capital to meet the business's short-term and long-term needs (see Unit 11 in this textbook)

■ deciding on the most suitable and tax-efficient structure and form of ownership for the business (see Unit 1 in your AS textbook)

■ identifying the key assets which the business needs to survive (see Unit 2 in your AS textbook)

Assessment

The assessment for this unit requires you to produce a fully developed business plan for a sole trader or a partnership. In doing so, you will be drawing on some of the knowledge and skills you will have developed throughout the entire Applied Business course. The plan needs to be presented as a viable business idea, suitable to support a request for finance for the venture.

This unit will guide you through the production of a business plan, helping you to focus on key areas such as aims and objectives, resources issues, and financial analysis and planning. The business in practice case study in Topic 9 gives you an opportunity to put your knowledge and skills into practice in drawing up a business plan.

Setting the scene: an innovative smoke detector

FireAngel's Plug-In Smoke Alarm is an innovative smoke detector. It is inserted between a pendant light fitting and the bulb, and self-charges from the mains every time the light it is connected to is switched on. This means that users don't have to worry about batteries going flat and the alarm not working, thereby putting people and homes at risk.

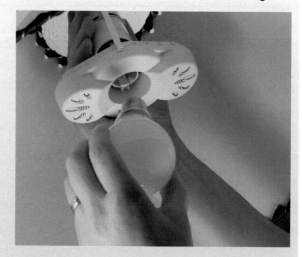

The alarm detector is the brainchild of Sam Tate and Nick Rutter, two design engineering graduates. They set up in business in 1998 to develop their idea further and, in time, to manufacture the commercial product.

Once Sam Tate and Nick Rutter had the initial idea for the mains-powered smoke alarm, they did not immediately assume they had a viable product. Instead, they carried out extensive market research to test and develop their thinking. This research included:

- talking to the fire brigade

- working with the Office of the Deputy Prime Minister (ODPM)

- looking closely at competitors' products

- analysing customer demand and consumer preferences.

Part of this research involved going out on the streets and getting feedback by showing people a prototype of the detector. Responses were collected by asking each interviewee to complete a questionnaire. Price was also considered. The company analysed competitors' pricing strategies and found out what people would be willing to pay for a premium smoke detector.

The Plug-In Smoke Alarm has been a considerable success. It is widely available, and retails at a considerable premium above the prices charged for conventional battery-powered stand-alone detectors.

KEY TERMS

Ideas are the initial thoughts or suggestions that produce a mental picture of a potential product or service.

Innovation is the process of developing new and original goods and services. Examples of innovation include re-engineering an existing product to make it smaller and lighter, using new technology to create an original product like the iPod, or finding a new way of using an existing product.

A **viable** business idea is one that is capable of working successfully, and which makes a profit for the business in the long term.

Product development involves harnessing ideas, innovation, new technology and market research to make a product that meets consumer needs.

Finding ideas

Look around you at the products in your bag, the products and services that are available in high street stores or on the internet. These products don't just materialise: each results from an idea and a business that is prepared to take that idea and develop it into a commercially viable product. But where do people get their business ideas from?

- Is it from comments by friends and families?

- Do they know about a particular subject, and use that knowledge to develop product ideas?

- Do they want to make money, so they try to develop a product that might be very profitable?

- Do they just sit down with the intention of inventing something?

There are huge numbers of new business ideas. What determines whether these become commercial goods and services, and what determines whether these products are going to be successful or fail? There are no easy answers; after all, about 60 per cent of businesses fail within five years of being set up. However, what is crucially important is the way you develop your ideas, and learn from the successes and failures of others.

Having an idea is just the first step on a long road. Business ideas need to be researched further to find out if they are viable, and they all need developing if they are to meet customers' needs. Look at some of the case studies and advice on these websites:

- Shell LiveWIRE (www.shell-livewire.org)
- DTI best practice (www.dti.gov.uk/bestpractice)
- The Prince's Trust (www.princes-trust.org.uk).

Look through these websites and find a case study that you could share with your class and that you think you could copy.

business practice
Catherine's cards

Some people try to develop their hobby into a business. Catherine has been making handmade cards for friends and family for several years. Everyone thinks her cards are very beautiful and far better than the cards on sale in shops. Catherine decided to book a table at a local craft fair to test out her business idea. She had a stock of over 100 cards, with various themes – flowers, birds, landscape. Each card took her about 15 minutes to make, and cost about £0.75 in materials. Catherine prices the cards at £3 each.

At the craft fair Catherine faced stiff competition. There were six other stalls selling cards, and most had cards that are either substantially cheaper than hers or had some very special feature. One stall stocked a card manufacturer's products, and the franchisee operating this stall had been well trained in sales techniques. Another stall was run by a couple as a hobby – it gave them an opportunity to do something together. They were just interested in covering the £30 cost of the stall and the cost of their materials.

By the end of the day, Catherine had not even covered her costs and she went home, abandoning the idea of a business altogether.

If Catherine is serious about starting a business she would need to take several vital steps:

- research her competitors, find out about the card marketplace, and find out about other card businesses, including the style and quality of their cards, and their customer profile
- research her costs, including her time, and determine the amount she wants to earn from making cards

- research consumer tastes, and find out how the card market fails them or meets their needs
- research other alternatives or innovations that might provide a more secure niche market.

Catherine isn't unusual in finding it difficult to make a transition from a hobby to a viable business.

One Young Enterprise company that hoped to succeed in the card market found that making cards involved long, hard work that took concentration and diligence. In despair, the business used their remaining raw materials to run a workshop helping children to make cards. Parents were far more willing to pay £5 to allow their children to make and decorate a card for 30 minutes, than they were to pay for a handmade card. By developing their original idea – if only by chance – this Young Enterprise company was able to produce a service for which there was a market demand.

Refining your ideas

Anyone researching a business idea will find that as they learn more about the marketplace, their initial sketchy suggestions will be refined into more solid proposals and suggestions. This analysis and development is likely to draw on the marketing tools that you have already studied (see Unit 3 of your AS textbook).

The marketing mix can be used to refine product ideas. Say, for example, you have the idea of starting a handmade greetings card business. Your initial research suggests that this market is over-supplied and that it would not be possible to operate a business profitably.

Some people might give up at that point, but successful entrepreneurs look for innovative ways into a market. In this case, you might undertake further research to see if there is any demand for some kind of greetings card kit.

This research suggests that there is very strong demand from parents for new types of activities for their children. Parents are attracted by an activity set that would enable children to make greetings cards and simple card-based toys such as masks and swords. Providing the activity sets are relatively cheap (up to £5), there seems to be a good potential market for the product.

People are willing to buy these card ideas in various ways: as an activity set to do at home, from a party organiser as an activity for groups of up to 20 children at a private party, or from a stall at a market or other event when they are out with their children. Museums have also expressed interest in card activity sets that can be designed as tie-ins with their current exhibitions.

To analyse the idea further, use the four Ps of the marketing mix:

- price
- product
- place
- promotion.

Product

You need to specify and cost the components of each packaged set. You might decide to provide a range of masks, hats, swords and shields to decorate the cards, plus some other decorations like glitter, crayons or paint, and plain cards, if you can keep the material cost per pack to, say, £1.

Price

Parents seem willing to pay up to £5 for packaged sets, but which parents and for what age of children? What is the socioeconomic profile of the parents that are likely to be attracted by the idea? If a shop sold these packs, what is the price the shop would buy the packs for?

Party organiser and market stall sales might yield £7 a pack, but you would have to pay staff to run the activities. Would this be a profitable venture? What price per unit could you charge a museum that wanted to place a bulk order?

Place

How are you going to get your product to customers? Which shops might stock the product? Would museums sell or use the packaged sets? Are party organisers likely to want to stock the group activity sets? Could you make sufficient sales to be running a stall each week outside a big local supermarket?

Promotion

Can you get any publicity free of charge? Perhaps you can promote the business through word of mouth and by attracting the attention of people walking past the stall. You might be able to get some free press coverage in local newspapers if you put out an interesting press release.

If you have some money available to spend on promotion, what is likely to be the most cost-effective method? You will need to investigate the cost and potential effectiveness of cold-calling shops and museums, getting a Yellow Pages entry, developing a simple website, printing personal business cards and a brochure, and placing adverts in magazines targeted at schools and parents.

Competitor analysis

Anther tool that you can use is competitor analysis. Go out and research the particular niche of the market that you think has potential. Consider both direct and indirect competitors.

Direct competitor analysis involves researching other businesses offering themed card kits for children, parties and museums. Don't restrict your review to greeting cards but look at similar products pitched at children that involve making a finished object from a purchased kit. If these products exist, are they successful? What prices do businesses charge for these products? Where do these competitor businesses operate? Do they have ideas or concepts that could be copied? Consider whether there are any market areas that seem untapped.

Indirect competition analysis involves considering the other products at possible sales venues that would compete for the child's pocket money. Most museum shops, for example, sell pencils, erasers, rulers, and small books and toys. The children's party market is highly competitive: there are a host of competing themes and attractions, from sport centre parties to clowns. Markets and craft fairs can be variable, and traders get to know which fairs suit their products best. This aspect of the research can be an expensive and slow process.

Planning in practice

Remember, the first step in business planning is to thoroughly research the viability of a business idea from the start. As data is collected, go through your market research and think about what you might need to develop a proper business plan. Any business looking for finance to support its development would be expected to produce a professional business plan.

You are tested on business planning skills for the external assessment of this unit. You will need to demonstrate:

- knowledge, skills and understanding of the market and product research – do you understand and have the skills to carry out this work

- application of knowledge – is your market research focused on your target market, is it asking appropriate questions

- research and analysis – think carefully about what you have found out and present your findings using tables and graphs to illustrate and analyse the data

- evaluation – use the data to make recommendations about how the product or service should be developed to meet customers' needs and to produce a viable business.

stop and think

Undertake an exercise in competitor analysis by researching competitors for a particular product with which you are familiar. Choose a product that you are interested in. This could be a good or a service.

First, examine the direct competition. How many companies offer your chosen product? Where is it available? Do prices vary much? What is the price range?

Second, consider the indirect competition. What products might consumers buy as a substitute or alternative for your chosen good or service?

Third, identify any gaps in the market, based on your own dissatisfaction with your chosen product type, or using any ideas you have for how the product could be improved.

Emily is 18 years old and is employed full-time as a trainee accountant. She likes to work hard, and is quick and questioning at work. Emily is determined to be financially independent, to buy her own home without running up massive debts. She has tried her hand at evening work. This involved debt collection, which was well paid, but miserable.

She decided that the only way to realise her dream was to set up her own business in the evenings. Emily had no access to working capital, and she was not willing to borrow money. So, Emily looked for opportunities where she could work as an agent for someone else and be paid on commission on sales.

There is a wide range of opportunities for people to sell parties for party organisation companies. The standard offer from a party organiser is 20 per cent commission on each sale. Emily went through several party-organising companies, working out which met her criteria. She was looking for something which:

- required no deposit
- offered training
- could earn at least £150 in an evening
- could fit in with her day job
- would be fun and tasteful.

She researched various companies and ideas on the internet, visiting these websites:

- www.likisma-online.co.uk – cosmetics
- www.tnjp.co.uk – gifts
- www.essentially-yours.co.uk – organic cosmetics

- www.eBay.co.uk – various party plan products
- www.savannahspartyplan.co.uk – a small party plan business involving tarot card readings
- www.thirtyfifty.co.uk – wine tasting.

Emily eventually chose to run ladies-only lingerie parties, selling to her friends, acquaintances, and leads given to her by the main company.

Emily aims to work three nights a week as a party organiser and to bank her earnings after tax (income tax is, say, 30 per cent; value added tax is 17.5 per cent). Emily must go to other peoples' homes to hold the parties, which are on average ten miles away. She has access to a car, which gets 50 miles to the gallon, and her annual insurance on the car is £1,500. Seventy per cent of her car usage is business-related.

Emily has to store stocks in her home and spend one night each week on administration, chasing up orders and making payments. HM Revenue and Customs allows Emily to charge 5 per cent of her housing costs as a valid business expense: annual housing costs are £8,000, including rent and utilities. Emily also has sundry expenses of £20 per week that can be charged against income for tax purposes.

A Assuming that Emily achieves a gross profit of £150 per evening and that she works a 50-week year, how much will she have banked after tax in her first year? What unexpected events might arise to disrupt Emily's plans? What contingency plans could Emily make?

B Emily found that she could increase her gross profit to £200 each night if she invested £500 in stocks of goods to show customers. Assess whether Emily ought to make this investment.

C Emily eventually ceased to trade as a party organiser due to delays in receiving payment of her commission. She ceased trading being owed £10,000 by the main company. Advise Emily on what steps she should take to recover her commission.

D Suppose Emily wanted to start another party plan business. Analyse and evaluate Likisma, the cosmetics party plan organisers, as a party plan opportunity to meet Emily's needs. Use the company's website (www.likisma-online.co.uk) to get background information, and visit the other party plan websites for comparisons.

E Emily could have set up her own small business, running trips for schools, retirement homes and work places to the theatre by coach. She estimated that she could have made £1,200 on average for each evening she organised. The steps involved were to arrange publicity, book the coaches, book the theatre tickets and accompany the trip on the evening. Analyse and evaluate the possible reasons why Emily might have preferred to work as a party organiser.

Legal status and business planning

Setting the scene: getting it wrong

Bill, Ted and Sam set up in business running a nightclub. It was a great idea, and everyone really loved the concept: a light, fun club with an 18–30 tropical theme. The club quickly attracted many members, who paid a year's membership fee up front.

As the club became established, the three partners were advised to write a business plan and make a formal partnership agreement by Sam's younger sister Penny, who was an accountant. But Bill, Ted and Sam ignored her because they had always done everything their own way ever since they were at primary school together. Penny suggested keeping proper controls on money, but the partners took money from the till when they needed it: they could trust each other.

The club opened seven days a week, from 7 pm through to 4 am. The partners worked on rotating shifts, and shared in running the club. They took on duties as they needed doing, everything from banking the cash, keeping the accounts, making up and paying staff wages, supervising the cleaning and reordering stock for the bar, to promoting the bar to existing and potential customers, recruiting and training staff, and filling in endless documentation for government agencies (VAT, PAYE and national insurance returns, health and safety and food hygiene documentation, licensing applications).

Eventually, the months of running the club without a break began to take their toll, and the partners were getting tired and bad-tempered. Worse still, the business was experiencing a cash flow crisis. Penny was asked to pull their accounts together and she sorted out some basic accounts and costings. She pointed out some home truths.

- There was a lot of cash missing – presumably this had been taken by the partners, but as there were no proper records it could have been stolen by an employee.

- The club was not selling enough new memberships, and sales in the bar were only just covering the cost of running the club.

- There was no money to pay for a professional manager, or to meet a tax bill, or to bring in temporary staff to allow the partners to take a holiday.

Within days the club closed. The partners stopped working together and blamed each other for the mess. Bill, Ted and Sam had to sell the business for next to nothing, and they had to pay off all the debts owing on the business. They were grateful to have got rid of the club, as the lease they had signed had another five years to run, with a rent of £1,000 per week. As partners they had unlimited liability for all the business's debts.

The new owners have installed a professional manager, introduced tight controls on the bar sales and cash, ran a special offer for new members, and set up a series of other businesses that appealed to club members and visitors.

A **sole trader** is a business owned by a single person. It is not a legal entity. Sole traders are liable for all the debts of their business, but they also receive all the profits.

Partnerships are groups of two or more people operating in business together. Partnerships are regulated by the Partnership Act 1890.

Partnership agreements set out formally the way in which the partners will run the business, be paid, and share profits and losses. There is no legal requirement for partnerships to have a written agreement, but it is good practice to do this at the start of the partnership before any problems arise. In the event of there being no partnership agreement, the terms of the 1890 Partnership Act apply.

Unlimited liability means that a business's owners are liable to pay off all the debts that they have incurred in the course of running their business. They can be sued for their personal assets to pay the business debts. Sole traders and partners have unlimited liability.

Sole traders and partnerships

Sole traders and partnerships are sometimes called unincorporated businesses. These businesses have not formed themselves into companies – a process called incorporation. Owners of companies – the shareholders – have limited liability, which means that they have some legal protection against being held liable for any debts the company incurs.

In contrast, sole traders and the partners in a partnership have not limited their liability. They are legally responsible for any debts their business incurs, and they can therefore risk all their personal assets (houses, cars, etc.) as well as any money they have directly invested in the business. In some ways, partners risk even more as they are "jointly and severally" liable for a partnership's debts. This means that if one partner cannot pay his or her share of the debts, any creditors can sue the other partners until all the debts are cleared.

It is very easy to set up as a sole trader or as a partnership. Window cleaners and market traders can simply get up one day and set up in business either as a partnership or as a sole trader. There are few formalities to complete. If the business trades under a name other than that of the owners, then the names of the owner(s) need to be displayed at the business premises and on its stationery.

Partnerships are regulated by the Partnership Act 1890. The terms of the Act govern all partnerships, unless they are specifically excluded or amended by a deed of partnership. A deed of partnership is a contract between the partners laying out the terms of the partnership, and it usually includes details of how much capital is to be introduced to the partnership, details of any partner salaries, the profit sharing ratio of the partnership and any other arrangements the partners wish to include. The 1890 Act is brief, but very well written, and can be found on www.hmrc.gov.uk/manuals/bimmanual/BIM72505.htm.

It is advisable to notify HM Revenue and Customs when starting an unincorporated business. This ensures that the business makes up-to-date national insurance payments and does not incur penalties for failure to submit tax returns on time. Profits are taxed, whether they are withdrawn from the business or not, and losses can be offset against any other taxable income of the individual.

Sole traders and partnerships enjoy several benefits:

■ considerable privacy – they do not need to publish their accounts

■ total control over their own decision-making

■ there are no limits to their activities – the owners of these businesses can take up any trade they like as long as it is lawful.

There are, though, some drawbacks to setting up as a sole trader or a partnership. These businesses do not always have a strong capacity for growth. They can be constrained by the difficulties of raising finance – banks are often reluctant to lend to these businesses – and many find it hard getting supplies and materials on credit terms. It is much easier for potential lenders or creditors to find out about a company than a sole trader or partnership: they can check the company's directors, and find out their connections to other businesses and their credit rating. Sole traders and partnerships are often insecure business units, as the illness, retirement or death of one of the owners can threaten the survival of the whole business.

There are some financial incentives to becoming an incorporated company. There can be tax advantages: company profits are subject to corporation tax, whereas sole trader and partnership profits are taxed as self-employed income which can increase the overall tax liability. More generally, unlimited liability can financially ruin a business owner for life, whereas limited liability provides the entrepreneur with a relatively safe framework in which to take risks. (Entrepreneurs need the opportunity to make mistakes and recover – that is the nature of a vibrant business community.)

Despite the drawbacks and limitations, however, many business people enjoy the freedom and relative lack of business regulation that comes with operating as a sole trader or partnership. Many owners do not want their businesses to grow very large: they enjoy their personal freedom, but they do not want to be burdened with employing many other people or taking the risk of expansion into another town or country. Their aims are to produce a reasonable profit rather than maximise sales and profits.

Formal business planning

Business planning is a vital skill. It is just as important whether you are planning for the development of a small part of a large established corporation or are planning to set up an operation from scratch. Formal business disciplines such as business planning allow sole traders and partnerships to ensure that they are not exposed to any unnecessary risks. Planning was introduced in Unit 2 of the course (see pages 60–69 of your AS textbook.)

Planning for an unincorporated business is a very serious matter. It has to ensure that:

- the business is successful and provides the owner(s) with a living

- the business continues for the foreseeable future

- the business does not run up huge debts that could result in the owners losing their homes and other personal assets, and risking bankruptcy.

If the business is to grow, or if it takes on any significant risks, then the plans should also include changing the business into a limited company.

Structure of the plan

Business plans should have a clear structure and format. The plan you submit for assessment needs to include:

- aims and objectives of the business

- a marketing plan

- a resources plan

- financial analysis and planning.

Your plan has to be suitable to support a request for finance, so this should be its focus.

There are other formats for business plans, and it is useful to familiarise yourself with some of them. You can find out more about different formats, as well as pick up useful help and guidance on business planning from the internet. We featured three useful sites in Topic 1: Shell LiveWIRE, DTI best practice and The Prince's Trust (see page 13 for web addresses). Another useful site on business planning is operated by Palo Alto Software (see www.bplans.co.uk).

The business plan is a summary of all the relevant research that is undertaken to investigate a business proposal. It should include analysis of any data collected to assess the viability of the proposal and draw conclusions from that research. To make your business plan comprehensible, pay close attention to both content and presentation.

To ensure good content:

- analyse and evaluate as you go along through the report

- make sure that all findings are supported by research, and that all research used is analysed and leads somewhere

- make all the data easy to read, and make good use of tables.

In terms of presentation, the plan should be written in a format that is easy to read, and broken into short paragraphs. Remember to:

- number all pages

- provide a contents list

- have an executive summary at the front that sums up the whole plan on one sheet of A4

- use very straightforward graphs that communicate quickly and clearly, label all axes on your graphs, and list the source of any data you present

- avoid diagrams that are difficult to interpret, such as pie charts and three-dimensional bar charts.

assessment practice
Wendy's fish restaurant

Wendy wanted to set up a new restaurant in a busy part of town. She researched the competition in the area. There were five Indian restaurants, four pizza parlours, three greasy spoon cafes, two Thai restaurants, a French bistro and an Indonesian restaurant.

All the restaurants seemed to be full on Friday and Saturday nights. Most customers were young people, 18–30 years old, mainly single, with no children. Customers tended to eat three-course meals and order alcohol to go with the meal. After the meal, many people went on to clubs and pubs in the area. The restaurants that offered a takeaway service stayed open until 1–2 am.

On Fridays and Saturdays, most establishments could fill their restaurants twice in an evening, with first groups coming in at 7:30–8 pm and a second wave of diners coming in between 9:30 and 10:30 pm. Most restaurants were only about 40 per cent full for lunch on Saturdays and Sundays, because the restaurant area is well away from the shopping area.

On Monday to Friday, all restaurants offered business lunches consisting of two light courses for about £5 each. In the evenings during the week (Monday to Thursday), occupancy rates varied tremendously between restaurants. The most successful restaurants during the week tended to have reasonably priced menus, with the average meal costing about £15 per head excluding drinks. They are typically small family businesses, providing a friendly atmosphere, with visible seating for a maximum of 30 customers, although there might be more seating downstairs in the basement.

Wendy had managed to get some data from a survey of customers leaving restaurants in the area during one week. This showed that 55 per cent of restaurant customers were female (45 per cent male). Figure 8.1 summarises some of the survey data, providing a customer profile of midweek restaurant users.

Figure 8.1: Customer profile of midweek restaurant users, by age, spend per head and distance travelled from home

Age	Profile
18–30 years	40%
31–45 years	20%
46–65 years	25%
66+	15%

Spend per head	Profile
£10–£15	30%
£16–£20	30%
£21–£25	20%
£26–£30	10%
£31–£35	8%
£36+	2%

Distance travelled from home	Profile
0–3 kilometres	20%
4–6 kilometres	30%
7–9 kilometres	25%
10–12 kilometres	10%
13–15 kilometres	10%
16+ kilometres	5%

Wendy decided to run a restaurant that specialised in fish meals. She found vacant premises on the main street of the restaurant area with seating capacity for 45 customers. The lease on the premises was £250 per week. Business rates were a further £150 each week. Light, heat and fuel were expected to be £40 per week. Wage costs for three staff (cook, waiter and receptionist) should have been around £600 per week including all other employment costs. Wendy was going to set her prices so that it was possible to buy a meal for around £16 per head on average. The cost of the ingredients would be no more than £4 per head.

A Draft an outline business plan for Wendy.

B What further information would you like to collect, if you had to prepare a full business plan for Wendy?

C Go through your business plan with a partner, and mark on it where you have used analysis and where you have reached evaluations.

D Redraft your plan if your evaluations and analysis need strengthening.

Physical resource management

Setting the scene: total quality management

After the Second World War, the Japanese were faced with the challenge of rebuilding their shattered economy. Resources were scarce, and they needed to be very carefully managed. The situation required businesses that could minimise waste and maximise the output that could be sold for a premium.

Entrepreneurs like Morita Akio and Masaru Ibuka, the founders of Sony, and Taichi Ohno at the Toyota Corporation, set up systems of manufacturing that were based on the idea of total quality management. This is a system of manufacturing that uses the principles of kaizen (or continuous improvement) and just-in-time stock control.

Using these techniques, Sony and Toyota were able to reduce the quantity of stock held at the company premises at any one time, and reduce the number of defects in their products and services. This helped make these companies become very low-cost, high-quality producers.

These lessons can be copied by entrepreneurs today. A total quality management approach will increase any business's chances of surviving into the long term.

Kaizen, in particular, can be applied to any business, not just those involved in manufacturing. Rather than a one-off initiative, kaizen is a long-term strategy of continuously working at improving every aspect of the production and delivery of goods and services. It is a business culture that requires everyone in a company to be thinking all the time about how to make the business better and more efficient.

SONY

COMPUTER ENTERTAINMENT ®

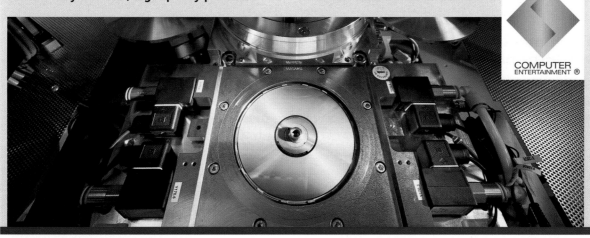

KEY TERMS

Quality control is the process of ensuring that products and services meet a set minimum standard.

Kaizen is a management philosophy that aims at continuous improvement in all aspects of the operation of a business.

Resource management is the process by which a business monitors and controls the use of all the resources it needs to operate and trade.

Capacity is the upper limit of a business's ability to produce and deliver goods and services.

Constraints are factors both inside and outside a business that restrict its activities and output.

Resource management

As you saw in studying Units 1 and 2 as AS level, businesses have a range of resources at their disposal. These can be classified under the headings:

- physical resources

- human resources

- financial resources

- intangible, knowledge-based resources.

All these resources are interconnected. A problem with one resource can impact on a business's use of other resources. For example, if a business making computer games cannot recruit skilled computer programmers this could impact on its use of physical resources. If it is not able to make high-quality games, sales will fall and it will need to make less product. It may cause human resources problems as other employees are put under pressure to deliver a product that is beyond their ability. Further, lower sales will have a long-term effect on finance and the business's ability to raise capital. Consequently, when focusing on the management of one resource area, it is important to be aware of the implications for other resource areas.

All new businesses tend to be short of resources, simply because of the demands of starting up a business. In the start-up, a business has to move from a position of having no resources, when it is just an idea in the founder's mind, to one of having all the resources necessary to run on the first day of operation. This takes considerable planning and preparation. Making the first expansion is also resource-intensive. Opening a second outlet, for example, often forces the business to make a 100 per cent increase in resources in one step. Anita Roddick exchanged 50 per cent of her share capital to get the money to finance the second branch of Body Shop.

From market research to resource planning

Once product and market research has suggested that a business idea is viable, an entrepreneur comes to the point of deciding to go into business. This requires obtaining and setting up the resources necessary to produce and deliver the products and services.

Clearly, a decision needs to be made about the amount of resources needed to start the business. This will depend, in part, on the planned level of output. This, in turn, should be informed by market research. When starting a business, it is good practice to use market research to set targets for production levels, or the volume of goods and services that are likely to be demanded by potential customers. However, even with very best of market research, entrepreneurs need to be cautious not to commit themselves too heavily into a new venture until actual sales are realised.

In the early stages, starting a business is like putting up a circus tent – a huge number of resources need to be in place, all ready at the same time. This is a time of considerable strain, as the business owners set up premises, machinery, finance, licences, etc. There are phone calls to field, potential employees to interview, potential premises to view, and so on.

Time needs to be managed very carefully with a well controlled diary or scheduler. It is useful for the business partners to have access to each other's diaries so that they know what the others are doing. Online diaries are a real asset for busy people, and IT can make a significant impact on an individual's time efficiency. Regular meetings between partners are important to ensure that everyone's time is used most effectively and that there is no duplication of effort.

Physical resource management

The main types of physical resources that any business owns or leases are:

- premises
- machinery
- tools and small equipment
- motor vehicles
- stock.

The combination of resources that a business can afford to bring together will determine the speed and quality of the final product. A business needs to ensure that its physical resources can deliver its products and services in sufficient quantity and to the required standard or quality. For example, any machinery that a business is considering acquiring needs to be assessed in terms of efficiency, speed and quality of outputs, as well as other factors such as maintenance costs, emission of pollutants, and type and cost of inputs.

The business needs to be aware of capacity constraints. The physical resources that a business acquires – and the number of hours that those assets can be used each day – will shape its physical capacity to produce and supply its products. A business needs to put in place contingency plans for increasing physical resources if demand exceeds the business's capacity. These plans should include alternative sources of supply (for machinery, raw materials, premises, etc.).

Quality standards can vary greatly, depending on the product or service being supplied. For example, a much higher quality standard might be expected in the production of medical products than household bricks. Likewise the standard of service – and the physical resource input – which is acceptable at a football match is completely different from that expected in the tearooms of the Ritz hotel.

Buy or lease?

Many physical resources can be rented (leased) from a supplier or a finance house. A decision therefore has to be made whether the business will buy or rent key resources. This has important implications for the capital requirements of the business. Generally it is cheaper (in the long term) to buy assets outright, but that might not suit the cash flow needs of the business.

Consider a hypothetical example. Suppose it is possible to rent office space in second-rate office blocks in the centre of a town for about £5,000 per annum, but the same premises could be bought for £200,000. After 40 years the business will have paid £200,000 in rent, but own no asset. If the company had bought the premises, it would also have paid £200,000 but it would have a potentially valuable asset. A new business, however, is probably not interested in the position in 40 years' time. The critical matter of concern to them in the present is managing their cash flow, and they probably cannot afford to spend a significant chunk of their capital on buying premises.

New or second-hand?

If a business is considering buying assets, then the next question that needs to be considered is whether the assets are going to be new or second-hand. This will depend on the type of asset, and what is available in the second-hand market. Let's consider some specific examples.

Computers only have a business life of about three years, and there may be a risk of viruses or other problems being present in second-hand computers, so it is more usual to buy new computers. Second-hand motor vehicles, on the other hand, are not only significantly cheaper than new models but are likely to be mechanically and physically sound if they are relatively new. With modern vehicle quality, it makes good sense for most businesses to buy vehicles that are already run in. However, vehicles that are really old and cheap can be a costly liability: they can be prone to break down at critical moments, spare parts can be costly, and they might struggle to pass the MOT each year.

Office equipment can be bought cheaply in second-hand stores, or can be picked up for a minimal price in insolvency sales. If no customers are ever going to see the office, then this is one way of keeping costs very low. Kitchen equipment also has a very lively second-hand market, as there are so many restaurants which set up in business only to close within months of opening. Industrial-standard kitchen equipment tends to be robust and have a long life.

There are not second-hand markets in all types of industrial goods. Some manufacturers gain a market advantage by using very high-tech machinery, and they would rather destroy their old machinery than sell it to their competitors and risk losing some of their lead in technology.

Health and safety issues

Any industrial machinery, whether new or second-hand, must meet relevant health and safety standards. Any restaurant business, for example, must ensure that its kitchen has proper ventilation systems that meet safety standards, and that its kitchen equipment is clean and sufficiently efficient to produce food that meets customer needs and complies with health standards. It must be possible to clean all the equipment, and the business must take steps to comply with food handling and hygiene regulations. All machinery needs to be insured for loss or damage, and for accidents involving the equipment.

Stock

Good stock management can be an important part of getting a competitive advantage. As the article on total quality management at the start of this topic shows, this approach has paid dividends for some Japanese firms. Stock management is a fine balancing act between having enough stock in place so that the business can always meet the needs of customers at any time, and not committing vast sums of working capital on stock that may stay on the shelf for months.

Small garages often have excellent stock control, just going out to collect spare parts from a supplier's depot as the need arises. Their premises are not cluttered with piles of parts and components, and their capital is not used on holding large quantities of stock. Instead, parts are sourced in the few hours between customers leaving their vehicles for service and returning later to pick up the repaired vehicle. If the garage has a credit agreement with its component suppliers, it receives payment from the customer for its work before it has to pay the supplier for the spare parts. This greatly assists the garage's cash flow position.

Not all businesses can operate with stocks as low as the modern garage, but they should strive to find ways of keeping their stock costs low and minimising stock waste.

Alex wanted to set up a small shop selling ice cream. He worked out that he needed these physical assets:

- a shop, something like a small sandwich bar where nobody would mind if he set up tables outside in the summer

- two freezer units, one for storage and one for display

- tables and chairs for 12 people, plus bar stools for six people

- a counter for serving customers, plus interior décor such as travel posters from Italy

- sufficient stock of at least 12 flavours of real Italian ice cream, plus paper cups and cones

- a music centre and some CDs to provide some background music

- a pinball table to keep at the back of the shop to provide more atmosphere.

Alex had seen great furniture he really liked on a website, www.cafereality.co.uk. He also found a website (www.mercuryleisure.co.uk) that sold pinball machines, and he thought that this should make it easy to get the pinball machine. He thought that he and his friends could decorate the café and make the counter.

He found a supplier of Italian ice cream on www.milking.co.uk, but he has discovered that he would need to negotiate prices with the suppliers. He has an appointment with an estate agent to go and look at commercial property, and he has got a feel for the market and prices in his area from www.daltonsbusiness.com. Alex has found the freezers on www.meritcoolers.com, but does not know whether it would be more sensible to buy two smaller freezers or one large freezer for display purposes.

Alex only has £10,000 to set up his business.

A How should Alex go about choosing his physical resources in order to gain value for money?

B Should Alex and his friends make the food counter?

C What strategy could Alex use to keep his stock costs low, given that producers do not publish their prices?

D Identify five key health and safety features that he should look out for, and five features that will make it possible for him to maximise sales.

Human resources

Setting the scene: people problems

Bill had been in business for many years. He had an outstanding CV, giving an image of a highly successful individual who had been in senior posts in large companies for most of his professional life. Bill had a strong network of friends and contacts throughout the world.

Bill decided to go it alone, producing and selling an innovative telecommunications product. He asked Phil, a bright young software engineer, to join him in setting up a new company. Phil was flattered to be asked to join an exciting business project, and he imagined that with Bill's capital and contacts they would soon be millionaires running the ultimate hi-tech firm. Phil's contribution to the project was his time and expertise.

The partnership soon ran into difficulties. In his previous jobs, Bill always had a personal assistant to do everything for him, and now he was working on his own he found it difficult to perform even the simplest tasks on his laptop. Phil soon found that he was frequently interrupted by demands from Bill for help with basic tasks. The funding only covered basic IT equipment. Progress on product development was slowed through lack of other software engineers and the necessary IT equipment. As he was working on his own, Phil also found it difficult to check the technical accuracy of his own output.

The business finally closed. It was not possible to produce a viable product with the limited resources available, and no venture capitalists were willing to finance such a weak team. Bill and Phil found that running a small business required a far greater range of skills and commitment than had been required of them as employees.

The challenge

It takes a considerable commitment to set up and run a small business. Owners must be able to do all the tasks necessary to run the business or have sufficient funds to buy in appropriate external help, and even then they must be able to check the quality of the service they are receiving.

Anyone planning to start a business must be realistic about what can be achieved, and in what time frame. Entrepreneurs often work extremely long hours, not just during trading hours, but also after hours, doing all the associated paperwork.

Long hours of work may be necessary to set up the business but, over a sustained period, they are not good for the health of either the business or the entrepreneur.

- If entrepreneurs get exhausted, their work gets slower. They would in fact produce just the same amount of work if they took proper breaks and worked shorter hours.

KEY TERMS

Multiskilled workers are able to perform many different tasks in the workplace. Multiskilling is increasingly expected. Many routine tasks, previously done by support staff, are expected to be undertaken by all employees interfacing directly with their computers, such as word processing and creating spreadsheets.

Flexible working is a way of organising work so that staff work as and when required by a business. A small business can find it useful to have casual staff available to work if big orders come in.

Skills audit is the process of identifying the skills available in a business's workforce. The skills audit can determine skill gaps which may need to be filled by recruitment or by training in-house staff.

Work-life balance is the relative priority individuals give to their work life and their home life. If people do not give enough priority to their home life, then they risk their close relationships, and their personal life can suffer.

stop and think

To get a feel of what running a small business is like, ask in one a small local shops if you can shadow the owners for a week, or get them to tell you what they do during the working week.

- If entrepreneurs overwork, they will find it difficult to make good decisions and will lack the energy to analyse and evaluate marketing and finance data.

- If entrepreneurs become over-tired and anxious, they can undermine their businesses by giving the impression that things are bad and the business is just about to close down.

To combat the strain, many organisations provide support networks for entrepreneurs running small businesses. These networks provide training and access to experienced business mentors for little or no charge. The Business Links network, funded by Department of Trade and Industry, is one source of this kind of support. If entrepreneurs are under 30 years of age, the Prince's Trust also provides training and mentoring for business start-ups. There are various other privately run business networking groups which can be both fun and mutually supportive.

Human resource management

In small businesses, the personnel are usually critical to the success of the business. In particular, the owners of the business set the tone and the standards of the enterprise, and they have a crucial role in quality control.

As start-up businesses grow, and they begin to take on more staff, quality management of the human assets in the business becomes both more important and potentially complex. In large businesses, companies often employ human resources managers (see Unit 1 in your AS textbook); in most small businesses, these tasks are undertaken by the owner. Owners need to consider four key issues.

Training

Investment in training is necessary to ensure that staff have the skills to do their jobs efficiently and can meet the requirements of current legislation in areas such as health and safety. Staff may also need training to develop skills to meet internationally recognised quality standards for product and service delivery. Research shows that small and medium-sized firms often find it very difficult to organise effective training.

Leadership and team development

Ideally, workplace teams should be happy, creative, smooth-working groups of individuals who support each other, work to each others' strengths, and work towards the business's goals. This might require the owners to undertake self-assessment and target-setting reviews to ensure that the business is staying focused on its objectives. Team development can be fostered by organising events such as team lunches and days out walking together. It also could be fostered by mentoring a Young Enterprise team, allowing team members to reflect on and contrast their problems with those of the YE team.

Delegation

Owners should employ appropriate people to do the tasks that they cannot do or do not have time to do. By freeing themselves from some of the more basic day-to-day tasks of the business, owners can spend their time monitoring the overall business and thinking strategically about where the business should be going.

Certainly, if the owners are passionate about the business, they need time to step back and focus on the long-term goals and vision of the organisation. They also need time to network, to build up sales leads and to explore further investment opportunities for the business.

Management systems

In time, owners need to be able to let go of control of some aspects of the business and to develop more formal management systems. This is probably the most difficult task for any entrepreneur. Many entrepreneurs find it very difficult to trust paid employees to run their businesses.

At this stage in their development, without outside help and guidance many businesses simply reach their "natural" capacity, and they do not develop or grow any further. Entrepreneurs need to decide whether they want to keep their business small – so that they retain control of all decisions – or whether they want to go on growing their business and therefore accept that this will necessarily change their role in the business.

Time management

Setting up any new business can run into problems if the timing of resource inputs is not well synchronised. It would be amazingly lucky if everything came together in a perfectly co-ordinated fashion, but life is usually not like that.

Various problems can arise. For example, fixed assets might be delivered before the premises which will house them are available, resulting in one of the owners having a pile of assets sitting in their house or garage which have to be transported later into the final premises at additional cost. The business might also run out of cash and find that there is no money to pay for vital last-minute purchases. The owners assume that they can help with everything and cover any resource gaps, only to find that this isn't possible as there are simply not enough hours in the day.

Sometimes the problems are not of the business's own making. Staff may be recruited and trained for a big contract, and then the client delays the start of the contract by several weeks. Staff may then be sitting around the office annoying each other, or they have to be sent home on full pay.

To overcome these problems, it makes sense to keep detailed plans of when everything is due to happen, what dates, what times, which people are involved, what equipment is involved. There will still be problems, but these should be minimised.

assessment practice
Jen the temp

Jen worked as a temporary clerk clearing up administration messes in large companies. She was well respected by those who employed her, as she needed very little supervision, she worked extremely quickly and when she ran out of work she looked around to find more. The employment agency that she worked for received many positive comments about Jen from their clients.

Then one week the agency sent Jen out to Fred's Flowers, a sole trader that needed help to set up some basic administration systems for the business. Fred, the entrepreneur, and Jen did not get on well. Fred wanted to supervise Jen closely, and by lunchtime they were snapping at each other. Close supervision did not suit Jen's personality, she hated being questioned all the time about every move she made, and she could not bear to do things in an inefficient manner. As Jen worked fast, no manager had every really questioned her skill for designing the fastest route for completing a task before.

Fred felt that it was his business and that he should make all the decisions, however small. He did not like an 18-year-old telling him how to run his business. He was irritated that Jen seemed to have slowed down her pace of work by Tuesday and was just doing what was in front of her. By Tuesday afternoon neither of them was speaking to each

other, and the afternoon finished with Fred telling Jen that she was no longer needed.

The job did not last the week, Jen was back at the agency by the Wednesday without all the glowing compliments that usually followed her.

A Why did the relationship between Fred and Jen break down so quickly?

B What are the costs to a business of this type of breakdown in working relationships?

C What strategies could Jen or Fred have employed to stop this problem arising?

D If Fred had employed Jen to organise the move of the business to a new location while he got on with dealing with his customers, what advice would you give to Fred?

Identifying financial needs

Setting the scene: DJ Carl

Carl has recently started working as a freelance DJ. He has financed the business by borrowing £2,000 from his Dad, investing £3,200 of his own money, and using a finance house loan of £10,000 to fund his van purchase.

He has the record stock, the deck and speakers, some great lighting effects and a second-hand van in good condition to get him to and from home venues. He has bookings for every Thursday, Friday and Saturday night over the next two months, with each venue agreeing to pay his £250 a night fee.

He has set up his draft balance sheet and cash flow forecast on a spreadsheet (see Figures 8.2 and 8.3). This shows that he would be able to repay his Dad within the month. Carl is all ready to go to his first booking. The problem is he needs to borrow another £100 to pay for some petrol *now* as he has absolutely no cash left.

Figure 8.2: Carl's draft balance sheet as at 1 June 2006

Fixed assets	
Motor vehicle	£10,000
Music deck and speakers	£2,500
Lighting units	£1,000

Current assets	
Stock of music	£1,600
Stock of light bulbs	£100
Debtors	£0
Cash	£0

Current liabilities	
Loan from Dad	(£2,000)
Net asset value	£13,200

Long-term liabilities	
Loan from a finance house for van (loan guaranteed by Dad)	£10,000
Capital	£3,200
Capital employed	£13,200

Figure 8.3: Carl's cash flow forecast

Income / Week	1	2	3	4	5	6	7	8	9	10	11	12
	£	£	£	£	£	£	£	£	£	£	£	£
Bookings	750	750	750	750	750	750	750	750	750	750	750	750
Expenses												
Loan repayment			100					100				100
Petrol	60	60	60	60	60	60	60	60	60	60	60	60
Telephone	10	10	10	10	10	10	10	10	10	10	10	10
Net cash flow	680	680	680	580	680	680	680	580	680	680	680	580
Opening balance	0	680	1360	2040	2620	3300	3980	4660	5240	5920	6600	7280
Closing balance	680	1360	2040	2620	3300	3980	4660	5240	5920	6600	7280	7860

Financial planning

All new businesses need to keep simple straightforward accounts that will help owners keep control of initial set-up costs. From these early costs, it is possible to project realistic plans, budgets and targets for the business.

You have already studied aspects of financial planning during the AS course (see unit 2 of the AS textbook). In this topic, we look at four key tools or measures that help in the financial planning of a new business. These are:

- start-up budgets
- working capital requirements
- cash flow forecasts
- breakeven.

Start-up budgets

Start-up budgets are estimates of the costs that a business is going to incur in getting ready to start operation. In Carl's case (see Figure 8.2), the start-up cost of his DJ business is the money he has spent acquiring his fixed and current assets. This adds up to £15,200. As the balance sheet shows, this spending has been financed through a £10,000 loan from a finance house, a £2,000 loan from Carl's Dad and £3,200 capital from Carl's savings.

In practice, any entrepreneur setting up in business will think carefully about the needs for both fixed and current assets. This involves considering a range of possible models and looking for assets that would ideally suit the business's purposes. Each potential asset would be assessed in terms of affordability and suitability. The objective is to get value for money from a purchase, but not be left with a cheap asset that is not fit for its purpose. In Carl's case, he may well have looked at several vehicles before he decided on the van as he weighed up cost versus suitability.

In most business plans there needs to be a contingency fund built into the start-up budget so that any unexpected costs do not bring the whole project to an abrupt stop. Jamie Oliver, for example, incurred significant unforeseen costs when starting his Fifteen restaurant because he had to install an essential extractor fan. He found the money to put things right and keep the business on track. However, in our case study, Carl has left no leeway at all. He has got to the point where he has absolutely no working capital, he does not even have the money for the petrol to get him and his equipment to his first venue.

An entrepreneur will often have to look for economies in the budget if costs overrun in one area. It is essential that entrepreneurs regularly review their actual costs against the budget for particular items, and their total spend against the start-up budget, to ensure that they do not run out of funds before the business has even opened.

Working capital requirements

Working capital is a measure of a business's short-term net current assets. It is calculated using the formula:

$$stock + debtors + cash - current\ liabilities$$

Essentially, working capital is a fund that circulates between current assets and liabilities. A business pays out cash to suppliers for raw materials and other inputs, which it turns into finished stock and services, which (hopefully) results in sales, which generate invoices to trade customers (debtors) and cash from consumer sales.

Sometimes problems arise and the fund fails to circulate sufficiently quickly. This might happen, for example, when a business's debtors do not pay on time or, worse, become bad debts. Then a business may not be able to pay its own creditors. Some creditors may then sue for payment, which if the business cannot pay because it is still short of cash could, in the worst-case scenario, lead to the business being closed down. It is essential, therefore, that any business has access to sufficient working capital.

Calculating working capital requirements is quite difficult until one has actual business experience. Banks, business advisers and accountants can often give expert help in this area, based on their experience of working with other businesses. However, it is possible for a new business to estimate its working capital requirements. This worked example, which involves several steps, shows the process.

1   Use market research to estimate the business's annual sales. For our example, we'll assume the business expects annual sales of £12,000.

2   Identify the expected spread of these sales over the year. Are there likely to be any seasonal peaks or troughs, as this will affect all aspects of the working capital? In our example, we will assume that sales are steady at £1,000 per month.

3   Identify the credit terms that apply to any purchased stock or raw materials. Lets assume that for the business in our example stock and raw materials is 50 per cent of the sales value – that is, £6,000 over the year. These are purchased in the month before the finished goods are sold, and our business settles this debt a month later.

4   We also need to know the credit terms that apply to the business's sales. Let's assume that all sales are on credit (they are sales to trade customers), and customers will settle two months after a sale.

5   Finally, we need to take into account the starting cash position and other business expenses that may draw on cash reserves during the year. Assume that the business started with £2,000 in cash at the beginning of month one, and assume that it incurs no other expenses, such as salaries, heat and light, etc.

Figure 8.4 shows the working capital position after five months' trading. The cash position is calculated by adding actual receipts from customers (three months' worth of sales) to the starting cash position and deducting cash payments to suppliers (five months' worth of sales). Check the calculation of the working capital. Do you agree with it?

Figure 8.4: A working capital requirement calculation

Stock (50% of a month's sales)	£500
Debtors (2 x £1,000, two months' sales)	£2,000
Cash	£2,500
Less trade creditors (1 x £500)	(£500)
Working capital	£4,500

In our working capital example, the business could probably manage with at least £1,000 less working capital at the start, but the entrepreneur may not feel comfortable operating in such a tight situation in case of unexpected expenses. It is not unusual for a business to arrange an overdraft facility, which it does not intend to use but is there in case of emergencies. Because the overdraft facility has been negotiated well in advance, the bank will have agreed that, as long as the business stays within its overdraft limit, it will not incur any additional bank charges and penalties. Businesses which go into overdraft without the prior consent of their bank can incur very high charges and interest rates.

Working capital requirements are difficult to estimate until a business is operating, and then the margins that are needed are dependent on the type of business and the experience, confidence and attitude of the entrepreneur.

Cash flow forecasts

Cash flow forecasting is a vital tool in calculating working capital requirements. In taking steps to forecast and manage cash flow, entrepreneurs show the bank and other investors that they really understand the financial side of business and their business's finance needs. Banks and investors feel a lot more confident if they can see that the entrepreneur is planning ahead.

Carl's cash flow forecast, Figure 8.3, clearly shows that Carl foresees his business building up a positive cash flow, represented by the ever-growing closing balance. The bottom line – the closing cash balance each month – is the critical line for businesses to watch and manage. If they can see in advance that the bottom line is turning negative, they can take steps to manage or avert that situation or they can make arrangements with investors for short-term finance to cover the problem.

The advantage of using spreadsheets for cash flow forecasts (like Carl) is that it is easy to assess the impact of various changes to a business by changing elements in the budget. For example, Carl could assess the impact of doing two more evenings' work each week at £200 a night, or he could assess whether he should invest in more equipment and a regular supply of new records, and he can see straight away how this would affect his business.

Cash flow forecasts are moving entities, and they should be updated regularly to reflect any revised situations. However, remember that they are a *forecast*: they are only an estimate of the future to help a business manage uncertainty.

Breakeven point

Breakeven is the point at which a business's costs equal its sales revenue, so that it makes neither a profit nor a loss. To calculate breakeven, first calculate the contribution of any sale. This is given by:

$$\text{contribution} = \text{sales price} - \text{direct costs}$$

Now use contribution in this formula, to obtain:

$$\text{breakeven point in units} = \frac{\text{fixed costs}}{\text{contribution}}$$

For example, if the sales price of a product is £10, the direct costs of production are £8, and the fixed costs associated with that product are £2000. Then, the contribution is:

$$\text{sales price less direct costs} = £10 - £8 = £2$$

And the breakeven point in units is the fixed costs divided by the contribution, so:

$$\text{breakeven} = £2,000/£2 = 1000 \text{ units}$$

Up to this breakeven point, the business will be making losses. The contribution after direct costs merely contributes to fixed costs. After the breakeven point has been passed, the contribution is profits. It is possible to calculate the net profit at 3000 units by this calculation:

net profit = production above breakeven point x contribution
= (3,000 units less 1,000 units) x £2
= 2,000 x 2 = £4,000

This calculation can be repeated to test out the impact of changes in costs and sales price on the breakeven point and profitability.

assessment practice
Personal alarms

Jane and Karen developed a small electrical personal alarm. In their market research, Karen and Jane discovered that people were willing to pay £5 on average for a reliable alarm with no special features that fitted on a watch strap or key ring. They believe that they can sell 12,000 units in a year. The direct cost to them would be £2 for the components and labour.

If they developed the alarm further and incorporated mobile phone technology, then they found that they could sell the product for £25. Each alarm would directly cost £8 to make, and market research suggests that they could sell 2,400 units in their first year.

The annual fixed costs for both types of personal alarm are £48,000. These are spread evenly throughout the year.

Jane and Karen have each invested £25,000 in the business. Sales are spread evenly throughout the year and all payments are received one month after the sale is made. Direct costs are paid in the month in which they are incurred.

A Calculate the breakeven point for both products.

B Produce two cash flow forecasts, assuming that Karen and Jane can only afford to develop one or the other of these products.

C Produce budget profit and loss and balance sheets for both products.

D Advise Karen and Jane on which product would be best to develop. Give your reasons, using both quantitative and qualitative arguments.

Financial resources

Setting the scene: desperately seeking finance

Alex, Stuart and Susan had been working together for a few years in a large company when they decided that they would set up in their own partnership.

They planned a gourmet food service that would deliver top cuisine to businesses that required lunches and dinners served in their own offices. They hoped that the ability to offer something better than a sandwich or a microwave meal on their own premises would attract plenty of businesses.

The partnership estimated its capital needs at £60,000. The partners reckoned the business needed two delivery vans at £16,000 each, a new industrial oven in Stuart's kitchen costing £6,000, and working capital to cover running costs, raw materials, advertising and their initial cash needs – as they planned to offer commercial customers 30 days' credit.

Each of the partners was prepared to contribute £10,000 to the business start-up, and they called a meeting to discuss how they might raise the other £30,000. Before the meeting, they researched the potential sources of finance for small businesses on the internet. This research showed some of the problems they would face in raising finance:

■ many providers of capital only lend money to companies

■ many lenders expected unincorporated businesses to pay premium interest rates – some quoted a premium as high as 25 percentage points above base lending rate

■ all potential lenders wanted to see a detailed business plan.

Their difficulty was compounded when they discovered that none of their potential suppliers would offer them credit terms until they had a six-month track record. This meant that they would have to pay for all supplies upfront, increasing their working capital needs by a further £2,000.

KEY TERMS

Risk, in relation to finance, is the probability that a borrower will repay the capital and interest on a loan.
A high-risk loan would be one to a borrower who could not provide any assets to secure the loan on or anyone to guarantee the loan.

Base rate is the rate of interest set by the Bank of England.

Premium, in relation to interest rates, refers to the number of percentage points above the normal lending rate that would have to be paid by a business considered a risk. For example, if the normal rate for lending to a business is 6 per cent and the lender offered a loan at 8 per cent, then there would be a 2 per cent premium on the loan.

Credit terms are the terms set out in any credit agreement and will cover aspects of the contract such as repayment dates, interest rates, and the consequences of failing to keep up with loan repayments.

Understanding risk

In this topic we look at the principal sources of finance available to sole traders and partnerships. Most of these sources are also available to small limited companies. At the outset, we need to consider why it can be so difficult (and expensive) for new businesses to get finance. The short answer is *risk*: lenders are reluctant to risk lending money unless they have some assurance that the recipients of the loan will be able to pay it back.

Sole traders and partnerships are unincorporated businesses. They can set up in business with few formalities, and they enjoy a high degree of privacy in their business affairs. They do not need to file annual accounts, or other information, with Companies House which would be open to public inspection. As a consequence, lenders can find it difficult to fully evaluate unincorporated businesses for investment potential and credit-worthiness, and this generates uncertainty.

All lenders have guidelines on the level of risk that they are willing to accept. Uncertainty increases a lender's calculation of the risk associated with a loan to a business. If a lender feels that too much is uncertain about an unincorporated business, then it may simply refuse to lend a business money.

Other lenders may recognise that an unincorporated business is a risky proposition, but they may be prepared to lend money providing that a partnership or sole trader pays a high interest rate on the loan. Interest rates on many loans are set in relation to the current base rate. (Set by the monetary policy committee of the Bank of England, the base rate is used as a means of controlling inflation in the economy.) Lenders will often charge a considerable premium on top of the base rate, both to reflect the level of risk involved in making the loan and to make money (lenders are commercial businesses themselves).

For example, if a lender is prepared to lend at an 18 per cent premium to the Bank of England base rate, this means that at the February 2006 base rate of 4.5 per cent, a business would be paying 22.5 per cent interest on any loan. This makes the finance very costly, and the business would need to be able to generate sufficient revenue not only to pay back the loan but to meet these interest payments (usually monthly) for the duration of the loan.

Consider an example. Suppose the gourmet food business featured above manages to arrange a £30,000 loan. The lenders have offered a fixed rate loan rather than pegging their interest rates to the Bank of England base rate, which can fluctuate. This can be attractive, as the partners will know exactly how much they will have to repay. In this case, the lender has offered a five-year loan at an annual interest rate of 20 per cent. Full repayment of the

Figure 8.5: Cost of borrowing: a worked example			
	Interest	Capital	Total cost
Year 1	£6,000		£6,000
Year 2	£6,000		£6,000
Year 3	£6,000		£6,000
Year 4	£6,000		£6,000
Year 5	£6,000	£30,000	£36,000
Total			£60,000

loan is to be at the end of the fifth year. Interest payments are to be made monthly. Figure 8.5 shows the total cost of the £30,000 to the partnership.

The business will have to generate sufficient profits not only to pay these interest and capital repayments but also to support the partners and to create a fund to reinvest in the business. Suppose that the three partners only expect to draw a modest annual salary of £10,000 each and aim to reinvest £15,000 per year into the business. Over five years, the business partners would therefore draw £150,000 in salaries and aim to reinvest £75,000 in the business: a total of £225,000. Add in the £60,000 cost of the loan, and the business needs to generate a total return of £285,000 (£225,000 + £60,000) in its first five years of the business. This is an average annual return on capital of £57,000, a significant return on an initial investment of £60,000 (95%). This is probably an impossible target for most businesses.

Funding sources

As Figure 8.5 shows, business finance can be expensive. In this example, the £30,000 loan will cost the partnership a further £30,000 in interest payments over five years. To keep business costs down, many entrepreneurs will look for alternative sources of finance that have more reasonable interest rates. So what are the options?

1 Family and friends

Family and friends are most likely to be the first group an entrepreneur will approach for a business investment. They are also the most likely group to lend money. In practice, the ability to raise business funds from a family and social network will depend to some extent on that network's culture and socioeconomic background. Social groups that possess a strong business and self-employment culture are far more willing to lend money and be supportive to a new entrepreneur than a group where, say, public service is the norm.

Although an entrepreneur's social network may seem an easy and cheap source of funding, it does bring potential problems and pressures. It is best to place the investment on a clear business footing, otherwise there can be misunderstandings which might ultimately lead to family rifts that may never be healed. It makes sense, therefore, to draw up a clear contract laying out the terms and conditions of investment, setting out when (and if) the money has to be repaid to the friend or relative, and whether the loan attracts interest (and, if so, at what rate).

2 Leasing

Leasing and hire purchase agreements are a way of acquiring assets that can be used immediately without having to meet the full costs of those assets upfront. By spreading payments over time, these arrangements reduce the immediate capital needs of the business. In the gourmet food business (see above), for example, it might make far more sense for the three partners to lease the vehicles and the industrial cooker. Rather than investing £38,000 in these assets before the business has even started trading, they could lease the assets by paying an agreed deposit and then a regular sum each month. This would allow them to put more of their resources into their working capital.

Unincorporated businesses can find it difficult to lease some items, or to get lease agreements on reasonable terms. The leasing company is in effect loaning the business the asset, and it may expect the business to make a high initial down payment and pay a high interest rate on the "loan". However, there are companies that specialise in leasing to businesses, including unincorporated businesses that find it difficult to arrange lease agreements.

3 High street banks

Traditionally, high street banks have not been very open to small businesses that come looking for finance. However, the banks have worked very hard in the last few years to understand small businesses. Branch managers have been sent on business-awareness sessions at leading universities. As a consequence, banks are now more willing to lend money to small businesses than before.

While small businesses are likely to get a more sympathetic hearing, banks remain commercial organisations: they must keep their shareholders satisfied, minimise their exposure to risk, and maximise their own return on capital. This means any small business granted a bank loan can expect to pay a relatively high interest rate, and it will have to meet quite tight terms and conditions that the bank sets to ensure that the loan can be repaid.

Before granting any loan application, banks would require the applicant to submit a business plan. Most banks now offer an online service to help businesses prepare and set out this plan. The advantage of filling in a bank's own forms is that it makes it relatively easy for the bank manager to read and process the application. The disadvantage is that this can take a considerable time in completing different paperwork if a business is submitting loan applications to several lenders.

In addition to the general business plan, banks expect entrepreneurs to plan their capital needs in advance in order to take advantage of the best terms and conditions on loans and overdrafts. Banks will charge very high interest rates if businesses come to them at the very last minute for loan and overdraft facilities. They also expect entrepreneurs to have demonstrated their own commitment by investing a significant amount of their own savings in the business.

If a bank agrees a loan application in principle, it will look for one final condition before handing over any money – this is security. Banks will not make unsecured loans (though they may offer a limited overdraft facility). They expect entrepreneurs to secure a loan against their personal assets, such as their houses. If the loan is not repaid, the entrepreneur can have these assets seized by the bank. In other words, many small business owners have to risk their homes to get bank finance. If the entrepreneur does not have sufficient assets to secure the loan, then the bank may ask for a guarantor. The guarantor will be someone with an adequate income or assets who would be legally liable to repay the loan if the business defaulted on its interest or capital repayments.

stop and think

Some of the supermarket banks offer very competitive loan rates; some can be as low as 6 per cent compared to say 28 per cent on some credit cards offered by major banks.

Think through the consequences of running a £1,000 debt that bears a 28 per cent interest rate for five years, compared to having a £1,000 loan on a five-year fixed interest rate of 6 per cent.

How much more interest would you pay in five years at the 28 per cent rate?

4 Credit cards

A credit card can be the easiest source of funds for an entrepreneur who is in a crisis. However, the interest rates charged on credit card debts are extremely high. It is often possible to switch a credit card debt to a loan with much lower interest rates or to another card that offers low (or zero) interest for some introductory period.

5 Grants

There are some grants available for small businesses. Some grant-awarding bodies require the business to be incorporated, but there are some that will consider unincorporated businesses.

Grant schemes are very specific about the type of business that is eligible for support. Funding depends on a whole range of factors, such as where the business is located, what sort of capital purchases the funding is for, what sort of business the entrepreneur is trying to set up (hi-tech industries are more likely to get support than traditional industries).

Most grant schemes are set up for a fixed period, and the rules governing eligibility change frequently. It is important, therefore, to research grant schemes at the time funding is needed. Good places to start this research are the three business advice websites we noted in Topics 1 and 2: the DTI best practice site (www.dti.gov.uk), the Prince's Trust (www.princes-trust.org.uk) and Shell LiveWIRE (shell-livewire.org.uk). These websites can direct you to the schemes that are currently operating.

Note that some grant-awarding bodies also operate some loan schemes, enabling businesses that are eligible to raise finance (usually for specific acquisitions) at interest rates below those available from banks and commercial lenders.

6 Business investment

Occasionally, a new business might develop an idea that interests another company. For example, the company might be interested in the new business because it has a commercial interest in the development of the new business's product.

In these circumstances, the company may be prepared to provide some finance to the new business. However, it is unlikely that any company in this situation would want to invest in an unincorporated business. Usually it would want a stake in the new business in return for its investment, and that is best arranged by the new business becoming incorporated and issuing shares.

7 Venture capitalists and other business angels

It is very rare for venture capitalists to fund sole traders or partnerships. These investors are likely to want the legal safeguards that are offered by limited liability company as well as a stake in the company – that is, a share of future profits in return for their investment. This is easy to organise through a limited company.

8 New partners

A final option for an unincorporated business is to look for additional partners to bring more capital into the business. This is not as easy as it sounds, as it is often quite difficult to find suitable people who are passionate about the business and have spare capital available to invest.

There are a number of questions that need to be addressed here. First, there is a need to establish the format of ownership. In other words, if a new partner is brought into the business, is a new partnership to be formed or would a limited company be more appropriate? It would be difficult to continue operating as a sole trader.

Second, it is necessary to establish the ownership shares – the entitlement to a share of any profits – of each partner. This would be done by amending a partnership agreement or, in the case of a company, by issuing shares.

Third, roles need to be established. It needs to be clear who takes the decisions – are they taken jointly or does someone have the final say if the partners can't agree? The partners need to be clear who is responsible for the various parts of the business.

Working capital management

As we have shown, it is not straightforward to raise finance for a new business. It can also be costly, and the interest repayments on business loans can be a considerable burden for a new enterprise.

One way of lowering this financial burden is to find ways of reducing the business's capital requirements. Working capital management is a set of tools and strategies that can be used by small businesses to reduce the amount of working capital required. This is the money any business requires to fund its ordinary day-to-day operations.

Stock management

New businesses should try not to tie up too much capital in stock. They can buy stock as and when it is needed. The disadvantage of this approach is that by buying stock in relatively small quantities, a small business may lose discounts for bulk buying. It may also misjudge demand, and risk losing orders through running out of stock.

Debtor management

Any business that provides goods and services on credit terms to its customers has to have working capital to cover the period between the supply of the goods and services and the receipt of payment from customers. Clearly it's in the business's interests to get paid as soon as possible.

One way to speed up payment is to use a factoring service, such as Alex Lawrie Factors. You can find out more about the service provided by Alex Lawrie by visiting its website (www.alexlawrie.com).

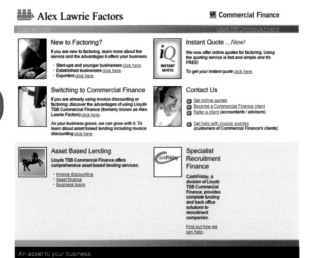

A factoring service will pay the business a proportion of an invoice as soon as it is issued to a customer. The factoring service usually then takes on the responsibility for recovering the debt. Of course, it charges for this service, so although the business gets paid promptly, a proportion of every invoice it issues is taken by the factoring service. The terms of trade offered by a factoring service to a new business are likely to be poor as the business does not have a track record, so the factoring house will not know how well their debtors pay. For established businesses, factor's fees are unlikely to exceed 5 per cent of the total value of sales invoices.

Debtors can also be managed by the business itself. Most new enterprises feel too vulnerable to insist on very tight terms of credit because they are wary about turning away potential customers who will not accept the credit terms. However, it can be good practice to offer very tight terms of credit from the start. In the short term, a business may lose some custom. In the long term, though, this may be prove to be a useful way of screening out poor credit risks and avoiding bad debts.

Cash

Cash and sundry expenses need to be controlled very tightly. It is very easy to let expenses drift out of control or to increase gradually. Considerable money can be saved by being rigorous about expenses management. It is not mean – this is about good business and survival. Cash flow forecasts should be regularly used, reviewed and revised to keep the business solvent and on target to achieve its goals.

Suppliers

Clearly any business would like to be able to buy stock and supplies on credit terms, as this will free up cash for other expenses. This credit, in effect, is a form of interest-free finance. However, most suppliers are unlikely to offer credit terms immediately to a new business. They will want to get to know the business and see how well it is managed before offering credit terms. Once credit terms are offered, they are usually limited – it will take time before a business is trusted to pay its debts as they fall due. It is therefore imperative that a business treats its suppliers with respect. Debts need to be paid on time to build up a good credit history, so that in due course a business is able to obtain credit from suppliers.

Tax planning

Finally, any business needs to consider tax benefits, the tax advantages that it might get when taking a particular course of action. If a business can reduce its tax liability, then it should have more money available to reinvest in the business. One issue to consider is the tax position of different types of businesses, because they are taxed in different ways. For example, depending on their profit levels, some unincorporated businesses may pay 40 per cent tax on their profits compared to about 19 per cent for incorporated businesses. This does not mean that every unincorporated business should incorporate and operate as a company, but there may be a case for some to take this course of action.

assessment practice
Abdul's renovation business

Abdul wants to set up a small building business. Initially he intends to do the work himself, taking on medium-sized house-renovation jobs. He can always hire in specialists when he needs them. Abdul reckons he needs £30,000 start-up capital for a van, some tools and the working capital to purchase raw materials, hire larger equipment and pay the fees of any specialists he takes on. He already has £10,000 in savings, so he wants to borrow an additional £20,000. He is now considering his options.

- Abdul's father has offered to give him £5,000. This is his life savings, which he would need to draw on in his retirement. The news of the offer has made Abdul's brother and sister jealous – they always said that Abdul was their Dad's favourite.

- Abdul could lease the van instead of spending £10,000 to buy it outright. This would spread the cost of the van. The effective rate of interest would be 14 per cent.

- Abdul's friend Sachin is in the building trade. Sachin suggests he adopts his policy of getting clients to go to the wholesalers and buy the big building material items themselves. This could reduce his working capital needs by somewhere between £5,000 and £10,000.

- Abdul has a credit card with an interest rate of 14 per cent and a credit limit of £5,000.

- A loan company has offered to lend him up to £30,000 at an interest rate of 25 per cent.

- A high street bank has offered a loan of £10,000 to Abdul at an interest rate of 12 per cent.

- Sachin has offered to go into partnership with Abdul. He is prepared to bring £10,000 into the business. Abdul is not too sure about Sachin. He has seen him at work, and he has a habit of irritating his clients by doing daft things like raiding their fridges.

- When he looked online, Abdul could not find any grants that were available to him, but then he was not very confident or patient with computers.

A Advise Abdul on each source of finance he has considered. Should he consider it further or reject it outright?

B Recommend to Abdul which sources of finance he should use to fund his business. Give your reasons.

C Search the internet to see if there are any grants available to builders in your area.

D Are there any other funding strategies that you would recommend to Abdul?

Planning for success

Setting the scene: dealing with change

Elizabeth ran a high-class tearoom in a small historic town. There were few other businesses in the town, but many tourists came to visit to see the views and the old houses.

Elizabeth was keen to sell the business because she wanted to move on and start a new career in hotel management. She started looking for a potential purchaser informally as she did not wish to pay commission to an agent.

Jim, a complete stranger, walked into the tearoom one day and gave Elizabeth some useful free advice. Elizabeth implemented his ideas immediately and found that her turnover increased quite dramatically. Then Jim said that he wanted to buy the business as it seemed like a great money-spinner, but first of all he would have to write a business plan.

It took Jim forever to write the business plan. To begin with Elizabeth was patient, then it became obvious that Jim could not deal with change. The business was not static: its sales were affected by several external factors such as the weather, roadworks, big sporting events and such like. Jim could never write his business plan,

Sally & Richard Greenhill 0207 607 8549 © Sally Greenhill

because he could not produce a "correct" plan.

Elizabeth dismissed him as a time-waster and started looking for a serious buyer. Jim might have had an MBA, but ultimately he could not deal with planning for the variety of ways a business develops.

Long-term viability

Businesses fail for a wide variety of reasons. Business failure is often nothing to do with the viability of the underlying product or service idea. Entrepreneurs simply get too busy and isolated to stand back and think strategically about their businesses. They lack the time to plan properly, to find out what is going on in their markets and to see what their competitor businesses are doing.

All businesses operate in a dynamic environment which creates new challenges and new opportunities. A business could be affected by a multitude of factors, from global events like changes in government policy, Chinese exports undercutting their market and long-term climate change, to local events such as changes in demographics or the closure of a nearby factory.

Profits and cash flow need to be actively managed in the short and the medium term in order for the business to maximise its potential and survive. This means looking at the potential impact of changes in

the environment. Consider a business like Saga, that has many customers that live off their savings. Saga will want to assess the impact on its business of anything that might affect its customers, such as changes in interest rates. So the company may carry out what-if analyses to assess the effect on its business of different changes in interest rates.

There are several vital steps that every business can take that will help it survive and prosper. A business needs to:

- avoid over-trading – staying busy by selling at very low profit margins – so that it fails to make a significant profit (or may even make a loss)

- manage its cash flow, so staying solvent

- take advantage of opportunities as they arise

- find solutions to any problems and constraints

- plan the long-term management of assets and loans to develop the business for the foreseeable future, say the next three to five years.

Profit management

When business owners do their market research and plan their position in the market, they need to think carefully about their long-term profitability. It is generally not possible for a new business to grab a significant share of the market through penetration pricing, and then to raise its prices to return its profit levels to an acceptable level. Once a price has been established, customers expect that price to be maintained.

Most businesses therefore need to decide at the outset whether they are going to be a high-volume low-cost producer, like McDonald's or Coca Cola, or whether they are going to be a small niche producer that sells a specialist product at a premium price. For most small businesses, the niche market is the most realistic option. To do well in a niche market, prices need to be high because turnover tends to be low.

Many small businesses are not able to maintain premium prices, so their owners often work long hours for low profits. For example, chemists often struggle to compete with supermarkets. So although they supply a valuable service in providing prescription drugs (often out of main shopping hours), studies have shown that many chemists who run their own shops only make about £10,000 a year, even though they are working six days a week and every fourth Sunday on a rota.

When entrepreneurs are planning their businesses, they need to assess whether they can provide product features that are so highly prized by customers that they are willing to pay premium prices. Even seemingly straightforward services can be made different from their competitors. For example, all hairdressers and barbers provide essentially the same service – they cut and style customers' hair – but they present themselves in many ways. This is why there is such a wide range of prices even for basic hairdressing services.

At the bottom end of the market, the customers are packed closely together in a small shop with few frills. Customers might be charged £3–£10 for the service. At the top end of the market, you might get a head massage, coffee and snacks, magazines, your own personal hair consultant and the pleasure of experiencing a top hairdressers where the "best" people go. This pampering comes at a price, and you can easily pay over £100 for a haircut.

Entrepreneurs have often chosen the independence of working for themselves over a high income. Whatever their motivation, they still need to ensure that the profit levels are high enough to secure the long-term viability of the business. Owners should regularly monitor their profit margins and overheads to keep them at acceptable levels. This can be done through monitoring profit and loss accounts on a monthly basis, comparing actual expenditure to planned budgets, and doing simple ratio analysis such as calculating profit margins.

Cash flow management

In Topic 5 we showed how cash flow forecasts are an important tool in forecasting a business's working capital requirements. They are also a key management tool in their own right. It might be tempting for any entrepreneur to treat all funds coming into a business as profit, or as cash that can be spent immediately. However, any business will have regular expenses, and needs to have ready funds to cover those debts. This is where cash flow forecasting is essential.

Cash flow forecasts do not give an indication of the profits of the business, but they indicate the cash position over time. The owner can use cash flow forecasts to see if the business is likely to experience a cash shortfall, and they can then plan accordingly, perhaps by organising a short-term loan. The forecast might show a period in which there is a good flow of cash funds, and the owner might decide to use that surplus cash to develop the business.

Cash flow forecasts ideally should cover the life of the business's loans (which are typically taken out for three to five years). The forecast will show whether the business is likely to generate the revenue to meet the regular interest payments and the eventual capital repayments. Drawing up long-term cash flow forecasts isn't a precise science, and further into the future the forecasts may only be rough estimates, but there should be a basic outline of expected cash flows. This enables an entrepreneur to:

- plan the future development of the business

- set targets for cash inflows and outflows

- think of strategies to control cash outflows, or increase cash inflows in relation to cash outflows.

This long-term strategic thinking needs to take place two or three times a year. Successful entrepreneurs regularly take time out to think through their future plans, and to try and get their businesses into perspective. It is often useful to have someone from outside assisting with this process, as everyone closely involved in the business will find it difficult to stand back and ask difficult questions about how the business is run.

Managing opportunities, facing challenges

Opportunities and challenges often come together. The development of mobile phone technology and free internet telephony is both a big opportunity for telecoms businesses but also a direct challenge to the traditional companies that rely on calls on land lines. Businesses need to be sufficiently flexible to be able to respond to change. The management guru Peter Drucker writing in 2003 urged large corporations to embrace a more entrepreneurial model.

The challenge for small businesses is to select the best opportunities given their very limited resources. A

assessment practice
Le Picard Camping, Normandy

Paul and Lucia Palmer own Le Picard Camping, a peaceful, friendly campsite in Normandy that mainly caters for English and Dutch families. The site has 37 camping spaces and seven mobile homes. It has 170 spaces for caravan storage, allowing customers to leave their caravans at the site rather than taking them home. The Palmers' supporting businesses include a restaurant and laundry service, and they get further income from caravan and mobile home sales, and ground rent from their seven mobile homes.

The business is highly successful. Families looking for reasonably priced, long summer breaks are happy to make their own entertainment around the beaches, countryside and history of Normandy. A high proportion of customers return each year. After the summer season, the campsite tends to be taken over by retired couples, and caravan enthusiasts who enjoy camping in a relatively small community.

The campsite is successful because it offers a highly personalised service. The Palmers treat their customers as guests who have come to share their home and their relaxed French lifestyle for the summer. It is a small and friendly campsite, with a relaxed attitude: customers are left to their own devices, there are few site regulations, but behaviour tends to be reasonable.

Why do customers keep coming back? When asked, you get comments like:

- for the combination of camping and caravan storage – there are not many sites that do that

- we feel like paying guests and enjoy a personal relationship with the owners

- the Palmers appear to know everyone really well when they arrive

- the peace and quiet

- pleasant company, nice food, quite rural site, good weather

- good value for money

- the site features in Dutch guide books as a good location for family groups.

The Palmers started their business in 1990. They had both worked on the cross-Channel ferries and were looking for a more settled life to bring up a family. They decided to move to France and set up a new home. Lucia's brother had asked if he could store his caravan at their new home. As they were thinking about starting a business, they decided to run an advert in some English newspapers to see if anyone else wanted a caravan storage service. The calls came back from interested potential customers, so they built a parking area for caravan storage. Paul and Lucia had found a market niche: it is cheaper to store your caravan in France than to bring it back and forth on the cross-Channel ferries.

As the caravan storage business built up, the Palmers landscaped the remaining grounds of their home for their own benefit. It was not long before caravan owners asked if they could camp for a night in the grounds when they picked up and dropped small business must not be afraid to turn down opportunities that would keep it very busy but not yield much profit. Instead, small businesses must operate to their strengths, and often that means focusing on offering high-quality personal service. For example, small stationery shops have to meet the challenge presented by the threat posed by the large out-of-town superstores. The local stationery stores that are doing well are those that now offer support services, such as basic administration, faxing and photocopying, to people who work online at home. These customers find it convenient to use a local shop: they are willing to buy at a premium in return for good personal service.

It is useful for all entrepreneurs to get out and see what their competitors are doing. This can be as simple as going for a walk past other shops and services. It might involve listening to radio stations such as Sunrise Radio which has regular discussions on small business strategies, going to business network meetings, or visiting the DTI website to read through new business case studies.

It is also valuable for all businesses to build up relationships with their customers. Many customers are very keen to promote local businesses, and most people want a successful local economy with a good variety of local services.

off their caravans. In June 1995 the Palmers built five camping/caravanning pitches and a shower block. According to Paul Palmer, "it was a gamble, we just wanted to see if it would pay off. Now demand has built up such that we are turning away business".

In the winter, when business is quiet, the Palmers maintain the site and the caravans and plan their long-term strategy. They have always drawn up careful cash flow forecasts to see if the income of the business will repay loan finance. The Palmers like to plan five years ahead, to map and cost out various ways in which they could develop the business further.

Further development, however, is constrained by several factors.

- It is generally felt that the campsite is now at an optimum size – if it gets any bigger it will lose the village atmosphere where everyone knows everyone and children can roam freely.

- It is not possible to access any more adjoining land to expand the caravan storage any further.

- It is difficult to get staff with the same passion for the business as family members.

The Palmers are reluctant to build up another business which would require them to travel between sites or to manage paid staff. It has been suggested that they might consider franchising the operation, so that the same sort of facility could be located near other ferry ports. Several customers have remarked that they could not find any comparable business of the same quality near other ports.

For more information on Le Picard Camping visit www.camp-france.com.

A Identify the ways in which the Palmers have managed their risk and their working capital as they built up their business.

B Identify the ways in which the Palmers have developed a service that has a very loyal customer base.

C From the website (www.camp-france.com) and the case study, consider how you might develop the business further if it were yours.

Setting the scene: TL Retail

Tony and Louise run a small clothes boutique. They have been doing this for 14 months. They researched small businesses before opening the shop, and realised that many entrepreneurs do not set aside time to plan and evaluate their businesses. Consequently many small businesses seemed to fail as a result of lack of sustained vision and strategic planning. Tony and Louise therefore built in time to evaluate their business planning.

Tony and Louise decided to carry out a formal review of their business each year in January, when their stock was at its lowest and business was quiet. They close the business for two working days in order carry out a structured business review. This involved several stages.

■ First, Tony and Louise "walk the business". They approach the business with a fresh, critical eye, assessing their own strengths and weaknesses by walking around their business from all angles and making notes. They plan to rethink the whole image – the branding, interior décor, the store layout, the website – and they want to see afresh what the business communicates to the customer.

■ To get a different perspective, they look through photographs of the business taken back in November, when the shop was busy and fully stocked.

■ They invite a small group of trusted customers

to carry out the same exercise. After the customers have "walked the business", they ask them to discuss its strengths and weaknesses. This session is videoed.

■ They meet with their accountant, who gives them a set of financial accounts, management accounts, and a brief written report.

■ They bring all the evidence together by trying to group it into common themes. From this exercise they try to prioritise the most urgent issues and identify five key targets for the coming year.

■ Tony and Louise then formalise their thoughts into a business plan. A copy of the business plan is sent to their bank – even though they are not currently seeking additional funding, they believe that it is important to maintain their bank's confidence in the quality of their management so that it will be easier to borrow money in the future.

KEY TERMS

Evaluating the business is the process of reviewing all aspects of a business to identify its current position and to pinpoint where it could develop to in the future.

Walking the business is the process of physically looking at all aspects of a business and how it actually works. A good manager will be doing this at least every week informally. Management teams often walk the business formally once a year.

Analysing is the process of bringing evidence together and processing it further by written comparison or further calculations in order to gain further insight into a situation.

Evaluating is the process of deciding between various alternative solutions, with the aim of choosing the course of action that will overcome constraints and meet the business objectives.

Reviews and evaluations

It is not possible to really get to know a business from a desk by poring over the financial data. The financial data is important, but the analyst needs to go out to the business's premises and see the business in action. It may be useful to observe where the business sells its goods and services and to carry out some market research with customers and employees.

All businesses need to carry out a review of their operations at least once a year. This is necessary preparatory work to setting strategic goals for the coming year and reviewing the long-term business plans. These reviews often use evaluation tools such as SWOT and PESTLE analysis, as well as an examination of key financial information. The main purpose of the review should be to identify the constraints on the business and to collect the information that will enable the business to develop strategies that it can implement to overcome these constraints and maximise its goals.

SWOT analysis

SWOT analysis is a management technique used to analyse a business under the headings of strengths, weaknesses, opportunities and threats. Strengths and weaknesses are internal to the business and cover the areas of marketing, finance, human resources, and production of goods and services. Opportunities and threats are those factors outside the business that affect the performance of the business. These opportunities and threats may come from a wide range of factors, but are generally classified under these headings: political, economic, social, technological, legal and environmental.

PESTLE analysis

PESTLE analysis is a management technique to analyse a business's external environment and its impact on the business. PESTLE is an another acronym, each letter stands for:

P = political, such as changes in government and fear of terrorism

E = economic, such as interest rates, exchange rates and level of consumer demand

S = social, such as changes in people's lifestyles, changes in fashion, and changes in the size of households

T = technological, such as changes in hardware and software capability, and developments in links between different pieces of technology

L = legal, such as changes to the laws on health and safety at work, changes to the rights of working mothers and fathers, changes to EU laws on competition policy

E = environmental, such as increasing congestion, levels of pollution of all types, and vermin control.

Carrying out an evaluation

Evaluation exercises can be quickly undermined by human factors, particularly in small businesses. Evaluations can make people in the business feel that their position is under threat or that their work is being criticised, and this can lead to tensions, difficulties and problems.

This can be exacerbated by an individual's position in the business or their relationship to other people in

the business. Here are some typical examples of the problems that can arise.

- Mr and Mrs Jones are in a business partnership as well as a marriage. Mrs Jones is a very strong character with firm views on how to run the business. Mr Jones does not want to challenge her opinions for fear of any business disagreement affecting their marriage.

- Amy is 22 years old. She works for Mr Smith, the owner of a small business. Amy knows that Mr Smith is losing business as some of his silly comments and embarrassing jokes turn away potential customers, but she does not know how to tell him.

- John and his four daughters are in business together. John built the business up over 30 years. He does not like to delegate and he still treats his daughters as children, even though they are all over 30 years old. When any of John's daughters question his judgement they get shouted at, often in front of other people in the business. They are just waiting for John to die or retire. Meanwhile the business is missing opportunities to expand internationally.

Implementation

Once a review is carried out, its findings and recommendations need to be implemented. They need to feed into the management plans for the coming year, the strategic plans for the next, say, five years, and people's personal targets for the year. If there is a need to raise additional finance, the review should feed into the business plans that might be submitted to potential lenders.

Everyone should know who is responsible for implementing the business review recommendations. During the year there should be regular checks to ensure that the outcomes of the business review are being followed up and that the business is performing more effectively.

These regular checks of strategy should be with the clear understanding that businesses are dynamic – sometimes a target that was valid six months ago becomes obsolete and needs to be updated during the year. Businesses must update their targets if circumstances change. It is not unusual – but highly unproductive – for businesses to keep revisiting out-of-date targets for meeting after meeting because the senior partner wants to keep going back to the review targets set at the start of the year. Sometimes you just have to accept that the world has moved on.

Look back through the case study about Tony and Louise's business TL Retail (on page 42). Figures 8.6, 8.7, and 8.8 contain the financial data. The analysis prepared by their accountant is also produced below. Imagine that you are in the position of Tony and Louise and want to continue the evaluation of the business.

Before presenting the financial data to Tony and Louise, their accountant told them: "You need to have a feel for the business in numbers. Work through the numbers yourself.

"Take it step by step, doing a calculation, and then think what other information do I have that makes more sense of this information, as I have done for the gross profit margin in my report.

"Then you need to think how you can increase the effectiveness of the business. In this case, the evidence points to increasing cash sales and to increasing sales throughout the year. Go back to your market research and see if that yields any ideas that might offer some solutions. Assess each of the ideas and select the best one (evaluation). If you want to borrow money, a bank manager needs to see both analysis and evaluation in your business plan to support your strategy."

Accountant's report

The gross profit margin looks very healthy at 66%. However, this could be even better if you made more cash sales. The credit card companies are taking a fixed percentage of each credit sale and they are slow to pay up: this is causing cash flow problems for the business.

Actual cash received for cash and credit sales totalled £163,500 by the end of the year, but as you made £300,000 sales in the year, this means you are still owed £136,500 at the year end stood. Debtors at year end therefore represent 45.5% of annual sales, though this is skewed by the fact that the bulk of sales were over the months of November and December. November's sales at £75,000 and December's sales at £120,000 represent 25% and 40% of the year's sales respectively. So you made 65% of all sales in the last two months of the year.

Figure 8.6: Profit and loss account for the year ended 31/12/05	
Sales	£300,000
Cost of sales	£100,000
Gross profit	£200,000
Overhead expenses	£35,000
Net profit before appropriation	£165,000

Figure 8.7: Balance sheet as at 31/12/05	
Fixed assets (NBV)	£238,500
Current assets	£155,000
Current liabilities	–
Net asset value	£393,500
Capital	
Partners' capital	£228,500
Retained profit	£165,000
Capital employed	£393,500

Figure 8.8: Management accounts

Monthly accounts	Jan	Feb	Mar	April	May	June	July	Aug	Sept	Oct	Nov	Dec	Total
Sales	10,000	10,000	10,000	11,000	11,000	10,000	10,000	10,000	12,000	11,000	75,000	120,000	300,000
Cost of sales	3,334	3,333	3,333	3,667	3,666	3,334	3,333	3,333	4,000	3,667	25,000	40,000	100,000
Gross profit	6,666	6,667	6,667	7,333	7,334	6,666	6,667	6,667	8,000	7,333	50,000	80,000	200,000
Expenses	2,916	2,917	2,916	2,917	2,916	2,917	2,916	2,917	2,917	2,917	2,917	2,917	35,000
Net profit	3,750	3,750	3,751	4,416	4,418	3,749	3,751	3,750	5,083	4,416	47,083	77,083	165,000

2005 cashflow	Jan	Feb	Mar	April	May	June	July	Aug	Sept	Oct	Nov	Dec	Total
Sales cash	3,000	3,000	3,000	3,000	3,000	3,000	3,000	3,000	4,000	3,000	22,500	36,000	89,500
Sales credit	0	0	7,000	7,000	7,000	8,000	8,000	7,000	7,000	7,000	8,000	8,000	74,000
Cost of sales	3,334	3,333	3,333	3,667	3,666	3,334	3,333	3,333	4,000	3,667	25,000	40,000	100,000
Expenses	2,916	2,917	2,916	2,917	2,916	2,917	2,916	2,917	2,917	2,917	2,917	2,917	35,000
Net cash flow	-3,250	-3,250	3,751	3,416	3,418	4,749	4,751	3,750	4,083	3,416	2,583	1,083	28,500
Opening balance	-10,000	-13,250	-16,500	-12,749	-9,333	-5,915	-1,166	3,585	7,335	11,418	14,834	26,585	
Closing balance	-13,250	-16,500	-12,749	-9,333	-5,915	-1,166	3,585	7,335	11,418	14,834	17,419	18,502	

A Pick out three pieces of information from the data available to Tony and Louise. Use that data to *analyse* the business – find other supporting data, carry out further calculations or make written comparisons.

B Suggest and recommend (that is, *evaluate*) alternative ideas that might increase the business's effectiveness.

C Calculate the cash flow forecast for 2006 assuming that sales remain the same and expenses do not change.

D What would be the impact on the business if Tony and Louise decide to invest in an additional store? They plan to buy the store in April for £200,000, and to be open in May. They assume it will have the same sales pattern as the first store. The purchase price of the new store will be funded out of cash and a bank loan. Tony and Louise do not want to have a bank overdraft above £20,000. What is the minimum value of loan that they need to take out?

E Visit two retail stores selling similar types of goods. Walk the stores, observe the customers, the sales staff, the layout of the store, the quality of the stock, and so on. Imagine that you work for one of the stores, and write a report suggesting five ways in which it could improve its sales. Use the other store visit for ideas and comparisons. Your report must include clear analysis and evaluation.

Business in practice: La Spezia Delicatessen

La Spezia Delicatessen opened in South Croydon in 2004. The business is a partnership. It is run by Georgio, who brought some capital but mainly his expertise to the business. Georgio's business partner is a sleeping partner – he has contributed capital to finance the business (and shares the business's profits) but takes no active part in managing the enterprise.

Georgio has been working in niche food retail and restaurants nearly all his life. His most recent job had been running the Little Bay, a very popular restaurant opposite his current shop. Georgio's customers at the restaurant all thought that a delicatessen was a really good idea, and said that they would all shop there.

The partners have signed a five-year lease on the premises. The shop was a mess when they took it over, and it needed to be cleaned and renovated. This meant that they were paying the rent on the lease from September 2003 although they only started trading at the beginning of 2004. The quarterly rent on the premises is £2,200. In addition, they must pay local business tax, which is about 50 per cent of the rental value. There are also lighting and heating bills to be paid, which amount to around £300 a month.

At Georgio's previous shop in north London he worked with a 45 per cent mark-up on cost, and intended to continue this practice at the delicatessen. The core of the business is groceries, cold dried meats and cheeses, and takeaway lunches for local office and shop workers. At present, the delicatessen does not have an alcohol licence.

The shop sells 25 lunches on average each working day. In the run-up to Christmas, Georgio also reckons to sell around 1,300 panettone, a special Italian Christmas cake, plus other cakes and sweets. Georgio is occasionally asked to prepare food for Italian parties. He organises delivery to the party venues and can even provide waiting staff.

Trading hours

The shop is open seven days a week. Bread is delivered at 5 am on six days a week, and Georgio must be there for the delivery as there is nowhere safe for his supplier to leave the bread outside. The shop closes at 8 pm on Monday to Saturday. On Sundays, it opens from 10 am to 4 pm.

Georgio employs another person to help him in the store at busy times. This makes it possible for him to do the business banking and to take some time off. He pays his assistant an annual salary of about £12,000. He must also pay about a third more in national insurance contributions and other sundry employment costs.

Customer profile

The customers who use the store are from various socioeconomic groups. There are the early morning commuters and local office workers who come in for coffee and snacks. The shop also attracts some commuters in the evening as they return from work. These are mainly young single people who live in the neighbourhood's flats and bedsits, who are looking for something for an evening meal. Some local residents with families use the store, finding it cheaper and more convenient than the large out-of-town supermarkets. The business also attracts many Italians, Spaniards and Poles, who specifically come to South Croydon to buy speciality foods.

Location

La Spezia is close to South Croydon station. The surrounding streets are home to many commuters who work in London. Though not on a main road, the business is on a very busy roundabout. Many cars pass daily, though the situation makes it inconvenient to stop. (For information on the immediate area use the www.upmystreet.com website – La Spezia's postcode is CR2 6PW.)

Whitgift School (www.whitgift.co.uk), a well-endowed private school for 1,200 boys is nearby. Annual school fees are £11,259. Parents of Whitgift pupils rarely pass the shop – they either drop their sons off at school by car or the boys arrive by train or bus unaccompanied. Occasionally some of the older students go over to the shop for lunch, but this tends to vary depending on the students' other social and extracurricular demands.

The business is located at the end of the popular restaurant and nightlife area in South Croydon. There are a variety of other retailers and businesses in the same area including:

- three mini-supermarkets and an English bread shop
- printing and stationery shops
- hairdressers
- small cafes and takeaway restaurants
- some medium-sized businesses including the Croydon Advertiser Group
- an NHS dentist who attracts clients from up to 15 miles away.

There are a few other very good stores in the area, including an art gallery and an interior design and fabrics store.

The nearest car park is at the railway station. Parking in Croydon is highly restricted and expensive. There are significant penalties for parking without a ticket, parking in a non-parking location, overstaying on a ticket and for residents parking in the wrong zone. It is not unusual for cars to be taken away and impounded by the council. There are residential parking bays on most streets, but not enough for all residents with cars. Parking restrictions usually apply until 5 pm.

Outlook

Georgio has been disappointed with sales. He is averaging £200 a day throughout the year (and working seven days a week, 52 weeks a year). When he ran a shop in north London, his turnover was at least £800 a day. His friends complain that it is difficult to park so they go to the supermarkets, which are more expensive and lower quality, but more convenient for parking.

He is very popular with his regular customers who got him into the top three of the LBC Living London Awards for the last two years. He just doesn't seem to be able attract more custom in his current location.

activities

Imagine that you have been asked to join the partnership to help reinvigorate the business. Georgio will give you free rein to implement new ideas and initiatives if you can show that you can raise sales to an average of £800 a day.

You need to do further research on all aspects of the business. Find out about the area, research what attracts people to shop at delicatessens, and consider strategies for increasing the effective market of the business.

Georgio has no spare cash. If he is to improve the business, he will need to take out a bank loan. In order to do that, Georgio will have to write a business plan. He has no spare time, so you must write the business plan on his behalf.

1. Collect a file of research evidence that you can draw on in developing ideas to improve La Spezia Delicatessen. Build up a picture of the business under various headings, including aims and objectives, marketing plan, resource plan, and financial analysis and planning.

2. By analysing your research file, produce proposals for Georgio on how he can develop the business. You should cost out your proposals, so that Georgio knows how much money he needs to borrow to implement your ideas. Write a business plan for Georgio.

3. Georgio decides to request a bank loan so that he can implement your ideas. Write a covering letter to the bank to go with the business plan.

4. Swap your business plan with a fellow student. Read your fellow student's plan carefully, and mark where you can see evidence of:
   - knowledge skills and understanding of business studies
   - application of knowledge skills and understanding of business studies
   - research and analysis
   - evaluation.

5. The bullet points in activity 4 (knowledge skills, etc.) are the exam criteria. Edit your business plan to ensure that it meets these criteria. Ensure that your final draft is an appropriate piece of communication to a bank and makes a well-supported case for a bank loan.

PEOPLE ARE THE MOST IMPORTANT RESOURCE OF ANY business organisation. Without people, nothing would get done. Even a car production line at Citroën that is operated entirely by robots needs people to turn the production line on and monitor output.

This unit examines how businesses manage, train and motivate their employees in order to achieve their goals. At its core is a recognition that when planning how to use human resources effectively, organisations must consider the needs of their employees as well as the needs of the organisation. Sometimes these needs conflict, and this conflict must be resolved.

Motivation plays an important role. This unit reviews the motivational theories of Maslow, Herzberg and McGregor, and practical issues of financial and non-financial incentives. It examines the motivational aspects of working in teams – and the other benefits and limitations of teamworking – and considers the factors that affect the performance of a team. It considers how the style of management influences the motivation and performance of employees.

People need developing in order that they can be used in the most productive way in an organisation. Individual employees have different needs for training and development, and organisations must meet individual development needs in a way that fulfils organisational objectives. Some businesses use personal development planning as a basis for drawing up plans for staff development, and the final sections of the unit introduce some tools for identifying individual development needs.

Managing and developing people

Setting the scene: the Hellespont swim

For a long time I had wanted to swim the Hellespont, the narrow channel between the Sea of Marmara and the Aegean. It was here that in Greek mythology Leander, who lived on the Asian side, fell in love with Hero, on the European side. Leander visited every night, and Hero would light a lantern for him to swim towards. One night the wind blew out the lantern and Leander was lost. Hero hurled herself into the waters of the Hellespont.

It had always been assumed that the Hellespont could only be swum by gods. But after one failed attempt Byron did it, and it has been done from time to time ever since. We should do it, I said to Steve and David (fat, pale, thirty-something pie-eaters like me).

There was a surprising amount of paperwork. The European shore is a military zone rumoured to be mined. The Hellespont itself carries a huge volume of traffic between the Mediterranean, Istanbul and the Black Sea. The Turkish authorities don't like the idea of Englishmen's bodies choking the propellers of container ships, and insist on everyone getting permits.

We trained in municipal pools, but never seemed to get faster or less tired. It was difficult to motivate ourselves, because there really didn't seem to be much connection between the heated human soup of the public baths and the swimming of a major shipping lane. The calendar ticked on, and we found ourselves in Turkey.

With the dawn came renewed incredulity at our stupidity. It was cold, there were some vast tankers in the channel, and the current was throwing up white horses that looked like Grand National winners. Also there was a launch full of photographers following us. Failure would not be private.

As the sun came up, our clothes came off. The lads on the boat rubbed us down with axle grease and we committed our bodies to the deep. As soon as I hit the sea, I was on my own. Behind was the grumbling of the escort boat's engine. Somewhere ahead Steve was swimming furiously towards fame. David on one side was grunting and swallowing water. But I was in my own world. I felt lonely and disoriented. There was no sense of movement. From the boat there were occasional shouted words of advice like "sewage slick ahead: keep your mouth shut" and "this is where blood started to pour from the Ukrainian's ears".

There was a vague sense of pressure against my chest as I ploughed into the current, but there was no visible fixed point against which I could measure any progress. Failure, though, was unthinkable. Too many people knew about this venture. If I didn't reach Sestos I could never return home. Then, suddenly, the current eased. A shout from the boat told me to turn up the strait. That was the indication I had been waiting for. It meant that the back of the Hellespont was broken. I began to realise that there was no need to keep a lot in reserve any more.

From then it all happened quickly. Looking up, I could see Sestos castle on the gorse covered hills of Asia. Seemingly a thousand miles away there was some cheering as the press men hauled Steve out of the shallows and asked him what on earth he had done this for. And then suddenly we were there too, stumbling out into towels and a posse of television cameramen.

Demotivation is a sense or belief that a course of action will not benefit a person in any way and may go unrecognised.

Motivating factors are incentives for taking a course of action.

Motivation is a sense or belief that a course of action will benefit a person in some way.

Motivation

People behave in certain ways because they believe it is in their best interests to do so. For example, you get up in the morning to come to school or college because you believe that you will benefit more than if you stayed in bed. Similarly, people go to work because they believe that they will benefit more by going to work than by not working. The belief that a course of action or certain type of behaviour is in your best interests is what motivates you to take that course of action or behave in that way.

The difficulty comes when trying to decide why people think certain courses of action or types of behaviour are in their best interests. For example, do you get up and come to college because you want to do well and get a good career or place at university? Or is it because you will get into trouble with your parents or guardians if you don't? And does somebody go out to work for the money, or for some other reason such as to be with workmates or to exert power?

There is a considerable body of theory that attempts to understand and identify the factors that motivate people. If businesses knew what motivated their

Figure 9.1: Motivational theories

Mayo:
Hawthorne studies

Maslow:
Hierarchy of needs

Motivation theories

McGregor:
Theory X and Theory Y

Herzberg:
Hygiene and motivating factors

employees to work harder and to contribute more, the success of the business would be assured. In this topic, we look at the work of some major theorists and consider their ideas about motivational factors.

Elton Mayo

Between 1924 and 1933, Elton Mayo, an Australian, undertook a series of studies into staff productivity at Western Electric's Hawthorne Works in Chicago at the request of the company. They developed into one of the largest investigations into motivation and employee attitudes at work that has ever been undertaken. Four major studies were carried out by Mayo and other researchers from Harvard University.

The illumination study

The illumination study involved women working with small components. It was believed that improving lighting conditions would result in improved productivity. The women were therefore split into two groups: a control group, where lighting conditions remained unaltered, and an experimental group, where the level of lighting could be manipulated. The productivity of both groups was then monitored.

As the lighting conditions for the experimental group were improved in stages, their productivity did indeed go up. But so did the productivity of the control group. In fact, there was little difference between the levels of productivity for the two groups throughout. What was even more baffling was that when, at the end of the experiment, the level of lighting for the experimental group was reduced to a level lower than it was before, and lower than the control group, productivity was maintained at the higher level.

From these results, it was apparent that while lighting may have been a factor in employee productivity, it was by no means the only or even the most significant factor. A second study was therefore undertaken, using a smaller group, to try and identify other factors affecting the productivity of employees.

The relay assembly test room study

The relay assembly test room study involved a group of six women, all assemblers of telephone relay equipment. The women were placed in a separate room where they worked a normal 48-hour week, including Saturdays, without any tea breaks, in conditions that were as close as possible to the room in which they worked before.

During the study, various working conditions were changed, including introducing and taking away rest periods, altering the number of hours worked, and changing the daily start and finish times. The women were observed by a researcher who tried to put them at their ease by talking to them, explaining what was happening and discussing with them each change that was being made to the working environment.

When rest periods and other improvements to working conditions were introduced, productivity increased. Yet, surprisingly, the increased productivity was maintained by the women when conditions in the test room returned to normal. Discussions with the women at the end of the test revealed that other factors than working conditions had influenced the way they worked, including:

- a feeling of importance taking part in the test, which was reinforced by the interest in them shown by the researcher and the company

- being involved in decisions on changes in working conditions

- developing friendships with the other women in the group.

It was apparent that the attitudes and morale of the women were as important factors in their productivity as improved working conditions.

The interview programme

The interview programme was intended to find out more about attitudes and morale at work, to discover how these are shaped and how they affect performance at work. Some 20,000 interviews were carried out which ranged from fairly tight questioning about work to more general discussions about home life and social issues.

One of the findings of the interview programme was that informal groups with their own rules and hierarchy developed within and across the formal work groups organised by the company. These informal groups seemed to play an important part in the behaviour and productivity of members. In order to investigate the development and workings of these informal groups further, a fourth and final study was undertaken.

The bank wiring observation room study

The bank wiring observation room study involved three work groups of three workers plus a supervisor. From these three formal groups, two informal groups developed, each with their own leader and rules or norms, and it became apparent that these informal groups controlled the actual output both of the individual workers within the groups and of the groups themselves.

Conclusions

The main conclusions of the Hawthorne studies are:

- pay and working conditions are not the only, or even the main, motivating factors affecting behaviour at work

- behaviour and attitudes are influenced by feelings of recognition, belonging and acceptance

- groups exert a powerful influence on people's attitudes

- informal groups can both motivate members and control their behaviour.

Abraham Maslow

In 1935, Abraham Maslow identified five categories of human needs:

1. physiological needs (basic life-supporting needs such as food and water, reproduction and warmth)

2. needs for safety and security (such as the need for living in a stable, predictable and ordered environment without fear)

3. social needs (such as the need for social interaction, belonging to a family or group)

4. needs for recognition and esteem (such as the approval and respect of others, influence and power over others)

5. needs for self-realisation (in order to develop as a person, fulfil one's potential and achieve one's goals).

It is the drive to meet these needs that provides the motivation to action and shapes a person's behaviour. Maslow suggested that the five categories of needs build upon each other. That is, a person will only strive to fulfil the higher-level needs when the lower level needs have been met. In other words, a person who is starving will seek for food before he or she worries about whether they have the respect of others. For this reason Maslow described his five categories as a hierarchy.

An attempt to simplify Maslow's need theory was put forward by the US psychologist Clayton Alderfer in 1969. Alderfer identified three categories of needs:

- existence needs

- relationship needs

- growth needs (needs for personal growth and achievement).

Frederick Herzberg

In 1966, Frederick Herzberg put forward a theory based on research he had carried out by asking a sample of employees what actually motivated them at work. On the basis of their responses, he concluded that factors such as pay, working conditions, organisational policies and administration, management, and supervisio, did not actually motivate them. If these factors are inadequate, employees will fight for them to be improved, but they do not actually motivate people to work harder. Herzberg called them hygiene factors. The real motivating factors were connected with the job itself, such as how interesting the job was and the opportunities it provided for achievement, recognition, promotion and responsibility.

Some of the ways in which Herzberg's theory can be implemented are by trying to improve the nature and content of the actual job. Several strategies have been adopted by businesses which attempted to use Herzberg's ideas.

- **Job enrichment** – employees are given a wider range of tasks (though not necessarily more tasks), and are encouraged to take part in decision-making and consultation processes. This may be accompanied by a reduction in supervision and involvement in setting targets.

- **Job enlargement** – employees are given a greater variety of tasks to perform in order to make the job more interesting. A greater sense of achievement may be felt by employees, for example, if they can see a process through to completion rather than concentrating on just one operation in the process.

- **Job rotation** – this approach seeks to give employees greater variety and interest in their work by enabling them to try a range of associated jobs at different times. In this way, employees may also gain new skills and opportunities for advancement.

One important factor which will influence the way employees feel they are perceived and treated at work is the amount of positive feedback on their performance they are given. Many business organisations now operate appraisal schemes – the individual performance of employees is assessed, and discussed with the employee at an appraisal meeting, usually once a year.

At these appraisal meetings, an employee is given feedback usually by an immediate manager on his or her work performance. It is important that this feedback is positive, encouraging the employee to build on his or her strengths and to strengthen any weaknesses, perhaps through additional training. Positive feedback given in this way serves to demonstrate an organisation's interest in the development of its employees, rather than just in whether they are making sufficient contribution to profits. It reinforces the effect of other motivators and helps to make employees feel valued and committed to the organisation and the job. Feedback given orally at appraisal meetings is often confirmed in writing, and both parties to the discussion will agree and sign the written appraisal report.

Douglas McGregor

In 1960, Douglas McGregor, a social scientist, put forward a theory of motivation at work based on assumptions about what workers are actually like. In fact McGregor put forward two theories: Theory X. which was based on the way most organisations and managers viewed their workers, and his own Theory Y, which was based on the way he considered people work best.

Theory X suggests that people dislike work and avoid it if they can. They must be persuaded with high wages, controlled with strict supervision, and threatened with punishment to ensure they put in the maximum amount of effort.

Theory Y, on the other hand, suggests that people actually enjoy working and will strive to meet targets and objectives to which they are committed. Their commitment to work is increased when they feel ownership of their job or task through increased responsibility and participation in decision-making.

The implications of McGregor's theories for the way employees feel they are perceived and treated at work are obvious. Some of the ways in which Theory Y management could be implemented are through

- delegation of responsibility
- consultation
- participation in decision-making.

assessment practice
Absenteeism in the UK

It is estimated that absenteeism is costing UK businesses over £11 billion a year. In 2004, workers took 176 million days' sick leave – up 10 million on the 2003 figures.

Obviously every employee (well, nearly every employee) has to take sick leave some time. But the problem is serious, with employees increasingly taking a "sickie". Businesses are looking at different ways of tackling this issue. It pushes up costs, because production cannot go according to schedule if people are missing every day.

Tesco recently said that it would withhold pay for the first three days of sickness. At British Airways, where employees take an average of 17 days off sick a year, the company has tried offering rewards for good attendance.

Another company has employed a nurse to answer the calls from people ringing in sick. This is aimed at discouraging people from taking a "sickie" as they have to describe their symptoms to the nurse – who can probably tell whether they are genuine. They also receive advice to help them get better quickly.

This has triggered a debate about the best way to get staff back to work, and many human resources departments are considering which method works best – the carrot or the stick. At Standard Life Healthcare, for example, a masseur is brought in by the company with the aim of keeping employees healthy and stress-free. This has resulted in a 9 per cent fall in absenteeism, a 5 per cent increase in productivity, and an improvement in customer service.

Another stress-buster that's laid on by the company is a 45-minute Pilates class. The employees who take it vouch that it works. National sales manager Claire Ginnelly says: "Because we have implemented different things throughout the company, that has made people realise what a good place it is to work. It makes for more loyal and productive employees."

The company hopes that fitness classes, healthier food in the canteen and a less stressful day will encourage staff to want to be at work and keep healthy.

Source: adapted from BBC News Website 10 September 2004

A Why is absenteeism a problem?

B Explain the statement "many human resource departments are considering which method works best – the carrot or the stick".

C Compare the approaches to absenteeism of Tesco, British Airways and Standard Life Healthcare.

D What advice on improving absenteeism would you give to Tesco?

Motivation in practice

Setting the scene: motivation at Marks & Spencer

Marks & Spencer is one of the largest UK high street chain stores. As a major retailer, the company is aware of the importance of providing a high level of service to customers.

Marks & Spencer offers a range of incentives and benefits to attract, motivate and retain the best people in retail. The company's benefits package includes competitive rates of pay and performance-related rewards that are regularly checked against other retailers to ensure they are competitive. Every employee's basic pay is reviewed every year and performance rewards are given to recognise individual achievement.

The company's retirement plan is one of the best of its type in the UK. All employees who have worked for the company for over a year can save up to 15 per cent of their salary in the plan, with the company making matching contributions.

Employees are also entitled to:

- a profit-sharing scheme

- a 20 per cent staff discount on M&S's products

- a generous holiday entitlement that increases with length of service

- optional subsidised health and dental care

- discount offers on holidays, theme parks and sports club membership.

Recognising the importance of striking a balance between working and home life, Marks & Spencer has introduced a range of initiatives to help employees with family responsibilities. These initiatives include flexible working, support for working parents, and career development. Many go far beyond the company's legal obligation as an employer. To ensure all employees are aware of the choices available to them, they are provided with a booklet setting out the various options.

Source: www2.marksandspencer.com

Incentives

Theory is all very well, and theories proposed by Mayo, Maslow, Herzberg and McGregor are very valuable in helping us to understand motivation. But how does it help an individual business decide on the best way of motivating its employees?

Most businesses have a limited – but practical – range of factors at their disposal that they can use to motivate their workforce. This includes financial and non-financial incentives. Financial incentives are those that can be given a monetary value, such as wages and salaries, pension schemes and health insurance. Important as these are, however – and few people would work without being paid – theories of motivation have shown that employees also look for other, non-financial incentives.

KEY TERMS

Incentives are anything offered to a person to encourage them to take a course of action.

Financial motivators are incentives that have a monetary value.

Non-financial motivators are incentives that do not have a direct monetary value.

Increasingly, therefore, businesses are developing strategies to motivate staff which involve a mix of both types of incentive. Money is always in the mix, but businesses also recognise the importance of offering praise and responsibility and providing opportunities for career development and advancement.

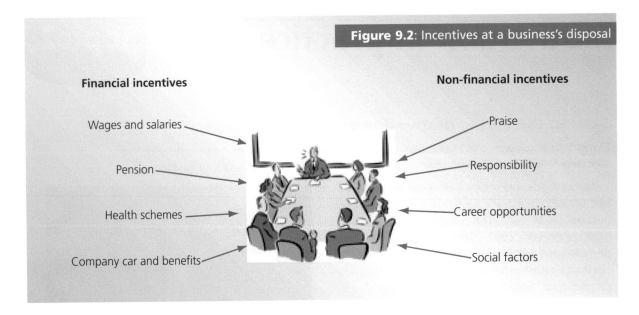

Figure 9.2: Incentives at a business's disposal

Financial incentives

Wages and salaries

Pension

Health schemes

Company car and benefits

Non-financial incentives

Praise

Responsibility

Career opportunities

Social factors

Money

Money is necessary for people to obtain many of the most basic needs, such as food, shelter and warmth. These needs are the first rung of Maslow's hierarchy of needs. Even once the basic needs are met, many people want higher salaries in order to afford a larger house, a better car or more Christmas presents for the children. Such things satisfy higher-order needs such as esteem needs.

Money is also an important factor in establishing differentials: wage and salary levels reflect the position and importance of employees, not only in the organisation but also in society. Other financial incentives may include pensions and health insurance.

Praise

Praise helps employees feel that they are valued and their work is appreciated. People who feel that their employer values them and appreciates their efforts are likely to contribute more to the business.

Responsibility

Responsibility can motivate people in the same way as praise. If an employee is given more responsibility, he or she is likely to feel that their employer considers them highly and that they are an important part of the organisation. This increases motivation, and people who feel that they are an important part of the organisation are likely to put greater effort and enthusiasm into their work.

Career opportunities

Career opportunities are an important motivating factor for many people. Employees who feel they are

in a dead-end job have little incentive to work harder – they may simply do the minimum required to keep their jobs. Employees are more likely to be motivated if they feel that by working hard and efficiently they can develop their careers. They will strive harder in the knowledge that by contributing more to the business they are also helping to develop their own careers.

Social relationships

Social factors are also important motivators for many people. As we shall see when we consider teams in Topic 3, people are not naturally solitary, and normally form groups. Working with others is a way of developing social relationships and encouraging a feeling that you are part of a group with similar aims and ambitions.

Conflicting needs

Sometimes the individual needs and motivating factors of employees may conflict with the needs and aims of the organisation. For example, in a small business there may be few opportunities for promotion. There will therefore be little incentive for people whose main motivation is career development. However, if the business can provide valuable experience and skill development, perhaps through job rotation, then working for that business might be seen as an important step in a career.

Conflict may also arise when employees look for higher salaries and wages. Labour is often one of the largest costs of a business. If a business is trying to reduce expenditure, it may keep increases in salaries and wages to a minimum, which can have an adverse effect on employees' motivation.

Lloyds TSB is one of the UK's leading financial institutions, with interests in corporate and private banking, insurance, credit cards, loans and mortgages, pensions and investments. With a history going back to 1765, the company now has offices throughout the European Union and in Japan and the United Arab Emirates.

Staff are at the core of the company's success, and Lloyds TSB actively recruits high-quality people. Entry is mainly at graduate level. In order to attract the best, the company offers a range of incentives. These include competitive pay, with bonuses and other financial incentives, a minimum of 22 days annual holiday, and training and development programmes designed to help employees achieve their full potential.

The company has a share plan, which allocates free shares to eligible employees each year based on Lloyds TSB's financial performance. Employees can also buy partnership shares – additional Lloyds TSB shares – each month, and some partnership shares are matched with free Lloyds TSB shares.

Lloyds TSB wants to give employees choice and flexibility. It offers staff the opportunity to choose their own benefits package to reflect their individual circumstances. For example, staff have the option of holiday trading – any staff member can buy or sell up to five days of his or her annual holiday entitlement each year.

Employees receive a sum each month with their salary, which they can use to take advantage of a range of offers and benefits – though they can simply opt to take the cash. They can use some of their salary to top up this cash sum to take advantage of additional benefits. Lloyds TSB call this scheme "flavours". Some of the offers and benefits that can be accessed through the scheme include:

■ discounted retail vouchers to use in a wide range of well-known stores and restaurants

■ sharesave – a savings scheme with a guaranteed tax-free bonus and the option to use savings plus bonus to buy Lloyds TSB shares at a 20 per cent discount on their market value

■ staff offers – a range of discounted offers on Lloyds TSB products as well as holidays, car hire, health clubs, etc.

■ health cash plan– offers cash-back on a range of medical treatments from hospital stays to dental care and physiotherapy

■ health screening and/or private medical and dental benefits

■ childcare vouchers

■ computers for staff – from standard desktop models to laptop and handheld computers

■ a matched learning fund

■ pension extra – an additional pension scheme that Lloyds TSB Group will also contribute to

■ personal accident insurance and/or life assurance.

Lloyds TSB is also committed to helping employees strike the right balance between work and home. In addition to the benefits above, the bank considers requests for flexible working arrangements such as job sharing, compressed work week and variable daily hours.

Source: Lloyds TSB website, www.lloydstsbjobs.com

A How would (i) Mayo and (ii) Herzberg have viewed Lloyds TSB's approach to attracting high-quality applicants?

B Identify the incentives offered by Lloyds TSB. For each identified incentive, state whether it is a financial or non-financial motivator.

C Do you think Lloyds TSB's system of motivation is likely to be effective? Give reasons to support your views.

D How might Lloyds TSB's system of motivating its employees conflict with some of the company's other aims?

Setting the scene: the finance team at DC Foods

The finance team of DC Foods plc is run by Mary Tilly, the chief accountant. Mary's job involves co-ordinating the work of the other team members, reviewing the financial information produced by the team such as budgets and cash flow forecasts, and reporting to senior managers.

Sometimes Mary must liaise with other managers over cutting costs, or taking action to meet the financial targets of the company. This is not always popular – nobody likes to be told they must spend less or do more. Mary also prepares the financial accounts, and arranges additional finance with the bank or other lenders if the company needs a new cash injection.

Reporting directly to Mary is Bianca Read, the management accountant. Bianca prepares monthly accounts, presenting detailed information on the expenses and income of each department of the company. These are compared with the budget, to show differences between planned and actual performance. Each department is asked to carry out a variance analysis to explain any major differences and to plan appropriate action to ensure that it achieves its overall targets.

Information for the management accounts is produced by Chris Nugent. He obtains financial information from each department and collates it on a computer database so that accounts can be produced quickly at each month end. He produces the latest sales figures and other analyses for the weekly senior management planning meetings. Chris also carries out the credit control function, checking credit references of customers and chasing overdue accounts. Chris rarely has to take a customer to court over an unpaid bill.

Also in the finance team are four wages clerks and a cost clerk. The wages clerks are responsible for preparing and paying the salaries of all staff. They calculate the wages of hourly-paid employees, deduct the correct tax, national insurance and pension contributions, and arrange for pay to be transferred to the bank accounts of individual employees on a weekly or monthly basis as appropriate. The cost clerk is responsible for checking the costing of the company's products to ensure that the margin between the selling price and the cost of producing the product – the profit margin – is maintained.

"Working together is important," says Mary. "The work of the finance department is essential to the efficient running of the company. We rely on each other for information, and for support in the work we do. If we didn't pull together as a team, none of us could carry out our function."

KEY TERMS

Teams are groups of people working together towards common goals.

Project teams are groups of people brought together to undertake specific projects, such as to build a hospital or to install a new computer system.

Team members are people working as part of a team. Each team member fulfils one or more roles within the team

Teamworking is a system of managing work by organising employees into teams. This increases motivation and productivity.

Teams in business

People are not generally solitary beings. Outside work, people often associate in groups or teams. This can be for many reasons. Take a moment to think why you, and people you know, form groups. Here are some of the principal reasons:

- to satisfy social needs for love and belonging

- to establish relationships

- to gain recognition as a member of an identifiable group

- to exert influence, either within the group or as a group, on outside events or circumstances

- to gain help in carrying out objectives

- to share in an activity.

In business, teams are often formed for a particular function, task or project. Other groups in a business may be less formalised, and some may take on a permanent aspect. For example, the employees in the finance department at DC Foods (see opposite) work together as a team in which each member contributes to the overall work of the department.

There are several reasons why a business may organise its staff into teams. One of the motivations for setting up teams is the nature of the work. Teams are formed to undertake tasks and procedures which cannot be successfully undertaken by one person working alone. Many teams are organised to make the best use of the skills and experience of the workforce as a whole, both in undertaking tasks and solving problems.

Other reasons for setting up teams are more concerned with efficiency and productivity. Teams can be managed much more easily and effectively than many individuals each doing their own thing. Teams make it easier for a business to disseminate information to all employees. Teams also increase commitment and motivation: people in a group are likely to feel a commitment to that group and want to work for the success of the group.

How teams form

Teams go through a fairly clearly defined pattern of development. As Figure 9.3 shows, there are four main stages in team formation.

Forming

The team members come together as a collection of individuals. At the outset, there is likely to be some discussion about the objectives and composition of the group. At this stage, team members begin to establish their roles within the team, to seek recognition and position.

Storming

Conflict between group members can occur in the early stages of team formation as members' personal agendas come to the fore. There is often a degree of jostling for position within the group. During this storming phase, team objectives and roles identified during the forming stage are refined. The division of roles within the group becomes established.

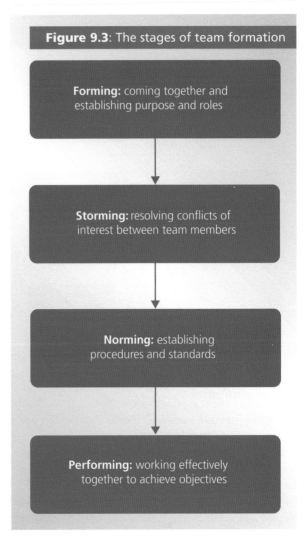

Figure 9.3: The stages of team formation

Forming: coming together and establishing purpose and roles

Storming: resolving conflicts of interest between team members

Norming: establishing procedures and standards

Performing: working effectively together to achieve objectives

Norming

The team attempts to establish norms and standards of behaviour and practice. Some team members may "test the water" to see how far they can get away with not conforming to team norms.

Performing

A team can only be fully effective when the team has come through the previous stages – of forming, storming and norming – successfully. At this stage, a team will have fully developed its approach to achieving its objectives. It now needs to deliver results.

Team members

Generally, team members fall into two categories: leaders and followers. However, within these two broad categories, there are many other roles that members fulfil which are essential to the successful performance of the team. R M Belbin has developed a computer program to identify nine basic roles which must be fulfilled for a group to be fully effective.

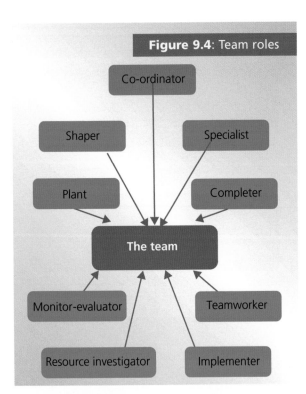

Figure 9.4: Team roles

Co-ordinator

Shaper

Specialist

Plant

Completer

The team

Monitor-evaluator

Teamworker

Resource investigator

Implementer

The monitor-evaluator

Someone who analyses the ideas and plans of the group to point out inconsistencies, difficulties and flaws. The monitor-evaluator may remain on the periphery of the group, stepping in to make a contribution before final decisions are made.

The resource investigator

Someone who identifies and locates the resources needed to complete a task, often from sources and contacts outside the group. The role of resource investigator suits an extrovert personality keen to take on the ideas of the group.

The implementer

An implementer is usually a good organiser and administrator. The implementer sees to the practical planning and scheduling of the task.

The teamworker

By themselves, teamworkers do not take a leading role in the group, but rather support and encourage other group members in their roles by listening and helping. A teamworker will often help to smooth things over if there is a disagreement within the group.

The completer

The group member who consolidates the efforts of the group as a whole. It is the completer who ensures the group meets its targets, both in terms of time and quality. The completer is usually finicky about details, checking that the task has been completed fully and on time.

The specialist

People with the specialist knowledge and skills required for the task or parts of the task.

Allocating roles

Belbin stresses the importance of each role being fulfilled in a group. If too few of the roles are fulfilled, there will be a risk that tasks may not be completed satisfactorily. In small groups with a few members, each member may have to fulfil more than one role.

Team roles are rarely allocated through a conscious decision process. Some roles are adopted because a member wants that particular role, either because he or she feels most comfortable in it, or because it fits in with their personal agenda. Other roles are adopted by members subconsciously, because their personality or temperament best suits them for the role.

The co-ordinator

Any group needs a leader, an overall chairperson who can co-ordinate the efforts of all members in the team. This role calls for someone who is an effective and well-disciplined organiser. The co-ordinator must be able to communicate well with others, to focus their minds and efforts on the objectives of the group as well as the job in hand. He or she must be able to work with and through other group members. In formal project and work teams, the co-ordinator is often appointed before a team is formed, although in informal groups a leader or co-ordinator is likely to quickly emerge.

The shaper

In many ways, the shaper acts as the co-ordinator's second-in-command, and will often take charge in their absence. The shaper can be the catalyst who turns plans or ideas into action. The role of shaper suits someone with an outgoing and dominant personality, ideally a person who is committed to the successful performance of the group and enthusiastic about the task.

The plant

The innovator of the group, the plant tends to be intelligent and imaginative. It is the plant who comes up with original ideas, suggestions and proposals. Often the role of plant suits a more introverted personality who needs to be encouraged in order to contribute fully.

Katrina wasn't so sure about the weekend. She was chief accountant of Torrey Miller plc. In fact, she had to break the news of the company's poor performance last year to Michael Adobe, the managing director. And that was the catalyst for the team-building weekend.

Michael Adobe had immediately called for a full review of the company's procedures and working practices. Consultants were brought in. The main criticism in the consultants' report was teamworking – in the consultants' view, there was not enough of it. People were put together in teams, sure enough, but they didn't *work* together as teams.

So Michael asked the human resources manager to come up with some team-building ideas. This was the result: weekend outdoor multi-activity courses for each department or team.

Katrina looked at ProAdventure's web page again and shook her head. Teamworking was all very well, but that's what it was about – working: not playing games as this weekend course was going to be.

Multi-activity Courses

All the following activities plus white-water rafting are provided on our standard two-day multi-activity courses. This is available every weekend of the year (bar Christmas Day). For our multi-activity week, visit our holidays page.

Abseiling
As you may have heard, going over the top is the hard part, it certainly is whether you are 10m, 30m or 50m above the floor. This is the second-fastest way down a cliff, and the most recommended way to get a real thrill and prove to yourself that you can do something really scary. You'll be safe as houses but your legs may tremble. Everybody comes back for more.

Rock climbing
Rock climbing and abseiling on the limestone cliffs of the Eglwyseg escarpment is one of the great unmissable experiences in life. High on a rock face, perched on a steep slope high above the beautiful Dee valley. On sunny days the sounds of the International Musical Eisteddfod drift a mile or two to the warm white rock, and the occasional sound of a steam engine gives the feeling of halcyon summers and times gone by. Come and try this exhilarating sport under the safe guidance of a qualified instructor. We can teach you a lot on our wonderful cliffs, and you may well decide to come back for our Learn to Climb weekend.

Canyoning
Gorge walking, or canyoning as it is known in other parts of the world is a surprisingly satisfying activity. Going up (or down) a narrow, deep cleft carved in the side of a mountain by the deceptively small stream through which you are wading, or swimming. Climbing up raging torrents, secured by your instructor's rope, jumping into deep pools and abseiling down waterfalls are all part of the fun. A well-earned lunch can sometimes be had sitting in the dappled sunlight on a sun-warmed slab of rock, by a deep pool with the sound of flowing water and the distant roar of the wind outside this sheltered place. After lunch perhaps you can try to traverse that pool, but remember even the instructors fall in sometimes.

Kayaking
I'm wet, again, but at last I'm going in a straight line. It took a while but now I can paddle forwards without spinning round. I didn't know why we had to make a raft with the kayaks, but I've rarely had so much of a laugh even when I fell in. The instructor made this so much fun that I learned so much without realising it. I'd really like to come back soon and learn some more, and get my own back for the dunking.

Source: www.proadventure.co.uk

A Explain the importance of teamworking to a business such as Torrey Miller plc.

B Discuss Katrina's attitude towards the team-building weekend.

C Evaluate the benefits of courses such as the one chosen by the human resources manager. Make reference to the theories of team-building in your answer.

Team performance

Setting the scene: kaizen groups at Doncasters Precision Castings

One of the main pillars of the introduction of lean manufacturing at Doncasters Precision Castings is continuous improvement, or kaizen.

The company has three full-time "lean sigma black belts" to facilitate changes within all areas of the business. The company runs a minimum of two week-long kaizen events each month. These involve a team of between five and eight employees assembled from across the company. A member of senior management (sometimes the managing director or the financial director) is also assigned to each team.

In conjunction with this internal continuous initiative, Doncasters is working closely with its customers, reviewing opportunities to drive costs down. It is important that quality is inherent in all products and procedures.

Like many other businesses, Doncasters realises that new product introduction is vital to sustain and grow its business. Mindful of this, new rapid prototyping capabilities have been introduced, and the time to market has been reduced by up to

12 months with concurrent solid modelling and tooling and a fast-track system for the manufacture of development products. A technical development team has been established to focus on enhancing existing products and processes.

There has been the development and introduction of key performance indicators across the business, with a suite of measures designed to highlight and pre-empt any potential problems. All measures are customer-focused and designed to improve customer service relating to on-time delivery, customer arrears, lead time, aged works orders, scrap rate, customer returns and non-conformance reports.

Source: www.manufacturingtalk.com

KEY TERMS

Life of a team is the period over which the team is expected to operate. The life of a project team might be limited to the period it takes to complete a project; other teams may continue indefinitely.

Team objectives are the tasks or purposes that the team has been set up to achieve

A **team's structure** is its size, members and stage of development.

Stages of development in teams are the four identifiable processes of forming, storming, norming and performing. Forming is when the team members first come together; during storming, team members establish their roles and functions within the team; norming is when standards of behaviour, attitude and performance levels are agreed; performing is when the team is working at its optimum and delivering on its objectives.

Kaizen groups are workplace teams that aim to find ways of continually improving an organisation's operations and business. Kaizen is a Japanese word meaning continuous improvement.

Factors affecting team performance

As Figure 9.5 shows, the performance of any team can be influenced by several factors. These range from the structure of the team itself – its size, members, stage of development, etc. – to the task it has been set. Other influences on team performance include the leadership style and the level of communication within the team, and the life span of a team. In this topic, we consider each factor in turn.

The effects of size on team performance

There are two aspects of team size which can impact on its performance:

- a large team can include members with a greater range of skills and with knowledge appropriate to the team's objectives

- a small team can offer more opportunities for individual members to participate fully.

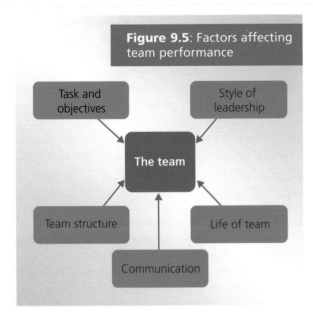

Figure 9.5: Factors affecting team performance

- Task and objectives
- Style of leadership
- The team
- Team structure
- Life of team
- Communication

The fact that a large team contains more members, and therefore can recruit people with a greater range of skills and knowledge appropriate to the team's objectives, may seem fairly obvious. You would think that the more people with the right skills and knowledge there are in a team, the more effective that team will be in carrying out its tasks. To be completely effective, however, each member must participate fully in the team's activities. Unless all team members actively participate in its work, some may make little contribution to the team's performance, and the team will not achieve its potential.

Some people find it difficult to participate fully in a large team. Someone who finds it easy to contribute when working in a team of four or five people may be unable to interact successfully when confronted by a larger group, with each team member equally wanting to make a contribution. This difficulty in interacting with a larger team may be due to shyness. It may be a reaction to the increased competition from other team members. Think how much more difficult it is to take an active part in a conversation at a party when you are in a large group than when you are in a group of three or four.

We all have what is known as a threshold of participation. A team member with a high threshold of participation finds it more difficult to participate in larger teams. In a large team, therefore, active participation tends to be concentrated on those members who have low thresholds of participation.

Studies have shown that those who participate most in team activities also have the most influence within the team. Those with influence in a large team are often the most forceful and persuasive, rather than those with the greatest skills and knowledge. This

means that some members in a large team can become marginalised. Some potentially valuable ideas are never explored, or some specialist knowledge is disregarded, because the size of the team inhibits some members from making effective contributions. This can have a negative and even destructive effect on team morale and performance, arising in part from the resentment of those members who feel their contributions are being repressed.

Qualities of team members

To a large extent the effectiveness of a team depends upon how its members work together. Collectively, group members must have the skills and abilities necessary to carry out the tasks of the group. Team members with different skills can support and supplement each other by

- co-ordinating the activities of others

- acting as a catalyst to turn the ideas of other team members into action

- finding the resources needed to carry out team plans and ideas

- analysing and suggesting new ways of approaching tasks and problems

- helping to carry out the suggestions of others.

Other factors connected with the characteristics of team members also have an impact on team performance. When members share similar attitudes, values and standards of behaviour, the team will be more stable and individuals will gain more satisfaction from working together as a group. In contrast, when there is a wide range of attitudes and values, the team is actually likely to be more productive but it will have more internal conflict. In general, teams in which members have a high level of compatibility are better at carrying out complex tasks, especially when the task requires some interaction between members.

Team members are individuals. They have their own needs and goals. In any team, individual members will seek to pursue their own objectives as well as those of the team. These personal (hidden) agendas can very greatly, but some common examples include:

- impressing the boss or leader in order to gain personal advancement

- proving oneself better than another member of the same team

- promoting the interests of the team, or protecting the team from outside influences

- making alliances with other team members.

Hidden agendas sometimes conflict with the overall objectives of the team. It is important that both the leader and the team as a whole are aware of the individual objectives of members, and work towards fulfilling these agendas as well as those of the team. This can avoid individual members concentrating on their own objectives and working against each other and the team. Obviously, the performance of the team will be more effective if individual members' objectives are in line with those of the team.

The stage of development

As we have seen, a team will only perform effectively when it has reached a stage of maturity. There will be some performance at each stage of a team's development, but once individual members are beginning to work together, the team will enter the norming stage, when it will establish:

- acceptable levels of work
- acceptable standards of behaviour
- procedures for arriving at decisions
- levels of openness and trust.

During the norming stage, individual members will often see how far they can push their own ideas and standards, to test the commitment of other members towards enforcing group norms, and to see how much leeway they have to pursue their own agendas. This is therefore a key stage of development, which is likely to have a significant impact on a team's performance in the long term.

If potential conflicts and personal agendas can be resolved at the norming stage, a team can establish a strong sense of commitment to group norms. This commitment, combined with a spirit of co-operation between team members, will play an important part in ensuring the effective performance of a team and in helping it to meet its overall objectives.

The task

A team may have been formed to undertake a particular project which will only last a limited time, or for the longer-term provision of a good or service.

An example of a project with a limited time span is the development of a computerised accounting package. It may take months to complete this type of project, from understanding the requirements of the system, through design, to testing, completion and installation. At the end of that period, however, when the new system is up and running, the team's task will have been fulfilled. The team can be disbanded.

The task of a company's sales team, on the other hand, is ongoing and continuous, with no set time span. The team may be set specific objectives with a limited time span, such as to achieve a sales target of £100,000 in August, but as soon as one target is met, the next takes its place. Indeed, as a team becomes more successful, it is likely to be set more ambitious targets. So if the team reaches its August sales target, it may be set a sales target of £150,000 in September.

There are four aspects of a task which can affect the team's performance.

- **The perceived importance of the task**
  A team that believes the successful completion of its task is important to the organisation is also likely to believe in its own importance as a team. This can be a strong motivating factor, resulting in greater commitment and enhanced team morale.

- **The timescale for completion of the task**
  If the timescale is limited, considerable pressure may be exerted on the group to finish within the set time. For example, a team developing a new football stadium may be under pressure to complete the project in time for the new season.. The team will have to adopt a more structured approach to the task, leaving less freedom for individual members to pursue their own hidden agendas. Placing a team under time pressure does not always produce a positive outcome – if the deadline seems unreasonable or unachievable, it can result in frustration, a loss of overall effectiveness, and negative attitudes from team members resentful of the pressures.

- **Clarity of the task**
  Any team will complete its task more easily when it can see exactly what it has to do. Unclear or ambiguous requirements and instructions simply generate uncertainty, and give rise to confused and ineffective performance. This may also lead to conflict within the team, as individual members may interpret the team's objectives differently.

- **Criteria for successful completion of the task**
  Not only does it help if a team knows what it has to do, it also contributes to effective performance if a team is given clear criteria for success. This means that teams need clear criteria for the quantity and quality of work to be produced, and information on the constraints under which they will be expected to work, such as any limits on costs. Just as placing a team under intense time pressure can be counterproductive, setting very high criteria which allow little margin for error can also inhibit the performance of a team.

Leadership style

Ultimately, the performance of the team is the responsibility of the leader. However, any team is only as effective as the combined efforts of its members, and all members must play their part. A leader must therefore be aware of and sensitive to the varying needs of the organisation, the team and individual members. So a team leader must draw out contributions from all members by co-ordinating their activities and by making sure that they work positively towards the team's objectives. A good leader will listen to the opinions, ideas and concerns of members. If conflict exists, the leader must decide on a course of action that is in the interests of the team and the organisation.

The life of the team

A team which has been formed to undertake a specific project may have a limited life span. A life span linked to the progress of a task can have a serious effect on the motivation and effectiveness of a team. Individual team members may find it difficult to commit themselves to a team that is soon to be disbanded. Members will question the value of the team if they become unsure of their own value to the organisation and uncertain of their future. This will be especially the case if the future of the project itself is unsure, perhaps due to funding problems. In these circumstances, team members may become more concerned with pursuing their own interests than meeting the objectives of the team.

assessment practice
New hospital development project

In 2005, a project team was set up by St Helens and Knowsley Hospitals Trust to oversee the construction of two new hospitals at St Helens and Whiston. These new facilities will complement developments in primary and social care, which together will deliver comprehensive modern services to the residents of St Helens and Knowsley.

The new hospital facilities will be funded through the private finance initiative (PFI) scheme. The St Helens and Knowsley Hospitals Trust selected NewHospitals as its private sector partner after a rigorous competitive process. Work commenced on both the Whiston and St Helens sites during the summer of 2005. St Helens Hospital is scheduled to take two and a half years to build, and Whiston Hospital four years. The schemes are expected to cost over £300 million.

Whiston Hospital is planned to be the main centre for emergency and more complex care, with over 900 inpatient beds. The redevelopment of the St Helens site will see the removal of outdated buildings and their replacement with modern purpose-designed accommodation. St Helens will be the main centre for outpatients, day case surgery and treatments. There will be a state-of-the-art diagnostic and treatment centre, a day care unit, and an intermediate care unit with 120 beds.

The trust's project team consists of a project director, personal assistant, project manager and team members from the several departments – including estates and construction, finance, and healthcare planning – as well as staff from Regeneration Opportunities and operations personnel from NewHospitals.

Source: www.sthkhealth.nhs.uk

A **Identify the functions and roles of members of a project team.**

B **Describe the ways in which a team can be influenced by the team leader.**

C **Explain the term "hidden agendas" in the context of a team such as the project team set up by St Helens and Knowsley Hospitals Trust.**

D **Discuss the factors that might influence the performance of the project team set up by St Helens and Knowsley Hospitals Trust to oversee the construction of two new hospitals.**

What does a manager do?

Setting the scene: David Phelps, manager

David Phelps is production manager of Argon Furniture Ltd, a medium-sized manufacturing business. His responsibilities include planning production, managing staff and resolving problems. This is a typical day for David.

08.30 Arrive at the factory. Collect the latest batch of customers' orders from the sales department. Go through production schedules with the shop-floor supervisor and allocate individual jobs to production workers and machines.

09.10 Meeting with six production workers who are operating the new woodworking machines. They are unhappy that they are expected to use the new technology without a pay rise. The machines call for new skills, and the staff feel that they should be paid a higher rate. David manages to avoid a dispute by promising to take the matter up with personnel .

11.00 David attends a meeting with other departmental managers about a new range of furniture to be launched later in the year. After the meeting, he speaks to the sales manager about the sales forecasts for the new range and the levels of production that will be required. He tells his production staff about the new furniture, as they will have to be prepared to do some additional overtime working to produce sufficient before the launch. It may mean that he will have to negotiate a bonus payment for those involved on the new furniture.

13.00 After lunch, David spends some time on the factory floor, talking to each of his staff. He checks that the production scheduled for the day will be completed. One production worker complains that some of the equipment is old and keeps breaking down. They do not seem to get a sufficient allocation of time from the maintenance department. David promises to raise the problem at the next weekly management meeting.

16.00 Two production workers who are working on a special one-off order come to David to ask for his help. They are having difficulty with one of the joints and, knowing David has been making furniture for a long time, want his advice. David readily agrees to show them. He is aware that the other workers respect him for being able to do any job he asks them to undertake.

17.00 The day's production has now been completed. David has some returns to complete for the finance department before getting things ready for tomorrow. He makes sure to say good night to as many of his staff as he can as they leave. He is normally the last one in his department to go home.

KEY TERMS

Decisional roles are those parts of a manager's function that involve decision-making.

Informational roles are those parts of a manager's function that involve gathering and distributing information.

Interpersonal roles are those parts of a manager's function that involve working with others both within and outside the manager's department or team.

Emotional intelligence is the effective awareness, control and management of one's own emotions and those of other people.

Managerial roles

An essential factor in the success of any business is the effectiveness of its management. Since managers are so important, it must be in an organisation's interests to employ the best managers it can.

This has led to many attempts to try and identify exactly what qualities, skills or knowledge combine to make an effective manager. Before you can begin to identify these attributes, however, you must define exactly what you mean by the term "manager": what roles managers fulfil, and what tasks managers perform for an organisation. In other words, you must find out what managers actually do.

The problem is that every manager's job is different from that of every other manager. People who run departments in a business organisation, who oversee a shop or a bank, who look after the interests of a football team or a pop group are all called managers – yet their jobs are very different. The picture becomes even more complicated when you remember that many people who undertake a management function are not actually called "manager" in their job title.

Mintzberg's ten roles

In *The Nature of Management* (Harper and Row, 1973), Mintzberg identified ten roles which all managers fulfil. These fall into three general categories:

- interpersonal roles
- informational roles
- decisional roles

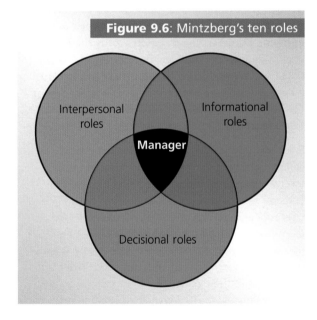

Figure 9.6: Mintzberg's ten roles

The interpersonal roles of a manager are those concerned with dealing with other people. They are:

1 acting as a figurehead

2 leading

3 liaising with others

The informational roles of a manager are concerned with gathering and distributing information about specific tasks and the general work of the manager's department or organisation. The tasks may be routine, and part of the day-to-day running of the department, or one-off events, such as the

manufacture and delivery of a special consignment. The informational roles identified by Mintzberg are:

4 monitoring the progress of the task

5 disseminating information

6 acting as spokesperson for the department or people for whom the manager is responsible

The decisional roles of a manager are concerned with planning for the work of his or her department and taking decisions to ensure this work is successfully carried out. Mintzberg identifies four decisional roles:

7 acting as an entrepreneur in order to get the task started, obtain the necessary resources and so on

8 acting as a "disturbance handler" to facilitate the smooth and successful completion of tasks

9 allocating resources

10 negotiating with others to get the best for and from the people for whom the manager is responsible in order to ensure that tasks are completed on time and to the required standard

Managing people

In this unit we are primarily concerned with the responsibilities of managers in relation to people. In each role identified by Mintzberg, managers are likely to have to deal with people. In doing so, they must take account of the factors which influence people's behaviour at work. These factors include their:

- motivation
- morale
- welfare.

All these factors are important to individuals at work. They affect people's attitudes and willingness to work, and they impact on how much they contribute to the success of the organisation. Managers must take account of their staff's motivation, morale and welfare if they are to get the best out of the people for whose work they are responsible. To do this, managers must listen to the views, opinions, complaints and needs of their staff, no matter what the work demands of the organisation.

Above all, in dealing with people, any manager must be an effective leader. A manager must be someone whom others are willing to follow, who will look after their interests and who can get them to work to the best of their ability for the good of the organisation. In Topic 6, we consider what makes a good leader, and how styles of management and leadership affect performance.

During his period as team coach of the England football team, Sven-Göran Eriksson's approach to management came in for considerable scrutiny and some criticism. This analysis of Eriksson was written by Tessera Consulting when he was still in charge of the England team, and well before the event on which his managerial reign will be judged – the performance of England in the 2006 World Cup. Read the analysis carefully before attempting the questions.

Eriksson's management style

Eriksson's restraint is legendary: he is a lesson in emotional control and charm. His ability to control his emotions in the past has led to him being nicknamed the Ice Cold Swede.

Hysén (a team-mate when Sven was managing Fiorentina) claims that in all the time he played for Eriksson, he never once heard him raise his voice. Indeed, it is difficult to think of an instance when Eriksson has publicly criticised his players, or indeed risen to the tabloid baiters. To his critics, Eriksson has said: "I know there are people who don't want me here, and I am sorry for them. But if people have an opinion about me, I try not to respond."

These are great attributes indeed for a leader. For example, it has been shown that the emotional flow within organisations tends to flow from the top down (rather than the other way around) and the emotional state of those in senior positions often rubs off on those they manage

Sven-Göran Eriksson has brought a certain calmness to the England team. You don't see him ranting and raving on the touchline when his team goes down, and this seems to have a very positive effect on the team's concentration and morale.

Another part of what it is to be emotionally intelligent is to be understanding of other people's feelings, needs and concerns. This kind of empathy is vital for a leader if he is to be able to inspire his team, and the ability to "take the temperature" of the group should never be underestimated. Unsurprisingly, Eriksson has shown competence in this area too. He repeatedly emphasises the need for team spirit, and is adept at spotting those players who may have a negative influence on the team, dropping them from the squad if necessary.

Indeed, when it comes to giving himself an honest appraisal, Eriksson also demonstrates great insight. He seems unusually prepared to admit to failings (a characteristic seldom seen in some of the less successful England managers of the past) and rarely claims to be omniscient. He has claimed: "If you have been doing a job for 20 years without ever feeling like you failed, you are either a very happy man, or a little bit stupid." He rarely believes he is as good (or as bad) as others make him out to be.

However, perhaps what Sven is most famous for is his ability to instil a high degree of trust in his team. He seems to have time for everybody (except perhaps the media) and he communicates clearly to the players that he trusts them to make their own decisions. Daniel Goleman would classify this kind of emotional mentoring under the heading of "social skills" and would further suggest that "the ability to induce desirable responses in others" is a key part of this particular competence, especially when it comes to leadership

Eriksson's own particular brand of management competence seems to be very much linked to his motivation and diligence. On his first trips to England he would visit clubs to see how teams like Liverpool and Ipswich operated. He has attended more league matches than any other England manager in living memory. Most importantly, people see that he's working tremendously hard. When a team looks to their leader as a source of inspiration, they are unlikely to react well if they feel that their leader is doing significantly less work than they are. Eriksson's approach is to set by example, and his diligence can be extremely motivational.

So, what is Sven-Göran Eriksson's personality type? Firstly, the evidence suggests that Sven-Göran Eriksson may well be an introvert. For example, others have said that his intelligence shines through most clearly not in the things he says, but in the things he does not say. Indeed, it is often the case with introverts that their contributions may not be as plentiful as an extrovert's, but what is said is often well judged and full of insight.

The British press of course would have to agree. Though he does not offer much to the media, what he does offer is certainly well thought through. An introvert's style of leadership is likely to be less up-front but can be equally as authoritative. Indeed, others have noted that his "calm" and "mysterious" approach has brought a little bit of authority back into the England manager's position. Players will say that he is not always easy to get a handle on, but is nevertheless able to convey the feeling that he knows what he needs to do.

On first appearance, Eriksson can come across as fairly traditional and conservative, but he has taken risks in appointing both David Beckham and Michael Owen to England captaincy (both of whom have risen to the challenge with honours) and is always looking for new players to bring new perspectives to the England game. This innovative approach may suggest a more intuitive preference.

People who have a preference for intuition often prefer change and something radical to a continuation of the status quo. They tend to have an eye on the future, as opposed to the past, and seldom ignore insights or the challenge of learning something new. One of the things that Eriksson has brought back to the English game is the pursuit of a long-term strategy, an approach consistent with a more intuitive outlook.

Source: www.tesseraconsulting.co.uk

A Explain how Sven fulfils Mintzberg's ten managerial roles.

B What are a football manager's responsibilities in relation to people?

C How effective do you think Sven was a manager of people? What alternative approaches could make him more effective? Justify your answer with reference to general management theories (rather than football tactics!).

Setting the scene: APQ Enterprises

Nisha Kotecha and Ken Masters are both managers at APQ Enterprises plc. Nisha is the chief executive while Ken is the production manager.

Nisha's role is to see to the day-to-day running of the company and to plan for its future. "I am ultimately responsible for the success of the company," she says, "although, of course, I rely on the efforts of my management team and everyone who works for us.

"I hold a regular management meeting each Monday morning to discuss the week ahead, and I try to get to see all my managers and as many other employees as possible. Of course, I have to resolve problems and take decisions that an individual manager cannot deal with, and keeping in close contact with employees helps me to be aware of any grievances or conflicts. I want to know what is happening within the company, as well as listening to the views of our customers."

As production manager, Ken's job is to see that production meets customer demand and departmental targets. "If my workers don't produce on time, we can lose an important order," he says. "Customers don't want to know about my problems – they want the goods, and they want them when they place an order, not when it's convenient for my workers to make them. And I think that's right. It's all part of customer service.

"So when there's a rush job on, and we have quite a few of those, I may have to lean a bit hard on my people. But it's for their own good really. Satisfied customers mean more profits for the company – and that's got to be good for us all.

"I don't hold department meetings – after all what have we got to discuss? I make sure that my workers have the jobs they have to do each morning. If there are any problems, then I sort them out."

KEY TERMS

Autocratic management is a style of management centred on the manager and in which the manager takes all decisions.

Democratic management is a style of management in which the manager takes decisions only after consulting team members and considering their opinions.

Laissez-faire management is a style of management in which decisions are left to those responsible for actually doing the work, the manager keeping a watching brief but only becoming involved when requested or in order to resolve a problem.

Proactive management leads from the front, with managers instigating actions, procedures and change to meet anticipated challenges. Proactive management may be autocratic or democratic.

Reactive management responds to the needs of the situation and team members. Reactive management may be autocratic or democratic.

Autocratic, democratic and laissez-faire styles

The style of leadership or management adopted (whether intentionally or not) by managers has an impact on employees. It can affect employee motivation and morale, and therefore affect their work, with consequences for the performance of the organisation.

Obviously, any business organisation wants to get the best performance out of its workforce. A considerable amount of research has therefore been undertaken into the effectiveness of different management styles and approaches to business leadership. The underlying goal of this research is to find the style – or styles – of leadership which is more likely to encourage subordinates to work better.

Theories of management have usually contrasted three styles:

- autocratic

- democratic

- laissez-faire.

In an autocratic management style, power and authority are exercised by the manager without reference to others within his or her department or team. The autocratic manager plans and controls the activities of the team, dictating what is to be done and spelling out how it should be done. Autocratic management tends to be task-centred, and more focused on the satisfactory completion of the task than on the welfare or motivation of employees.

In a democratic management style, on the other hand, while power and authority still lie with the manager, plans and decisions on future activities are made by the team as a whole. A democratic manager may even delegate some power and authority for making decisions to others in the team and may encourage staff to take some independent action. Democratic management is employee-centred, being based on the theory that employees will be more motivated and work better when they are involved in decision-making.

A manager who adopts a laissez-faire management style allows members of the team to carry out their functions and tasks without interference. This type of manager will remain in the background, co-ordinating and supporting the work of the team members, and representing them at management meetings.

s t o p a n d **t h i n k**

Look again at the mini case study on APQ Enterprises opposite. Examine how managers Nisha Kotecha and Ken Masters describe their different approaches to management. What style of management do you think they most clearly exhibit: autocratic, democratic or laissez-faire?

There is no "right" or "wrong" management style, and each approach may be suitable in particular circumstances. The important point is to understand that each style has an impact on employees and can affect – for better or worse – the performance of a business. Figure 9.7 briefly summarises some of the advantages and disadvantages of each style.

In practice, the management style that is usually adopted is likely to reflect both the personal characteristics of the individual manager and the culture of the organisation. Some organisations such as the armed forces and the police have an autocratic culture; others such as a housing co-operative or a creative business like an advertising agency may have a more democratic or laissez-faire culture. In business, a company's culture is likely to reflect the attitudes and ethos of its founders, its history, and its mission and strategic objectives, as well as the values of its current senior management.

Figure 9.7: Some advantages and disadvantages of different management styles

Style	Advantages	Disadvantages
Autocratic	Ensures uniform approach to tasks Provides strong direction Speeds decision-making	Can cause staff resentment Discourages teamwork and initiative Demotivates employees
Democratic	Improves staff job satisfaction Decision-making is more informed Builds manager-employee relations	Can slow down decision-making Can seem condescending Open to hidden agendas
Laissez-faire	Encourages innovation and initiative Less stressful work environment Motivates staff	Can lower productivity if lack of focus Open to exploitation by lazy staff Can lead to empire building

Theories of management

Of course, in practice, management styles do not always fit neatly into the three categories of autocratic, democratic or laissez-faire. There have been many other attempts to characterise different management styles and to offer advice to managers on how they can adapt their approach to get the best from their staff. Some of the more well-known theories are summarised in the rest of this topic.

Likert's four systems

Rensis Likert, in *New Patterns of Management* (McGraw-Hill, New York 1961) identified four basic styles or systems of management.

System 1 – exploitive, authoritarian

Management is seen as having no trust or real confidence in subordinates. All decisions are made at the top, and communication is one-way – downwards (from management to workers). This system of management operates through fear and threats – the most common being the threat of being fired.

System 2 – benevolent, authoritative

Management shows some trust and confidence in subordinates, although this is often seen as condescending by employees. Decisions are still made at the top and imposed on team members, but there is some involvement of staff in problem-solving. There is some reward for good performance, and some upward communication.

System 3 – consultative

Management shows much more confidence and trust in subordinates. Attempts are made to make constructive use of team members' ideas and opinions, and there is some participation by staff in decision-making. Overall policy, and all major decisions, are made by management. Communication is two-way between management and team members.

System 4 – participative

Management demonstrates complete trust and confidence in subordinates. Full use is made of team participation in decision-making and setting targets. Communication flows freely in all directions, and there is a supportive atmosphere in which the leader helps and advises rather than dictates and commands. Responsibility for decisions and performance are shared throughout the team.

Likert asserts that, in general, the most successful leaders are those who are able to establish work teams that are fully co-operative and have a high level of job satisfaction. In his view, this is best encouraged by a system 4 style of management.

Continuum-based theories

While Likert's four systems still place management styles into four basic categories, other theories of management have proposed a whole range in which each style shades into the next. For example, social psychologists Tannenbaum and Schmidt have constructed a continuum of management styles. The position of a leader or manager on the continuum depends on his or her personality, the nature of the work team, and the policies of the organisation.

Contingency theories

The theories of management style which we have reviewed so far are based purely on the personal characteristics of managers and leaders. They suggest that each manager has a single distinctive style. However, what is an appropriate management style in one situation may not be appropriate or effective in another set of circumstances.

This has led to the development of what are known as contingency theories of management. These are based on the idea that managers and leaders must first assess the circumstances in which management is taking place and then decide what style will produce the best results. In other words, the most effective management style to be adopted will be contingent upon the circumstances.

Fiedler's contingency theory

Fred Fiedler, an American management consultant, suggested that the ability of a manager or leader to manage or lead effectively depends upon the situation facing the team. According to Fiedler there are three critical "dimensions" or factors which have to be taken into consideration:

■ position power – the power and authority given to the leader by the organisation

■ task structure – the extent to which tasks and outcomes can be clearly defined to those responsible for carrying them out, as opposed to tasks that are unclear or ambiguous

■ relations between the leader and other team members – the extent to which the members of a team like and trust their leader, and are willing to follow his or her lead.

Fiedler also identified three conditions (or sets of conditions) which can affect the effectiveness of management styles.

Condition 1 where position power of the manager is high, the task highly structured and relationships with team members are good. Fiedler suggested that in this condition an authoritarian, task-centred management style is most appropriate, as relationships are already good and the manager is able to maintain control.

Condition 2 in which the position power of the manager is relatively low, the task is poorly structured or ambiguous, but relationships between the manager and team members are moderately good. In this condition, Fiedler suggested that a democratic, employee-centred management style is more appropriate in order to maintain relationships and to enable the manager to exert some influence.

Condition 3 where again the position power of the manager is low and the task poorly structured, but relationships between the manager and team members are also poor. In this condition, Fiedler suggested that an authoritarian, task-centred management style is more appropriate, giving rise to more positive action and better performance than a more conciliatory democratic, employee-centred style.

Vroom's decision tree

An alternative contingency theory has been proposed by the US psychologist Victor Vroom. In his model, Vroom identified these five styles of management from which managers can choose the most appropriate to their situation.

1   The manager makes all decisions and solves problems without reference to team members.

2   The manager obtains relevant information from team members, and then makes the decision or solves the problem.

3   The manager consults team members individually for opinions and suggestions, and then makes the decision or solves the problem.

4   The manager consults with the group as a whole, and then makes the decision or solves the problem.

5   The manager consults with the team, and a decision is taken or the problem solved by the team as a whole.

Modern approaches

Modern theories of management and leadership are mainly derived from contingency theories. They assert that there is no one "right" style of management: the most effective style depends on the situation.

In deciding which style of management to adopt in a given set of circumstances, a manager should consider his or her own characteristics, the characteristics and personalities of the group members, the specific nature of the task and its objectives, and the wider organisational environment.

What the manager should strive for is a style of management which takes into account these factors. In many situations this is not possible, and it is necessary to adopt the style that is the "best fit". A manager must be both proactive and reactive, changing those factors which can be changed, responding to those which cannot.

Meetings

A meeting is a gathering of people called together to discuss or investigate problems, give information, consult the views of others, take decisions or plan courses of action, when more than one person is involved. As methods of communication, involving employees in the management of the business, and spreading information, meetings have an important part to play in motivation. They are, therefore, an important management tool, and any manager needs to have the skills and experience to use meetings effectively.

Meetings are an important part in the management of any business and are called on several levels.

■   At director level, meetings are called to discuss and take decisions on the future strategy of the business and to set aims and objectives.

■   At senior management level, meetings are called to decide on plans of action to implement strategy and achieve objectives.

■   At department or team level, meetings are called to disseminate or give information, investigate problems or ways of doing things, consult the views of team members, and plan the work of the team to achieve its targets.

Many organisations spend too much money on unproductive meetings, however, and many managers and team leaders waste time which could otherwise have been spent more profitably. Running an effective meeting requires a degree of discipline and a structure. These guidelines set out seven steps for organising and chairing an effective meeting.

1   Define the purpose of the meeting, and be sure that it is really necessary. Consider whether a short face-to-face conversation or written communication with those involved wouldn't be more appropriate.

2   Prepare an agenda, and stick to it.

3   Circulate the agenda and any other papers for the meeting in advance, so that people attending are able to come to the meeting prepared.

4   Start promptly and finish within an allotted time.

5   Let people have their say, summarise and obtain a consensus of opinion.

6   Get a full range of views. Be aware of anyone who has a point to make, but is nervous or hesitant.

7   Make sure that all decisions are noted down in writing so that everybody involved can have a formal written minute (record) of the meeting as soon as possible afterwards. This acts as a reminder of any action they have to take.

As with any team activity, the effectiveness of a meeting is also affected by the style of leadership and decree of control exercised by the person chairing the meeting. This may vary according to the purpose of the meeting. For example, a meeting called to resolve a problem or consult on a specific issue may require a higher degree of control than a meeting whose purpose is a more general discussion.

assessment practice
Sarah Buchanan, leader of control team at APQ Enterprises plc

Sarah Buchanan was recently appointed credit control team leader at APQ Enterprises plc. She is responsible for a team of three assistant credit controllers. Sarah's own inclination is towards a democratic style of leadership, and typically she would wish to consult with the other team members about problems and courses of action.

Soon after she was appointed, the financial director spoke to Sarah, and explained that the company was experiencing cash flow problems – too many large customers were delaying payment of their accounts. This meant that the company was receiving too little cash and, unless the situation improved, it would have difficulty in paying its own bills. Sarah and her team must find a way of reducing the amount of outstanding money that was due to the company.

Sarah's first reaction was to discuss with the other members of her team how they could tackle the problem. On reflection, however, she realised that this course of action would not produce the innovative ideas she wanted. None of the other three in the team had been in credit control for more than three months. They did not have the experience – or the desire – to come up with new ways of reducing the outstanding debt to the company.

So Sarah took some statistics home that evening, and sat working out a new credit control strategy. She abandoned the democratic style of management she preferred and the next morning called a team meeting, during which she detailed the new strategy and told each team member exactly what they had to achieve and what was expected of them. It was easier to do than Sarah had expected. The team members supported her fully, and were obviously happy to be told what to do.

A Explain Sarah's style of management in terms of continuum-based theories.

B To what extent is Sarah proactive rather than reactive?

C Suggest ways that Sarah should organise the meeting with her team to explain the new strategy to ensure its effectiveness.

D What advice would you give Sarah regarding her management style? Justify your answer.

Developing people

Setting the scene: Tesco's approach to developing people

Wherever Tesco operates it tries to give every customer the very best. This simple philosophy has been the key to the company becoming the leading UK retailer.

Tesco also feels the same about its employees. At every level, from warehouse staff or general assistants at the start of their careers, through to the company's most senior managers, Tesco believes everyone should benefit from the best support and training the company can provide.

Tesco's commitment to people has led to an emphasis on training and development. In addition to on-the-job training and off-the-job coaching, the company has a specially designed learning programme.

With a business as big and varied as Tesco, the company is able to provide "exceptional people with exceptional opportunities" through career development. It can offer its people a range of roles, not just in retail but covering areas from human resources to finance, IT to marketing, and logistics to site and strategic research.

Teams work together, not just across functional boundaries but international ones. According to the its careers website: "Tesco's constant and rapid expansion means the company and its employees are always embarking on new ventures ... and adventures".

Based on Tesco careers website, www.tesco.com/careers/

Learning and development

People learn in order to develop. From birth, human beings learn about the world around them. What they learn enables them to adapt to and manipulate the environment into which they are born. How good someone is at learning largely dictates the effectiveness with which that individual can adapt to and control their world.

In the main, learning and development is controlled and channelled by society, through family, education and socialisation. It is an ongoing process, extending way beyond the period of compulsory school education. People continue learning new things and new ways of adapting and manipulating their environment throughout their lives.

Sometimes this learning is formal and encouraged, and takes place within a recognised education and training environment such as a school, college or university. Sometimes it is informal and a spontaneous reaction to circumstances. Sometimes the outcomes

> ### KEY TERMS
>
> **Induction training** is designed to introduce a new employee to an organisation, its structure and procedures.
>
> **Off-the-job training** takes place away from the normal work environment. Off-the-job training is often provided in skills that are not job-specific, or in a situation where on-the-job training may be dangerous or costly.
>
> **On-the-job training** takes place in the normal work environment while employees are carrying out their jobs.

are valued, sometimes not. People learn in school and college and at home, at work and in their personal and social lives.

The concept of lifelong learning recognises the importance of development throughout life. It values the continuous adaptation of the learner through training and education. This is because increased knowledge and improved skills widen a person's ability to adapt to and change their environment. This, in turn, increases self-esteem, confidence and motivation – factors which businesses seek to build on by promoting the development of their employees.

Barriers to learning

Although everybody continues learning to some extent throughout their life, as Figure 9.8 shows, there are sometimes barriers that make learning ineffective.

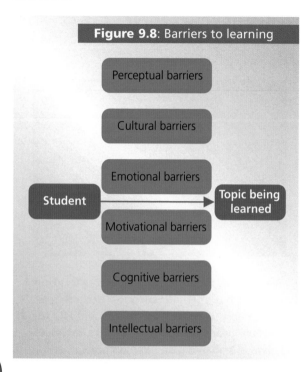

Figure 9.8: Barriers to learning

- **Perceptual** barriers arise when someone does not see that they need to learn.

- **Cultural** barriers arise when the learner is over-reliant on the way things have always been done.

- **Emotional** barriers arise out of fear or insecurity, perhaps through someone being unsure of their ability to learn new ways of doing something.

- **Motivational** barriers arise from an unwillingness to take risks or change from familiar ways.

- **Cognitive** barriers arise from prejudice based on previous learning experiences.

- **Intellectual** barriers arise if somebody has poor learning or communication skills and finds it difficult to understand the training or the trainer.

Barriers also arise if there are few opportunities to learn, or if the organisation does not support learning.

Training and development

Training and development is largely the responsibility of the human resources department in a business organisation. Through it the organisation can ensure that employees reach their full potential in the business and are used in the most productive way. This benefits both the organisation and the employee. Opportunities for training and development also have an impact on staff motivation and turnover.

Types of training

An organisation's strategy for training and developing its employees will make use of a range of training techniques, according to the needs of the individual employee and the needs of the organisation. Figure 9.9 shows main types of training.

Induction training

Induction training is one of the most important initial steps in the training process. The aim of induction is to familiarise the new employee with the organisation, to welcome them and make them feel at home. A new employee who feels comfortable with their new employer is more likely to settle in and become productive quickly.

On-the-job training

There are many forms of on-the-job training, and each has some advantages and benefits.

- "Sitting by Nellie" consists of the inexperienced employee watching a more experienced person carry out the job. The inexperienced employee is expected to remember and apply what he or she has seen. This method has the advantage of being cheap, but it can be an ineffective training method.

- Learning by doing takes "sitting by Nellie" a stage further in that the trainee actually does the job they are learning. In this way, the organisation does get some production out of the trainee. However, in the early stages of training especially, output and quality are likely to be low, and wastage from mistakes high.

- Mentoring schemes match an experienced with a less experienced employee so that the more experienced (the mentor) acts as an adviser and guide to the less experienced (the trainee).

- Shadowing aims to give trainees experience of working in different departments and job roles by following and watching another, usually more senior, job holder.

- Job rotation is a method of raising productivity by increasing job interest. It is also an effective way of widening the skills of employees and creating a multi-skilled workforce.

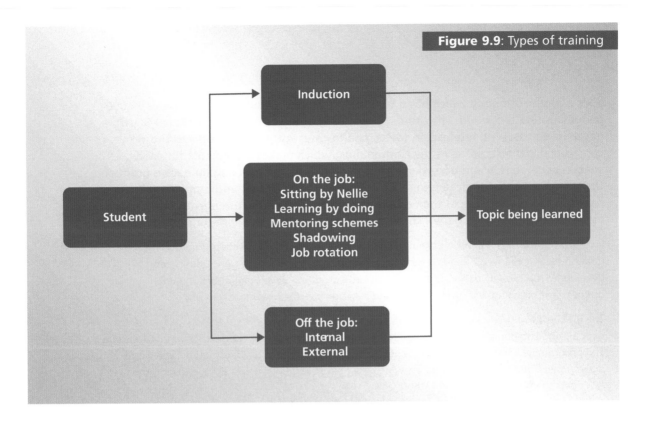

Figure 9.9: Types of training

Induction

Student

On the job:
Sitting by Nellie
Learning by doing
Mentoring schemes
Shadowing
Job rotation

Topic being learned

Off the job:
Internal
External

Off-the-job training

Off-the-job training is most useful for generic and transferable skills such as communication. Off-the-job training can be run on the organisation's own premises or can involve the trainee taking courses with an external institution.

Internal forms of off-the-job training include induction training and attendance on courses run by an organisation's own staff or by outside trainers using the organisation's facilities. Employees undertaking internal off-the-job training are unproductive during the time of the training, but they are able to give the training their whole attention without distraction.

External forms of off-the-job training include courses run by professional training organisations (which tend to be expensive) or by colleges (less expensive).

Constraints on training

When developing a training strategy, there may be constraints that limit the scope, type and delivery of the training. These include:

■ financial constraints – training can be expensive, and businesses must consider both the direct costs (the cost of running a training course and buying materials and external training resources as appropriate) and the indirect costs (the loss of production when people are being trained)

■ availability of resources within the organisation influence the type and quality of training provided – training may be more comprehensive in organisations with dedicated human resource functions and with facilities to undertake off-the-job training

■ existing skills and attitudes of staff being trained will determine the type of training offered – businesses will clearly invest more in training in areas of perceived skill shortages or areas in which the organisation is weak

■ equal opportunities legislation and policy must be observed and implemented when developing training programmes as in all areas of business – businesses must take care not to discriminate by, for example, only offering training programmes at times when employees with family commitments are unable to attend.

ICI is a global company which has a turnover of around £6 billion and employs 35,000 people around the world. The group comprises four major divisions: National Starch based in the US, with interests in foods, health care, automotive products and construction; Quest, based in the Netherlands, which makes ingredients for foods, snacks, beverages, fragrances, personal and oral care products, and homecare products; Uniquema, a specialised chemical business based in the Netherlands; and ICI Paints, based in the UK and one of the world's leading paint manufacturers with brands such as Dulux and Polycell. Together these divisions produce 55,000 different products.

ICI takes the training and development of its employees seriously. Individual programmes are defined by an employee's role and based on their ambition and motivation. Training and development is broadly delivered on three levels: a graduate development programme, business-level training and development, and function-specific training.

The ICI European graduate development programme has been developed to provide graduates with an understanding of the ICI group as a whole and a network of contacts throughout Europe. The programme consists of four key events – designed to enhance business-based knowledge, and management and teamworking skills – which are held in locations across Europe during the first few years of employment with ICI. These are:

- the "ICI World" forum – two days plus an evening

- delivering value – four days

- business understanding – three days

- self, people and teams – four days

Business-level training and development provides a mix of practical experience and formal training designed to support an employee's development in his or her role. The emphasis is on taking the initiative and learning by doing. Each division has its own range of relevant training courses for individual development. Often a mentor, who could be a recent graduate themselves, or a senior manager, will also support the employee's progress, helping them to reach their full potential and build an exciting and rewarding career.

The function-specific training employees receive will depend entirely on the function they are a part of and the job that they do. It will be tailored to their specific responsibilities and development needs. In some countries this may include working to gain appropriate professional qualifications, such as CIMA, CIM and CIPS for finance, sales and marketing, and purchasing professionals respectively.

Based on information from www.icigraduates.com

A Distinguish between training and development.

B Explain the importance of training and development in a company such as ICI to (i) the employees and (ii) the organisation.

C What other methods of training and development could ICI use?

D How might the training and development provided by a large company such as ICI differ from that organised by a medium-sized firm of builders with 60 employees?

Personal development planning

Setting the scene: Personal development planning at Tesco

Tesco operates in a highly competitive retail environment and, as we saw in the introduction to Topic 7, learning and progression from within the company is core to its operation.

All Tesco staff have personal development programmes (PDPs) to ensure they have the right skills to do their job and can access learning tailored to their own personal development needs, from induction and operating and leadership skills to core skills, such as project management, personal efficiency, effective meeting management, presentation skills and facilitation.

Each individual has a career discussion with their manager to plan their career progression. They are then placed in a "talent pool", and this information is used to determine who fills future vacancies and to identify cross-functional movement and development opportunities.

Based on Tesco careers website, www.tesco.com/careers/

What is a personal development plan

A personal development plan is a plan of action showing how the career aims of an individual can be achieved. Personal development plans can be constructed by individuals for their own use or by employers in respect of their employees.

While personal development plans constructed by individuals help the individual plan their own career aims and see what action they need to take in order to achieve those aims, plans constructed by organisations enable the organisation to see what training and development each individual employee needs in order to achieve organisational aims.

A good personal development plan can improve employee motivation. It will provide a focus for discussion and interaction between an organisation and an employee when devising a strategy for staff training and development. However, conflict may arise if the individual career development aims of employees differ from the aims and needs of the organisation. Employees can become demotivated if appraisal is poorly carried out, or if the organisation

KEY TERMS

Appraisal is the process of assessing the development needs of an individual employee. This may be done through interview and questionnaire, and/or by getting the views of peers and others with whom the employee comes into contact.

Learning gap is the difference between the skills and knowledge a person already has and those he or she requires in order to achieve career goals.

Job analysis is a method of identifying the requirements of a job by breaking it down into discrete tasks.

Peer assessment is a means of employee appraisal undertaken by colleagues whom the employee works with and who are on the same level.

Personal development plans are action plans constructed to identify the steps required for individuals to achieve their career or other goals.

does not take account of the personal development plans of employees when determining staff development strategies.

There is a range of tools available to help an organisation identify the individual development needs of its employees.

Job analysis

Job analysis looks at the job an employee is doing, and evaluates the skills required to undertake the role successfully. It is usually carried out with reference to a job description. The job description details the specific and general tasks carried out by the job holder. When carrying out a job analysis, it is important to consider the function of the job and to anticipate future developments that might alter this function or the current job tasks. For example, developments in technology may require different skills or lead to increased productivity so that some employees have to be redeployed within the organisation. Each case requires different types of training and development.

Observation

Observation is perhaps the simplest and most obvious way of assessing the needs of an employee for training and development. Observation normally consists of an employee's manager or supervisor being aware – through day-to-day contact – of the employee's productivity in terms of throughput, errors or waste, capabilities, etc., and the employee's strengths and weaknesses. This can be used to decide whether there is any need for training to improve the employee's skills and abilities. Employees can, however, feel intimidated if they feel they are being observed too closely or judged too harshly, and this will affect both motivation and productivity.

Self-observation

Self-observation seeks to avoid any feelings of intimidation by letting employees consider their own performance and make a judgement about the skills they need to develop in order to become more efficient in their jobs. Being given the responsibility of assessing their own abilities and training needs can lead to increased motivation. The main problem with self-observation is that it is likely to result in a subjective assessment.

Peer assessment

Peer assessment is where the performance of an employee is assessed by his or her colleagues. This is likely to be more objective than self-observation and give a more all-round assessment than simple observation by the employee's manager or supervisor. However, colleagues may feel they have to support an employee and this may bring bias into the assessment. In 360° assessment or appraisal, the assessment is made by everyone who has working contact with the employee, including the employee's manager or supervisor, colleagues, subordinates and others in the organisation, and even customers and suppliers where this is appropriate.

Appraisal

Appraisal normally involves an interview between the employee being appraised and his or her manager or supervisor. The interview must be conducted in an atmosphere of trust and support, and the employee should not feel intimidated or threatened in any way. A well-conducted appraisal interview will help an employee feel valued and identify areas of concern for the employee as well as the employer. Poor appraisal interviews can demotivate employees.

Performance review

A performance review is the most wide-ranging method of establishing the training and development needs of an employee. Usually a performance review includes use of the tools described above to provide an in-depth analysis of an employee's training and development needs.

Constructing your own personal development plan

We make plans every day, but do not always write them down. Writing a personal development plan helps you to define your aims and see how you are going to achieve them.

Your personal development plan is an action plan that shows the actions you are going to take to meet your career objectives. It can also be used to check your achievements and progress towards your aims. It is not a fixed statement that cannot ever be changed, but it presents a way forward. To be effective, you must review your progress against your personal development plan at regular intervals so that you can make any amendments that are appropriate.

There are three basic questions to ask when constructing a personal development plan.

- Where am I now?

- Where do I want to be?

- How can I get there?

Answering these will help you bridge the "learning gap" – the distance between where you are now and where you want to be in the future.

Where am I now?

Your first task is to decide where you are now. Consider these questions.

- What have I achieved so far?
- What am I good at?
- What do I know that I need to work on?
- What might stop me?

For example, you may feel you have good interpersonal skills, and sound organisational and IT skills, but lack formal qualifications mainly because you do not like – and therefore do not do well in – exams. You may also see money, time and lack of opportunities as obstacles.

If this is the case – and, of course, each individual will be different – you might want to consider improving your educational qualifications by concentrating on vocational skills rather than more formal exam-based qualifications. As money and time are obstacles, work-based learning would be an ideal situation. The skills you gain would also be transferable and you could continue your development anywhere.

Where do I want to be?

This is an exciting but difficult question to answer – and only you can answer it. There are many factors to consider, and it is important to remember that your answer can be altered in the future as your own aims develop and your ideas change. Again, develop your thinking by considering a series of questions.

- What do I like doing?
- What is my real motive for learning and development?
- What is my timescale?
- Are there any imminent changes to my lifestyle?
- What is my ultimate goal and how will I measure success?

As you consider these questions and other factors that you think of – and some will apply to only you – a future goal will form in your mind. Or you may have more than one goal. Your goal should be a job or career profile that you will find interesting and satisfying. Your learning gap is the difference between where you are now and where you want to be.

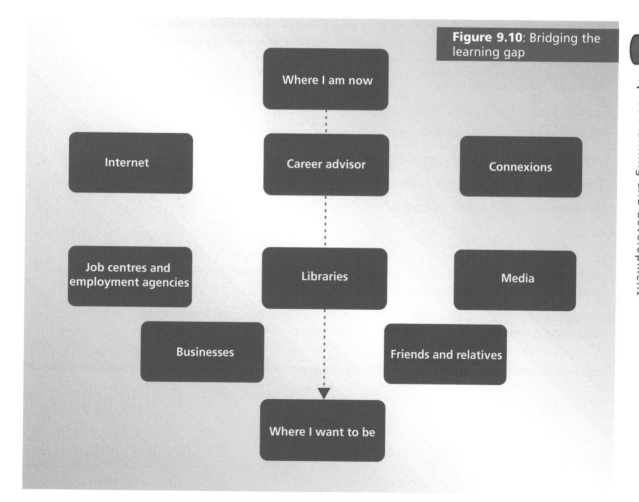

Figure 9.10: Bridging the learning gap

How can I get there?

The question "how can I get there?" can best be answered by splitting it into bite-sized pieces. Achieving small objectives on your way to achieving your overall goal will help to motivate you. The best way to do this is to set short-term, medium-term and long-term objectives, but remember that these are relative terms and mean different things to different people.

Completing this part of your personal development plan requires research into the type of job or career profile that you have identified as your aim. You need to find out what it takes to bridge the learning gap. As Figure 9.10 shows, there are many sources that you can draw on in your research. These include:

■ the internet – a wide variety of sites with a wealth of information

■ careers advisors at school, college or university

■ Connexions partnerships – local sources of information for school and college leavers

■ jobcentres and employment agencies – for job opportunities

■ libraries – most school, college and university libraries have comprehensive careers sections

■ the media – jobs sections of local and national newspapers, and trade and industry journals

■ businesses – write to the human resources manager of an organisation in your chosen sector and ask for advice

■ friends and relatives – do you know anyone in an interesting career or organisation?

The final piece of advice is to simply observe. Look around at other people you see, come into contact with or hear about, perhaps on the news, and use them as a resource and to learn a little more about what it takes to achieve your aims.

assessment practice
Your own personal development plan

Now is the time to start constructing your own personal development plan. Begin by identifying SMART objectives that you want to achieve. Identifying SMART objectives ensures that they are meaningful and you can achieve them.

Remember SMART objectives are:

Specific – be clear and precise about what you want to achieve

Measurable – so that you will know if you have met your objective

Attainable – be sure that you can realistically achieve the objective

Realistic – check that you have the means to achieve the objective

Time-bound – set yourself a deadline by which you will have achieved your objective.

Use the information in this topic to identify your objectives. Once you have identified your objectives, go on to plan how you will achieve them. Be realistic and as specific as you can. If you are not sure of anything, undertake research.

Remember, you must produce a personal development plan as part of your assessment for this unit. If this is well-researched and realistic, it will help you achieve your career ambitions.

Skills audit

Setting the scene: skills audit at Croydon College

Croydon College is one of the largest providers of further and higher education in south-east England. The college offers a wide range of qualifications at different levels and across many subjects, with over 600 staff delivering programmes to more than 13,000 students.

Many of Croydon College's teaching staff consider themselves competent or advanced in their personal use of IT. However, not all curriculum areas benefit from a well-trained body of staff with the skills to know how and when to use ILT (information learning technology) to best effect.

The college therefore decided to undertake a skills audit so a general ILT staff development programme could be devised to meet the training needs within the college. The ultimate goal was to narrow the gap between IT competence and ILT competence, and to encourage staff to integrate ILT into their day-to-day roles.

Five short questionnaires were devised, targeting both academic and support staff. (You can see examples of the questionnaires on the FERL website http://ferl.becta.org.uk.) Questions sought information ranging from access to PCs and basic IT skills to more advanced capabilities such as using online resources and interactive content. They focused on three aspects:

- technical skills
- ILT in the classroom
- ILT equipment and online resources.

To encourage staff to complete these questionnaires, online versions were uploaded to the college intranet and appeared as the first screen after staff logged in to the PCs. (Online returns also made it easier for the college to collate the data.)

Paper copies were also made available via departmental administrators and ILT champions. And, as a further incentive for staff to participate in the survey, those submitting questionnaires were entered in a prize draw, with prizes including mini digital cameras, memory sticks and WH Smith gift vouchers.

This survey was kept online for a period of two months. By the end of this period the college had received around 800 responses. After collating and analysing the results, Croydon College organised an ILT training day.

This training day marked the start of an ongoing training and staff development programme, and information learning technology skills are now reviewed regularly as part of the standard staff appraisal and auditing process in the college.

Source: FERL website, http://ferl.becta.org.uk

What is a skills audit?

A skills audit identifies and records the skills currently possessed by employees within an organisation, group or team. It allows a business to consider whether the skills available within the organisation are being effectively utilised, and to identify potential skills gaps or skills shortages.

A skills audit can be conducted on an individual basis. This is good practice when drawing up your personal development plan. You need to know your current abilities – in other words, undertake a personal skills audit – before you can properly assess your training and development requirements. This is the first part of personal development planning: the "where am I now" element.

For businesses, a skills audit is concerned with the totality of skills that are generally available within the business as a whole or within specific teams or groups. The skills audit should reveal any gap between skills currently available and skills needed by the organisation now or in the future.

Some organisations conduct skills audits on a regular basis as part of their staff appraisal process. However, auditing involves management time and some expense, so many businesses only undertake an audit if they are aware of an underlying problem or if they think that some change in their operating environment could place different skill demands on the organisation. For example, a skills audit may be carried out by an organisation if

- changes in working methods or practices are likely to lead to a requirement for new skills or the redeployment of existing skills

- the performance of a particular team or group within the organisation indicates that skills either need strengthening or are not being effectively utilised.

Conducting a skills audit

Employees can feel threatened by skills audits. In situations in which working practices are undergoing change, they may feel that the audit may be used to determine who has a future within the business and who might be made redundant.

More generally, employees may feel that they will be judged too harshly, or that the team undertaking the

audit isn't qualified to assess their skills and qualities. This might particularly be the case if a business brings in outside management consultants to undertake the skills audit.

It is important, therefore, that employees must be made aware of the reasons for the skills audit. They should be informed how it will be carried out, and what actions might result from any findings. In this way, managers can minimise any potential disruption, and are likely to retain staff support and maintain motivation levels.

A skills audit can be carried out using many of the tools used in developing personal development plans (see Topic 8). For example, an audit could be conducted using instruments such as:

- self-observation

- peer assessment

- appraisals.

Sometimes these tools may need to be adapted for the skills audit exercise. For example, the audit at Croydon College (see page 83) was conducted by self-observation, as staff were asked to record details of their own capabilities in using information learning technology. However, this process needed careful planning by Croydon College managers to ensure its success. It required a specially designed set of questionnaires, a degree of organisation, and some incentives to ensure that there was an adequate response to the audit.

Another way of conducting a skills audit is through observation. This can take many forms, from spot checks to sitting in on shifts or interactions with customers. Observation may be carried out by the leader of a team, the manager of a department, a senior manager within the organisation, or an outside human resources professional or management consultant. The observation will be of the whole team, department or organisation, although individual employees will be observed.

As with any form of observation, employees can feel intimidated and vulnerable, and this can have a detrimental effect on both their motivation and productivity. It is important that the reason for the observation and the way in which it is to be conducted is explained fully, and that any concerns that employees have are addressed. A report on the observation, including recommendations for strengthening particular teams or redeploying skills to other areas, will normally be given to senior management in the organisation.

Petfood Products plc is a manufacturer of animal food. Based at a purpose-built office and factory complex near Preston, Lancashire, the company manufactures and distributes cat food and dog food which is sold throughout the world.

The market for pet foods, although vast, is fiercely competitive, with other companies such as Pedigree Petfoods competing for a share. Cost-effectiveness, efficiency and quality are essential to survive in this market.

Falling sales and a decreasing market share have led to a new chief executive, Shona Dalby, being appointed. She immediately began an investigation into the company's poor performance. This found that:

■ the management and organisational structure of the company was too rigid and autocratic

■ the company was product-driven rather than customer-driven

■ production methods were outdated and unable to meet the needs of today's market.

The company had been making the same pet foods in exactly the same way, to exactly the same recipes, since the early 1950s. However, the market had changed, the competition was tougher, and pet foods had developed in taste and nutritional value. Customers wanted new flavours and better nutritional value for their pets – and these products were being offered by competitors.

Part of the problem lay in the fact that the company undertook virtually no market research or marketing. Research and development was the responsibility of a small section in the production department, while the company's administrative systems were antiquated – there was hardly a computer in sight. Obviously, the situation called for a major overhaul of the company.

A **You work in the human resources department of Petfood Products. In view of the impending changes necessary, Shona has said that new people with new skills would be needed. Write a formal report to Shona explaining the importance of a skills audit, the method you would use, and the benefits to the company and its employees.**

Business in practice: managing people at Aviva

Aviva is the world's sixth-largest insurance group, and the biggest in the UK. It is one of the leading providers of life and pensions products in Europe and has substantial businesses elsewhere around the world.

Aviva's main activities are long-term savings, fund management and general insurance. The group has 60,000 employees serving 30 million customers worldwide. In 2004, its key financials were:

- £2,344 million operating profit before tax
- 25.36 pence full-year dividend
- £12.9 billion shareholders' funds.

This case study is drawn from material on the company's website. It presents, in the company's own words, Aviva's approach to people management and development.

Working for Aviva

Aviva offers high-calibre people the opportunity to build a career in one of the world's most challenging and fast-moving business environments. To be a part of this, you need to be able to share our values and goals and have the skills and motivation to play a major part in our future. If this is you, then we can

offer you professional training, excellent career prospects and a competitive salary and benefits.

At Aviva we consider people to be our greatest asset. Professional, self-motivated individuals in every part of the organisation are the key to achieving excellent customer service and continued growth of our organisation. From the moment you join, you will have a stake in our success.

Benefits

Aviva is guided by our aim to be the employer of choice in all countries in which we operate. In this respect, we aspire to have competitive and fair reward policies in place set by the local human resources departments.

In order to recruit and retain high-quality individuals who can deliver our business plans, we offer competitive salaries and benefits that, as a minimum, comply with local legal obligations, such as minimum wage and equal pay for work of equal value. Only through this can Aviva hope to retain the staff who will ultimately ensure the continued success of our company worldwide.

Working for Aviva means taking advantage of the benefits that only one of the world's leading financial services companies is able to provide.

Pensions

Aviva recognises that long-term security is important to all staff so, in the UK for instance, both full-time and part-time employees are provided with pensions that they can enhance by making additional, voluntary payments. Also, in the event that a member of staff dies while in employment, their dependents may be eligible for a payment of up to four times the employee's salary. Pension provision outside the UK is determined by local legislation and market practice.

Flexible working

In view of our changing customer demands and technology, we recognise that we need to adopt a flexible approach to working. We have an increasing number of staff worldwide who choose to work from home, and the number of people who choose to job-share or work part-time continues to grow.

Staff discounts

Aviva staff in the UK enjoy very real savings on high street prices every time they click on the "Your Offers" site on the intranet.

Home entertainment, jewellery, cameras, bicycles, white and brown electrical goods, carpets: the product list seems endless. Or for bigger purchases, staff can bid for items such as former company fleet cars or, for the more energetic, there are discounts on leisure club memberships across the UK.

Staff can also take advantage of special rates for home, vehicle and travel insurance, for example, as well as for goods and services as diverse as a boat trip on the Norfolk Broads or buying books.

Share scheme

We understand that how our workers feel about Aviva is more than just what they do and how they do it. So, where possible, we offer share-based schemes that allow them to recognise their real and influential role in our ever-expanding organisation.

In the UK, as part of the rewards package available to staff, the company runs several share-based schemes so staff can benefit from the future success of the company. Most of Aviva's UK schemes are optional, and we encourage staff to think carefully about the advantages and risks before making their decision. Many of these schemes do have tax advantages for participants, but also inevitably bear the same risks as any other investment in shares.

The only company scheme in which eligible staff participate without a choice on whether to take shares is the Share Award scheme. This is a scheme where free shares may be awarded to eligible staff based on the group's profits, and released from trust tax-free after five years. This is a UK government-approved scheme that does not allow us to offer a cash alternative.

Reward packages for most staff are overwhelmingly cash-based and we encourage all staff to view share participation schemes as longer-term investments.

Holidays

Promoting a balance between work and home life is very important to Aviva, which is why we offer staff, wherever they work, the holidays that they need. In the UK, for instance, as well as public holidays, staff holiday entitlements are worked out based on length of service with the company and type of role. Where staff are needed to work on public holidays to fulfil their roles, they generally take a day off in lieu in agreement with their managers.

Health and wellbeing

All around the world, Aviva aims to help staff to pursue their professional goals, which can only make Aviva a more successful company. However, we also understand that employees may sometimes be faced with situations – either personal or professional – where it would be helpful to discuss issues with someone outside the organisation.

In the UK, Aviva runs an Employee Assistance Programme which is a free, confidential personal support service, available 24 hours a day, every day of the year. In Ireland, the Hibernian Group offers all employees a health-screening option every two years. And our Polish operation, CU Polska, offers employees a package of free medical care services and promotes healthy lifestyles by providing all employees and their families with free access to fitness clubs.

Culture and values

Aviva is a value-driven company. We strive to develop products that offer value to our customers. And we measure our success as employers by our ability to incorporate four core values into everything we do:

- progressiveness
- integrity
- teamwork
- performance.

Put simply, the Aviva group values are what Aviva stands for and believes in. They help Aviva to manage and create behaviours that it needs to display as a powerful, international financial services brand.

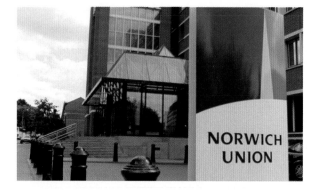

The values capture the spirit, philosophy and day-to-day behaviours which Aviva staff are expected to follow, both internally and in relationships with customers, partners and other external parties.

Progressive

Being progressive is having a vision of the future, encouraging innovation and improvement, and championing continuous learning. It is about leading the industry by listening and responding to customers and keeping ahead of the competition.

These behaviours are typical:

- welcomes new ideas; is open to diversity
- challenges the status quo and suggests ideas and improvements
- is tuned in to the changing needs of customers and employees
- always aims to be the best (in the industry)
- constantly keeps knowledge and skills up to date for continuous improvement.

Integrity

Integrity is behaving in a way consistent with professional and ethical standards and with Aviva values. It is being open and keeping commitments, taking personal responsibility for what we say and do. It is about earning trust through honesty and fairness.

These behaviours are typical:

- shows consistency between words and actions
- keeps promises and commitments
- speaks up when something is not right
- trusts others and is trustworthy
- maintains confidentiality
- actively deals with under-performance
- handles issues firmly but fairly.

Teamwork

At the core of Aviva's values is teamwork – this is what brings them together and makes them effective. Teamwork is commitment to a shared vision and objectives, depending on one another, pulling together and sharing knowledge and learning. It is creating a sense of community and pride in how Aviva operates as a business. It means taking pride in Aviva's achievements and putting the company ahead of personal interests.

These behaviours are typical:

- actively contributes to teamwork
- treats others with respect
- shares knowledge and information with others
- is able to fulfil different roles in teams
- works with customers towards common goals.

Performance

Being performance-driven is having clear goals and achieving them by everyone working towards them in an efficient way. It is taking personal responsibility for achieving results and superior service, by being committed and focused, and having a desire to excel.

These behaviours are typical:

- consistently hits deadlines and exceeds customer expectations
- has a "can-do" attitude and shows initiative
- admits and learns from mistakes
- shows perseverance and flexibility
- respects the need for work-life balance
- encourages and motivates others to achieve more
- is motivated by the need to deliver shareholder value
- takes tough decisions when the need arises.

Career management

We believe our people are a source of competitive advantage and therefore we invest in our employees' training and development. The overall aim of our career management system is to:

- maximise the potential of all staff in terms of productivity, job satisfaction and career aspirations in line with organisational needs

- ensure the needs of management succession are satisfied in line with company strategy
- attract and retain high-quality people.

We expect all our employees to take an active role in managing their own career development; however, we have created a range of programmes and processes that offer support and guidance. Our performance management system gives an opportunity for biannual feedback on a formal basis. This facilitates discussion based on performance in the current role, and your skills and aspirations moving forward.

Organisational development reviews take place across Aviva and we have set up UK-wide cross-business forums for our actuarial, accountant, legal, human resources and IT communities. These processes enable effective management succession, provide greater active career management across the group, identifying talent as early as possible and providing opportunities to develop skills and capability in our people.

All roles below director level within our UK businesses are advertised on internal job boards.

Education and training

We believe that it is essential for our business and the development of our employees that effective training and development activities are in place. On joining the group, an employee will participate in an induction or employee orientation programme in the business.

Training needs are identified as part of our performance management process, and the technical/personal skills development required is linked with the training requirements of the business. Evaluation of programmes takes place in all business units, and programmes generally exceed 3.5 out of 5 in terms of favourable scores.

International group development programmes have continued to encourage and develop our talent for their future roles and to bring the company together by building mutual understanding and international networks.

Training methods used within the group are varied, and are related to subject matter. They cover development centres, 1:1 coaching, management skills programmes and further education provided by professional institutes, universities and job-related learning. As such, it is difficult to quantify worldwide the total amount spent on learning activities for employees.

Increasingly our businesses are grouping together their learning opportunities to give a supermarket of

activities for employees: Delta Lloyd's example is called Course Shop. Also there is innovative use of computer-based training. Two examples are Aviva Canada's "e.learn" system which gives access to materials which can be downloaded at home or work, and Hong Kong's e-learning centre.

Aviva's Leadership Academy

Aviva's Leadership Academy provides an opportunity in an environment of learning where like-minded colleagues from all over the world can form networks, exchange ideas and share best practice, whilst experiencing some of the best facilities in the world.

Aviva takes its responsibility for developing its people seriously and has formed strong partner relationships with some of the top business schools in the world, including Columbia and Wharton in the USA, London Business School in the UK, and CEDEP on the INSEAD campus in France. The company also enjoys a strategic partnership with the Corporate Leadership Council and the Cranfield Change Management Consortium.

Aviva runs a series of programmes for staff at all levels, from its business leaders through to its younger manager programme, all with the aim of developing its high-potential people.

activities

1 Discuss the methods of motivation at Aviva, making reference to motivational theory. How effective do you think they are? Justify your answer.

2 Evaluate the different styles of management that might be used in a business such as Aviva. From the material provided, what do you think Aviva's preferred style of management is? Explain your answer with examples from the material.

3 Describe and evaluate the methods of developing individual employees at Aviva. Suggest how these might be improved.

4 Construct a personal development plan for a new accounts assistant who has just started work at Aviva's head office, and has dreams of becoming a senior accountant or even financial director with the company.

Topic 10 Business in practice: managing people at Aviva

THE BUSINESS OF MARKETING IS EVERYBODY'S BUSINESS. We are exposed to marketing every day of our lives. Whether willingly or unwillingly, we see advertising, promotional incentives, brand images and messages that encourage us to buy and buy again.

Although marketing theory seems to concentrate on the commercial sector, public and voluntary sector organisations also invest time, money and effort in the process. There is nowhere to hide from the influences of the marketing industry.

This unit explores how marketing decisions are made and what goes into the planning of marketing activities. It shows how businesses aim to understand the behaviour of the customer, respond to that behaviour and even generate particular behaviours as part of the bigger marketing process.

The business of marketing is complex. There are many specialities, ranging from marketing research to advertising, from internet marketing to customer relationship management. This unit helps you explore effective decision-making and planning in the marketing process.

Marketing decisions

Setting the scene: the exchange process

At the heart of marketing is an exchange process between the provider and the customer. The customer expects something from the provider, and vice versa. In the simplest terms, this is money for goods. But in a more complex world, the buying process involves a range of different satisfactions. For example, value for money is not the only reason why people like to buy particular brands.

On one side of the exchange process is the customer. The target customer is at the centre of all marketing decisions. Target is the key word here, and this point will be stressed throughout this unit. Target customers are the businesses and/or consumers most likely to buy your product and the ones at which you are aiming all your marketing activities.

On the other side of the exchange is the business. The business is looking for a profit or some other benefit, so that we can describe the marketing process as an exchange between the two parties for mutual benefit.

The Chartered Institute of Marketing defines marketing in this way:

■ marketing is the management process that identifies, anticipates and satisfies customer requirements profitably.

This definition, therefore, incorporates the beneficial exchange between the business and the customer that we will look at in marketing decisions. By understanding what motivates customers (as explored in pages 111–13 of the AS textbook), the business can maximise the benefit it gains from this exchange.

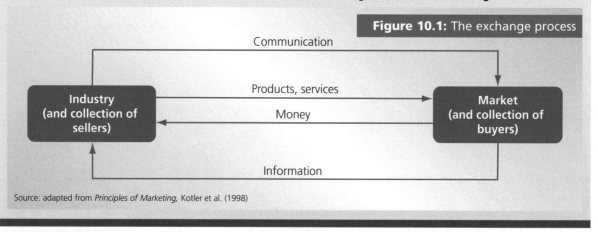

Figure 10.1: The exchange process

Source: adapted from *Principles of Marketing,* Kotler et al. (1998)

KEY TERMS

Target customers are the typical customer. They are the focus of an organisation's marketing mix.

Macro environment is the wider external environment in which an organisation operates, which directly or indirectly influences its decision-making.

Micro environment is an organisation's immediate external environment and the internal environment which mostly directly influences and is influenced by its decisions.

PESTLE analysis describes the macro environment in terms of political, economic, social, technological, legal and environmental factors.

SWOT analysis describes the micro environment and macro environment in terms of strengths, weaknesses, opportunities and threats.

Direct marketing is a form of promotion in which producers communicate directly with individual customers rather than through, say, advertising on television.

A **supply chain** is the different businesses involved in producing and distributing a product.

Distribution channels are the means of getting products from producer to consumer.

Marketing communications are all aspects of promotion which convey messages (including images) between producer and consumer.

The business environment

All marketing decisions are based on identifying, meeting, anticipating, and even generating, the target customer's needs and wants. Everything that is marketed should be what its target market wants.

This requires a systematic collection and processing of information about all the factors that influence the target customer's decision-making processes. If you want to know your customer – if you want to develop new products within a framework of managing relationships with customers – you need to know what is going on in your customers' lives and what is likely to affect their behaviour in the future.

Marketing decisions are taken about every aspect of the whole marketing process. These include the four Ps of the marketing mix – product, promotion, price and place (see Unit 3 of your AS textbook to revise these concepts) – as well as distribution, processes, branding and targeting. These are decisions key to the organisation's success. They need to be informed by the organisation's understanding of its target customers but they are also influenced by the organisation's environment.

This environment in which a business operates is the wider context that helps to shape a marketing decision. If you take a business from any part of the world and in any industry, the way that it operates is influenced in many ways by its environment. In this topic, we start to look at some of the key factors that determine the business environment. We begin by dividing the environment in which businesses operate into:

■ the wider environment – the macro environment

■ the immediate (internal and external) environment – the micro environment.

The macro environment exerts pressures and influences on any business. These factors can be categorised using the acronym PESTLE: this stands for political, economic, social, technological, legal and environmental. This analysis can then be developed within a SWOT analysis, in which a business categorises its strengths, weaknesses, opportunities and threats.

The macro environment is also one over which an individual business has little or no direct influence. That does not mean it can be ignored. Charles Handy, the management thinker, illustrates the importance of the macro environment in his parable of the boiled frog:

> It is said that if you place a frog in cold water and heat it gradually, because the temperature change is so slow it will ignore the increase. It is so comfortable with the continuous, gradual change in its environment that in the end it will allow itself to be boiled alive!
>
> Charles Handy, *The Age Of Unreason* (1989)

See the dangers of failing to keep a close watch on the environment. The point for business is to scan the environment continuously in order to assess appropriate responses to external changes. The purpose is to identify those external factors that might have an impact (positive or negative) on current and future marketing decisions.

PESTLE analysis

The macro environment comprises many factors. The value of PESTLE analysis is that it allows the macro environment to be monitored and analysed in a systematic and coherent fashion. Let's consider each element of the acronym in turn.

Political factors

Political factors clearly have an impact on businesses and the public. They can bring about (as well as reflect) social changes, and political decisions obviously shape and determine legislation. The political environment may influence decisions about product use, the import or export of certain goods, aspects of promotion, such as advertising, and so on.

The political environment isn't simply the sphere of the mainstream political parties and parliament. Marketing professionals in large companies need to manage their relationships with powerful pressure groups, such as the environmental group Greenpeace (see below), or representative bodies such as trade unions – to fail to do so can be commercially damaging.

Economic factors

One of the government's key responsibilities is to control the economy. The economy essentially represents how much people spend, what they spend money on and the distribution of wealth. Marketing is also concerned with people spending money, so you might expect the overall effectiveness of marketing by businesses to be reflected in the performance of the economy. Of course, it is not as simple as that, but the economic environment – whether the economy is

In 1995 there was a dispute between Shell and Greenpeace over a redundant oil platform called the Brent Spar. Shell wanted to sink the platform in the North Sea but Greenpeace said that it contained toxic chemicals and launched a publicity campaign against Shell.

Shell did not respond quickly, and faced a consumer backlash. There was an effective boycott of Shell's petrol stations in Germany and the company lost a great deal of revenue. Shell changed its plans to sink the rig, and instead towed it to land for decommissioning

It was later revealed that some of Greenpeace's information about the chemicals on the platform was incorrect. However, it has been difficult for Shell to shake off the adverse publicity and build a reputation as an environmentally responsible company.

growing (prospering) or declining, for example – will have an impact on consumers' and businesses' buying decisions and spending power. And this is obviously a very important influence on marketing decisions.

The government's main method of controlling the economy is through taxation and public spending. In the past, governments also controlled interest rates – this is now the responsibility of the monetary policy committee of the Bank of England, which is charged with setting interest rates so that the economy stays within inflation targets set by the Chancellor of the Exchequer. Decisions on taxation have direct and indirect effects on businesses. Increases in direct business taxes will reduce the amount of post-tax profit which could be used to reinvest in a company. A general tax rise will reduce the amount of disposable income available to spend on a company's products. Conversely, reductions in taxes are likely to benefit businesses.

The overall effect of government macroeconomic policy is to speed up or slow down spending. At the time of writing (late 2005), it seems that the economy is slowing down, and the Chancellor has revised his growth forecasts downwards. High street spending has slowed, and many retailers report falling or sluggish sales compared to the previous year.

It is not sufficient to monitor overall economic trends, however, as individual businesses need to know what impact a particular economic situation has for their particular sector. The effect of, say, a cut in interest rates or a cutback in consumer spending will not be the same across all business sectors. The fundamental point is to understand the impact of any economic change on customers. For example, a company that sells luxury holidays may find that an economic slowdown results in its customers looking for cheaper deals. This may make the company see if it can offer better value or design new products that will attract customers reluctant to spend too lavishly on holidays.

Social factors

Social factors include public attitudes and behaviours. These don't remain static, although changes sometimes take place over a long period of time. Attitudes can modify as a result of changes in societal structure. Today, for example, there are increasing numbers of single-parent families, an ageing population and people getting married at a later age. These demographic factors not only help shape attitudes but also create new markets for business.

Saga has become an extremely successful business by recognising that there was an untapped market for services targeted at the over-50-year-olds. Saga now offers a wide range of products (see www.saga.co.uk). The company's current target market is the "baby boomers", people born in the first years after the Second World War. Many in this generation have had successful careers, their children have left home and they have high levels of disposable income. While many firms have focused on younger consumers, Saga has recognised and exploited a lucrative market.

Changes in attitudes and tastes also shape the demand for particular products and services. For example, increasing concerns over environmental issues is driving demand for "green" products such as organic food and "ethical" holidays. Changes in jobs and incomes may lead to changes in aspiration and expectations. People's lifestyles change – where people live, what they do, what they buy are all factors that impact on marketing decisions.

The terrorist events of 9/11 had a major impact on consumer confidence. The airline industry was particularly affected. Worst hit were the traditional long-haul carriers such as British Airways. The transatlantic trade suffered as UK consumers appeared to feel safer travelling shorter distances.

Other factors have also had an impact on the air travel market. The low-cost airlines have found that they could gain market share, and grow overall customer numbers, by using a price-driven ("no-frills") marketing model.

One effect of these market and social changes has been that UK consumers now tend to take more short holidays in European countries. Time will tell whether this change – partly, but not solely, resulting from an unforeseen external event – has been a permanent one.

Technological factors

The term technology applies not only to digitally based technologies (such as the internet) but also to the development of new materials and enhanced technical, mechanical and electronic processes.

The impact of technological factors used to be relatively minor compared to the other PESTLE factors. However, this has completely changed in the past ten years or so, as technological changes have driven business processes and increased the speed of new product development (NPD).

In marketing, it would not be an exaggeration to say that each aspect of the marketing industry has been transformed by technological change. This goes right from NPD to distribution to the processes used in managing relationships with customers.

Impact of the internet

Modern marketing strategies emphasise the importance of building and developing long-term relationships with valuable customers. This is made much easier with digital information and communication technologies, with the internet playing an ever more important role. This allows a business to conduct much of its communication with customers and information-gathering about customer behaviours electronically.

As an example, visit the website of Kettle Chips (www.kettlefoods.co.uk). The company encourages customers to visit its website, and uses the site as a key part of its marketing to announce new product launches, special offers and other news about its products. This encourages brand loyalty.

Telecommunications

Mobile technologies are being seen as the next phase in the integration of technologies. Not so long ago, it was thought that the mobile industry was self-limiting – that once everyone had a mobile phone, they would only replace them very infrequently. However, not only has that prediction proved wrong – with the mobile phone becoming a fashion item as much as a functional product – mobile telecommunications offer new opportunities for business. They allow new ways of transmitting information, increasing the speed and volume of data that can be transmitted, and providing a different medium to carry marketing messages. The mobile itself offers opportunities to deliver new products such as ring tones and text services.

Satellite and cable

Satellite and cable systems have enabled the massive growth in the number of media channels. This poses a problem for the advertising industry. As the number of channels has grown from five main terrestrial channels to hundreds of satellite and cable stations, the average audience for any particular programme has declined, and marketing managers face a difficult choice about where to place television advertising. So how are advertisers going to reach their target customer? One response has been a trend away from advertising to forms of direct marketing. In addition, there is much greater use of the internet as a marketing medium, giving businesses direct access to individual customers, sometimes with customised or personalised messages.

Supply chain impact

Electronic technologies have enabled the speeding up and linking of many business processes. They have made significant changes in the supply chain, the way that all businesses in a particular distribution channel are linked together (see Figure 10.4, page 99).

Electronic and communications technology allows businesses to communicate efficiently with each other and to introduce better and more secure methods of arranging transfer of payments, monitoring and ordering stock, and managing financial transactions. Many supply chain processes can be automated, leading to greater speed and manpower savings.

New technology also allows businesses to communicate in new ways with their customers, the final destination in any supply chain. For example, the use of loyalty cards and credit cards generates information which marketers can use for targeted communication with customers. The internet allows new ways of making sales and, for digital products like music downloads, distributing products to customers.

Other key technology changes

Technological change also includes non-electronic developments, and has resulted in product and service tranformations in many industries. Health services could not operate as they do now if polymer-based materials and plastics had not been developed. Research into new fuel sources, like biodiesel, will have an impact on the car industry. The fashion industry uses fabrics, such as Lycra and Teflon, which did not exist, or had not been used for chic clothing, thirty years ago. New packaging and preserving processes allows food manufacturers to store products longer and transport them further, allowing, for example, supermarkets to sell strawberries in March.

stop and think

How has your use of new technologies changed in the last two years? Has your use of products such as mobile phones, MP3 players and the internet changed? If so, how?

Legal factors

Every year the government introduces new legislation. Some has a direct impact on businesses. Of course, many new laws are responses to particular social, political or economic changes. For example, the Disability Discrmination Act was introduced partly in response to greater social awareness about the impact of discrimination. This legislation has affected many businesses: service companies, such as retailers and restaurants, must alter their premises to accommodate people with reduced mobility or other disabilities.

Environmental legislation means that companies have to think about materials used in the manufacturing and packaging of products. Legislation to protect consumers from potentially harmful products, such as cigarettes, alcohol and pornography, has an impact on product and promotional decisions. Food standards legislation affects all businesses preparing and selling food. EU regulations require that nutritional information is clearly stated on food packaging. This has an impact on a company's costs and profitability.

Environmental and ethical factors

As businesses and consumers alike become more aware of the impact of economic activity on the environment and the wider world, decision-makers are increasingly incorporating ethical considerations into their marketing, and strategic, planning.

Of course, environmental and ethical issues are often inextricably linked with social and political factors and changes in attitudes and behaviours. Political and consumer pressure is often brought to bear on businesses to change their practices. If businesses don't change voluntarily, then today's ethical factor can become tomorrow's legal factor, as governments legislate to outlaw socially unacceptable practices.

In recent years, some corporations have used their marketing communications to reassure customers that they operate on an ethical basis with consideration for the environment. Waitrose includes fair-trade information in its adverts for tea, and Shell produces an environmental audit with its annual reports.

assessment practice
An environmental audit

Suppose that you work for a travel company that is undertaking an environmental audit to inform its future planning processes.

A Using recent media sources or the internet, identify one current issue from each PESTLE category which might have an impact on business performance and marketing decisions.

B Explain how these issues might affect the business. Suggest ways in which the marketing mix can be used to respond to the changes.

C Develop your findings into a presentation that you could deliver to your class or group for discussion.

The micro environment

Setting the scene: the influence of stakeholders

Topic 1 dealt with the wider background environment that influences marketing and business decisions. In contrast, the micro environment is much closer to the business.

A key feature of any business's micro environment is its stakeholders, those people and organisations that have a direct interest in a business's affairs. Whether these stakeholders are inside or outside the organisation, it is important that a business listens and responds to stakeholder groups.

Customers may seem to be definitely external stakeholders. By building brand loyalty and managing relationships with customers, a business generates a valuable internal resource of information – providing data that can be used in product development decisions, for example.

Tesco gathers valuable marketing information from its Clubcard loyalty scheme. The Clubcard allows Tesco to record the purchases of customers that participate in the scheme. This helps the company to decide how to expand its product range and to target its marketing offers more accurately. The customer therefore becomes a valuable asset to the company.

The immediate external environment

The micro environment describes the more immediate environment in which a business operates. This includes the internal market of employees, owners and shareholders, and the immediate external market of customers, competitors, creditors, suppliers and intermediaries. These are the groups that the organisation interacts with on a day-to-day basis, through, for example, the management of employees or a marketing response to competitor activity. Some of these stakeholders are more important at different times than others, depending on a company's particular situation.

When making marketing decisions, the process of scanning the external environment to get a picture of the current situation is called an external audit. This includes looking at the macro environment (see Topic 1) and the immediate external environment.

We can use Porter's five forces analysis to describe the scanning of the immediate external environment. As Figure 10.2 shows, Porter's model outlined the forces that shape the immediate competitive environment of a business. We shall consider each in turn.

KEY TERMS

Micro environment is an organisation's immediate external environment and the internal environment which mostly directly influences and is influenced by its decisions.

B2B markets consist of businesses selling to other businesses. **B2B markets** consist of businesses selling to end consumers.

Suppliers are enterprises which supply goods or services to a business for use in producing the end product.

Intermediaries are businesses which are involved in the distribution chain between producer and consumer.

Stakeholders are people and organisations with a direct interest in a business's affairs.

A **monopoly** is a market with only one seller. A monopsony is a market with only one buyer.

Vertical integration is a strategy of a owning all, or a considerable part, of the supply chain, from source to outlet.

Niche marketing involves targeting products to a small and very specific market segment.

Gaps in the market are market segments which other companies are not exploiting and which offer marketing opportunities. These may be small niche markets or they may be potentially sizeable markets, such as the market for cheap furniture spotted and exploited by Ikea.

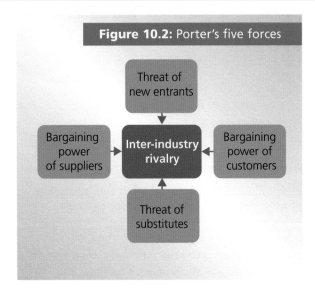

Figure 10.2: Porter's five forces

Inter-industry rivalry

At the centre of any company's competitive environment are its competitors. It is important, therefore, to monitor what the competition is doing and to respond accordingly. Businesses understand what their competition is doing by undertaking a competitor analysis using research data.

They want to know who their competitors are, which are the greatest ones, and whether there are any that are likely to pose a greater threat in the future. Once this is known, a business can estimate the relative positions of competitors in the market and use this information to make marketing decisions. One useful tool in deciding on an appropriate strategy to deal with competitors is Ansoff's product-market matrix (see Figure 10.3).

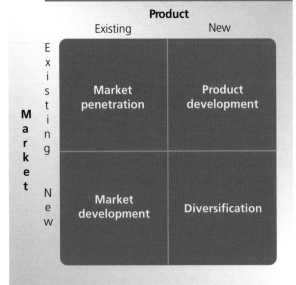

Figure 10.3: Ansoff's product-market development matrix

Not only is it important to know about the immediate competition, it is also important to understand who might be less obvious competitors. This means a company needs to look further than businesses that produce similar products, but must consider those that produce alternative products that might be purchased by the target group in preference to the company's products.

Consider, for example, Kettle Foods, the company that manufactures Kettle Chips. Are its competitors other crisp makers such as Smiths or Walkers? Or are they manufacturers of other types of snacks, such as olives, pretzels and corn chips, which might be more relevant to Kettle Foods' target market?

Bargaining power of suppliers

Few businesses can provide goods and services without relying on suppliers for raw materials, components, ancillary services (light, heat, power, etc.), office and IT equipment, and a whole range of other inputs.

As Figure 10.4 shows, the production of any product or service can be represented by a supply chain, the network of companies that are involved (in some way) in producing and getting the product to the final customers. Suppliers are those companies that supply goods and services to a business that produces the final product. They are called business-to-business (B2B) enterprises.

The power of suppliers depends on a number of factors:

- relative size of supplier and the business
- scarcity of supplier's service
- importance of reliability of supply
- level of dependence (related of course to the other factors)

In some cases, a business can completely control its suppliers. Consider the situation in which there is only one customer in the market, so that suppliers can only trade with that customer. This relationship is called a monopsony, and it gives the customer a considerable degree of power in setting the terms of trade. The supplier may benefit from the efficiency of selling its entire output to a single customer, but it risks serious consequences should that customer choose to buy from someone else and sever the relationship. It is somewhat similar to a monopoly situation: if a single business has the entire market for a particular product, customers have to accept that business's terms as there are no alternatives.

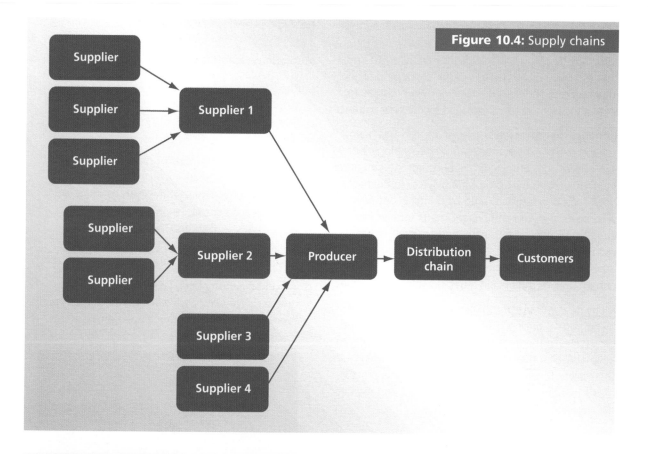

Figure 10.4: Supply chains

stop and think

When Marks & Spencer was going through a reorganisation, it moved production of some of its woollen garments from a Scottish firm to an overseas contractor. This meant that M&S was able to reduce its costs, and could keep prices low for its customers. But the Scottish firm which had produced exclusively for M&S for many years was suddenly faced with a drastic situation in which it didn't have a customer for its goods.

Think of three ways in which the Scottish producer might have dealt with this situation and suggest ways in which it could avoid this risk in the future.

Most suppliers try to avoid situations in which their customers can exert too much power. However, they are not always successful. There has been controversy over the power that some of the UK's largest and successful retailers exert over their suppliers. The supermarket industry is dominated by a small number of companies, and there is considerable media and public concern about the way they exploit their powerful position.

Another way for a firm to gain more control over its supply chain is to vertically integrate. This describes a strategy in which a company aims to owns all, or a considerable part, of the whole process from source to supply. An example is Shell, the oil and gas company, which owns gas and oil wells, refining facilities, transport systems and petrol stations.

Threat of new entrants

New entrants to the market can pose serious threats to the long-term market share of a business. The internet, for example, has made it relatively easy and cheap to gain access to new customers. So small companies have entered the clothing retail market, threatening the larger established clothing retailers.

In some industrial sectors, new entrants find it difficult to enter the industry: the scale of production and the size of investment required to compete successfully deter all but the largest organisations. In most industries though, if some businesses are doing well, then other companies will want to enter the market to compete. Ansoff's product-market development matrix (see Figure 10.3) is also a useful tool for a business to assess the threat of new entrants to its market.

Often new entrants identify a niche or gap in the market for a particular product type or a particular type of customer. If successful, they may expand into other areas. However, this will not be easy – while they may be trying to expand, they are likely to find that established companies will be responding to their initial success and developing their own products to exploit the niche markets exploited by the new entrants.

Consider the success of Apple's iPod. This has been leading the market in mobile music technology, but its very success has attracted several competitors to enter the market with their own MP3 players. Apple has been forced to respond, both by bringing out new versions of the iPod and enhancing its functionality, and also by moving into new markets itself. It has used the success of the iPod to enter the music download market, gaining market share as a new entrant against established music download businesses.

Many new entrants try to gain a foothold in markets by aggressive pricing. This can then drive established companies in the market to develop their products to keep ahead of the competition – or to cut costs themselves to lower their own prices. By this process of competition, you can see that product and market development is a continuous process.

Threat of substitutes

The threat posed by substitutes is that demand may fall away for a business's product because the new product – the substitute – does the same job better and/or more cheaply. So, for example, music CDs have largely replaced vinyl records, and now CDs are threatened by DVDs and music downloads.

The world is full of examples of new products which are substitutes for old ones. Often, the new product not only provides the same function as the old product (but often better), but it offers added functionality. Personal computers, for example, have completely replaced typewriters in offices: they not only replicate the function of typewriters but offer much more besides. This continuous development process means that companies must make decisions about whether to be proactive or reactive to change. Those that are proactive are the ones that generate most of these substitute products.

Bargaining power of customers

Last, but definitely not least, of Porter's five forces is the power that customers have to bargain with the business. As with the relationship with its suppliers, a business will always try to have the power advantage. Just as a business would like to have some control over its suppliers, so it also wants to exert some power over customers.

Thomas Edison first invented a way of turning a virtual product (music) into a tangible product (a wax cylinder, later a flat disc), which stored and played the music.

Over time new methods of music storage were introduced as substitutes for their predecessors. So shellac discs replaced the cylinder, then vinyl discs replaced shellac, then came CDs, mini-discs, DVDs, and so on. The advent of each substitute generated new products (and the equipment on which to play the music).

Around a century later, Edison's process has been reversed. We can now dispense with the physical product and listen to downloaded music at our leisure (a virtual product).

A business would have ultimate control in a monopoly situation. This used to be the case when the utilities in the UK were publicly owned. You could only get your electricity and gas from one government-controlled supplier. When these industries were privatised, they were placed under the scrutiny of watchdogs to ensure that customers were not exploited.

Some businesses are powerful because of their size and, arguably, success. The government protects the consumer from potential exploitation through the Office of Fair Trading. This body watches over the activities of large and powerful companies, and it can get the Competition Commission to investigate cases of monopoly or market dominance. The government has the power to prevent a particular company merger or a proposed acquisition if the Competition Commission judges that the merged company could use its size to prevent fair competition.

On a smaller scale, much of the response to the bargaining power of customers is through the marketing techniques and tools that are examined in this unit. Encouraging strong brand loyalty, through successful marketing, can deter customers from moving to another brand. Loyalty card programmes are designed to add value and nurture the relationship with the customer to discourage brand switching.

Internal environments

As well as conducting an external audit, businesses also need to consider their own internal environment when making marketing decisions. The questions that an internal audit needs to address concern the way the company is run, the competences, attitudes and commitment of staff, the vision of the management, and the risk attitude of shareholders. These give a flavour of how likely plans are to succeed or be supported. The internal audit also looks directly at the performance of the company's marketing and other business processes, its financial situation – levels of debt, investments, etc. – and its production levels and capacity. This includes considering the effectiveness of current product mix, pricing strategy, distribution methods and promotional activities.

A SWOT (strengths, weaknesses, opportunities, threats) analysis is a widely used method of starting a situation analysis. You are likely to encounter SWOT

analyses many times in your future education and career. Any SWOT analysis should take the external and internal audit findings into account.

Figure 10.5 shows an example of a simple SWOT analysis. Strengths and weaknesses are factors that are related to the internal environment. Businesses, therefore, have a degree of direct control or influence over these factors. Opportunities and threats come from outside the organisation – from the micro and macro environment. These are factors which affect the business directly or indirectly, and decisions need to be made about how to respond to threats and how to best exploit opportunities.

Figure 10.5: A SWOT analysis

Strengths	Weaknesses
Strong brand	Slow customer enquiry response times
Good product range	Lack of spare capacity
Loyal customers	High financial liabilities

Opportunities	Threats
Overseas markets expansion	New entrants into the market
Production opportunities in Eastern Europe	Potential economic downturn in UK
	Rise in interest rates

assessment practice
The education environment

All organisations need to assess their own internal and external environment in order to plan effectively for the future. This applies to public sector bodies like schools as much as companies operating in the private sector.

Increasingly schools, colleges and universities are in direct competion with each other for students, funding and, ultimately, status. So education managers are required to use marketing techniques to attract students and fulfil commitments to the wider community.

In this exercise, you are required to carry out a SWOT analysis of an educational establishment. You can choose you own school or college, in which case complete tasks A and B. Or, choose two universities that you are considering for higher education, in which case complete tasks C, D and E.

A **Carry out a SWOT analysis of your own school or college.**

B **Identify ways in which its performance might be improved by focusing on how the institution could:**
   – attract more applications
   – improve its public image
   – improve student satisfaction.

C **Carry out SWOT analyses of two universities which you are considering (and may have visited) for your higher education.**

D **Explain which features of each university impressed you or disappointed you.**

E **Identify areas for improved performance in each university. How would you build on strengths and address weaknesses in these organisations?**

Product decisions

Setting the scene: Cadbury's product range

Cadbury Schweppes produces a range of chocolate and confectionery products. The company's product range includes many well-known brands such as Dairy Milk, Boost, Snaps, Creme Egg, Crunchie, Easter Egg Delight, Double Decker, Flake, Heroes and Picnic.

All these products provide a similar "core benefit" for customers – a chocolate and sugar snack in a convenient package. However, each product has a distinct way of delivering this benefit.

Cadbury Schweppes makes each product different by using:

■ additional ingredients such as nuts and fondant fillings

■ different packaging, creating a distinctive shape and wrapper for each product

■ new combinations of ingredients, producing different chocolate textures.

Why do you think Cadbury Schweppes produces a range of different chocolate products? How do competing businesses, such as Nestlé, try to make their products different?

KEY TERMS

The **product life cycle** is the stages of launch, growth, maturity and decline that a product goes through during its time on the market.

Innovators are customers who are the first to buy new products.

Early adopters are customers who like to buy new products when they first establish themselves on the market, but not as soon as innovators.

Majority are the customer group that buys at the mature, stable phase of the market.

Laggards are customers that buy at the end of the market cycle.

What is a product?

In this topic, we introduce some of the concepts and techniques used by businesses to make product decisions. In doing so, we expand on concepts introduced in the AS textbook (see pages 136–8).

The traditional way of viewing a product is in terms of the benefits and satisfactions obtained by the customer in its consumption. This applies both to tangible products – something that can be seen and felt such as a pair of jeans or a car – and to intangible products such as services like banking, a holiday or a nightclub. However, another way of describing a product, from a business point of view, is to use the layered product model (see Figure 10.6).

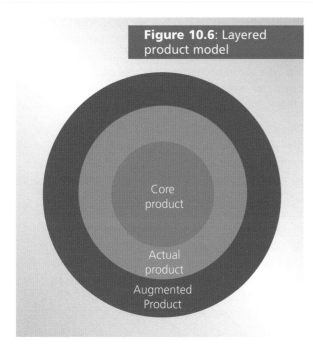

Figure 10.6: Layered product model

Core product

Actual product

Augmented Product

Without marketing, many products would simply be core products. This is the very basic level of any product; the basic satisfactions and benefits it delivers. For example, at its most basic level, a soft drink satisfies thirst.

At the actual product stage, there is a degree of differentiation through branding and product development which provides some extra value to the customer. In the soft drinks industry, a company like Coca-Cola has a strong brand and it offers a range of products linked to that brand such as Coca-Cola, Diet Coke, Vanilla Coke, etc. The product experience is no longer simply about satisfying thirst, but includes the added value provided by the particular product characteristics – such as distinctive taste, or fewer calories in the diet versions – and the associations of the brand itself. If customers feel that drinking Coca-Cola is a cool thing to do, they will get an extra good feeling from being associated with the brand.

The augmented product adds even more value through supporting features such as after-sales service, special deals for loyal customers, etc. A retailer (or manufacturer) may offer customers "free" support services for a period of time when they buy electronic equipment. A new car may come with free insurance, good-value finance deals and service offers. It is in the area of augmented product that much of the loyalty building can take place.

New product development

New product development (NPD) covers a range of changes to products, from improvements to existing products to the design and development of innovative (completely new) products. Companies must incorporate product development into their overall marketing management. They may adopt a proactive or reactive approach. A proactive approach involves introducing products continuously as part of a strategy of continuous product development. A reactive approach involves developing new products in response to competitor or customer activity.

Figure 10.7 shows a simple process model for new product development. The starting point for any development is idea generation. Ideas for improving existing products may come from research into customer perceptions and changes in the marketing environment. Ideas for an innovative product are more difficult to come up with, and the whole development process is riskier, because by definition the product has not been made before. However, regardless of whether a business is planning an improvement to an existing product or a completely new departure from its current product range, it should follow the same process of idea generation, evaluation, feasibility, testing and launch.

A large proportion of new product ideas fail to reach the market; they get rejected at the evaluation, feasibility or testing stages. Even if the new product is launched, it may not be a success and it could fail to get established in the market. There is a trade-off between risk minimisation and speed to market: rush the product development process and you risk failure through skimping on feasibility and testing; take too long is assessing the idea and you risk your competitors introducing a similar product to the market first.

The product development process (as illustrated in Figure 10.7) can appear to be product-oriented rather than consumer-driven, suggesting that companies create new products and then attempt to market them. This would go against current marketing theory, which places the customer at the heart of all marketing activity. In reality, of course, if products were only ever produced in response to stated customer needs and wants, then product lines would not move forward. However, this does not mean that the customer plays no role in the development process, and the key to product development success is involving customers in assessing the market potential of new products.

Product life cycle

Another useful concept when discussing marketing decisions is the product life cycle. Figure 10.8, which plots the volume of sales of a product against time, shows a typical product life cycle. In practice,

Figure 10.7: The new product development process

Idea generation
- From research into customers' perceptions
- From research into the current market
- From a bright idea

↓

Evaluation and idea screening
- Of the benefits of the development
- Of potential market opportunities
- Of alternative options

↓

Feasibility and business analysis
- Financial – costs and profitability calculations
- Production capacity and competence
- Sustainability of the market
- Accessibility of the target customer

↓

Idea generation
- From research into customers' perceptions
- From research into the current market
- From a bright idea

↓

Development and testing
- Prototypes may be used in a restricted market (test market) to test different concepts
- Focus groups may be used to test ideas or prototypes
- Perceptions of how the marketing mix elements work together can be tested on a representative sample

↓

Launch
- Pricing decisions to be made
- Promotional plan to launch the product needs to be designed
- Performance measurements need to be devised
- Success or failure needs to be monitored

individual products will have their own distinct life cycles: some may be relatively short (because, say, the product is quickly supplanted by newer and better technology), others may have a long life and slow decline. Brands, for example, tend to come and go more quickly than generic products, so the life cycle for branded goods is usually (though not always) shorter than for the generic product.

At each stage of the product life cycle we can identify different types of customers. The motivations of customers that buy a product in its early stages of its life cycle are very different to those of customers that buy when a product is in decline, and we can use these differences to guide marketing decisions.

Some people (called innovators) are keen to be the first to buy new products. They will be less concerned with the price than with the kudos of being the first to get the product. Similarly, early adopters also like to be up to date with product developments, though they will take some more time in deciding whether and when to buy a new product. Both innovators and early adopters may be prepared to pay a premium price to be among the first to buy a new product. This was the case, for example, with plasma and LCD television sets, which were very expensive when they were first introduced to the market.

The majority – sometimes split into early and late majority – are the customers who buy the product in its mature phase. They are likely to pay what is approaching the "true" market price. The majority are more price-sensitive, so they will wait for prices to stabilise and become more "reasonable", in their opinion, before buying plasma and LCD televisions. In a product's mature phase, a company achieves the highest volume of sales. This is when the product is likely to be most profitable. A company may be able to set a price during the growth stages that yields a higher profit margin per unit, but it is likely to make greater profits during the mature stage because of the higher overall sales volume. Companies will usually try to maintain the mature phase of the product life cycle as long as possible to generate maximum revenues.

In the decline phase, buyers are called (perhaps rather unkindly) laggards. These people are not concerned with buying the latest products – with being seen to be fashionable – but they probably like a bargain. It is likely at this stage that the pricing policy will be aimed at covering costs and shedding any surplus stock.

How long any particular product life cycle lasts is dependent on the type of product and the nature of the market itself. Some products (see cash cows below) have very long life cycles, with no decline being evident for decades. A good example of a product with a long life cycle is petrol. The market for petrol is not likely to reach the decline stage until the invention of cheaper (and perhaps greener) alternatives that provide similar performance for people's cars. Other products, such as some high street fashion items, have a life cycle that may be measured in just a few weeks or months: they are "in" one season, then fall completely out of fashion.

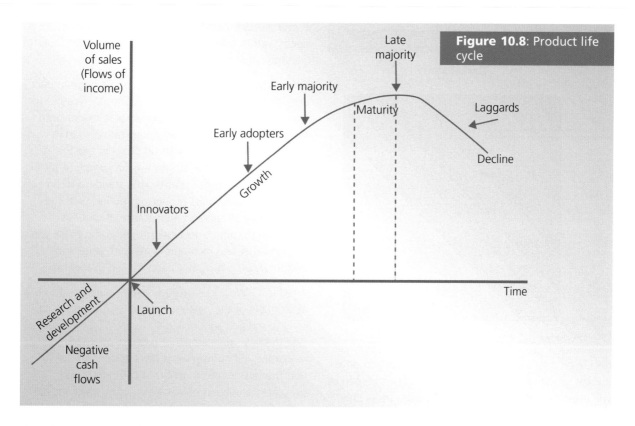

Figure 10.8: Product life cycle

Optimum product mix

Most companies do not rely on just one product. They will offer a range of products, each at different stages of their life cycles and with different levels of success. One way of analysing a product range, and describing how each product works within the product mix, is to use the Boston matrix (see Figure 10.9). This is an analytical tool, devised by the Boston Consulting Group, which divides products into one of four types.

Cash cows

Cash cows tend to be long-established products, and will often be very familiar to customers. Many typically have a very long product life cycle. Examples of cash cows include KitKats, Mars bars and Heinz tomato ketchup. Products like these, which have high market share and low market growth, can generate revenues to fund product development. This is where the term cash cow comes from – the idea being that the product generates cash that can be "milked" year after year.

Market growth is slow because cash cows tend to be in the mature stage of the product life cycle. Note that this does not mean that there is no product development. KitKats, for example, have been produced in new chunky versions and with orange and lime flavours. These product developments are not designed to take sales away from the original KitKat product, but aim to reach new customers or to persuade existing brand-loyal customers to buy more.

Promotional activity for cash cows is likely to concentrate on maintaining brand loyalty and customer awareness. Pricing is likely to be at a competitive market level.

Stars

A star, with its high market share and high market growth, is likely to be a product establishing itself a new market (hence the high market growth). An example of a star is the iPod, which (as of 2006) dominates the MP3 player market. There are competitors, but (at the time of writing) the iPod has its own iconic brand status.

New and successful products, of course, attract interest from competitors, so stars may be relatively short-lived and may only benefit from their advantage of having a high share of a growing market for a short time. For example, Apple will have to find ways (through promotion, pricing or product differentiation) to fend off competition if the iPod is to maintain its market-leading position. Even if Apple is successful, overall market growth will eventually level off as the MP3 player market reaches maturity.

In the early stages of the life cycle, the prestigious status of the brand can be important in maintaining stars and managing revenue flows. Remember that innovators and early adopters, the likely target customers for stars, are less price-sensitive. Not all stars are priced relatively highly. A company may

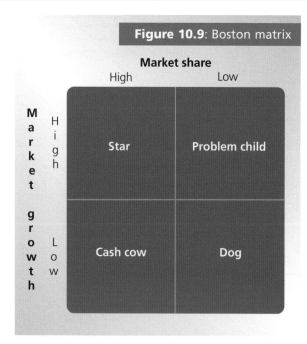

Figure 10.9: Boston matrix

Market share

	High	Low
High Market growth	Star	Problem child
Low Market growth	Cash cow	Dog

decide on a very competitive pricing strategy to drive market growth and deter competitors, but the market will need to be sustainable for long enough for the business to recoup expensive development costs.

Problem child

The problem child has a small share of an increasing market. It might be a rival product that is newly entering a growing market to compete with the star product of another company. Following the success of the iPod, for example, many companies have introduced MP3 players which are jostling for market share with each other and Apple. The key challenge that any company with a problem child product faces is to change its status to a star rather than to a dog.

Dogs

The low market share and low market growth is not good news for the dog. This product has probably come to the end of its life cycle and needs to be withdrawn. This is not always the case. A dog could be used with other products to get a competitive advantage. For example, a supermarket might use a dog at a rock bottom price to entice bargain hunters into the store in the expectation that they will also buy other products. However, a company would not aim to keep a dog in its product portfolio for long.

A customer-oriented approach

Modern marketing theory argues that marketing should be focused on customers (consumer-oriented) rather than on the product (product-oriented). It suggests that businesses should find out what

customers want and develop products to meet those needs, rather than develop products and then look for customers for those products.

One particular product that has made a huge impact does not seem to adhere to this concept. This product was designed by technical specialists in response to their technical development needs rather than in response to customer needs. In order to use the product, the customer has to learn a complete set of new skills. The product comes in a standard design, with all manufacturers producing models with the same colour, shape and appearance. It requires supporting products to work properly, and these can be unreliable and incomprehensible to potential customers who have not been trained in their use.

What is it? Well, in case you haven't guessed, this is a description of the personal computer (at least in its early years) and supporting software. You could argue that this was an example of product-oriented marketing. Of course, what has happened since is that the design and function of computers and software have been refined so that the products are more accessible to more consumers.

stop and think

How might you have designed the personal computer if you had done so from a customer's point of view?

So what are the characteristics of a customer-oriented approach to product development? Five factors are worth highlighting.

■ Target customer's wants, needs, aspirations.

■ Pay attention to design as well as function: the introduction of the iMac challenged the idea that all computers had to be in beige boxes.

■ Use appropriate technology: customers' technical ability and technological acceptance does not progress at the same speed as technological development.

■ Be flexible: products which are designed to serve particular functions can transform into something else. The mobile phone is now as much a fashion accessory as a practical communication tool.

■ Add value: a business wants to add value in terms of profitability and longevity of the product life cycle. The way to do this is to add value for the customer through generating, anticipating and exceeding needs and wants.

assessment practice
Cargo and Nail's Snails

Two entrepreneurs, Simon Cargo and Sarah Nail, have been researching the catering market and looking for a niche in this growing industry. They have discovered that there is a shortage of edible snails for the restaurant businesses. Their initial plan involved setting up a snail farm and supplying fresh and frozen snails directly to catering businesses.

After a year of reasonably successful trading – dealing directly with individual restaurants – Sarah feels that the company needs to develop a stronger brand image. She wants to explore possible ways of adding value and increasing profitability for the business.

Simon and Sarah decide that they should look for ways to add value to the products they supply to existing customers and research the potential market for end consumers, such as keen home cooks.

You have been asked to devise a product and marketing development plan which might help the company to achieve its aims of adding value to its existing products, extending its markets and increasing profitability. You approach this project by completing the set tasks below.

A First, undertake a situation analysis. What is the current situation? Suggest, with reasons, where Simon and Sarah's product is in its product life cycle.

B Now define objectives for the product development project. Use Ansoff's matrix to help you identify your objectives.

C What product development ideas can you come up with to add value? Suggest ways that you can try out your new product ideas.

D End consumers such as home cooks represent a new market for the company. What type of people are these customers likely to be? Profile this new target market, and suggest types of promotion that could be used to reach these customers. (Note, you will study promotional planning in Topic 5, so for now just set out some initial ideas.)

Pricing decisions

Setting the scene: Tesco's brands

In the past, supermarket own-label products provided a cheaper alternative to established brands. They offered value for money, and often the goods came in simple packaging to emphasise the lack of promotion and hype.

Today, the supermarkets' own-label ranges are more sophisticated. Tesco, for example, has three different own brands: its Finest range, a regular Tesco brand and its Value brand. Each brand is targeted at different customers who expect them to be priced at an appropriate level.

This product differentiation allows Tesco to offer premium-priced and cheaper-value products under the same umbrella brand – Tesco.

How does the store set different prices for what are essentially very similar products? As we shall see in this topic, some of the key factors are that a price should:

■ target customer expectations

■ be in harmony with other aspects of the marketing mix

■ reflect supply and demand conditions.

KEY TERMS

Cost-plus is a method of determining prices by calculating costs and adding a certain amount of desired profit.

Price leadership is a method of determining prices by adopting the market leader's price.

Market price is the price determined by the interaction of supply and demand.

Cost leadership is a pricing strategy based on achieving the lowest costs of production.

Normal profit is the minimum level of profit required by a producer to enter a market.

Elasticity is a measure of the sensitivity of customer demand to price changes.

Contribution pricing is a pricing strategy that sets prices (for a period) so that they cover variable costs and make a contribution towards fixed costs.

Discriminatory pricing is a strategy of offering the same product at different prices to different groups of target customers according to market conditions.

Price skimming is a strategy of setting prices at a high level at product launch in order to recoup some development costs.

Penetration pricing is a strategy of pricing below market price in order to gain market share and/or squeeze out weaker competition.

Some pricing strategies

In this topic, we look at some of the ways in which businesses determine the price of their products. At the outset, it is worth emphasising that a business may use a variety of pricing policies and strategies at different times to achieve its objectives. There is no "best" method – it requires selecting the most appropriate approach to meet the business's objectives, given the particular product and market conditions. We start by looking at three general approaches to setting product prices.

Cost-plus

In cost-plus pricing, the price of a product is determined by calculating the cost of production and adding the required amount of profit. This approach is often used by new start-up businesses, and as long as the competition does not have lower costs then it can work for a while.

The disadvantages of this approach are that:

- the market price (see below) may be higher than the cost-plus price, so the business may be missing an opportunity to charge a higher price and make more profit

- established competitors may be able to undercut the price because they have lower costs

- real unit costs may be difficult to calculate because they vary with output.

Price leadership

In a price leadership approach, a business looks at what its competition is charging for similar products and follows their lead. (Of course, if the business is one of the main players in the market, it might be the price leader itself and find that its competitors tend to follow its lead.) This approach has the advantage that a business is likely to set a price closer to the market price (see below). It is based on the assumption that consumers have an idea about the price level to expect for a particular type of product.

Price leadership may also be driven by cost leadership. A business may be able to drive down prices by being the lowest-cost producer. Competitors are forced to follow suit if they wish to retain their market share. This approach has been perfected in the supermarket industry by the US corporation Wal-Mart (which owns Asda in the UK). This can make it very difficult for small businesses to compete, because the cost advantage comes from the purchasing economies of scale enjoyed by large corporate buyers.

Market prices

Market prices are determined by the interaction of supply and demand. The market price is the point at

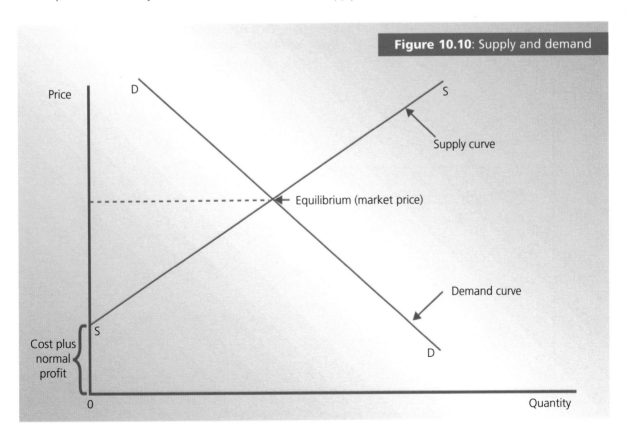

Figure 10.10: Supply and demand

which supply and demand are in equilibrium. What this means is that the market price is the price at which the marketing activity of a company matches the customer's expectations. The customer and producer are, at this point, both "happy" with the price.

Figure 10.10 shows simplified supply and demand curves (represented here by straight lines). It shows that demand falls as prices rise, and supply increases as prices rise (because producers can make higher profits). Note that the price at which a company will start to produce will include an aspect of cost-plus pricing: that is, a business will want a minimum amount of profit on top of costs – called normal profit by economists – before it is willing to enter a market.

Does this mean that the customer is in control? Well, perhaps. But the job of marketing is to try to influence customers in such a way that they will pay more for the product. Arguably the best way to do this is to make customers think they are in control. Businesses can do this by strong branding, good design, good promotional campaigns, and, in general, successful, integrated marketing. If they are successful, they will be able to generate an overall increase in demand. In effect, as Figure 10.11 shows, they are shifting the demand curve to the right – customers are buying more at a higher price – and creating a new, and higher, market price.

Pricing for particular purposes

We have considered above three general approaches to pricing that a business can take. But a business may also use a range of different pricing strategies to achieve specific outcomes and responses or in response to particular competitive situations.

Promotional pricing

A sales promotion is a campaign run for a specific length of time to increase product sales. Part of a sales promotion is likely to be a special price offer or a value offer such as BOGOF (buy one get one free).

Promotional pricing is often used when a product is launched to encourage trial, to achieve quick acceptance of the product, or to fight off competition and gain market share.

Contribution pricing

Contribution pricing is a particular type of pricing which allows spare production capacity to be used while not competing with a business's other products. It is perhaps easiest to explain by an illustration.

Tourism and hotel operators often offer holidays in Spain during the winter months at a very low price.

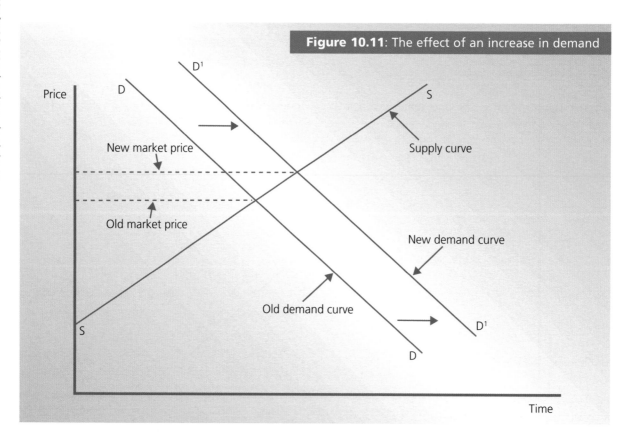

Figure 10.11: The effect of an increase in demand

These are very popular with pensioners who relish a month away from the cold UK climate. Essentially, these holidays are offered at such a low price that the operator doesn't make any profit. However, the reason these companies do this is that provided they cover more than their variable costs (costs which vary according to the number of customers being served), they generate revenue that contributes towards their fixed costs (costs which will be incurred whether the accommodation is occupied or not). The operators couldn't afford to operate on these margins throughout the year, but this winter revenue makes a contribution towards their fixed costs, and when added to the revenue generated by the high summer season, means they make a profit over the whole year.

The key point here is that the main product is not compromised by offering the product at a special price. Contribution pricing is often used in industries where there is spare capacity. Transport providers, such as airlines, would rather offer discounted fares, providing the revenue makes a contribution to fixed costs, than have empty seats. This concept also tends to be used in relation to time-limited promotions.

Discriminatory pricing

A business operates a discriminatory pricing policy when it offers the same product to different markets at different prices. Discriminatory pricing allows a business to take advantage of customers who are willing to pay more for the product than others. The rail and air travel industries use discriminatory pricing. Different prices are charged at different times of the day depending on the level of demand. Commuters who have to travel at peak times are "forced" to pay higher prices for the same product that is available at much lower prices during off-peak periods. A discriminatory pricing policy is likely to be used as part of a long-term marketing plan rather than a special time-limited offer.

Pricing and the product life cycle

At particular stages of the product life cycle, different pricing policies may be used to control the dynamics of the market.

Price skimming

Price skimming (or skim pricing) as explained in the AS textbook (pages 138–9) can be used in markets for new, innovative products. This approach takes advantage

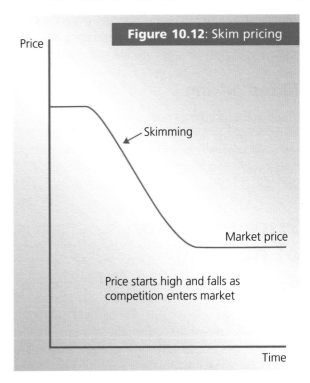

Figure 10.12: Skim pricing

Price starts high and falls as competition enters market

of the fact that for a time after launch of a radically different product, a business has a relative monopoly over the market. Even with prices set relatively high, there is little immediate competition, and innovators and early adopters are unlikely to be deterred if the product is desirable. Skimming allows some research and development costs to be recouped at an early stage in the product's life cycle before competitors start to undercut and eat away at profitability.

Penetration pricing

Penetration pricing is the opposite of skimming. In this approach, the product's price is set lower than the market price. This can be used for a limited time so that weaker competitors are squeezed out of the market or are deterred from entering. Penetration

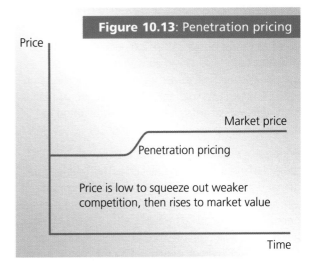

Figure 10.13: Penetration pricing

Price is low to squeeze out weaker competition, then rises to market value pricing can be used to gain market share quickly. When a strong market position is established, the price is allowed to float upwards towards the market price.

Mixed pricing

Mixed pricing combines both skimming and penetration. The price is high at the product launch, then as competitors enter the market it is lowered to repel competitors before stabilising at market price.

Price elasticity of demand

Markets are not generally stable, and businesses need to know what happens to sales when they change their prices. The simple supply and demand diagram (Figure 10.10) shows that if the price of a product falls then more will be sold, if it rises then fewer will be sold. However, the important point for a business is by how much sales will drop or rise and what happens to revenues as a result of a price change.

The key concept in understanding the impact of price changes on demand is, like supply and demand, drawn from economics theory. It is the price elasticity of demand. The term price elasticity can be described as a measure of sensitivity to price changes. If the price of a particular car rises, how does this affect the buying decision of the customer? Suppose the price of competitive mass-market model such as a Ford Focus increased by 10 per cent, how many potential customers would switch to another model such as a Vauxhall Astra?

Price elasticity of demand is defined by a simple equation.

$$\text{price elasticity of demand} = \frac{\text{percentage change in demand}}{\text{percentage change in price}}$$

If the price elasticity of demand is less than −1 (that is, it has values of say −1.5, −2 or −3), then demand is said to be elastic. This means that demand is price-sensitive. If prices are increased, proportionately fewer units will be sold and overall revenue will fall. So if demand is elastic, a business that wanted to increase revenue should reduce its prices.

If the price elasticity of demand is between 0 and −1, then demand is said to be inelastic. This means that demand is relatively insensitive to price changes. So if a business want to increase revenue, it should increase prices. This is because the fall in sales caused by the higher price will be more than compensated for by the increased revenue generated by the higher price.

This is a very simplified account of a complicated mathematical concept, but it gives an indication of the dynamics of pricing. Do marketing managers really sit down and attempt to calculate price elasticity? Well they might if they enjoyed the economics part of their marketing course at university, but in practice they should know from research what the likely effect of price changes are on the demand for their products.

In general, price elasticity depends on a number of factors. For products where there are many substitutes or alternative products that consumers can buy, price elasticity tends to be higher – that is, demand is likely to be significantly affected by price changes. For example, when people go to a street market to buy fruit and vegetables, they tend to look for the best prices. If, say, bananas are expensive one week, they might decide to buy pears. If one stall has a good price for apples, customers will buy its product rather than more expensively priced apples of similar quality at neighbouring stalls.

Price elasticity also tends to be high for products that are not considered to be necessities. Customers will buy these products when they can afford them, or when they see a good bargain. These products are desirable – like say an overseas holiday or a new fashion outfit – but not essential. Businesses selling these type of "treat" and luxury products can increase demand by reducing their prices through sales promotions, for example.

For products where the demand is price-inelastic, the opposite is generally true. Products which are necessities and for which there are few substitutes will generally have inelastic demand. Perhaps the most obvious example of a price-inelastic product is petrol. Though the price of petrol has increased substantially over recent years as world oil prices have risen, demand has not fallen significantly. In the long term, consumers might switch to more fuel-efficient vehicles or buy cars which run on other cheaper fuels. However, in the short term, people need – and want – to use their existing cars, and they do not have a choice of an alternative energy source: if you have a car that runs on petrol, you have to buy petrol to make it run.

Note that many businesses try to build strong brands so that they are able to retain customers even when forced to increase prices. Products with strong brand image, such as Nike trainers or Apple iPods, can attract a higher price than, say, a store's own brand or rival products because of that image. This is effectively a way of making demand more price-inelastic (or less price-elastic).

Factors which affect price

Market prices are determined by the market, by the interaction of supply and demand. This is not necessarily a given, and there are many factors that will impact on the price of any particular product.

- Customer expectations – prices should match the expectations of the target customer. There is on old saying that "you can't sell a diamond for sixpence". This means that diamonds are worth what the customer thinks they are worth, and if you tried to sell them cheaply they would lose their status. There must be a match between the image of the product and its price.

- Costs of production – this is most relevant in cost-leadership situations and in deciding at what price level it will be sensible to enter the market. Once a launch price is determined, a business would try to increase profitability by driving down costs.

- Competitor activity – in some situations and markets the activity of competitors can drive pricing decisions. If a competitor reduces its prices, a business may need to do the same. But it might also decide to run a special sales campaign or to add value to the product, so that it can keep market share while maintaining its prices.

- Branding – one of the main reasons for investing in brand building and brand maintenance is to ensure that prices can be held at a reasonable level. Essentially, a strong brand can make demand less elastic. Successful brands are worth a great deal of money to a company.

- Customer sensitivity to price changes – the ability to control prices and to reduce sensitivity to price changes (elasticity) is an advantage in very competitive markets. A key goal of relationship marketing (see page 122) is to cement customer loyalty and discourage brand switching if, for example, competitors reduce their prices.

assessment practice
Scrumptious cakes

You have decided to start up a home-made cake business with some friends. This type of business has relatively low set-up costs, and there is a growing market for fresh, locally sourced food products. You expect to sell your first batch at a farmers' market.

A **You need to decide on a price that meets your marketing objectives. How will you go about pricing the cakes? How will the prices fit in with your overall marketing mix?**

B **Explain how you intend to determine how your prices compare to those of competitors.**

C **Discuss how your pricing strategy could be used to achieve particular objectives, for example in relation to the product life cycle.**

Promotional decisions

Setting the scene: brand awareness

As consumers, we are exposed to promotional messages every day. Some of the ways that businesses communicate with customers is very obvious. Advertising campaigns and special offer promotions are very direct. Other methods of building product and brand awareness are less overt and depend on influencing opinion less directly, such as public relations and sponsorship.

Some advertisements are so memorable that people recall them many years after they were last shown. An example is the Cadbury's Smash advert, recently voted the best advert ever on a Channel 4 television programme. This used alien puppets to ridicule the earthling practice of boiling and mashing potatoes.

If you are asked to recall a particular brand of a product, such as a soft drink, a trainer brand, a model of car, a mobile phone, a make of crisps, etc., your first recall is likely to have been

influenced by your exposure to promotional campaigns.

Try this out on your classmates. List a number of products, and then ask each other to write down a brand of each product that first comes to mind See how many times the same brand is chosen. Why has this happened? How do you know about these products? Where have you seen them advertised or promoted? What factors influenced your choices?

KEY TERMS

The **marketing communications mix (MCM)** is the various tools used to communicate with target customers during a specific promotional campaign

Consumer response hierarchies describe the stages that consumers go through before they take action. The most well-known is AIDA.

Opinion leaders are influential personalities to whom customers relate.

Opinion formers are people whose opinion or authority informs customer choices.

Message is the image, impression or content that a promotional campaign tries to transmit.

Medium is the channel through which the message is conveyed.

Communication

In order to make decisions about marketing communications, it is important to understand the process of communication itself. As Figure 10.14 shows, there are two parties involved in the communication process. The sender encodes the message and the receiver decodes it. Note that non-verbal communication – the part not in words – is very important in the communication process. The receiver decodes body language, facial expression, attitude and tone of voice to aid understanding.

Something similar happens when we interpret advertisements. The advertiser encodes the message in a form that hopefully means something to the intended (target) customer. This message is then decoded and understood by the receiver. Again the non-verbal (non-textual) elements are important, as the visual style and tone of the advertisement often carries a key part of the message.

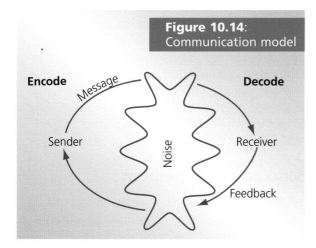

Figure 10.14: Communication model

In order for the communication loop to be completed there must be some kind of feedback. So what sort of feedback is there from an advertisement? This is a problem because advertising tends to be a mass coverage activity. The idea of advertising is to reach relatively large numbers of customers quickly and cost-effectively. In short, it is difficult to get feedback from advertising easily; it is not in itself a sound communication method.

So an additional (or different) method needs to be used. This can be a sales promotion, offering special deals for a short time, to create an incentive to buy – the sales figures could then be used as an indication of feedback. You could use personal selling or direct marketing linked to an advertising campaign, or you could use market research to gauge the response of target customers. The important point is to find a way of getting feedback.

Note also the feature of the communication model called noise. This refers to anything that gets in the way of the message being received (and decoded) or between decoding and feedback. In a one-to-one conversation, noise can be audible; loud background noise can prevent you from hearing what someone is trying to say. In terms of marketing communications, things that can get in the way (that is, noise) can be:

- the message is not targeted correctly
- the message is not clear
- the message is ambiguous
- the message is too similar to that of other brands
- the medium used is not appropriate
- the timing is not correct.

Consider the use of jargon in an advertisement on the television or a billboard. The assumption is that the target audience will understand the message. This is fine as long as the advertisers are certain that their target audience does "get it". But if they don't, the message may not be understood and will have been ineffective. In this case, noise has got in the way.

stop and think

The internet, through e-mails and websites, offers a relatively new way for businesses to communicate with target audiences. How does medium relate to the communication model in Figure 10.14? What forms of noise may be experienced online?

The promotional mix

A famous advertising guru once said that "we know that 50 per cent of our advertising is effective – unfortunately we don't know which 50 per cent it is". This is the problem facing every marketing manager in deciding how their business's promotional mix should be put together.

The promotional mix – perhaps better described as the marketing communications mix (MCM) – is the means and methods used to communicate with customers. In this section, we look at how promotional campaigns can be put together to make an effective campaign. This expands some concepts introduced in the AS textbook (see pages 140–1).

The MCM toolbox is made up of the different methods of communication used by marketing professionals in a promotions campaign. These methods include:

- **advertising** – paid-for mass media communications, with the potential to reach many people (wide reach)

- **public (and press) relations (PR)** – an attempt to get free media coverage to create a good image for a company or brand

- **personal selling** – direct marketing techniques such as face-to-face, telesales and internet selling

- **sponsorships** – enhancing the image of a business through association with other organisations or events, such as sports teams, music festivals and charity events

- **exhibitions** – giving customers information within a specific forum such as the Ideal Home Exhibition and the Motor Show; used extensively in business-to-business marketing

- **sales promotions** – time-limited campaigns, such as "buy one get one free", competitions and trial money-off offers, designed to increase sales in a short time period.

All these activities can be undertaken by a marketing department within a business or contracted out to an advertising or PR agency. Advertising is also known as 'above-the-line' promotions, with all other activities sometimes called 'below-the-line' promotions.

Consumer response hierarchy

The promotional methods in the MCM toolbox have different purposes and, therefore, tend to be used at different stages of a promotional campaign. To understand this process, we use the concept of a consumer response hierarchy. This describes the stages that a customer goes through before making a purchase. The simplest, and most widely used, consumer response hierarchy is AIDA. This is an acronym which stands for:

- **Awareness** – making the customer aware of the product or brand

- **Interest** – presenting something interesting so that the customer wants to know more

- **Desire** – persuading the customer that your product is what they want

- **Action** – getting the customer to buy.

As Figure 10.15 shows, each element of the MCM toolbox tends to work better at different stages of the AIDA model. This relates back to the communication model in Figure 10.15, in that activities which allow easy feedback or response – like personal selling and sales promotions – work best at the action end. But much work in generating awareness and interest needs to take place to get the customer in the right frame of mind for action.

Figure 10.15: Use of promotional methods within AIDA

Promotional method	Stage of AIDA
Advertising	Awareness, interest
PR	Awareness
Sponsorships	Awareness
Exhibitions	Awareness, interest, desire, action
Personal selling	Desire, action

A promotional campaign will often contain all the activities within the MCM toolbox at different stages. A television advertising campaign may be used to raise customers' awareness of a new product launch. A press release may be issued to encourage the press to run articles on the product or company. Special offers may be used as sales promotions at the product launch to encourage customers to try or buy. Personal selling or point-of-sale (POS) promotions might also be used to persuade customers, which is more likely to be successful if the campaign is backed up by strong advertising and offers.

Message and medium

In advertising, and to a lesser extent other broadcast promotions such as PR, a choice must be made about the message. How is the message going to be conveyed and what medium should be used?

The message may be explicitly stated – a slogan such as McDonald's "I'm lovin' it" – or it might be more subtle, such as the images used in advertisements for alcoholic drinks and cars where the message is about the kind of social life that is associated with the product.

The person giving the message can also influence customers. Advertisers often use opinion leaders and opinion formers to get their messages across. Because of his high-profile image, David Beckham is used to promote products ranging from M&S children's clothing to disposable razors. Glamorous female celebrities encourage the purchase of L'Oreal products with the "because you're worth it" slogan. These are examples of opinion leaders. They are people that many consumers would like to emulate.

Opinion formers are those who influence choice from a more authoritative position. They may be family and peer-group members, or they may be experts, or characters created by advertisers to represent experts. People in white overalls who tell us which cough medicines to use could be seen as opinion formers.

Advertisers also need to consider how to convey the message. They may want to create impact by repeating the message in two or three short television adverts screened separately within a single advertising break or over the course of a given programme. Some advertisements, Honda's Power of Dreams for example, have used a complete sequence which has then been chopped up to produce a number of smaller adverts that link together. The effect is to reinforce the message by repetition. In print media, the use of white space (areas in a newspaper advertisement left blank) can create visual impact. Music and sounds can also be used to create impact, allowing an adertiser to use a number of the senses to embed the message in the minds of the audience.

The choice of advertising medium depends on a number of factors.

- **Television advertising** is good for reinforcing brand image. It is good for products which are often impulse buys, for which a strong image association is important or which are in very competitive markets such as in FMCGs (fast-moving consumer goods) like confectionery, toiletries, bread, etc. Television advertising reaches many people in a short time. However, the proliferation of satellite and digital TV channels means that the target customers are less easy to pin down to a particular channel at a given time.

- **Radio advertising** is relatively cheaper, and commercial radio channels know their customers well. Radio listeners do less channel-switching than TV viewers and tend to be loyal to a particular station.

- **Cinema advertising** is more limited in reaching many people (by the audience numbers), but is often used for brand reinforcement as well as by local businesses.

- **Billboards** can reach large numbers of customers, but may be ignored as they are most likely to be viewed from cars. They are used to supplement other media and can be successful where visual impact is important. Adshels, the advertisements incorporated into bus shelters, work in a similar way to billboards, and suffer the same limitations.

- **The internet** is a way of advertising and publicising products and/or a business. In addition to a business's own website, it can use pop-ups to reach visitors to search engines or websites. Like direct mail and telesales, however, these can irritate rather than persuade. The main problem with using the website as a means of communication is the need to keep customers on the site and to stop them from navigating away before they get the message.

- **Newspapers and magazines** can be a good way of reaching the target market, as readers tend to be loyal to particular papers and magazines. A print advertisement can carry more information than a television or radio ad. For example, there is room to include technical specifications or more detail about specific features. This gives customers an opportunity to make informed decisions.

- **Direct mail**, though often regarded as junk mail, does work in that many people respond. It could be argued that junk mail is simply poorly targeted direct mail. Accurate targeting depends on good information being available to the marketing team. This has become easier for the marketing industry to obtain, as so much information is stored about individual customers.

Planning a promotional campaign

Any promotional campaign plan should have several components. These are:

- targeting and positioning
- objectives
- timescales
- budget.

Targeting and positioning

Who is the target customer and how will the product be differentiated from that of competitors? This is sometimes referred to as the USP (unique selling point). This relates to the layered product model (see Figure 10.6, page 103): the challenge for a business is to consider how to add value to its product and make it distinct within the market.

Objectives

What are the SMART objectives for the promotional campaign? For a new product launch these may be to generate so many trials of the product within a certain number of weeks within a certain target customer group. These objectives provide a means of measuring the performance of the campaign. In other words, success is judged on how far it has been successful in achieving the objectives set.

Timescales

Choice of timescales will depend on the campaign objectives. The greatest impact may be achieved by an intensive campaign, with schedules that concentrate promotional activity into a short period of time. Other campaigns may adopt an approach of gradually introducing the product so that customers become familiar with the brand name before the arrival of a new product. Daewoo used this approach when its cars first arrived in the UK. Its advertisements did not show any cars, they simply comprised landscape scenes with the word Daewoo. This created a sense of curiosity, and brought the brand name to the attention of the customer. The timescale also provides the planning framework, and will typically include review periods to check on whether the campaign is going to plan.

Budget

When deciding on the budget, there are a number of factors that help determine the appropriate level. For established businesses, budgets are often based on previous promotional spending. If a business is in a very competitive market, promotional spending will be higher than if it was in a market with few competitors. If a business operates in business-to-business (B2B) markets, expenditure on marketing generally tends to be lower than in business-to-consumer (B2C) markets – mainly because there are fewer customers to reach. Sometimes marketing managers base their budget on matching the competitor's spending. Of course, businesses also need to consider what resources are available and what returns they expect to get on their expenditure.

Finally note that, as with all the other elements of the marketing mix, promotion must be integrated with the other 4Ps – product, price and place. And target customers, their self-image, expectations and attitudes, must be at the centre of any decision about a promotional campaign.

assessment practice
Scrumptious cakes

Scrumptious Cakes (see the assessment practice at the end of Topic 4) has been a great success. You have decided to run a promotional campaign to launch a new home-made cookies range.

A Plan a promotional campaign for your product launch. Your plan should set out the promotional mix you intend to use and the messages you will seek to convey. Provide clear statements about targeting and positioning, and campaign objectives. Provide indications of an appropriate timescale. Give suggestions for a budget – approximately how much will it cost to implement your plan?

Distribution decisions and the extended marketing mix

KEY TERMS

Distribution channels are the chain of different businesses involved in conveying products from producers to consumers.

Franchises are businesses that buy the right to use another business's products, ideas, materials and brands. The franchisee is the business that buys the franchise. The franchisor is the original business that sells the franchise.

Vertical integration describes a situation in which a business owns all, or part of, the production and distribution chain from source to outlet.

Extended marketing mix (7Ps) covers factors of more relevance to marketing services, adding people, processes and physical evidence to the 4Ps of product, price, promotion and place.

Exchange describes the mutual benefits which are gained by consumers and producers in the marketing process.

Added value is an aspect or enhancement of a product that helps to differentiate it from the competition.

Relationship marketing is a strategy of building long-term relationships to encourage loyalty and repeat custom.

In the last three topics, we have looked at three of the four Ps of the marketing mix: product, price and promotion. In this topic, we focus on the fourth P in the marketing mix. This stands for place, as introduced in the AS textbook pages 142–3, and covers the process of distribution – the means of getting the product to the customer. We also extend the marketing mix to include other factors that are particularly relevant in the marketing of services.

Distribution channels

There is a huge range of distribution options facing marketing managers. Some companies only sell their own brands of products through their own outlets. Other companies, like Amazon, distribute directly to customers from their warehouses. The internet has enabled them to operate as an online business, and some traditional retailers like Marks & Spencer now use the internet as part of their distribution mix.

Not all companies are going down the online route. Some businesses, such as House of Fraser and Zara, prefer to encourage customers to visit their stores rather than buy online. So although they use promotional materials such as catalogues and websites, they want customers to come into the store so that they can see and buy their products at first hand. Some of the smaller clothing companies such as Boden and Toast operate as mail-order businesses, accessing customers via databases and electronically held information.

So why do particular companies choose a particular distribution strategy? To answer this question, we must first consider the distribution chain. There are usually several different participants involved in the process of conveying products to customers. Many businesses can be involved in the supply chain, as Figure 10.4 shows (see page 99). As well as using various suppliers, a business may choose to use other companies to distribute its products to customers. Figure 10.16 shows three typical distribution chains.

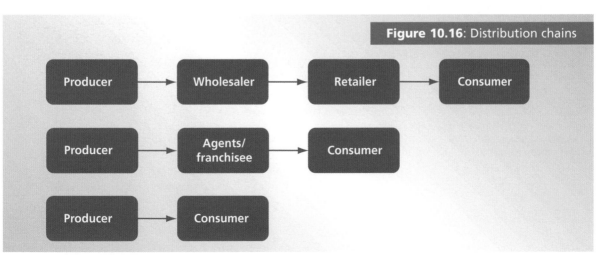

Figure 10.16: Distribution chains

Producer → Wholesaler → Retailer → Consumer

Producer → Agents/franchisee → Consumer

Producer → Consumer

Why use intermediaries?

There are several reasons for not distributing products directly to the customer. Many businesses see a commercial advantage in using intermediaries such as wholesalers, retailers and agents to get goods to their target customers. Let's consider the case for each type of intermediary.

Wholesalers

Wholesalers provide a link between a producer and retailers. By taking possession of goods in bulk, they offer a ready market for a business. They provide an opportunity to generate sales revenue more quickly (and perhaps more efficiently) than if the business has to deal with individual retailers and customers. Wholesalers also store and split consignments into smaller quantities which can widen access to more outlets. They may have access to more retail outlets, which can help expand the product's market.

Retailers

The use of retailers can help a business to reach its target customers. If a new fashion manufacturer sells clothes to Debenhams, for example, it benefits from the store's image and established customer groups. If a business is designing products for niche markets, such as skateboarders and snowboarders say, it may seek specialist outlets that are more likely to attract the target customer. What a business is doing here is using the retailer's name, expertise and accessibility to reach customers most efficiently. It relinquishes some profit and revenue for the benefits of customer reach.

Agents

Agents are another type of intermediary that can help a business to reach its target customers. Unlike wholesalers and retailers, agents work directly on behalf of the producer and take a commission on sales. Often agents have particular market knowledge or networks. Businesses that are looking to expand overseas will often use local agents based in the export countries to distribute their products.

Franchisees

Franchising is a method that allows a business a means of distributing its product quickly. In franchising, franchisees buy the right to use the franchisor's brand name but they work as independent businesses in their own right. This approach suits the franchisor, because it spreads risk – franchisees stand to lose if things don't work out – and it allows a company to quickly build a network of retail outlets. It also benefits franchisees, as they get to use an established brand name, often with the support of the producer (the contract between franchisee and franchisor will determine the levels of support and control). There are many franchises in the UK high street including some well-known names like The Body Shop and McDonald's. Both The Body Shop and McDonald's own their own outlets, but they have also expanded their retail networks by offering many franchises.

Of course, businesses do not need to use intermediaries – they can deal directly with customers. Direct distribution means that a business takes control

Figure 10.17: Advantages of different distribution methods		
Distribution channel	**Advantages**	**Disadvantages**
Producer – consumer	Control over channel Profits contained within company	Storage needs Transport needs Possibility of unsold stocks Reduced cash flow
Producer – wholesaler – retailer – consumer	Cash flow increased, as income generated before final sale to consumers No storage needs Intermediaries take ownership of stock	Reduced profits Reduced control
Producer – agent or franchisee – consumer	Use of agent's and/or franchisee's market knowledge Control can be maintained	Reduced profits, as agent or franchisee takes a cut Storage and transport needs Possibility of unsold stocks, unless franchisees required to take certain amount each period

of the whole process including storage, transportation and delivery. This enables all profits to be held within the company, but does require that resources are devoted to the whole range of distribution activities.

Figure 10.17 gives a brief summary of some of the advantages and disadvantages associated with different choices of distribution channel. Direct distribution – and/or using agents and franchisees – allows more control over the distribution process than using wholesalers and retailers, but there are some disadvantages to these approaches. In practice, large companies are likely to use a mixture of methods, depending on the particular business situation.

Some businesses seek to maintain control over the supply chain through vertical integration. This means that the company owns the businesses within the supply chain. In some cases there is total integration from source to outlet. For example, BP owns oil wells, refineries, transportation facilities and petrol stations. More typically, there is partial vertical integration, where one company owns and controls a section of the supply and distribution process.

Decision criteria

So how does a business decide on the best distribution method (or methods) for its products? Its choice will depend on several factors. The business will certainly want to examine carefully the potential impact of any distribution method on its profits and income flow. It will need to consider which methods provide the best access to target customers, and which allow access to overseas markets. It will want to consider the cost and benefits of direct and indirect methods:

- use of intermediaries – how much control does the business want over the distribution process; how much revenue is it prepared to sacrifice in order to speed up distribution?

- direct distribution – how will this be managed; what are the costs of managing distribution in-house; will distribution costs outweigh the benefits of retaining control of distribution?

There are wider management considerations linked to distribution. A business needs to consider logistical issues – covering everything from product storage, transportation methods, protection (packaging), timescales, insurance, etc. It will need to consider the packaging used to protect and preserve products in transit. If a company has perishable goods like foodstuffs, then it will require special packaging materials or equipment to ensure products arrive with customers in good condition.

Another factor to consider is whether technology could be used to improve the distribution process. New technology has had an enormous impact on distribution operations. It has enabled the growth of direct marketing, and the internet has spawned companies such as Amazon as well as whole new industries in virtual products such as music downloads, interactive games and gambling. Information technology allows businesses and customers more control over the distribution process, as a product can be tracked using internet-based systems through the entire distribution process from producer to final customer.

Choice of retailer

If a business decides to use intermediaries, it will need to choose partners with care. It will need to consider what kind of relationship it needs to build with the intermediary, and how this relationship should be managed. What happens, for example, if something goes wrong?

Customers, of course, will only experience the end of the distribution chain, so it is important that a business chooses its retail outlets carefully. The choice needs to take into account the image of the store. This image should be right for the business's target customers, meeting their expectations and aspirations.

Some companies use merchandising agreements to make sure their products achieve maximum exposure in shops. Coca-Cola provides chiller cabinets to retailers if they sign strict agreements about what products are displayed within the cabinets. Confectionery producers insist on a specific display position for their products, and sales representatives are used to ensure compliance. In France, cosmetics and beauty companies restrict the number of outlets in each town that are permitted to sell their products.

The aim of these merchandising agreements – and the choice of retail outlets – is to manage the customers' exposure to a business's products.

The extended marketing mix

The discussion on distribution (above) has been more appropriate to the marketing of goods rather than services. However, services have been a growth area in the UK economy for some years, and it is worth focusing on some of the decisions involved in marketing services.

The differences between goods (tangible products) and services (intangible products) are to do with the perishability and variation of the product. Many service products are specific to the person delivering the service. Services cannot be stored – this means that they are immediately perishable. Some services can be described as virtual products (such as music or bank services) and some are never experienced fully (such as insurance products).

Services may also be used to augment products. For example, a car manufacturer may offer added-value services such as financial deals, insurance and after-sales maintenance in addition to its main product (the car itself). In developing a service-product mix in this way, a business can add value to products in order to improve marketing outcomes.

As Figure 10.1 (see page 92) illustrated, an exchange is at the heart of the relationship between the producer and customer. What the customer values in this exchange is often more than the immediate satisfactions from the product itself. The benefits include all those personal and behavioural benefits that are attached as added value or add-ons. In the service sector, a business's people and processes are crucial in delivering those personal and behavioural benefits.

The extended marketing mix was conceived with the service sector in mind. It introduces a more integrated approach to marketing decisions, and shows how other functions within an organisation contribute to marketing success. The extended marketing mix adds three additional factors to the original four Ps of product, price, promotion and place. These are people, processes and physical evidence.

- **People**
  This acknowledges the fact that many services are provided by individuals, and the most important factor in determining the customer experience may be the skills, attitudes and behaviours of the people involved in providing the service. In a wider sense, the image of any business may depend on its staff displaying a particular set of values and behaviours. This means that recruitment and personnel decisions have an impact on the effectiveness of marketing.

- **Processes**
  This refers to systems that are important in making sure that services are delivered successfully. For example, distribution systems will influence how quickly and accurately orders are processed; systems used to back promotion campaigns will affect how well sales personnel perform.

- **Physical evidence**
  This relates to those aspects of a service that signal to the customer the brand identities and values of the business. Examples of physical evidence are very diverse – they include the particular décor and sound systems in a nightclub; the colour and typography (font) associated with a particular brand; the ambience of a hair salon, bank or even a website.

stop and think

What colour scheme is used by Marks & Spencer? What makes the atmosphere in Starbucks different from that in McDonald's? What colours and font do you associate with these three banks: First Direct bank, Smile bank, HSBC? (A visit to a few corporate websites may help.)

What image do you think each of these companies is trying to project? How would you describe their target customers? Is there a link?

Relationship marketing

The focus on people, process and physical evidence underpins the concept of relationship marketing. The idea behind relationship marketing – sometimes known as customer relationship management (CRM) – is to invest effort in building and maintaining a long-term bond between a business and its customers. For many successful businesses, this has been done as a matter of course through good business practice. This has been the key to their success, and others have tried to copy their approach.

The growth in the number of businesses offering loyalty card schemes is an example of this approach. It is evidence that more companies are adopting CRM as a key business strategy.

Most businesses will say they are committed to delivering good customer service. To do this in practice, however, requires more than good intentions. A business must have a clear understanding of what its customers demand. It must be able to meet ever higher customer expectations. It must be proactive, and not just treat its customer service obligations as a complaints-response issue. Companies that are interested in building long-term relationships with their customers embed customer service within the overall business culture.

The driving force in customer service and relationship management is that it is easier (and more profitable in the long run) to keep selling to existing customers than to try to get new customers. Businesses use a range of methods to keep customers. One approach is the use of loyalty cards and incentives to discourage customers from switching to other suppliers.

It is not only in services that relationship marketing is important. Look back at the layered product model (in Topic 3): the augmented product frequently includes the addition of added-value customer benefits which are designed to encourage brand loyalty.

assessment practice
Niche clothing markets

One of the key success factors in the clothing business is the ability to target customers through effective distribution and to build relationships with customers.

A number of companies have grown from relatively small specialist markets, such as surfing, skiing and snowboarding clothing. Three of these niche companies, Joe Browns, Fat Face and White Stuff, have used different marketing approaches.

Find out more about the contrasting apporaches used by these three companies by visiting the websites of the companies. Their websites are, respectively:

■ www.joebrowns.co.uk

■ www.fatface.com

■ www.white-stuff.co.uk

Get some of their marketing material from their websites. Examine the material and any other information you can obtain to complete the tasks.

A **Identify and evaluate the distribution strategy of each company.**

B **Who do you think are the target customers of each company? Are they from the same segment?**

C **How important is branding to the customers of each company?**

D **How might these companies build long-term relationships with their customers?**

Segmentation, targeting and positioning

Setting the scene: targeted marketing

Popular products like Coca-Cola and KitKat are bought by many different types of people. However, the manufacturers don't rely on a universal "one size fits all" approach to marketing.

They vary the marketing mix, particularly through variations in the product and promotion elements. In this way they can target particular customer groups to encourage higher sales or to reach new customers.

Coca-Cola now offers many variations on its basic product, such as Diet Coke, as well as vanilla and lemon and lime versions. Similarly KitKat, for many years the leading UK chocolate confectionery product, is available in chunky,

white chocolate and orange-flavoured versions.

Try to come up with descriptions of the types of customer that might be attracted to the various versions. Who, for example, do you think are the typical buyers of regular Coca-Cola; what type of customer is likely to buy vanilla-flavoured Diet Coke? Why has a chunky version of KitKat been produced – is it likely to appeal to a different type of customer than those who like the traditional KitKat bar?

KEY TERMS

Segmentation is the process of dividing a market into distinct groups of customers, with similar features and responses.

Target customers are the typical customers that should be the focus of the marketing mix.

Positioning is the process of determining a product's position in the market compared to competing products.

Positioning maps show how products relate to competitor products against two relevant factors – price and quality, for example.

Viability is the process of assessing whether a market segment will be easy to reach and profitable for the business.

The target customer

In business, your marketing efforts should be directed at target customers because they are the people most likely to buy your product(s). (For an introduction to this theory see the AS textbook pages 118–21.) The aim of focusing on target customers is to reach (the largest number of) the keenest customers, and to avoid wasting marketing resources on those that are not likely to buy your products. Segmenting the market – by breaking it into smaller chunks – also allows different marketing campaigns to be designed to create the required response from diverse target customer groups.

This approach requires a systematic analysis of the segmented market which will help a business identify the target market and position its product in the most promising place in that market. The process starts with segmentation. This means analysing the market into different groups of customers who have enough similarities that they will respond to marketing signals in the same way. Having segmented the market, a business can find out about the wants, needs and expectations of each "typical" customer. Marketing managers will then need to determine the position of their products in the market.

stopandthink

In positioning a product for a particular target group, does this mean that it will only be bought by the target customers? The answer is "no", of course, because for any product there are likely to be sales to some customers who are not typical of the target group. However, there will probably be something in the marketing mix that these "untargeted" customers can relate to.

Consider Burberry clothing. Burberry became quite upset that its premium brand of clothing (particularly its plaid pattern) was adopted as a badge of recognition by some young people on inner-city estates. These were not the target customers. Why do you think Burberry was selected as a brand by city youth culture?

Segmentation

The marketing challenge is to split the market into manageable groups – or customer types – that have similar traits and behaviours. This allows a business to predict the likely response of each group to a marketing campaign, and to focus effort and design promotional campaigns accordingly.

To do this, a business needs to decide on the basis for segmentation – the set of variables that are used to determine each segment of the customer population.

The marketing industry has become famous for its inventive descriptions to describe customer segments, with categories such as yuppies (young upwardly mobile), dinkys (double income no kids yet), skiers (spending the kids' inheritance) and silver surfers (older internet users).

Before we look at some of the most commonly used bases of segmentation, it is worth emphasising two points. First, any segmentation needs to draw on market research as this will provide information on customer behaviour and preferences as well as trends in a business's main markets. Second, any market segmentation should not be set in stone: markets are dynamic, and research into customer behaviour should include emerging as well as existing segments. This should be part of a business's ongoing environmental scanning.

Socioeconomic segmentation

Socioeconomic segmentation is widely used, though more often outside rather than within the marketing industry. The population is split according to income and status (roughly equivalent to social class). Figure 10.18 shows the definitions of the different groups. These were originally devised when occupations could be clearly linked with income and wealth. Today, the links are less clear but the groups are still useful in some markets – newspaper advertising, for example.

Demographic and lifecycle segmentation

Demographic (population-related) and lifecycle segmentation divides a population on variables such as age, sex, marital status, education, income and occupation. It can also be based on sociocultural factors like religion, stage in family lifecycle and ethnic groups. Examples of lifecycle segments include dinkys, silver surfers and empty-nesters (people whose children have grown up and left home).

Geographical segmentation

Geographical segmentation is useful for products for which sales are dependent on climate, regional factors

Figure 10.18: Socioeconomic class

Social grade	Description of occupation	Example
A	Higher managerial and professional	Company director
B	Lower managerial and supervisory	Middle manager
C1	Non-manual	Bank clerk
C2	Skilled manual	Electrician
D	Semi-skilled and unskilled manual	Labourer
E	Those receiving no income from employment	Unemployed

and country-specific issues. Geographical segmentation is also used on a smaller scale, using where people live as an indicator of their lifestyles and behaviours. This is based on the assumption that people tend to live alongside others who have similar tastes, behaviours and incomes. This type of small-scale geographical segmentation is done by postcode or by the ACORN (A Classification of Residential Neighbourhoods) categorisation.

Psychological, psychographic and lifestyle

Psychological, psychographic and lifestyle segmentations are more sophisticated methods of segmenting populations. They are favoured by marketing professionals because they describe in a fuller way the aspirational and behavioural factors of customers, giving a fuller picture of the target customer. Figure 10.19 shows the four Cs classification (cross-cultural consumer classification), which is an example of a psychological classification.

Figure 10.19: The cross-cultural consumer classification

Descriptor	Personality traits
Aspirer	Upwardly mobile; ambitious and fashionable; style and brand conscious; probably young
Achiever	Probably more mature; has achieved goals and likes to demonstrate status discreetly; concerned with maintaining social position and high standard of living
Mainstream	Moderate, conservative lifestyle; may be family-oriented; concerned with value for money and may be slow to change; often brand-loyal
Reformer	Non-conformist; may be interested in social issues; brand-switchers; uninterested in social status

Use-related segmentation

Use-related segmentation looks at how, when and where a product is actually used. For example, a business may segment its customers into frequent and infrequent users of its services, and tailor its marketing offer and promotion to different types of user.

Segmentation may be on the basis of how customers use the product. Credit card companies might offer one incentive for customers that settle their accounts at each billing date – such as cashback on purchases – and a separate incentive such as a low interest rate for customers that just pay off some of the bill each time. (Obviously, the low interest rate will not be attractive to the card clearers because they never have to pay interest.)

Loyalty cards allow businesses to gather useful data which they can use to segment their customers. Boots uses information it collects through its Advantage card scheme to offer different incentives and rewards to its low-, medium- and high-value customers. High-value customers receive a copy of Boots glossy magazine; low-value customers are only entitled to some special offers at in-store Advantage card kiosks. In this way, Boots invests more resource in trying to keep high-value customers loyal.

The best method?

In practice, marketing professionals may use a mixture of these segmentation methods to reach the most appropriate and useful way of describing the target customer. However customers are described and grouped, the point is to use market research and the business's own information to paint an accurate picture of target customers and to predict their behaviour as accurately as possible.

Assessing viability

It is little use identifying a target customer market segment unless that segment generates enough revenue for the company. So any market segment needs to be assessed for viability. Four factors are relevant in assessing viability:

- size – the segment needs to have enough potential customers to make the effort worthwhile

- durability – the market segment needs to be in existence long enough

- profitability – the segment must be able to generate enough profit over its potential lifetime

- accessibility – it must be possible to reach the target customer.

These points might seem obvious, but in the past there have been market segments that were difficult to reach, particularly with traditional marketing tools. For example, it used to be notoriously difficult to devise marketing strategies for 16–24 year old males whose tastes, attitudes and behaviours tended to change rapidly and who were difficult to reach using communications channels such as television and radio. As a market segment, this group of target customers was neither durable (in that their tastes changed rapidly) or easily accessible. That has changed to some extent in recent years, with the use of computer-based and mobile phone technologies, and there are now far more products specifically aimed at this group.

Targeting

Marketing research can provide information about the typical buyer of a business's products. This data should be used to understand the typical – or target – customer's set of buying behaviours, attitudes and tastes. This can then be used to inform how the business can develop its marketing mix. The marketing mix – of product, price, promotion and place – is then managed in such a way that the needs, expectations and tastes of the target customer are satisfied.

Kettle Foods, for example, targets its Kettle Chips product at higher socioeconomic groups. It is a premium product, with an image that conveys a sophisticated lifestyle. The product, its packaging and price, and the way it is presented to customers in-store through Kettle Foods display stands are all designed to differentiate the target customer from those of, for example, Walkers crisps.

The target customer expects that all the elements of the marketing mix will match their image of themselves and meet their other, perhaps more practical, needs such as their budget. The marketing mix should be designed to motivate the target customer. Indeed, nothing in business can be achieved without understanding what motivates the customer.

Positioning

Putting the product into some kind of market perspective, compared to competitors, is known as positioning. To do this, marketing professionals often use a positioning map. This takes two aspects of the product – features which are of importance in the product's performance – and compares them to competitor products.

One typical combination is to use price and quality as the two features to construct the positioning map, but we could use any relevant variables. For clothing brands, we could use style and price; for cars, we could use design and safety. We could use separate combinations of features for one product to construct several positioning maps which could be combined to produce a more complete picture of the product's performance.

A positioning map is also sometimes called a perceptual map because it is based on the perceptions of the products' positions. Figure 10.20 shows a practical example. This is based on small hatchback cars, and uses quality and price as the two features to construct the map. The UK car market is very competitive, and consumers are brand and image conscious – it is, therefore, a good industry to use to illustrate this aspect of marketing theory.

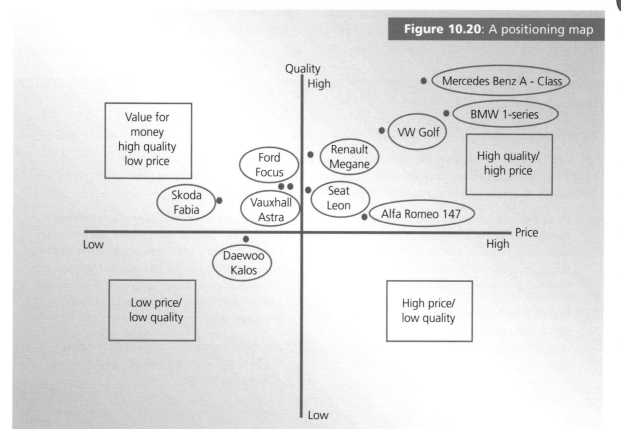

Figure 10.20: A positioning map

Figure 10.20 positions the Skoda Fabia in the high-quality, low-price quadrant. This position should be determined by collecting the perceptions of a representative sample of the public. You may disagree with some of the positions given to particular models on this map, but what is important to Skoda is the opinions of their target customers. These may be those who already buy Skodas and those who might consider buying a Skoda.

A few years ago, you might have expected to see the Skoda in the low-price, low-quality quadrant. But since Skoda was taken over by VW, the public's opinion of the quality of Skoda cars has steadily risen. The company has used the its previous poor image within its advertising and promotion campaigns by inviting potential customers to challenge their prejudices and to think about buying a Skoda.

In general, a business will use a positioning map to determine whether it wants to reinforce its product's current position in the market through its marketing mix, or to reposition the product by changing the marketing mix – through, say, altering its features, price, image or distribution – to take advantage of opportunities in other parts of the market.

The marketing mix

The process of segmentation, targeting and positioning is used to inform the decisions that need to be taken in determining the marketing mix. Not only must the product be right, it must be offered at a price that matches the target customer's expectations. All promotion must speak to the target customer, reinforcing their self-image and their relationship with the product and/or the business. Distribution, and the place that sells the product, must support these elements. The aim is that all elements work together to match the expectations and needs of the target customer in such a way that the company's marketing objectives are reached.

Note that this process of market evaluation and segmentation not only supports the marketing of existing products but can also suggest new business opportunities. By examining the market through customer segmentation and product positioning, a business might uncover a potential market segment in which customer's needs are not being met. In other words, there is a gap in the market, and new product development relies, to a large extent, on finding gaps in existing markets.

stop and think

Companies such as Ben and Jerry's, Body Shop and Pret A Manger have built a reputation and image for ethical and social responsibility. These three companies, however, have all been taken over by bigger organisations with different ethical and social images. How do you think their target customers might respond to these takeovers?

assessment practice
Positioning niche clothing

In Topic 6 you investigated the distribution decisions of three clothing companies: Fat Face, White Stuff and Joe Browns. Look back at the marketing material you obtained to undertake the assessment practice at the end of Topic 6.

A Using the methods outlined in this topic, describe the target customers of each of the three niche clothing companies. Describe their target customers in terms of, for example, age, lifestyle, income, occupation, aspirations, etc.

B Explain how you came to your conclusions in task A. For example, was it the product range itself that influenced your decision? Was it something in the promotional material? In which case, what? Was it the pricing or distribution aspects?

C Try to construct an appropriate positioning (perceptual) map to show where the companies are positioned within their market. The factors that you could use for the axes of this map could be price and quality, or size of range and fashionability, or any other features that you think relevant.

D Are there any gaps in these niche clothing markets that another company might fill, or already has filled?

Marketing research

Setting the scene: why businesses do marketing research

As explained in Unit 3 of the AS Applied Business course (see pages 122–35 of the textbook), research information is gathered by businesses as an ongoing process.

Market research is used to inform decisions about all aspects of the marketing mix and the business environment. It is, for example, used extensively to test new (innovative) ideas before committing to the cost of launching a new product on the market.

Market information is collected directly through specific research activities, such as surveys, focus groups and test markets, and indirectly through customer activity, such as purchasing patterns on loyalty cards and credit cards.

The UK's leading retailer, Tesco, was the first to make full use of its Clubcard scheme as a means of gathering customer data. Information on customer purchasing behaviour is used by Tesco to target particular promotional activities or product developments to groups of customers most likely to be attracted by the offer.

Kettle Chips uses a range of research techniques to find out the likes and dislikes of its existing customers, to test out new flavours, and to gauge the likely success of a particular campaign. Like many other companies, Kettle Chips' marketing success is based on knowing what its typical (target) customer wants and needs.

The role of marketing research

All marketing decisions should be based on marketing research. Successful companies integrate marketing research into their operational and strategic planning processes. This means that research is a continuous process so that the business can respond quickly to the dynamics of the market.

Marketing research forms a vital part of marketing management. A business may carry out its own research, but, as in many areas of marketing, a plethora of consultancies offer marketing research services, with some agencies specialising in particular markets and industries.

Note that, strictly speaking, "market research" is carried out to be able to understand the market in which the business operates; "marketing research" takes this wider and is research into the entire marketing process. So market research is part of marketing research, though in practice the two terms get used interchangeably.

Research data

Research information, or data, comes from a variety of sources. In Topics 1 and 2 we looked at the process of scanning the environment in order to carry out external and internal audits. This process generates research information on the current situation in a business's environment so that decisions can be made about marketing planning. We have also emphasised the vital importance of businesses knowing what their customers think about all their marketing activities – from product development through to pricing, promotional campaigns and distribution choices – so that they can respond to, and generate, future needs and wants. This is achieved using marketing research.

Market research involves an investment in time and money. Any business needs to balance the cost of collecting information against the value of that information. It needs to have as good a picture of what is happening in its market, and how well the business is performing, as it can reasonably afford. This means that sometimes it needs to settle for sufficiently good data rather than perfect information.

Marketing research is the systematic collection and analysis of data to enable a business to make better marketing decisions.

Qualitative data is non-numerical data. For example, market researchers obtain qualitative data on the in-depth attitudes and opinions of consumers.

Quantitative data is numerical data. Businesses want quantitative data about the size of markets, the number of potential customers for their products, etc.

Primary data is new information on a market. It is collected for a specific purpose by a market research agency or a business.

Secondary data is information on a market that already exists, having been collected by another person or organisation.

Cross-sectional research collects information on a number of variables from different sources at the same time.

Longitudinal data collects information on a variable over a period of time.

Sampling is the process of selecting a representative group of consumers from a larger population.

Trends of past performance over time are used to forecast future performance.

Test marketing involves using a small, representative market to test out marketing ideas.

Another consideration is how to get to the right information. Since the information technology revolution, the marketing research challenge has changed from one of a lack of information – and how to find what you need to know – to one of finding the right information in a situation of near information overload. So a systematic approach to research and information gathering needs to be adopted.

Primary and secondary data

Primary and secondary are the two basic categories of research data. These are also sometimes called field (primary) and desk (secondary) research, which is a little misleading as you can gather primary research information while sitting at a desk.

Primary research is the process of gathering new information for a specific project or activity. This may be done using surveys (by telephone, face-to-face, through the post, over the internet), focus groups, observations, experiments, etc. Figure 10.21 sets out the main advantages and disadvantages of each of these different methods.

Secondary research uses data or information that has already been collected, by the business or by someone else, for another purpose. This might be old primary research data, but it also might be more general data that provides useful background information. This allows a bigger picture to be seen, putting the primary research into context. Secondary data can be found in a business's own records, government publications and statistics, research agencies' databases, newspaper articles, industry bodies' information, and so on.

Quantitative and qualitative data

Another way of categorising research data is by whether it is quantitative or qualitative.

- **Quantitative data** is factual, and usually provided in numerical form. An example of useful quantitative data would be the total sales of a particular product type in a market, and the percentage change of those sales over time. This helps provide the "what" part of understanding customer behaviour. Surveys can be used to gather quantitative data. It can also be obtained from the company's own sales records and from information on changes in its market share. So quantitative data can be primary or secondary.

- **Qualitative data** is concerned with "why" people behave in a particular way. For example, qualitative data might report on customers' opinions of product performance or what brands mean to them. Qualitative data can also be primary or secondary. It can be collected using focus groups perhaps discussing the merits of a particular package redesign. This would be primary data. An example of secondary data would be general opinions about environmentally friendly products from articles and research papers.

Cross-sectional and longitudinal data

Cross-sectional data takes information on similar variables from a range of different sources. For example, a business might look at the sales of its own product, and get comparable information on similar products offered by its competitors. This would usually require primary research and would generate quantitative information.

Longitudinal data shows the values for a variable over a period of time – such as the month-by-month sales figures. This would also be primary quantitative data. If a business collected the results of focus group discussions over a period of time and compared the results to ascertain changes in customers' opinions, this would be longitudinal, primary, qualitative data.

Research methods

A business needs information about customer behaviour. It needs to be able to predict what will happen if it implements specific marketing plans. Marketing research, therefore, needs to provide information on the dynamics of the market. This might include information on:

- the size of the market – crucially, is the market growing or declining?

- competitor activity – what are competitors doing, how is their market share changing, are there any new entrants or potential new entrants?

- consumer tastes, attitudes and behaviour – are these changing and in what ways?

- the economic situation – is the economy looking good or do the latest trends show problems on the horizon?

- the business's own sales figures – how are sales performing, how can it improve performance?

- responses to particular marketing activities, such as promotional campaigns, new packaging design, new product developments, etc.

Figure 10.21 shows some approaches to marketing research, and lists some of the advantages and disadvantages associated with each method. As

Figure 10.21: Market research methods

Method and approach	Advantages	Disadvantages
Face–to-face survey Mostly quantitative Cross-sectional or longitudinal	Can use supplementary questioning People may talk for longer in face-to-face interviews	May be unwanted bias in choice of subjects Unit costs are high Small reach
Telephone survey Mostly quantitative Cross-sectional or longitudinal	Can reach many people easily Lower costs Allows opportunity for some supplementary questions	Perceived as intrusive Cannot easily target specific groups Only gets to those who answer the phone (so potential bias)
Postal survey Mostly quantitative Cross-sectional or longitudinal	Can reach large numbers Quick and cheap	Poor response rate No opportunity for supplementary probing
Internet survey Mostly quantitative Cross-sectional or longitudinal	Quick and cheap Immediate response	Only those with internet access can participate
Observation For example, using CCTV to record customer movements around the supermarket Mostly qualitative, some quantitative Cross-sectional or longitudinal	Gives valid information Can be unbiased	Expensive to process findings, as it needs trained specialists No opportunity for interaction with customers
Experimentation For example, trying out an advertisement on a selected group of target customers Mostly qualitative	Allows predictability Allows changes to be made based on valid (real) behaviour	Can be expensive to set up and process Small scale may be unrepresentative
Focus group For example, discussion on product packaging prior to launch Mostly qualitative	Allows understanding of response and predictability	Expensive to run Small scale

Figure 10.21 shows, there are many different research methods, and any business is likely to use a variety of approaches to get as good a picture of the market as it can. By mixing quantitative and qualitative research, it can find out why people behave in a particular way and what people actually do. When one approach is supported by another, this is called triangulation. So the numbers-based data may prove what the behavioural information indicates, and vice versa.

A business may obtain primary data to give up-to-date information about the market, for example, and secondary data to provide the bigger picture and put marketing activity into context. Cross-sectional research might provide information that can be used to compare different situations at the same period of time, such as rates of economic growth in different EU countries in 2005. Longitudinal information, such as data consumer spending in high street retailers in 2002, 2003, 2004 and 2005, might be used to identify trends. This trends information can provide the basis for forecasting future performance, which is a key part of marketing planning.

stop and think

Suppose you are working in the marketing department of a confectionery company. The company wants some information to help it develop a new chocolate product. Come up with a list of questions that would need to be answered to help you make decisions about this new product development.

Decide how you would go about the marketing research: what methods would you use, where would the information come from. Describe the methods that might be most appropriate (drawing on Figure 10.21) and categorise the different types of data you might collect.

Sampling

In trying to obtain information on the preferences, tastes and behaviours of target customers, ideally you might want data on every prospective customer. Obviously, with any large market segment, this would be ridiculously expensive and simply impractical to collect. Instead, businesses rely on data from a representative sample of the entire customer group (or population).

It is important to get this sample right, because if it is unrepresentative it could result in poor decision-making and wasted effort and money. The sampling method needs to ensure accuracy and lack of bias as far as possible. It needs to produce results that are accurate, reliable and valid so that sound decisions can be made on their basis.

The choice of sampling method should be determined by the given situation. You need to identify your objectives, and you need to find the best way of getting a sample that represents the whole of your target group. All methods require you to determine the sampling frame – this a list (or other record) of the population from which all sampling units are drawn. This might be the entire customer list of Tesco, for example. The sample itself is taken from the sampling frame.

Random sampling

In random sampling, any individual has as much chance of being selected as any other. But if a particular target group is being investigated, the sample should also be targeted. For example, if you are investigating the clothing market for shorter than average men, you might just sample males between 25 and 30 who are less than 1.7 m tall. In all cases, the sample should be representative of the population under investigation.

Quota sampling

Quota sampling is used when you need a certain number of respondents from each sub-category of an overall population. For example, if you are researching the market for a new chocolate bar, you may want opinions from 50 people aged 13–21, 50 aged 22–30 years, 50 aged 31–39 years, and so on. This method is widely used in marketing research.

Stratified sampling

Stratified sampling is used when the sample is relatively small, and pure random sampling might result in an unrepresentative outcome. For example, if you wanted to find out how shop staff have been affected by new customer service policies, you would need to get opinions from a representative sample. Your problem is that the response of management is likely to be different from those dealing daily with the customers, but random sampling may result in too many managers being selected (because it is random). In this case, you will decide on a sample from each layer in the organisation that reflects the true structure of the organisation.

Cluster sampling

Cluster sampling picks a random sample from a sampling frame of groups of subjects rather than individual subjects. All subjects in the selected groups are included in the sample.

Testing the market

Once marketing decisions, based on research, have been made, the marketing plan can be tested to see what happens in reality. Testing can also be carried out at intervals, for example during the new product development process.

Some test marketing uses a particular geographical region to see how a new idea or product performs. For example, Boots tested out its Advantage card in East Anglia before being launched nationwide. Alternative new product ideas can be tested out to see which variant is best received by the target customer group.

Testing in this way – like marketing research in general – is about minimising risk. It allows a company to be as informed as possible about customer wants, needs and behaviours. Note, however, that sometimes businesses go out on a limb and press on with a product despite their research findings. The Sony Walkman, allegedly, was predicted to be a flop when customer opinion was sought. Similarly, when Hovis commissioned a design company to come up with new ideas for its white loaf, customer opinion suggested that it should stick with the style used by competitors in the premium white bread segment. However, both these companies decided to take a risk and to trust their own instincts rather than go along with the customer research. Both products were huge successes. Often the customer prefers familiarity – or expresses a preference for the known over the innovative – so perhaps there are certain situations when a risk is worth taking.

assessment practice
Car valeting

Suppose you have decided to start up a new mobile car valeting business. Your business will undertake a full valet of a customer's car at their home or business.

Your task is to design a marketing research project to find out how to market your service. You will need to decide on all aspects of the marketing mix.

A First assess the competitive environment, and try to identify a potential gap in the market. How will your service offer something more or different from that of competitors?

B Consider what information you will need to gather to plan your marketing mix. For example, how will you promote your service? How will you decide on pricing?

C Draft a marketing research plan. This should set out:
- the most appropriate methods for collecting primary and secondary data
- how you plan to sample the population
- your research questions.

D Design a questionnaire to collect some primary data about your market. Test the questionnaire by running a pilot survey to see if there are any areas that need to be amended.

E Collate your findings and come to conclusions which will inform your marketing decisions.

F When you have completed the research, prepare a report on what went well and which elements did not work as planned. What would you do differently next time?

The ideas that underpin marketing planning were introduced in Unit 3 of the AS Applied Business course (see pages 110–17 of the AS textbook). This showed how marketing planning fits in with the overall business planning process.

In this unit, we have been looking at the decisions that need to be made about how to market products and services effectively, and examining the tools and techniques that businesses use in the decision-making process. In this summary topic, we show how the marketing decisions examined in this unit are used in practice to draw up a marketing plan.

The marketing plan sits within the corporate plan, which also incorporates plans for other organisational functions such as finance, human resource management, production, purchasing, design and administration. Similarly, the marketing plan will consist of operational plans for product development, pricing, promotion and distribution.

Any marketing plan needs to fit in with the overall plan of a business. As Figure 10.22 suggests, this is a two-way process: the corporate (or business) plan informs the marketing plan by, for example, setting overall business goals and objectives; and the marketing plan in turn informs the longer-term business plan.

Planning steps

Planning is a continuous process. It requires ongoing research to assess the performance of the marketing plan. It requires flexibility – plans may have to be adapted to meet changing market dynamics or to ensure that objectives are met.

There are a number of key stages in the planning process that provide a framework for effective and efficient decision-making. This process incorporates all the decisions that we have been looking at in this unit.

> ### KEY TERMS
>
> **Situation analysis** involves an audit of a business's external and internal environment to assess the current situation.
>
> **SMART objectives** are specific, measurable, achievable, realistic and timed.
>
> **Performance measures** provide the basis for assessing progress and are necessary for checking performance against objectives so that remedial action can be taken if necessary.

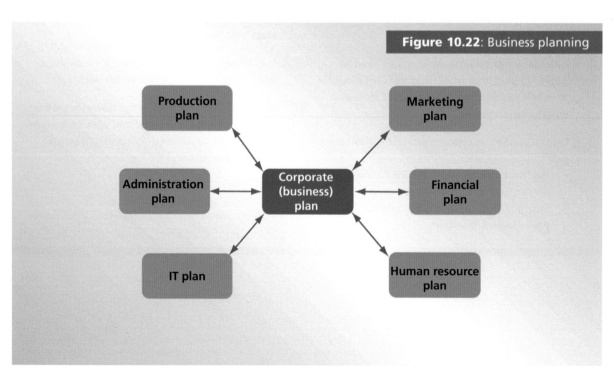

Figure 10.22: Business planning

- Production plan
- Marketing plan
- Administration plan
- Corporate (business) plan
- Financial plan
- IT plan
- Human resource plan

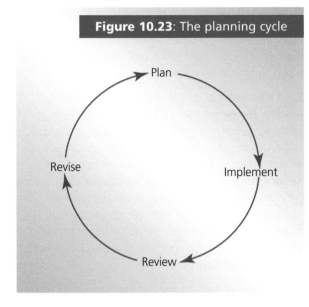

Figure 10.23: The planning cycle

Plan

Implement

Review

Revise

1 Situation analysis

This first step is an assessment of the current business situation. This requires an audit of the business's internal and external environment as described in Topics 1 and 2.

Consider the car valeting service, the subject of the assessment practice in Topic 8. A situation analysis for this business would require an assessment of the current state of the market:

- who are the competitors
- how well are they doing
- what market share do they have.

You would also want to know about the current economic climate – do people want to pay for this type of luxury service; do they feel it is affordable? Are there relevant social factors – is this a business that appeals to people who are "cash rich and time poor"? Are there any legal requirements? By answering these questions, you would be able to produce an audit of the business's environment and undertake a SWOT analysis of the enterprise.

2 Objective setting

What are the goals of the company? Is it new product development, or increasing market share, or entering new markets? All goals need to be expressed as SMART objectives. This means they should be:

- specific – with measurable outcomes, such as a 20 per cent increase in sales
- measurable – there should be a means of measuring what has been achieved, by say monitoring sales figures

- achievable – within the available resources
- realistic – it is obviously pointless to set unrealistic objectives, but it is good practice to set challenging targets
- timed – there should be a defined timescale setting out when the objective should be achieved, say a 20 per cent increase in sales over one year.

For the car valeting service, two initial objectives may be to get 50 regular customers within three months, and to generate £500 per week within six months. These are specific, measurable and timed. Are they also achievable and realistic?

Progress towards objectives should be regularly reviewed during the period of the plan. If at any review stage the objectives appear to be in danger of not being met, then tactics and strategies can be amended.

3 Strategies and tactics

These are the operational considerations – what is actually going to be done to achieve the objectives? Throughout this unit, we have considered the decisions that businesses must take to determine their marketing mix, including the targeting and positioning of their products. From these decisions on each part of the marketing mix, and on the key target customers, flow a set of strategies and tactics. These need to be put into a time frame.

- How long will new product development take?
- When will promotional activities be implemented (these will be in the form of promotional plans)?
- How will marketing research be used to inform the plan's implementation?

This is where a business will use its marketing information to make decisions about product, price, promotion and place.

4 Performance measurement

How will performance in each area of the marketing mix be measured? For example, the effectiveness of advertising campaigns can be assessed through using customer perception surveys or focus groups; sales figures over a specific period of time can be monitored against forecast sales levels; pricing decisions can be measured against planned profitability levels.

Measures of performance can be anything that is relevant to the marketing plan's success. These can include:

- sales figures
- trials of products
- numbers of new customers
- awareness of brand in a given group of customers
- increased profitability
- numbers of enquiries about products
- increased usage by existing customers

The important point is to use performance measurement to improve performance.

5 Resources

The plan must set out the resources that will be required. This will be a key section in assessing the plan's viability. It should clearly set out:

- financial resources – what are the costs of implementing the plan, and how do these compare against projected benefits?
- people resources – who will do what and when?
- external resources – does the plan require outside expertise such as advertising agencies, marketing research companies and website consultants?
- information – what information is needed, and where and how can this be obtained?

These decisions on resources, together with a clear time frame and all elements of the marketing mix, are the framework for marketing planning and management. Note that each part of the mix will generate its own type of plan.

Figure 10.24: The marketing mix constituents

6 Monitoring and review process

Every plan needs to be reviewed to ensure that planned outcomes are being met. The key question is when to monitor progress?

For a new product, a business is likely to want to monitor the performance of the marketing plan at relatively frequent intervals as it is crucial to identify any problems as early as possible. For established products, where patterns of consumer behaviour are better known, it may be more sensible to allow longer periods of time between reviews. In promotional planning, there may be "natural" review periods when performance is best measured against forecasts, such as after product launch or at the end of a sales promotion campaign.

The purpose of monitoring and reviewing is to allow corrections and/or improvements to be made in order to optimise overall performance. Certainly if objectives are not being met, the plan must be adapted and improved.

7 Implementation

Implementation is the process of putting the plan into action with continued reviewing and monitoring. In practice, planning and implementation are not really separate concepts but are part of a continuous management process in a dynamic business environment. There is a saying that "failing to plan means planning to fail", and this is certainly true in marketing. If the plan has been thought through well, the implementation stage can go very smoothly. If not, this is where planning mistakes will be exposed.

If, for example, a business is engaged in a new product launch, then it must ensure that it has the resources to implement its marketing plan. Remember in the product life cycle that there is often a need to try to recoup development costs, incurred before product launch, by pricing high in the growth phases. So this might need heavy and intense promotional activity to generate interest and raise brand awareness. The promotional campaign should include a costed media schedule, showing which media will be used and when and how much this will cost.

Using your own business idea or one that has already been suggested in this unit, devise a marketing plan for your product or service. You could use marketing research already carried out to help in the situation analysis.

Go through the stages described below to produce your marketing plan. This will help you think through all aspects of the marketing mix. At all stages, don't forget the target customers and their needs and expectations.

A Management and finance. You will need to decide on who is responsible for what aspects of planning and implementation. You will need to determine a budget for product development and promotion.

B Planning. You will need to undertake a situation analysis, set objectives for the plan, and decide on strategies and tactics.

C Product. A product development plan could include a product range. Do you offer the same product to everyone? Or will you differentiate your products for particular target groups?

D Price. What will your price be? Will you have a range of prices for different products?

E Promotion. How will you promote your product so that you reach your target market with the right message? Find out how much advertising costs are for different media. What about a website?

F Place. Distribution of services requires different solutions from distribution of tangible products. If you choose a perishable product, you will also need to consider packaging (remember this can also be used for promotion and branding) and transportation.

G Service. If your product or business idea is a service, think also about the extended mix. And have you considered relationship marketing aspects?

H Performance measurement. How wil you measure the performance of the plan? What will constitute success? You need to set out the steps you will take to monitor and review your plan during the implementation stage.

137

Topic 9 Marketing planning

Business in practice: Zara

Zara is a growing player in the fast-moving and competitive world of high street fashion retailing. It is regarded with envy within the industry because of its phenomenal growth and success. There are Zara stores in major cities in the UK and around the world.

Situation analysis

The high street fashion market is very competitive. There is frequent media coverage about the difficulties that many companies are having in this market.

Many businesses have relied on driving down costs in order to remain competitive. Many companies, such as Top Shop, Gap, Mango, H&M, Next and River Island, have moved production to the Far East, where labour costs are much lower than in the developed world.

Zara has not followed this approach; instead it is a vertically integrated company with production facilities in Spain. In the long term, however, a 2005 compromise agreement between China and the EU on textile imports could pose a threat to Zara and make it more difficult to continue manufacturing garments in Spain.

Target market and consumer behaviour

The target customer for the company is young fashion-conscious women and men. They are likely to be between 18 and 30 years old. They have sufficient disposable income to buy high fashion clothing frequently, changing their style to keep up with fashion. They are likely to be influenced by the styles worn by celebrities.

Because of the target customers' habits of frequent spending and high disposable incomes, this is a very attractive market. It is a large one and for all these reasons very competitive.

Product decisions

Zara only sells its own products and employs its own designers. It offers high fashion clothing and accessories.

Because the fashion business requires quick response times, Zara's production facilities are linked

ZARA

electronically directly to the shops. The factory and designer teams are able to keep up to date by using shop managers to identify which products are selling best in individual stores. Using a PDA (Personal Digital Assistant), the managers can then communicate directly with the factory to send orders for the right number of specific garments. These will normally be dispatched and received within a few days.

Pricing

Pricing is keen, and Zara is competing around the same level as Mango, Top Shop and River Island. The target customer has concerns over fashionable styling and price.

Promotion

Zara tends to use a limited amount of local advertising rather than national campaigns. But the stores have a distinctive style which is carried through on the web-based catalogue.

Because of the nature of the business, however, there is a strong reliance on PR. The company makes an effort to ensure that magazines aimed at the target customer group include models wearing Zara's clothes in their features.

Distribution

Zara only uses its own outlets to sell products to its customers, and it does not offer its clothes to other retailers. Many other retailers do the same, as they want to have control over the entire marketing process.

Quick response times are a key feature of Zara's integrated system, and it ensures this by having control over the logistics aspects of distribution operations.

Marketing research

Research sources for Zara include the fashion industry itself. The colours and styles of each season's

collection are not just a direct response to customers' tastes. The fashion industry is very well networked, and current styles, colours and fabrics are largely determined by the leading design houses. Indeed, the main design houses, and the fashion media, play a role in persuading customers that particular styles, colours and fabrics are fashionable. The high street chains, to some extent, follow in their wake.

This may sound like product-oriented rather than customer-oriented marketing. However, the high street stores, which are closest to most customers, are responding in many ways to past customer trends: fashions get adopted by their customers because of media coverage of celebrities. So the design houses provide the stimulus to these celebrity opinion leaders

and formers. The fashions which catch on are "chosen" by the target customer in response to these external influences. This goes to show that marketing theory is not always as cut and dried as it is presented.

The fashion design industry plans several years ahead, so it is planning now for the collections for two or three years' time. In the shorter term, the designers at Zara will be scanning the pages of celebrity magazines to see which fashion items are being worn by the rich and famous. They can then produce similar products, without stealing designs, and they can do this quickly. In the stores, staff will be observing which lines are selling best, and this information can be used to increase or reduce production back at the factory.

activities

The case study on Zara illustrates aspects of the marketing planning process in action. It shows how decisions are made in every area of marketing in an image-conscious, competitive, fast-moving industry to ensure both customer and producer satisfaction.

Before attempting these assessment practice activities, visit Zara's website (www.zara.com) to find out more about the company and to see how it promotes itself to its target customers. Also visit the websites of Zara's main high street competitors. Look at news sites to see if you can find any recent press articles about Zara or its competitors.

1 Can you tell who are the target customers from Zara's websites? Do its competitors target the same type of customer? What are the similarities and differences? Describe Zara's target customer using some methods covered in this unit.

2 Find out where Zara's stores are located. Why are the stores located where they are?

What is your impression of the style of the stores? Describe any physical evidence aspects.

3 Why has Zara chosen vertical integration rather than another method of distribution? List the advantages and disadvantages of choosing other distribution options.

4 Look through a batch of consumer and fashion magazines. Which magazines feature Zara's clothes? Why these magazines?

5 Produce PESTLE and SWOT analyses for Zara. Are there any threats or opportunities that the company should be particularly aware of?

6 Using the information you have gathered from websites and other sources, and your responses to question 1–5, write a report evaluating the effectiveness of Zara's marketing activities.

THIS UNIT IS ABOUT ANALYSING, EVALUATING AND USING financial information. It presents a range of tools that can be used to analyse business situations, to develop possible solutions to financial problems, and to choose between competing investment opportunities.

In working through the unit, you look at the financial constraints that affect all businesses and learn how these constraints can impact upon a business. You will learn how businesses monitor and control their operations in order to manage within their financial constraints, and the types of strategies that can be used to relax financial constraints in order to let a business grow and develop.

This unit is organised into four broad sections that help you understand the impact of finance on business decisions:

- identifying financial needs and constraints
- managing working capital
- investing in equipment and projects
- investing in other companies.

Impact of finance on business decisions

Introducing financial analysis

Setting the scene: the financial challenge

For many owners and managers of small and medium-sized businesses, once the day's work is done they have to then attend to the finances. It is not uncommon to work late into the night trying to sort out the business finances.

Some businesses shift as much of this burden as possible on to their accountants. They gather all their invoices, bank statements, recipts and payment vouchers for the year (or for each month) into a big bag and hand them over to an accountant – these are known as "brown paper bag jobs" in the accountancy profession. From these "bags" of assorted papers, the accountant will piece together the financial records of the business, usually for the benefit of both business owners and the taxman.

Personal computers, and sophisticated accountancy software now make it much easier for businesses to maintain their financial records.

Together with their accountant, they can use these records to analyse the financial health of the business and to forecast its future financial needs.

Financial analysis needs to be allied to a thorough understanding of the underlying business. It is crucial therefore that owners of small businesses and managers understand finance as well as the particular ins and outs of their own business. When one of the elements is missing, a business will struggle to meet its objectives, either through being undermined by lack of finance or by failing to understand the needs of its customers.

Why is finance important to business?

All business organisations need resources to operate. This is applies whether the business is delivering a service or selling products, whether it makes profits or it operates in the not-for-profit sector.

KEY TERMS

Finance is the resources available to a business to fund its operations. This includes income from profits on sales, investment by the business owners, investment by third parties, short-term finance from creditors, and bank overdrafts.

Financial constraints are the restrictions placed on any business because of its finite (or limited) resources. These constraints will restrict a business's options. For example, it might have to choose between two projects because it does not have enough funds to invest in both.

Monitoring finance is the process of using reports to feed back information to managers on the use of funds in the business.

Controlling finance is the process of actively managing the use of funds in the business to ensure that the best use is made of financial resources.

The assets and expenses that are funded by the capital that is invested in the business can be divided into two broad categories.

■ Long-term assets, such as fixed assets, are used in the business to generate further wealth. Fixed assets are expected to be held in the business for more than one year. Investment in fixed assets usually requires long-term finance.

■ Short-term assets, such as cash balances, debtors and stock, are used to fund day-to-day operations and pay immediate expenses such as wages and rent. These short-term assets and expenses change daily – they are very fluid. Short-term assets can be funded through both long-term and short-term sources of finance. A core of long-term finance ensures that a business does not experience shortages of cash, and short-term finance (from, for example, sales revenue) keeps the operation afloat.

There are various sources of business funding. The most efficient companies match that funding with the needs of the business. They also look for the most tax-efficient form of borrowing. These are skills that develop with experience.

The particular legal structure of the business will also determine to a certain extent the type of finance that is available. It is important to understand how the financial and funding options are different for each of the main types of business ownership structure – sole traders, partnerships. limited companies, charitable organisations and public corporations.

A business's aims and objectives are also a consideration when looking for finance, as is the culture of the organisation. For example the Cooperative Bank has a policy of ethically sound investment, and as a result the bank receives a large number of deposits from other organisations and individuals that consider an ethical stance a priority.

What this unit covers

This unit is designed to help you examine, analyse, evaluate and use financial information. It will help you develop the skills to use financial information to make business decisions, and to monitor and control finance – and overcome financial constraints – to achieve business goals.

Identifying financing needs and constraints

Working your way through the accounts of real businesses, you will identify ways in which they could grow. You will develop an understanding of how the availability of finance impacts on every decision a business makes, from taking on more staff to launching new products.

Managing working capital

Any manager needs a good understanding of working capital – from where it appears in the accounts to where you can see its physical impact on the business. You will learn how to use ratios to develop a deeper understanding of working capital. The unit introduces strategies to manage working capital and to improve working capital management.

Investing in equipment and projects

By building on your understanding of financial constraints, you will gain an insight into how to choose between competing investment options in order to meet a business's aims and objectives.

Investing in other companies

The final part of the unit considers investment options in the context of investing in other businesses. You will learn how to evaluate a proposal to invest in another company, and to assess the merits of different ways of making that investment.

Financial accounts

In order to understand the concepts introduced in this unit, it is useful to work from some real accounts. There is no point starting out with a multinational corporation that produces complex accounts. It is much more useful to have a bank of small and medium-sized business accounts to draw on. So in this unit, you will find the profit and loss accounts and balance sheets of some real businesses. If you need to refresh your understanding of financial statements, review your AS textbook: pages 74–87 for profit and loss accounts and pages 78–81 for balance sheets.

The featured businesses reappear throughout the text, although the accounts are only presented where the business first appears. For space reasons, these financial accounts are not reproduced in their entirety, and figures taken from the additional notes in the accounts have been used where appropriate. UK companies must file accounts on a regular basis with Companies House (www.companieshouse.gov.uk), and accounts can be downloaded for a small fee.

Although using financial information is fundamental to building up an understanding of a business, it is not the only evidence that should be used in making a business assessment. It is important that you understand the company's underlying business, so we have also added links to websites for the featured businesses. The featured businesses are:

- **Adventure Divers Ltd**, a scuba diving shop offering equipment and training courses www.adventuredivers.co.uk

- **Country Lanes Ltd**, an eco-friendly walking and cycling holiday company www.countrylanes.co.uk

- **Ecological Sciences Ltd**, a leading specialist in the field of composting www.ecosci.co.uk

- **LH Turtle Ltd**, a hardware store www.turtlescroydon.co.uk

- **Lush Cosmetics Ltd**, a leading maker of handmade cosmetics www.lushdns.co.uk

- **Nutec Centre for Safety Ltd**, the UK arm of an international company offering safety, emergency and contingency expertise www.nutecuk.com

- **Warehouse Theatre Company Ltd**, a small independent theatre www.warehousetheatre.co.uk

Topic 1 · Identifying financial needs and constraints

Setting the scene: LH Turtle Limited

LH Turtle Limited is a family-owned business that runs a hardware store situated in the centre of Croydon. Turtle is a traditional store, with experienced staff who can advise customers about the right machinery, tools and materials needed to undertake building and DIY work.

The store stocks hardware, tools, garden and DIY supplies. Visit the company's website (www.turtlescroydon.co.uk) to see examples of the product range. Ask yourself, what sort of a market does Turtle operate in? Who are its competitors? What is its location?

Figure 11.1 shows LH Turtle's profit and loss account for the year ended 31 January 2005. This shows that turnover fell 2 per cent in the year to January 2005, with sales of £1,408,474 in the year compared to £1,436,372 in the previous year. Gross profit on sales amounted to £668,097 compared to £660,413 in the previous year, an increase of 1.2 per cent. Gross profit as a percentage of sales was 47.4 per cent in the year to January 2005, a slight improvement on the 46 per cent in the previous year.

The company did not make an operating profit in the year, but recorded a loss of £871 (indicated by the brackets in the profit and loss account) compared to an operating profit of £9,184 in the previous year. Turtle made no profit from trading in its core activity. Its only income from operations was £2,468, from "other interest receivable and similar income", which leaves a net profit on ordinary activities after taxation of just £1,597.

Think about what these figures mean. It is important that Turtle keeps the costs of goods low and its sales revenue high in order to maximise its profit margins. However, does Turtle have a big enough turnover to get discounts from suppliers to keep the costs of goods low? What about the profits? Any business needs to reinvest to stay up to date, and it must generate enough profit in the long term to finance this investment. According to the notes to the accounts, Turtle only purchased additional fixed assets to the value of £696 in the year ending January 2005. This could be financed from its £1,597 profit on ordinary activities. Does this feel like enough investment for Turtle to compete effectively with the major DIY chains?

Figure 11.2 shows Turtle's balance sheet. This presents a snapshot of the business's finances. The top half records the business's fixed assets and working capital. The bottom half of the balance sheet records how the business has financed the fixed assets and working capital.

At 31 January 2005, LH Turtle owned fixed assets worth £8,473 after depreciation. The notes to the accounts show that these fixed assets were bought for a total of £105,005, comprising £30,301 for land and buildings and £74,704 for plant and machinery. When there is a large gap between the cost of fixed assets and their net book value – as there is here – it suggests that there has been little investment in new assets and that existing assets are being run down. What are the consequences of running down the fixed assets? The key questions, of course, are whether the business needs to reinvest in additional assets, and has it got resources to do so?

A business's working capital is its current assets less its current liabilities. Working capital is often recorded on the balance sheet as net current assets. Working capital is important because it is a measure of a business's ability to fund its trading activities. Turtle's working capital is £319,484 at 31 January 2005. It has short-term debts of £142,035, including (according to the notes to the accounts) £36,320 in bank loans and overdrafts. However, the company's cash balances are relatively healthy at £120,457. (It is important to make effective use of working capital, and this is considered in some depth in Topics 3 and 4.)

The final section of the balance sheet, under the heading "capital and reserves", shows that the business has been wholly funded by shareholders funds, through £50,000 invested in share capital with £277,327 in retained profits. The company has no long-term loans. If the business needs significant investment to secure its future, will this need to be financed through long-term funding?

Figure 11.1 LH Turtle Limited profit and loss account, for the year ended 31 January 2005

	2005	2004
	£	£
Turnover	1,408,474	1,436,372
Cost of sales	(740,377)	(775,959)
Gross profit	668,097	660,413
Administrative expenses	(668,968)	(651,229)
Operating (loss)/profit	(871)	9,184
Other interest receivable and similar income	2,468	2,212
Profit on ordinary activities before taxation	1,597	11,396
Tax on profit on ordinary activities	–	(1,856)
Profit on ordinary activities after taxation	1,597	9,540

Figure 11.2: LH Turtle Limited balance sheet, as at 31 January 2005

	2005		2004	
	£	£	£	£
Fixed assets				
Tangible assets		8,473		9,066
Current assets				
Stocks	247,926		225,493	
Debtors	93,136		94,342	
Cash at bank and in hand	120,457		154,318	
	461,519		474,153	
Creditors: amounts falling due within one year	(142,035)		(156,859)	
Net current assets		319,484		317,294
Total assets less current liabilities		327,957		326,360
Capital and reserves				
Called up share capital		50,000		50,000
Share premium account		630		630
Profit and loss account		277,327		275,730
Shareholders' funds		327,957		326,360

Financing businesses

For many businesses, although the long-term goal may be to maximise profits, the daily reality is survival. In practice this means that a business has sufficient finance to pay for the resources it needs to deliver goods and services. The key to survival, therefore, is the way that the business is financed.

It is worth walking through the accounts (as we have done in the LH Turtle case study) to get a feel for what is happening in a business, and for how it works and is financed. From going through the accounts of LH Turtle Limited, and from looking at its website, we now know that:

- the company operates in the DIY market, a highly competitive market dominated by large, low-price, out-of-town superstores

- its sales are not sufficient at present to generate significant profits, with income only just above total costs and expenses, and they may not be high enough to allow the business to demand substantial discounts from suppliers

- it operates from a town centre site, which potentially restricts large sales (although Turtle offers a home delivery service) and the numbers of customers because of the difficulty of parking

- it is financed through shareholder funds, and although it has a bank overdraft, it has no long-term liabilities.

In order to understand the possible options for a business, the financing options that are available and the financial constraints that it faces, it is useful to put yourself in the position of the owners of the business. Try to create a vision for the business. How would you like to develop it, and how are you going to fund that development?

In the case of LH Turtle, for example, you might suggest relocating to a larger site away from the town centre that affords customer parking space, or perhaps further investment in its online DIY store and home delivery service, or a focus on the current premises through upgrading fixed assets and redecorating the store.

All these options will require finance. Whatever option the business chooses, it is going to need some investment. Where can it find the necessary finance? It needs to review the options for long-term finance by considering several questions.

- Could existing shareholders invest further share capital?

- Could new shareholders be brought into the business?

- Would a bank offer the business a long-term loan?

- Would another organisation or a private individual provide a long-term loan to develop the business?

There are other options it could consider. Could it generate increased profits that could be reinvested in the business? Could it raise some short-term finance through, say, the bank authorising an increase in its overdraft facility? Could working capital be better managed to release resources for investment in the business?

Assessing the options

Suppose LH Turtle Limited needs to raise about £250,000 in order to be able to do any serious redevelopment of the store. In assessing its options, we can see some of the challenges its faces and the financial constraints that can impact on any business.

Existing shareholders

LH Turtle's three directors are its three main shareholders, with one director holding a majority (and controlling) shareholding in the company. The notes to the company accounts show that collectively they only earned £62,400 from the business in the year to 31 January 2005. If this is their only source of income, then it is unlikely that they have sufficient savings to invest a substantial sum in the business.

New investors

Any new investors would want a better return on their investment than they could make by investing in another business. Certainly they would expect a return greater than the interest that could be earned by simply leaving money in a bank account. At present, the prospects don't look good, as the business made a small operating loss in 2004/5. An investor would need to see a really good business plan, well supported by market research, that convincingly explains how the business could generate the profits to produce a good long-term return.

There is also the issue of control. The business is currently controlled by one major shareholder, but any new investor putting a substantial sum of money into the business would want to have some level of control over the company. Could this family business open up to working with non-family members at board level?

Banks

Turtle's bank would certainly have the resources to offer a long-term loan to develop the business, but that does not mean it would necessarily lend the business any money. Banks are required by their shareholders to manage their risks. Before making any long-term loan, a bank would require a business plan which was well supported by market research and by cash flow forecasts that clearly show how the debt (both interest payments and capital) could be repaid.

A bank is likely to want some security against the loan. Since LH Turtle has few fixed assets that could be used to secure a loan, a bank would usually expect the loan to be secured against the directors' personal assets. This typically means that small business directors offer their homes as security against bank loans, and therefore stand to lose their homes as well as their companies if they run into business difficulties.

Other investment agencies

There are other agencies, such as venture capital firms, that invest in businesses. The business would need a good business plan to convince the investment house that it could be confident of a sound return. The investment agency may well also want some control over the business.

To attract this type of financial backing, the business idea needs to be better than all the competing ideas that are available to the investor. Turtle would need to consider whether an investment agency is likely to invest in a DIY store. Can a DIY store compete with faster growing sectors of the economy for financial resources?

Retained profits

Turtle is currently not generating sufficient profits for reinvestment into the business. It is in a difficult situation here, because it is hard to see how the business could generate significantly more profits

without some investment. Attempts could be made to boost profits by cutting administrative expenses by inviting tenders for all services the business buys, or by reducing the cost of sales by taking on cheaper, less experienced staff. However, it might take time to see any benefit from this strategy.

Short-term financing

Additional resources could be acquired using short-term finance agreements such as leasing and hire purchase. This may be one way of obtaining resources and assets for redevelopment without needing to produce a business plan or detailed cash flow forecasts.

Assume, however, that the business upgraded its computers through a leasing deal so that it could run a more effective online DIY store. It is still likely to need some additional finance to set up the new computer systems and to pay for promotion of the online store. Turtle would then have to produce a business plan to support an application for a loan to take this development forward. It would also make sense to prepare cash flow forecasts to ensure that it could pay the lease or hire purchase payments as they fell due.

Overdrafts

The business could probably increase its overdraft. However, this can be a high-cost and risky option. Banks charge high interest rates for overdrafts. Banks can also withdraw the overdraft facility at any time, and sometimes demand immediate repayment of the overdraft. If this happens, it usually signals the end of the business.

Limitations of financial statements

The financial statements of a business provide a guide to the resources currently being used to finance the operation and give an indication of areas of strength and weakness. However, financial statements do not give the whole story of a business's finances. To create a detailed understanding of the business, it is always important to explore the business further, through visiting, analysing its website, searches for newspaper articles or any other published information.

This process will provide a fuller picture of a business's prospects, and an understanding of the financial constraints that may restrict access to finance and investment. These constraints are likely to be one of the major challenges facing the business, and they need to be overcome in order to develop the business.

Ecological Sciences is a leader in the field of compost technology. Its profit and loss account (Figure 11.3) and balance sheet (Figure 11.4) are similar in structure to those of LH Turtle Ltd.

The notes to the accounts provide additional information on the company's commitments under hire purchase agreements and operating leases.

- Creditors amounts falling due within one year includes £51,977 for hire purchase agreements.

- Creditors falling due after more than one year includes £20,642 for hire purchase agreements.

- Commitments under operating leases at 31 December 2004 were £1,250 on leases that expire within one year and £13,750 on leases that expire after more than five years.

For more information on Ecological Sciences visit its website at www.ecosci.co.uk.

A Study the accounts and website for Ecological Sciences Ltd. Set out the sources of income for the business, and identify any possible future investment potential.

B Suppose Ecological Sciences wants to invest £150,000 in a major fixed asset. Advise the company on all possible sources of finance. Evaluate the alternatives, and make a recommendation to the board on how it should finance this new investment.

Figure 11.3 Ecological Sciences Limited profit and loss account, for the year ended 31 December 2004

	2004	2003
	£	£
Turnover	1,127,618	988,233
Cost of sales	(556,494)	(525,075)
Gross profit	571,124	463,158
Administrative expenses	(385,963)	(356,255)
Operating cost	185,161	106,903
Interest receivable	2,926	2,610
Interest payable and similar charges	(10,750)	(11,026)
Profit on ordinary activities before taxation	177,337	98,487
Tax on profit on ordinary activities	(34,085)	(19,191)
Profit on ordinary activities after taxation	143,252	79,296
Equity dividends paid and proposed	(20,000)	(20,000)
Retained profit for the financial year	123,252	59,296
Balance brought forward	266,976	207,680
Balance carried forward	390,228	266,976

	2004		2003
	£	£	£
Fixed assets			
Tangible assets		262,663	227,321
Investments		4	4
		262,667	227,325
Current assets			
Stocks	4,489		2,467
Debtors	222,644		197,399
Cash at bank and in hand	224,673		143,436
	451,806		343,302
Creditors: amounts falling due within one year	(286,049)		(259,644)
Net current assets		165,757	83,658
Total assets less current liabilities		428,424	310,983
Creditors: amounts falling due.after more than one year		(20,642)	(28,892)
		407,782	282,091
Provisions for liabilities and charges			
Deferred taxation		(17,454)	(15,015)
		390,328	267,076
Capital and reserves			
Called-up equity share capital		100	100
Profit and loss account		390,228	266,976
Shareholders' funds		390,328	267,076

Figure 11.4 Ecological Sciences Limited balance sheet, as at 31 December 2004

Topic 2 Legal structures and obtaining finance

Setting the scene: Lush Cosmetics Limited

Lush Cosmetics supplies handmade cosmetics throughout the world. It is a private limited company and a multinational corporation.

Although Lush owns some of its overseas stores, it has also managed its expansion into markets around the world through a network of subsidiary and associate companies. According to the company's consolidated accounts for the year ended 30 June 2003, Lush Cosmetics Ltd has 12 subsidiaries, companies in which it has more than a 50 per cent stake, and nine associates, companies in which it has a 30–50 per cent interest.

Lush has used more than one source of funding to finance its operation. Much of the day-to-day operation is funded through retained profits, though the group also had a bank overdraft of £180,082 at 30 June 2003. In the year ended 30 June 2003, the group retained profit was £1,190,584.

Retained profits have also been used to invest in business expansion. Figure 11.5 shows Lush Cosmetics Limited's consolidated balance sheet. As you can see, the group has few long-term liabilities – this is shown as "creditors: amounts falling due after more than one year". Investment in subsidiary and associate companies has been financed by head office funds (presumably retained profits), and by local investment (the shareholdings not owned by Lush).

The company has obtained some lease finance. According to the notes to the balance sheet, Lush has liabilities under financing leases of £15,783 falling due within one year, and £13,645 falling due after more than one year.

Lush Cosmetics can issue up to 100,000 £1 shares. (This is its authorised share capital, set out in the notes to the accounts, and determined by the legal framework established when the company was set up.) Only 20,000 shares have been allotted, called up and fully paid. Therefore, the company has the option to issue up to 80,000 £1 shares.

	2003		2002	
	£	£	£	£
Fixed assets				
Intangible assets – goodwill		77,121		—
Tangible assets		3,870,704		2,101,766
Investments in associates		591,405		181,726
		4,539,230		2,283,492
Current assets				
Stocks	2,118,914		1,267,538	
Debtors	3,809,944		3,418,996	
Cash at bank and in hand	1,755,660		1,220,885	
	7,684,518		5,907,419	
Creditors: amounts falling due within one year	(8,820,123)		(6,343,064)	
Net current liabilities				
Due within one year	(1,135,605)		(539,645)	
Debtors due after more than one year	—		104,000	
		(1,135,605)		(435,645)
Total assets less current liabilities		3,403,625		1,847,847
Creditors: amounts failling due after more than one year		(13,645)		(36,274)
Provisions for liabilities and charges		(124,117)		(54,338)
Net assets		3,265,863		1,757,235
Capital and reserves				
Called up share capital		20,000		20,000
Other reserves		132,008		132,008
Profit and loss account		2,575,804		1,400,387
Equity shareholders' funds		2,727,812		1,552,395
Minority interest		538,051		204,840
		3,265,863		1,757,235

Legal structures

Businesses can adopt several different legal structures. There are advantages and disadvantages to each type of structure (see Unit 8, Topic 2, page 18), and this includes access to finance. The legal structure of a business significantly affects its ability to raise external finance and, to some extent, to generate internal funds.

Unincorporated businesses

Unincorporated businesses can find it difficult to raise finance. Indeed, some of the attractions for owners of operating an unincorporated business can deter potential investors.

A business owner may like the fact that as a sole trader or partnership the business can be set up and dissolved with little formality, and that it does not need to produce and publish audited accounts. However, this very informality makes it difficult for potential outside investors to assess the business. Outside investors may also regard unincorporated businesses as being too reliant on their owners: the business may not survive the retirement or death of a founding partner.

One source of finance for sole traders and partnerships is retained profits. However, tax law discriminates against unincorporated businesses, and they pay higher rates of tax than small companies. This can make it more difficult to amass retained profits to reinvest in the business.

Lenders also discriminate against unincorporated businesses. Some have a policy of not lending to sole traders and partnerships, others may charge premium rates on business loans. This not only affects loans – unincorporated businesses may find that they are charged premium rates for lease finance and hire purchase agreements.

Several grant-awarding bodies do not give grants to unincorporated businesses. In any case, grants available to support small business development tend to be small and specific. They are often targeted at businesses located in areas of deprivation.

Private limited companies

Raising finance for small private limited companies is relatively easier. However, small companies still face some restrictions on their ability to raise funds. In particular, any investors or lenders will want a detailed business plan and will want some measure of security or control before offering finance.

Business planning can be a stumbling block. Many directors of small businesses lack the skills and confidence to write a business plan to support their loan applications. They find it difficult to organise basic market research and produce appropriate forecasts. Although help is available for small businesses, through organisations such as Business Link, the high street banks and the Prince's Trust, many business people find it difficult to overcome the emotional and psychological barriers to using these sources.

Both banks and venture capital companies invest in small businesses, but any finance is likely to come with conditions. Banks often ask for directors to personally guarantee loans and to secure them against personal assets such as their homes. Venture capital companies often want a significant say in the running of any business that they invest in as well as a share in the company. The founding owners may not be prepared to give up that level of control.

Private limited companies do not have the option of raising finance through a share issue if they wish to remain private companies. This means they cannot advertise their shares for sale while remaining private companies. However, a private limited company can choose to become a public company. This process, known as flotation, usually occurs when a private limited company has grown to a reasonable size and it needs a fresh capital injection to fund the next stage of its business development. In making itself a public company through a flotation, a firm issues shares to the general public and, if it is a suitably attractive business proposition, it can raise substantial amounts of capital.

Public limited companies

Public limited companies (plcs) are subject to many more rules and regulations. For example, companies listed on the London Stock Exchange must follow the rules in the Yellow Books, which set protocols for financial reporting. All public limited companies face additional requirements under the Companies Acts.

In return for this degree of exposure and scrutiny, public limited companies are able to raise substantial finance through share issues. They are able to reach a much wider group of people who might invest in the business; although, of course, they also widen the company ownership because these shareholders ultimately own the company.

Large public limited companies are usually able to reap economies of scale. They can secure the best interest deals on loans from banks and finance houses – in part, because they have attractive assets (often shares in the company itself) against which to secure long-term loans. They can use top advisers to find ways to minimise their tax burden, thus retaining a higher share of their pre-tax profits for reinvestment in the business.

Charities

Charities and other non-profit-making organisations tend to rely on grants and income they can generate through fund-raising to finance their operations. Some non-profit-making organisations receive government grants if they undertake work that the government regards as socially beneficial and which meets its wider agenda. For example, grants may be offered to fund:

- service delivery, such as delivering ITC training to owners of small businesses

- overhead costs, such as running the central office function for a national helpline

- capital costs, to acquire fixed assets such as computers, minibuses and buildings.

Lenders tend to be cautious about lending to charities and non-profit-making organisations. They have to be very confident that they will get repaid. They will want to see a business plan showing an income stream that would allow the organisation to meet the interest payments and repay the loan. They will also want to ensure that the loan is not used to fund activities that lie beyond the powers and remit (ultra vires) of the charity.

Obtaining finance

There are certain basic steps that must be followed in any request for finance. All potential investors and lenders will want to see a business plan. A good plan is essential if a business wants to raise a loan from a bank, obtain funds from a private investor or a venture capital firm, or receive a large grant from a government body. A business plan needs to cover aims and objectives, a marketing plan, resource issues, and financial analysis and planning.

When external funders and investors consider funding a business, they often look at the non-quantifiable factors as well as the hard financial data in making their assessment. They look at the quality and skills of the management, the quality of the product and the business proposition, the customer base and brand strength, and the way in which the business operates and presents itself.

The information demands get more onerous as the amount a business wants to raise increases. Any public limited company looking to raise substantial capital through a shares issue will need to supply potential investors with a wealth of information. The company is required to issue a prospectus, which offers a complete review of the business, its performance to date, and detailed plans explaining how the business is going to develop as a result of the additional finance.

Any lender or investor is not likely to rely completely on the information provided by the business seeking finance. Many organisations carry out a credit review and other checks before they make a loan, enter into a hire purchase arrangement or complete a leasing agreement. Credit ratings are easy to obtain and are relatively cheap. You can carry out a credit rating assessment on a business known to you, using one of the many websites that offer this service such as www.busibody.com. The cost of any credit checking service is normally charged to the business applying for a loan as part of the normal costs of setting up the transaction. If a business does not have a good credit rating, it will either be refused a loan or have to pay a higher rate of interest for that loan.

Warehouse Theatre Company Limited

The Warehouse Theatre, Croydon is a company limited by guarantee. It is a registered charity. The theatre promotes new plays, emerging playwrights and alternative forms of theatre. The theatre is dependent on public funding, and without annual funding from the London Borough of Croydon it would not be a going concern. For more information about the theatre and its current programme visit www.warehousetheatre.co.uk.

Note, as the Warehouse Theatre is a charity, it publishes an income and expenditure account rather than a profit and loss account. In practice, there is not a lot of difference between the these accounts; it merely reflects the fact that as a charity the Warehouse Theatre is a "not-for-profit" operation.

A Imagine that you have been appointed general manager of the theatre. Write a report to the board of directors outlining the theatre's sources of funding in the financial year ended 31 March 2004.

B Suppose that you wish to apply for Arts Council funding for a particular event. Using the Arts Council website (www.artscouncil.org.uk), identify an event that would qualify for funding and fit the theatre's criteria of promoting new plays and alternative theatre. Identify what information the Arts Council requires to support an application for funding.

C The theatre wishes to develop its bar and coffee area into a viable commercial operation that is open for passers-by all day and theatre-goers at night. You need a loan of £30,000 to do the development work. Write a report to the directors outlining what sources of funding are available, if any, to develop this idea.

D A major coffee shop company offers to run the coffee and bar area for the theatre after the redevelopment. The coffee shop company would pay £5,000 as an annual rent to the theatre. The coffee shop company would take 75 per cent of the profits, which are estimated to be about

Figure 11.6: Warehouse Theatre Company Limited balance sheet, as at 31 March 2004

	2004		2003	
	£	£	£	£
Fixed assets				
Tangible		4,100		1,280
Investments		369		369
		4,469		1,649
Current assets				
Debtors	11,662		21,418	
Cash at bank and in Hand	357		178	
	12,019		21,596	
Creditors: amounts Falling Due Within One Year	101,181		68,792	
Net current liabilities		(89,162)		(47,196)
Net liabilities		(84,693)		(45,547)
Funds				
Unrestricted funds		(94,113)		(58,832)
Restricted funds		9,420		13,285
Total funds		84,693		45,547

£20,000 annually, providing the balance to the theatre. However as a condition, the theatre would not be allowed to have any other competing operations on its premises, and the coffee shop company wants quite a large area that could potentially be developed into an additional retail outlet for merchandise. Write a note for the theatre's directors assessing this offer in terms of access to finance and financial constraints.

Figure 11.7 Warehouse Theatre Company Limited income and expenditure account, as at 31 March 2004

	Total 2004	Total 2003
	£	£
Incoming resources		
Core funding	158,966	217,115
Box office	107,142	94,296
Bar rent	16,968	17,588
Membership fees	7,385	6,673
Donations and gifts	61,942	10,639
Interest receivable	85	173
Other income	8,853	9,502
Total income	361,341	355,986
Resources expended		
Direct charitable expenditure		
Purchases	2,532	5,974
Actors, musicians and directors	101,610	100,200
Touring companies	36,133	7,522
Production costs	16,406	43,268
	156,681	156,964
Other expenditure		
Publicity	33,948	30,293
Management and administration of the charity	209,858	182,349
Total resources expended	400,487	369,606
Net (outgoing)/incoming resources	(39,146)	(13,620)
Fund balances brought forward at 1 April 2003	(45,547)	(31,927)
Fund balances carried forward at 31 March 2004	(84,693)	(45,547)

Setting the scene: Country Lanes Limited

Country Lanes Limited (www.countrylanes.co.uk) is an active holiday specialist.
It organises holidays which are healthy for humans yet don't harm the environment.
The activities it offers include walking and cycling.

Working capital (also known as net current assets) is calculated by subtracting a business's current liabilities from its current assets at any moment in time. From the company's balance sheet (see Figure 11.8), we can see that Country Lanes Limited working capital at 31 October 2004 was £16,012.

The company had £24,168 worth of current assets, comprising stock, debtors and cash, and £8,156 current liabilities which are recorded in the line "creditors: amounts falling due within one year" in the balance sheet. In more detail, these components of working capital are:

- stock – for Country Lanes this might include sundry bike parts, tee shirts, souvenirs, maps and guides
- debtors – this is the money owing to Country Lanes, probably money from sales by credit which has yet to be passed on by the credit card companies
- cash at bank – this is shorthand for the sum of the company's bank balances and any actual cash it held on the account date
- creditors – this is the money owed by Country Lanes to its suppliers, such as the hotels on its tour routes.

Note that creditors can be regarded as another form of short-term finance, By paying its bills in arrears, a business can ease its immediate need for cash. However, this is a very short-term solution, and all businesses tend to play the same game – so what a business might save by delaying paying its suppliers, it might lose by delays in receiving payment from its business customers.

KEY TERMS

Liquidity is an assessment of a business's ability to meet its short-term debts. It is a measure of whether the business has enough cash (or assets which can be readily converted into cash) to pay bills and invoices as they come due for payment.

Working capital cycle is the movement of funds between stock, debtors, cash and creditor balances.

Ratios are calculations used to analyse a business's financial performance. They should be interpreted in comparison to other businesses or to previous accounting periods.

The working capital cycle

The working capital cycle describes the movement of short-term funds in a business, and the flows between short-term assets and liabilities. The cycle is closely related to the trading account – to sales, stock, purchases and gross profits.

Figure 11.9 illustrates the working cycle. It shows how cash is used to buy stock or supplies, which can be converted into finished goods, which are then sold,

Figure 11.8 Country Lanes Limited balance sheet, as at 31 October 2004

	2004 £	2004 £	2003 £	2003 £
Fixed assets				
Intangible assets		7,950		9,010
Tangible assets		46,483		19,591
		54,433		28,601
Current assets				
Stocks	1,899		3,515	
Debtors	12,856		14,498	
Cash at bank	9,413		10,426	
	24,168		28,439	
Creditors				
Amounts falling due within one year	8,156		16,692	
Net current assets		16,012		11,747
Total assets less current liabilities		70,445		40,348
Creditors				
Amounts falling due after more than one year		52,609		50,403
		17,836		(10,055)
Capital and reserves				
Called-up share capital		2		2
Profit and loss account		17,834		(10,057)
Shareholders' funds		17,836		(10,055)

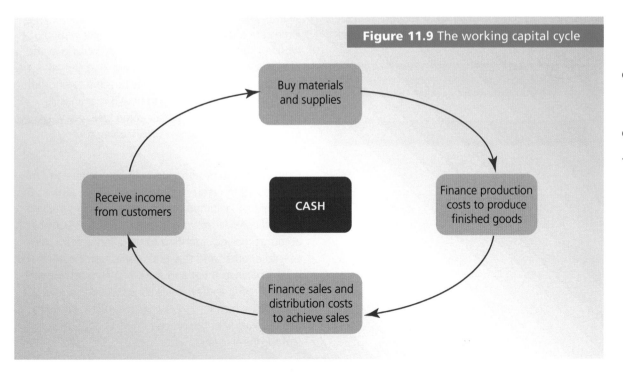

Figure 11.9 The working capital cycle

Buy materials and supplies

Finance production costs to produce finished goods

Finance sales and distribution costs to achieve sales

Receive income from customers

CASH

which then produces sales receipts back into the business. To show how the working capital cycle works, consider this simple example, looking in particular at the flows between current assets and current liabilities.

Point 1: the business buys £100 of stock on credit that it plans to sell

      Current assets = stock £100
      Current liabilities = creditors £100

Point 2: the business sells the stock on credit for £150

      Current assets = debtors £150
      Current liabilities = creditors £100

Point 3: the business receives payment in cash for the goods sold on credit

      Current assets = cash £150
      Current liabilities = creditors £100

Point 4: the business pays for the goods that it bought on credit

      Current assets = cash £50
      Current liabilities = creditors £nil

Note at the end of the process the balancing £50 is retained profit. This is outside the working capital cycle, and it would appear on the balance sheet as part of shareholders' funds.

It is important to understand the difference between profits and cash in the working capital cycle. Figure 11.10 shows the profit and cash balance at each stage of the working capital cycle in our simple example. Note that it is only when the transaction is fully complete that cash and profit match each other. Businesses need to take care that they do not spend funds that they have not earned: if managers assume that cash balances represent profit, then they might be tempted to take this money out of the business only to find that they do not have the resources to pay debts as they fall due.

In our working capital example, we assumed that the stock supplier was content to wait for payment until point 4, when the business had received payment for the goods sold. In practice, business life is rarely that simple. Some suppliers operate on "cash on delivery" terms and demand payment when the goods are delivered to the customers.

If the business in our worked example had to pay cash for its stock, then it would still have current liabilities of £100 at points 1 and 2, but this would be a bank overdraft of £100 instead of a creditor (assuming that the business had a zero bank balance at the start of this very hypothetical example). Again, bank overdrafts should not be equated with losses, in the same way that cash balance should not be mistaken for profits – the true profit/loss position is only reached when the transaction is complete.

Working capital is important because any business needs financial resources to operate. Many new businesses cannot access trade credit in their first six months of trading; they need to build up a trading history so that suppliers can see that they are steady, reliable businesses. Even then, in some trades, such as the building industry, cash on delivery is the normal way to do business. Businesses need to make sure that they have the funds (or the overdraft facility) to cover the purchase of the stock, to pay suppliers and to meet staff wages.

Ratio analysis of working capital

Ratios are a useful tool for assessing how well working capital is being managed. By looking at the ratio of elements of a business's working capital against other financial data, it is possible to find out more about the business and how it manages its short-term funds, and gather some ideas for ways of improving the business's management of working capital.

Ratio analysis is designed to help you understand the business. Before you calculate exact ratios, look at the accounts and estimate roughly what the answer will be, and consider what it means. Look closely at the accounts, paying attention to the change from one year to another and the relationship between items on the balance sheet and the profit and loss account. You are trying to develop skills in reading company accounts, which in time should mean that you only need to calculate the precise ratios to confirm your feel for the business.

Figure 11.10: Flows of cash and profit in the working capital cycle

Point	Profit	Cash balance
1	nil	nil
2	£50	nil
3	£50	£150
4	£50	£50

1 Monitoring liquidity

The reason for monitoring liquidity is to check whether a business has sufficient financial resources to meet its immediate liabilities. Put simply, it is a means of checking whether a business is in a position to pay its debts as they become due. There are two common liquidity ratios: the current ratio and the acid test. Both concern the relationship between current assets and current liabilities. In both, we are looking for a result of greater than 1 – ideally around or above 2 – which would indicate that current assets are greater than current liabilities.

current ratio = current assets : current liabilities

Using the data in Figure 11.8, we can calculate the current ratio for Country Lanes. Dividing current assets of £24,168 by current liabilities of £8,156 produces a result of 2.96 (or a ratio of 2.96 : 1). This indicates that Country Lanes can comfortably pay its debts as they fall due.

The acid test is calculated in a similar way to the current ratio, but the ratio differs in that stock is subtracted from the current assets before making the calculation. Stock is excluded because experience suggests that there is no guarantee that stock can be sold quickly (if at all) to realise cash to pay a business's creditors. The acid test therefore assumes only debtors and cash balances in the current assets should count when assessing a business's ability to pay its debts.

acid test = current assets less stock : current liabilities

We would not expect the acid test to differ significantly from the current ratio for a company like Country Lanes, because we know that its stock is a relatively small element of the business. (This would not be the case for a retail business, which might have significant sums tied up in stock.) Country Lanes' acid test is calculated by dividing current assets less stock (£24,168 – £1,899 = £22,269) by current liabilities of £8,156, which produces a result of 2.73 (or a ratio of 2.73 : 1). As predicted, the acid test (like the current ratio) shows that Country Lanes can easily pay its debts as they fall due.

2 Debtor collection periods

The debtor collection period (or debtor days as it is sometimes called) refers to how many days it takes for a business to collect its main trading debts. This figure on its own does not tell you much; however, it becomes useful when it is compared to the debtor days figures for other companies in the same type of business or to the debtor days figures for previous years. These comparisons tell you whether a business is doing better or worse than its competitors in collecting its debts, and whether its customers are paying more quickly or slowly over time.

$$\text{debtors days} = \frac{\text{trade debtors}}{\text{turnover}} \times 365$$

Note only trade debtors are included in this calculation because these are the debtors that relate to credit sales sales made by the business. A business may have other debtors – it may, for example, be owed money by its directors, by a parent company or by one of its subsidiaries – but these are not trading debts so they are excluded from the top line of the calculation.

To calculate debtor days, you need figures from the profit and loss account (turnover) and from the balance sheet (trade debtors). Many balance sheets only include a line for debtors (under current assets): in these cases, the figure for trade debtors is sometimes given in the notes to the accounts. However, some companies do not give a figure for trade debtors anywhere in their published accounts, which means that the ratio cannot be calculated.

This is the case for Country Lanes – there is not enough information in its abbreviated accounts to do this calculation. However, the information in the LH Turtle accounts (Figures 11.1 and 11.2, page 145) and the accompanying notes allow us to calculate the company's debtor days. In the accounting period covered by these accounts, LH Turtle had a turnover of £1,408,474 and total debtors of £93,136. This debtors figure looks high for a business that operates largely on cash sales, but the accompanying notes state that trade debtors only amount to £2,302.

Before calculating the ratio, it is apparent that the trade debtors figure is trivial compared to the firm's turnover, and we would not expect this ratio to reveal any problem with regard to debt collection. This is because of the nature of the business: Turtle is a hardware shop that sells primarily to customers who

Topic 3 Understanding working capital

stop and think

Imagine that you are running a small shop. Goods are bought on credit on day one of each month for £100. Goods are sold on credit on day 10. The debtors pay £500 cash for the goods on day 20. The trade creditors are paid £100 on day 25. Calculate the business's working capital on, respectively, day 5, day 15, day 22 and day 30.

visit the store. You would expect nearly all goods to be paid for when they are bought, either by cash, cheque, or debit and credit card. This means (with the exception of credit card payments) that Turtle receives payment when it makes a sale. Turtle's debtor days calculation is:

$$= \frac{£2,302}{£1,408,474} \times 365 = 0.001634 \times 365 = 0.6 \text{ days}$$

This calculation confirms the analysis. Note, however, we would expect a very different picture for a company that primarily sells goods and services to other businesses on trade terms. This company would be happy if it could get its debtor days ratio as low as 30 days.

3 Creditor payment periods

Another factor that impacts on working capital is the time a business has to pay its creditors. The creditor payment period is a similar in many ways to the debtor days calculation, but it measures the time it takes a business to pay its suppliers. Like debtor days, the ratio is concerned with the main business transactions, so it focuses on trade creditors (the business's suppliers), and the calculation excludes other creditors such as the tax authorities or the bank that may be owed money.

$$\text{creditor payment period} = \frac{\text{trade creditors}}{\text{purchases}} \times 365$$

Again the calculation requires figures from the balance sheet (trade creditors) and the profit and loss account (purchases). Again, it is not always possible to obtain these figures because some companies do not provide sufficient detail in their accounts. Some only record the cost of sales but not their purchases in the profit and loss accounts, and some only record creditors but not trade creditors in their balance sheets. Sometimes (though not always) these figures can be found in the notes to the accounts, which can provides a more detailed breakdown of the main entries recorded in the profit and loss account and the balance sheet.

Let's use LH Turtle again to illustrate this ratio. First, the balance sheet (Figure 11.2) only has a single line for all creditors (amounts falling due within one year), but the supporting notes state that the company owed £41,914 to trade creditors as at 31 January 2005. To do the calculation we need to know the purchases in the preceding accounting period. For this, we look at the profit and loss account (Figure

11.1). This only provides a figure for the cost of sales: this is £740,377. However, for a business like Turtle it is perhaps reasonable to make the assumption that all of its cost of sales are purchases. Therefore, Turtle's creditor payment period calculation is:

$$= \frac{£41,914}{£740,377} \times 365 = 0.0566 \times 365 = 20.7 \text{ days}$$

This looks quite reasonable. Standard trade terms typically allow 30 days for payment, and this ratio of 20.7 days suggests that some of Turtle's stock may be bought on a cash on delivery basis. LH Turtle's seems to be making good use of trade credit, without abusing these credit terms and paying its suppliers late.

Note that a supplier may look at a business's credit payment period before deciding whether to offer it credit terms. If the business looks to take a long time to pay its creditors, the supplier may demand some payment upfront or even decline to trade with the business.

4 Stock turnover

Stock turnover is a measure of how many times the stock turns over in a year. A business wants a high stock turnover because it does not want to tie up a large amount of working capital in stock that is just sitting in its stores or warehouses.

$$\text{turnover} = \frac{\text{stock turnover}}{\text{stock}}$$

As LH Turtle has a turnover of £1,408,474 (in the accounting period we have been examining) and stock of £247,926, it has a stock turnover of 5.68 (1,408,474/247,926). Ideally, the company might want a higher stock turnover, but the reality of the DIY business is that it needs to keep a large range of stock on its shelves so that it can offer a comprehensive service to customers.

In practice, stock turnover is partly determined by the nature of a company's business. A market trader that sells perishable goods will have a very high stock turnover because produce like fruit and vegetables doesn't keep for many days. Traditionally, clothing stores restocked their stores every season, so they might expect a stock turnover of around 4 (as there are four seasons in the year). However the clothing retail business is changing, and by using online ordering systems and tills linked to stock records, this industry like many others is looking for much higher stock turnover rates.

assessmentpractice
Nutec Centre for Safety Ltd

Nutec Centre for Safety provides training in safety and survival techniques and firefighting. Before undertaking these tasks, study its accounts (Figures 11.11 and 11.12) and visit its website (www.nutecuk.com).

A Write down the details of the working capital as at 31 December 2004. What item is missing from the current assets? Why might that be?

B Calculate the company's current ratio, acid test, debtor days and creditor payment period. The notes to the Nutec accounts state that the company was owed £859,107 by trade debtors and it owed £321,190 to trade creditors. Assume that purchases are equal to its cost of sales.

C Compare working capital in 2004 with working capital in 2003, commenting on any significant differences.

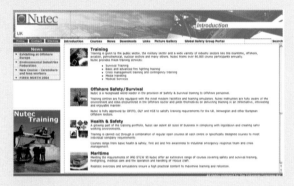

Figure 11.11 Nutec Centre for Safety Ltd profit and loss account, for the year ended 31 December 2004		
	2004	**2003**
	£	**£**
Turnover	5,644,855	5,000,648
Cost of sales	3,232,988	3,104,961
Gross profit	2,411,867	1,895,687
Administrative expenses	1,522,305	867,693
Other operating income	(23,230)	(32,101)
Operating profit	912,792	1,060,095
Interest receivable	1,834	21,182
Interest payable and similar charges	(145,312)	(188,391)
Profit on ordinary activities before taxation	769,314	892,886
Tax on profit on ordinary activities	248,974	69,491
Retained profit for the financial year	520,340	823,395
Balance brought forward	940,098	116,703
Balance carried forward	1,460,438	940,098

Figure 11.12 Nutec Centre for Safety Ltd balance sheet, as at 31 December 2004

	2004		2003	
	£	£	£	£
Fixed assets				
Tangible assets		3,368,071		3,520,406
Investments		60,000		60,000
		3,428,071		3,580,406
Current assets				
Debtors	2,288,227		2,205,335	
Cash at bank and in hand	7,933		1,875	
	2,296,160		2,207,210	
Creditors: amounts falling due within one year	2,114,058		1,709,861	
Net current assets		182,102		497,349
Total assets less current liabilities		3,610,173		4,077,755
Creditors: amounts falling due after more than one year		1,134,407		2,129,139
		2,475,766		1,948,616
Provisions for liabilities and charges				
Deferred taxation		65,083		58,273
		2,410,683		1,890,343
Capital and reserves				
Called-up equity share capital		950,245		950,245
Profit and loss account		1,460,438		940,098
Shareholders' funds		2,410,683		1,890,343

Managing working capital

Setting the scene: Adventure Divers Limited

Adventure Divers is a scuba diving shop and training centre. As you can see by visiting the company's website (www.adventuredivers.co.uk), the business runs dive trips, training sessions and courses at various venues, and has an equipment rental service as well as a shop. As Figure 11.13 shows, at 31 December 2004 it had £24,893 in working capital.

Consider each element in the working capital equation. First, look at the current assets. Stock is presumably the shop stock, which seems quite low, but the website directs readers to manufacturers' websites, so perhaps the company largely buys in stock on customers orders and holds very little stock in the shop. The bulk of the current assets are held in cash in hand or at bank. There are no debtors – it is not possible to pay by credit card on the website, and presumably all fees for training courses, diving trips and equipment must be paid in advance or at the point of sale.

Current liabilities – creditors amounts falling due within one year – are low at £1,178. This sum can easily be paid from current cash at bank. It presumably represents creditors for a few stock items and sundry bills such as electricity that were outstanding at the year end.

Working capital appears to be managed very tightly: stock is kept low, so that it does not get damaged in the store or become obsolete; there are no debtors, so the business does not have

Figure 11.13 Adventure Divers Limited, working capital as at 31 December 2004

Current assets

Stocks	£1,220
Cash at bank and in hand	£24,851
	£26,071

Current liabilities

Creditors amounts falling due within one year	(£1,178)
Net current assets	£24,893

funds tied up in other businesses, such as credit card companies, or with its customers; creditors are kept low, and it appears that advantage is being taken of credit terms.

KEY TERMS

Prepayments are bills that are paid in advance. In the year-end accounts, the proportion that relates to the next year is accounted for under debtors in the current assets section of the balance sheet.

Accruals are bills that are paid in arrears. In the year-end accounts, the entire bill is charged to the profit and loss account, and the proportion of the bill that is outstanding for the financial year is accounted for under the current liabilities section of the balance sheet.

Surplus cash is an excess of current assets. It is a difficult figure to quantify: a business needs enough liquid assets to be able to pay its debts as they fall due, but not hold too much so that it is leaving money idle that could be invested to generate further profits for the business.

Working capital management

For a business to survive and prosper, each element of working capital needs to be actively managed and controlled. The owners of a business need to consciously decide what stock levels they are going to hold, how much credit they are going to allow customers, how much cash they wish to hold in the bank and how the business is going to use its creditors.

1 Stock control

Stock are goods that a business holds for resale, or for use in delivering a service or in manufacturing its products. A business needs to hold enough stock to meet immediate customer, service or production needs, but not so much that it ties up capital in stock that is not going to be sold or used in the foreseeable future.

The level of stock that a company has to hold is partly determined by the nature of its business and the expectations of its customers. For example, Adventure Divers might hold relatively small amounts of stock because its customers are willing to wait a few days to collect specialised diving equipment.

LH Turtle, on the other hand, has to carry a large range of stock because its customers expect to get whatever they need when they visit: so the shop has to stock a whole rage of items – from sink plungers and three-quarter-inch nails to padlocks and clothes props – even though each item might not be requested very frequently.

In planning its stock-holding strategy, a business needs to consider:

■ the reliability of suppliers

■ the frequency of supplier deliveries

■ the willingness of suppliers to deliver small quantities of stock every few days

■ the value of individual stock items

■ the lead times – the time between the order being made and the goods being received

■ the shelf life for stock items

■ the discounts available for ordering larger quantities

■ the quality and reliability of the business's own stock information systems.

A business needs to get a balance between holding too much stock – and so tying up working capital and risking wastage if stock becomes out of date or perishes – and holding too little and risk failing to meet customer needs. Traditionally, many businesses have struck this balance by adopting an approach set out in the stock-holding model shown in Figure 11.14.

In following the traditional stock-holding approach, a business first identifies its maximum desired stock level – this might be dictated by the available storage space or the maximum amount that has ever been bought in one week or day. Then, it needs to determine its buffer stock level – that is, a safety stock level below which it does not ideally wish to fall. This is particularly important in businesses which need to maintain a steady supply of goods and services to their customers. The reorder quantity – the stock level at which the business places a new order with its suppliers – will be determined by the (historic) rate at which stocks get sold (or get used in production) and the time lag between placing an order and receiving a delivery.

Stock management has now changed dramatically since the model in Figure 11.14 was conceived. The model still provides a useful discipline, but businesses should not get caught following it too rigidly. Instead,

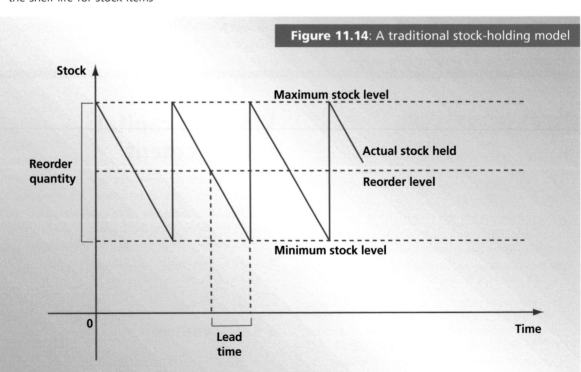

Figure 11.14: A traditional stock-holding model

Figure 11.15 Summary age analysis profile

Debtor	Total outstanding	Age analysis			
		Up to 30 days	60 days	90 days	120+ days
A. Smith	£100,000	£50,000	£40,000	£0	£10,000
B. Jones	£80,000	£80,000	£0	£0	£0
C. Patel	£90,000	£70,000	£20,000	£0	£0

an efficient business can exploit the potential of information technology and better delivery systems to remain responsive to customers while holding relatively lower levels of stock.

Monitoring stock levels

While efficient stock ordering can free up working capital, it is probably more important for a business to monitor individual stock items, and develop an understanding of how its stock moves. If a business has many product lines or separate stock items, it should use a computer system to record purchases. The computerised system ought to be able to generate sales reports and flag any slow-moving stock items. In practice, these reports suffer from some practical problems:

- managers often find them very difficult to read and understand

- systems do not automatically pick up the fact that some stock will have been stolen, damaged or withdrawn.

So although the computer-generated information is useful, managers need to get out to a business's stores and warehouses to develop their understanding of the stock situation. They need both systems and routines to ensure that all stock lines are moving at a reasonable level and that computer stock records actually tally with the physical stock (both in quantity and quality – stock must be fit for use).

If stock items are not moving, then managers need to consider ways the business can promote sales to move the stock faster. The relative cost of sales promotions needs to be weighed up against the costs of holding the stock.

Managers also need to regularly review stock order quantities. They should see whether the business could get a better deal from its suppliers, for example through bigger discounts, more special offers, support for promotions or a system of just-in-time delivery.

2 Debtor control

If a business offers its goods and services to customers on credit terms, then its stock asset has transferred into a debtor (on the balance sheet). A business needs to actively manage its debtors to ensure that they pay within the credit terms.

This process of active management should start before any sale is concluded. Before offering credit terms to a new customer (whether another business or an individual consumer), a business should check the customer's credit history and ask for bank references. Credit reports cost from about £5 upwards, which is a very small price compared to the potential losses that can be incurred if a customer fails to pay for a big order. Some reputable businesses will not offer credit terms to a new customer for the first six months, and then allow increasing levels of trade credit as the relationship develops.

A business's basic financial information systems are the first line for debtors management. Most accounting packages have the facility to produce an "age analysis" of debtors. This analysis provides a debtors ledger report that shows:

- the total value owed by each debtor

- the total value broken down by the age of the debt

- the transactions that make up the total balance.

Figure 11.15 shows part of a summary age analysis profile of debtors. These records need to be monitored regularly and used to chase up customers with large or longstanding debts. It is not easy to chase customers for debts, and there is a fine balance between ensuring that debts are paid promptly and not alienating good customers who always pay their bills eventually. It is often a good idea to work with the sales team that deals with the customer, or to phone the customer to find out if there has been a problem. For example, Mr Smith (in Figure 11.15) may be in dispute about the £10,000 which is still outstanding more than 120 days after issuing the invoice. This dispute needs to be resolved speedily.

If chasing outstanding debts by phone does not work, then the business needs to take more serious action. This requires time and effort, and comes at a price. First, a business needs to assess whether the debt is worth collecting. This depends on the philosophy of the business owners: some people will collect every debt on principle, others will be prepared to waive small debts and move on.

The debtor Smith (in Figure 11.15) owes £100,000 in total, including the £10,000 that has been due for more than 120 days – this is a significant sum for any business, and therefore will be followed up. The next step, if post or telephone requests have not produced a response, is to request the debt in person by going the customer's business address (or home in the case of an individual consumer). This is often a quick and successful strategy. Failing that, a business will take a debtor to court to enforce payment of the debt. If the debtor being taken to court has no income or assets, it might take a long time to get full payment.

Factoring

Many businesses do not want to spend time managing a debtors ledger. Instead, they contract out their debt collection to a factoring company. The factoring company effectively buys all the business's outstanding debts at a discount, and then takes on the job of debt collection. Factoring companies are experts in debt control, in managing bad debts and in the legal procedure for collecting debts.

The terms of a factoring agreement vary, but it is not unusual for the factor to buy the debts at 90 per cent of their face value, with the further proviso that the business will get another 5 per cent of the debt upon collection, although the factor may take a larger percentage if the debt cannot be recovered within an agreed period. So, for example, if a business's total debtors are worth £150,000, the factoring company would pay £135,000 (90 per cent of the debt) immediately, and then pay the business a further £7,500 (5 per cent of the total) if and when it collects the full £150,000 from the debtors.

So assuming all the debtors pay up, the business receives £142,500 (£135,000 + £7,500) for supplying £150,000 worth of goods and services. The benefit is that the business receives most of that sum immediately, therefore improving its cash flow, and it doesn't incur the time and expense of debt management. The factoring company receives £7,500 (5 per cent of the debt) for its trouble.

Some businesses have longstanding agreements with factoring companies, so that all their invoices are automatically passed to the factor for immediate (part) payment. There is a potential downside, as many customers do not like dealing with a factoring company, and they can be alienated if there are disputes or problems trying to determine that the correct payments have been made. However, businesses that factor their invoices regard the reduced income as a price worth paying for the quicker cash flow and the delegation of debtor management.

3 Cash management

Cash is like any other asset, it needs to be managed and understood. It is the only totally liquid asset. Stock may never be sold. Debtors are not a guaranteed source of income, as customers may go bankrupt owing large sums. So in a severe economic downturn, which could depress sales and lead to more bankruptcies, a business can find itself dependent on its cash reserves to pay its debts as they fall due.

Business managers need to consider what is a reasonable amount of cash to hold on a day-to-day basis. They need to be prudent about liquidity, but also keep the cash actively working to generate more profits for the business.

Cash is managed through a these basic techniques:

- cash flow forecasts

- bank reconciliations

- clear procedures for recording, handling and banking receipts and payments.

Cash flow forecasts are statements of expected inflows and outflows of cash in and out of the business. (For more information on cash flow forecasting techniques look back at Unit 2, Topic 7 in the AS textbook and at Unit 8, Topic 5 in this book.) The net impact of cash flows into and out of a business's bank account is calculated at the bottom of the forecast, so that the owners of the business can plan for shortages and surpluses of cash. For example, if the cash flow forecast indicates that a business is going to be short of cash for three months, then the owners can either arrange a short-term loan or overdraft to manage the situation. Alternatively, they could explore ways of moving the cash outflows during that period to ease the pressure, perhaps by delay buying a fixed asset until the cash flow shortage is over.

Bank reconciliations are an important discipline. They involve checking on a weekly or monthly basis that the balance on the business's bank statement can be reconciled to the company's own record of cash at bank. This procedure ensures that items that might be easily overlooked, such as receipts and payments by direct debit, bank charges and dishonoured cheques, are picked up in the company's accounts. Bank reconciliations also monitor and keep track of:

- the accuracy of the bank's records

- the accuracy of the business's own records

- any cheques issued by the business that have not yet been presented to the bank

- any receipts paid into the bank that have not yet been recorded on the bank statement.

Bank reconciliations ought to be checked and signed by a senior accountant or by the owner of the business. The cash balances should be checked against the cash flow forecasts, and the forecasts should be updated if necessary. In this way, the owners of the business are actively engaged in monitoring and understanding the impact of actual cash flows on their forecasts, and they will be better placed to take any necessary action if the business faces a cash shortage, or to manage a cash surplus.

The final element of good cash management is having procedures for all financial transactions. Any business needs clear procedures for recording, handling and banking cash and cheque receipts. As well ensuring the integrity of the business's financial records, good cash-handling procedures protect innocent employees from false accusations of theft and weak employees from temptation. Some of the basic elements of a good bank and cash system include:

- division of duties – don't make systems easy to defraud by letting the same person check stock received, issue invoices and authorise payments

- regular financial checks by a senior person regularly, including the petty cash reconciliation and the bank reconciliation

- large payments require more than one cheque signatory – in this way, two people must authorise any payment over a certain amount

- all significant contracts require prior board approval.

4 Creditor management

Creditors arise when a business's suppliers allow it to buy goods and services on credit. This is a really valuable privilege. The suppliers are effectively offering free finance to the business. Some businesses manage to fund their whole operation out of trade creditors, as Figures 11.16 and 11.17 show.

In order to keep this privilege of free credit, it is important that creditors are properly managed and paid on time. Other creditors, such as loans and overdrafts, should not be taken on lightly. A business needs to be confident that it is able to repay all its creditors as they fall due. If a business fails to repay its creditors, it can suffer several consequences:

- suppliers may not allow any further credit

- court action might be taken against the business for non-payment of debts

- court proceedings may adversely affect the business's credit ratings

- poorer credit ratings will mean that lenders are more likely to charge premium rates for any future loans and finance.

Figure 11.16 Trading on credit

Day	Transaction	Bank balance
Day 1	Buy goods for £1,000 on 30 days credit	£0
Day 6	Sell goods for £2,000 for cash	£2,000
Day 7	Buy goods for £1,000 on 30 days credit	£2,000
Day 13	Sell goods for £2,000 for cash	£4,000
Day 14	Buy goods for £1,000 on 30 days credit	£4,000

Figure 11.17 Balance sheet as at end of day 14

Current assets	
Stock	£1,000
Cash	£4,000
Current liabilities	
Trade creditors	(£3,000)
Net current assets	£2,000
Shareholders' funds	
Profit	£2,000

assessment practice
Warehouse Theatre Company Limited

You examined the accounts of the Warehouse Theatre in Topic 2. As Figure 11.67 shows (see page 154), at 31 March 2004 the company had current liabilities (creditors: amounts falling due within one year) of £101,181, and a working capital of –£89,162. In other words, at that date, current liabilities greatly exceeded current assets.

In the notes to the accounts, the company gave more detail about its creditors falling due within a year. These creditors were:

Bank overdraft	£41,555
Tax and social security	£11,207
Other creditors	£990
Grants paid in advance	£30,875
Accruals and deferred income	£16,554

The notes also state that the amount recorded in the balance sheet of £11,662 for debtors is all prepayments and accrued income; there were no trade debtors.

A **Write a report to the directors of the Warehouse Theatre Company assessing the working capital management of the theatre. Make recommendations to the directors on how the theatre could improve its working capital management.**

Investing in assets and projects

Setting the scene: Ecological Sciences Limited

Ecological Sciences featured in the exercise at the end of Topic 1. To carry out its business, the company needs vehicles, plant and machinery, including plant for composting and machinery for moving large quantities of compost. These are its main fixed assets.

The balance sheet as at 31 December 2004 (see Figure 11.4, page 149) shows fixed assets of £262,663. These are at net book value – that is, the cost of the assets less depreciation since acquisition.

The notes to the accounts provide details of the initial cost of the fixed assets and depreciation, so that you can see how net book value has been calculated, and details of recent acquisitions and disposals of fixed assets. In 2004, Ecological Sciences spent £100,858 in acquisitions of fixed assets, £97,208 in plant and machinery, and £3,650 on motor vehicles.

The company doesn't purchase all its assets outright. In total, £134,019 of the net book value of fixed assets relates to assets held under hire purchase agreements.

Fixed assets account for more than half of the net asset value of Ecological Sciences. These purchases are not made lightly – they have to be assessed to ensure that the business is making the right investment to maximise returns on its capital and to meet the business's aims.

Similarly, any investments into new projects need to be assessed to ensure that they will meet the aims of the business. If you visit the company's website (www.ecosci.co.uk), you can see the variety of projects that Ecological Sciences has invested in and the type of fixed assets that it owns.

Investment decisions

All businesses at some stage face opportunities to invest in new fixed asset purchases or new projects. These decisions usually require a substantial investment. The business needs to commit a large sum of money at the beginning of a project (or at the time of asset purchase). It does this in the expectation that it will receive returns on that investment at a later date, often over a period of several years.

A business needs to decide whether these investment opportunities are worthwhile. It needs to consider several questions.

■ Do the returns outweigh the investment?

■ Is there a cheaper alternative which requires a lower investment?

■ How will the investment affect the business's market position?

■ How will it affect cash flow?

■ Is technology changing in this area? Would it be sensible to delay investment until new technology becomes available or a new model comes out?

■ Does the business have staff with the right skills to work on the project or to use and exploit the new fixed asset?

A business must look at qualitative and quantitative factors before taking a decision on whether to go ahead with a new investment. A quantitative assessment may suggest that investment in new machinery could increase production, say, but this would not be achieved if the business lacks staff with the skills to operate the plant. So qualitative factors, such as skills levels, must also be considered.

A business needs to accumulate a portfolio of evidence which covers all aspects of the purchase decision. It needs to identify what is the need for the fixed assets purchase or project. How will the investment enable the business to fulfil customers' expectations better?

If it is considering a fixed asset acquisition, a business needs to undertake research into the type of asset that would best meet its needs. For example, would a second-hand model be adequate? It needs information on the performance and specifications of different models – with data on size, capacity, technical specifications, life expectancy, guarantees, service agreements, support needs, etc. The business's engineers need to evaluate this information and identify a shortlist of machines or models that would meet the business's needs.

KEY TERMS

Fixed assets are resources that are held by a business for the long term (more than one year) to generate products or services.

Investment is the process of putting money into a project or financial undertaking with the expectation that it will generate further wealth and provide a financial return.

Risk is a situation that exposes an investor to uncertainty. Investors expect to be rewarded for taking risks, and would expect the potential return to reflect the level of risk involved.

Returns are the profits yielded on an investment.

Cash flow forecasts and profits

Having established the basic data about a proposed asset acquisition or a planned project, the next level of research can take place. This involves assessing the impact of the purchase or the project on the business's future cash flows and profitability.

This is best illustrated by an example. Suppose a business wants to invest in a new piece of equipment that will cost £100,000 to buy, and which will be sold for £20,000 in four years' time. It is estimated that by using the new equipment the business will generate £40,000 in additional revenue (net of cost of sales) each year.

Figure 11.18 shows the impact of the investment on the business's cash flow. The investment will produce a net cash flow over the four years of £80,000. Note that the business will not earn back its £100,000 investment until half way through the third year, and the £80,000 will not be fully realised until the fourth year of the project. This is a relatively long time frame. The further into the future the return, the higher is the risk that the returns will not actually be realised.

Figure 11.18 Cash flow analysis

Year	Outflows	Inflows	Net cash flows	Balance
0	(£100,000)		(£100,000)	(£100,000)
1		£40,000	£40,000	(£60,000)
2		£40,000	£40,000	(£20,000)
3		£40,000	£40,000	£20,000
4		£60,000	£60,000	£80,000

Figure 11.19: Revised cash flow projections

Year	0	1	2	3	4
Net cash flow	£50,000	£50,000	£50,000	£50,000	£50,000
Impact of investment	(£100,000)	£40,000	£40,000	£40,000	£60,000
Revised net cash flow	(£50,000)	£90,000	£90,000	£90,000	£110,000
Opening balance	£10,000	(£40,000)	£50,000	£140,000	£230,000
Closing balance	(£40,000)	£50,000	£140,000	£230,000	£340,000

Although this analysis suggests that the investment will have a positive impact on a business's cash flow, the investment shouldn't be considered in isolation but assessed against the cash position of the business as a whole. This means assessing the impact of the investment on the business's current cash flow. This can be critical, and it is not unusual for one large fixed asset purchase or a new project to jeopardise the future of the whole business.

Assume, for the purposes of illustration, that without the investment the business would have a net annual cash flow of £50,000, and an opening cash balance of £10,000. Figure 11.19 shows the impact of the new investment. If the business can fund the short-term cash shortfall of £40,000, then the investment has a positive effect on the business's cash flow forecast and shouldbe seriously considered.

Finally the business needs to consider the impact on profits. We know that the asset will generate gross profits of £40,000 each year (that is, additional revenue net of the cost of sales). We need to offset the depreciation of the fixed asset against the gross profit it generates. Figure 11.20 shows the impact on net profits by assuming that the asset will be depreciated on a straight-line basis over the four

years. (The business has assumed it will be worth £20,000 after four years, so depreciation has been calculated by dividing the difference between the purchase price and the final sale price by four – that is, £100,000 – £20,000 divided by 4, which equals annual depreciation of £20,000.)

Figure 11.20 shows that (on our assumptions) the impact of the investment will be to increase profits by £20,000 each year. If one of the business's objectives is to maximise return on capital and to increase profits to shareholders, then this investment can be recommended.

Note that, in the short term, profits and cash flows are not the same. Figure 11.20 shows that the investment yields an annual profit of £20,000, but Figure 11.18 shows that the investment only yields a positive overall cash flow in year 3. This apparent anomaly is because profits are always calculated on an accruals or matching basis. This means that revenues are matched to costs over a particular time period, and the fixed asset is accounted for as an expense over its useful life to the business. But cash flows always reflect actual cash movements.

Consider what happens to the company's cash flow and balance sheet at year 0, if the £100,000

Figure 11.20: Impact on profits

Year	1	2	3	4
Gross profit	£40,000	£40,000	£40,000	£40,000
Less depreciation	(£20,000)	(£20,000)	(£20,000)	(£20,000)
Impact on profits	£20,000	£20,000	£20,000	£20,000

investment is financed through a cash payment from the company's bank account. The effect on the cash account is a net outflow of £100,000 – the company's cash position is reduced. However, the effect on the balance sheet is neutral: the company has £100,000 less recorded in cash at bank under current assets, but £100,000 more recorded under fixed assets – so its net assets (current assets plus fixed assets) are unchanged.

Risks and variability of returns

The future cash flows from any investment are not certain. Companies can make forecasts based on market research and past experience, but any business is subject to many internal and external influences that change the environment in which it operates. As cash flow forecasts are projected further into the future, we would expect the estimates to be more uncertain.

To deal with this uncertainty, businesses use different techniques to evaluate "what-if" scenarios. These exercises help managers plan for best-case and worst-case situations and to assess whether the business can risk and survive the worst-case scenario arising. Conversely, a business will also want to know if it is in a good position to exploit a best-case scenario.

Businesses also undertake sensitivity analysis. This tests the sensitivity of cash flow forecasts and profit estimates to changes in environmental factors or to changes in the assumptions that underpin the forecasts. In sectors such as the oil industry, in which companies make huge investments in highly risky situations, extensive systems are set up to test the sensitivity of every factor.

The purpose of any investment is to make an acceptable return. Individual businesses will take different views on what constitutes an acceptable return on an investment, and what constitutes an acceptable risk. As a minimum, however, any

business would expect to make a higher return than it could make by keeping money in the bank. If someone can earn 5 per cent annually without risk by investing in a high-interest bank account, it makes little sense to invest in a business venture (which is inevitably more risky and uncertain) that is only promising a 4 per cent annual return.

In practice, attitudes to risk and return vary from industry to industry. The oil industry seeks to make high returns from investments because of the huge risks involved in oil exploration. The industry risks losing assets and lives operating in dangerous areas such as the North Sea, it risks incurring the cost of exploration only to find that deposits are smaller than expected, it risks bringing the product to a volatile market and not getting the price its wants. Since the risks are so high, oil industry executives want to see high projected returns before they will commit to an investment. In contrast, for example, newsagents face considerably fewer risks and make much smaller investments, and would commit to projects with much lower projected returns.

Relevant costs

When making a decision about an investment, it is important to isolate the costs that relate to the actual investment and to set aside any costs that the business is already paying or that it would incur if it continued without making the investment. A business is trying to identify the potential impact of the investment on future profits and cash flows. It cannot make a fair assessment if there is double accounting or if the project is loaded with overhead costs that the business would have to pay anyway.

In the past it was common practice to allocate overhead costs rather arbitrarily when assessing investment projects. This resulted in some viable, profitable projects being rejected. Today, most businesses have a much better understanding of investment decisions.

Property development

A small property company is deciding on a new investment. It is considering a 1901 house in a considerable state of disrepair that is located on an inner city site near a railway station. The directors of the company believe that they can purchase the property at auction for £50,000 and turn it into three flats for rent.

The directors estimate that the building work to convert the house into three flats will cost £100,000. On completion, they will get the property revalued by an independent surveyor, but they estimate it will be worth at least £300,000. The property costs are to written off over 50 years.

In year 1, the property will only be available for letting in the last six months of the year. However, the company then expects each flat could be let for £700 each per month until the end of year 8, before it would incur any further significant repair and maintenance costs. The tenants will be responsible for all the bills related to the property, including council tax.

Figure 11.21 shows the projected net cash flows for the property company for the next 10 years for its core business – that is, without taking into account the impact of the new investment under consideration. At year 0 – that is, at the point of the investment decision – the company has an opening cash balance of £60,000.

A Calculate the cash flows that directly relate to this project for the first eight years.

B Calculate the impact of this investment on the cash flow of the business up until the end of year 8.

C Calculate the net profit that this investment will generate in the first 8 years.

D What other factors might affect the directors' decision to invest in this property?

E Identify three factors that are used in the cash and profit projections that could be subject to change. Explain why these factors could take different values when the property is actually bought.

F The company has a general policy of selling properties after 10 years. What factors might influence its decision about whether to sell this property after 10 years?

Figure 11.21: Projected cash flow for core business excluding the new investment

Year	Net cash flow for the year
Year 0	£250,000
Year 1	£300,000
Year 2	£300,000
Year 3	£300,000
Year 4	£250,000
Year 5	£200,000
Year 6	£200,000
Year 7	£200,000
Year 8	£150,000
Year 9	£150,000
Year 10	£100,000

Setting the scene: Nutec Centre for Safety

The massive explosion at the Buncefield oil depot near Hemel Hempstead in December 2005 showed yet again the critical importance of safety in the oil industry.

Nutec Centre for Safety, by providing training in safety and survival techniques and firefighting, helps industries update their health and safety readiness. However, in order for Nutec to stay at the forefront of its industry it needs to invest in new products and fixed assets

Look back at Nutec's balance sheet at 31 December 2004 (Figure 11.12, page 162). On that date, the company held fixed assets with a net book value of £3,368,071. This figure includes assets worth £62,618 held under hire purchase agreements. The notes to the accounts show the division of these fixed assets between land and buildings, fixtures and fittings, motor vehicles and training equipment. In total, they cost £5,198,662 when they were originally purchased.

The balance sheet shows the company held just £7,933 in cash at 31 December 2004. It had significant other (non-cash) current assets but also high current liabilities, so it did not have any

significant leeway to use current assets to invest in new fixed assets. New fixed asset purchases would probably have to be financed through a loan or through hire purchase or lease.

In this situation, Nutec must consider investments in new fixed assets or new business projects carefully. It needs to choose investments that help it meet client needs and which maximise the company's long-term return on capital employed.

Methods of investment appraisal

In the last topic, we looked at how businesses assess investments in terms of their impact on cash flows and future profits. However, businesses are often faced with a choice of investments. Businesses usually must make a decision between several competing projects, or between different fixed asset purchases

(either to do different jobs or the same job). In order to be able to decide between different options, they need to place a value on each option.

Investment appraisal is the process of assessing the worth of potential investment(s) to the business. This helps a business choose between alternative investments. It also helps a business decide whether any single investment is worth making at all. Most medium-to-large businesses have set minimum targets or returns that investments must deliver, and they will reject projects that do not meet these targets.

In this topic we look at four different methods of investment appraisal. These methods help businesses to make investment decisions and to get best value for money. More fundamentally, they allow businesses to fulfil their responsibility to use their liquid assets and its opportunities to maximise returns for their owners (or shareholders).

It is important to understand that no appraisal method provides a definitive answer. All the

KEY TERMS

Payback period is the time it takes to repay the initial investment in a project.

The time value of money is the concept that a pound is worth more to a business now than a pound in say a year's time. This concept is used to discount future flows of cash.

Capital rationing is the process by which companies have to choose between investment options because they do not have the capital available to invest in all opportunities.

techniques featured in this topic provide useful evidence. However, a business also needs to consider qualitative data such as the state of the markets in which it trades, potential changes in technology, and other factors which might impact on its environment. It is by bringing together this qualitative evidence with the quantitative valuations from an appraisal that a business makes an informed decision about a future investment in a project or a fixed asset.

1 Payback period

The payback period method is relatively simple. It looks at the time it takes for a project (or fixed asset) to repay its initial investment. To illustrate this method, Figure 11.22 shows the projected net flows for three projects under consideration by a business.

Figure 11.22: Projected net cash flows for three projects

	Project A	Project B	Project C
	Net cash flow	Net cash flow	Net cash flow
Year	£	£	£
Year 0	(10,000)	(25,000)	(60,000)
Year 1	3,000	12,000	20,000
Year 2	3,000	26,000	40,000
Year 3	20,000	8,000	30,000
Year 4	40,000	2,000	10,000

The initial investment for project A is £10,000. In the first two years, the business gets back £6,000. So it will make back its initial investment when it receives a net cash flow of £4,000 in year 3 (as £6,000 + £4,000 = £10,000). Assume the £20,000 net cash flow in year 3 is spread evenly through the year, then it makes £4000 after 0.2 of the year (£4,000/£20,000 = 0.2). So the payback on the initial investment in project A is just over two years and two months.

Project B is paid back part-way through year 2, when the business receives £13,000 (as £13,000 plus the £12,000 from year 1 equals the £25,000 initial investment). It makes back £13,000 half-way through the year (£13,000/£26,000 = 0.5). So the payback on the initial investment in project B is one year and six months. Project C has a net cash flow of £60,000

in its first two years, which is the size of the initial investment. So project C has a payback of two years.

So, in terms of payback, Project B looks like the best project. It is paid back in the shortest time. It is arguably the least risky of the projects, given that returns and cash flow projections become more uncertain over time.

The payback period is widely used throughout the world. It has the advantage that it is quick and easy to calculate, and easily to understand. Businesses find it a useful tool that can be applied to any investment situation, including projects that have a payback of, say, two years or less. The method implicitly takes into account that the longer a project takes to repay its initial investment, the higher the risk of the project.

The approach has some disadvantages. These include that:

- the payback method ignores the value of cash flows after the payback date

- it also does not attribute any significance to the time value of money, it just looks at straightforward cash flows.

2 Discounted cash flows

The time value of money is the concept that a pound is worth more to a business now than a pound in, say, a year's time. This reflects the uses to which that pound could have been put over the year, the decline in the purchasing power of the pound over that year, and the risk associated with the uncertainty of getting a pound in one year's time.

Applying this concept to investment appraisal means that a business cannot assess the worth of an investment by simply adding up the expected contribution of the investment to net cash flow over a given period. Instead, it needs to discount future flows of cash to reflect the time value of money. In other words, the appraisal needs to reflect the fact a £10,000 net cash flow in year 1 is worth more to the business than say a £10,000 net cash flow in year 5.

Discounted cash flow techniques work by marking down (that is, discounting) future net cash flows. The further the cash flow is into the future, the more it is discounted. The factor by which the cash flows are discounted depends on several criteria. If, for example, a business is paying 6 per cent interest on loans to fund the project, it estimates inflation to be 3 per cent on average over the course of the project, and it wants a 6 per cent return on its investment, it might use a discount factor of 15 per cent on investment projects.

Once a business decides on a discount factor, it needs to use this to mark down the forecast net cash flow in each year of the project to its net present value (NPV) – that is, it needs to convert future cash flows to present values. You do this by using present value tables. For any specific discount factor, these tables show the index to be used each year to convert future cash flows to net present values.

Figure 11.23 is an extract from a present value table, and shows the indices for years 0–5 for three different discount factors. This table can be used to calculate the net present value of the three projects in Figure 11.22. Suppose the business decides to use a discount factor of 15 per cent to evaluate the project. Then the forecast net cash flow for each project in year 1 is multiplied by 0.870, the index for year 1 in the 15 per cent column in Figure 11.23; the net cash flow for each project in year 2 is multiplied by 0.756; etc.

Figure 11.24 sets outs the net present values for the three projects at a discount factor of 15 per cent. This shows that project A comes out as the best project using the discounted cash flow method of investment appraisal, with a net present value for the project of £30,918.

The net present value method of investment appraisal has several advantages:

■ it is widely understood and used by investment professionals

■ it takes account of all cash flows associated with the projects

■ it takes into account the time value of money by discounting future cash flows by an increasing factor.

The choice of discount factor affects the final outcome significantly. This is a potential weakness, as the choice of discount factor can be quite arbitrary. The method also has the disadvantage that non-financial specialists may find it difficult to understand, and may be confused about the meaning of the final net present value figure.

3 The internal rate of return (IRR)

The internal rate of return (IRR) approach is a development of the discounted cash flow method. The internal rate of return is defined as the discount rate at which the net present value (NPV) is equal to zero. There are computer programs which can easily calculate IRR or, as we demonstrate here, it can be found by trial and error.

The trial and error methods relies on you being able to find two discount rates, fairly close together, where one gives a positive NPV for the project and the other gives a negative NPV. You know that the IRR (where the NPV is zero) will lie between these two discount

Figure 11.23: Present value table

Discount factor	10%	15%	20%
Year 0	1	1	1
Year 1	0.909	0.870	0.833
Year 2	0.826	0.756	0.694
Year 3	0.751	0.658	0.579
Year 4	0.683	0.572	0.482
Year 5	0.621	0.497	0.402

Figure 11.24: Net present values for three projects at a discount factor of 15 per cent

	Project A		Project B		Project C	
	£	NPV	£	NPV	£	NPV
Year 0	(10,000)	(10,000)	(25,000)	(25,000)	(60,000)	(60,000)
Year 1	3,000	2,610	12,000	10,440	20,000	17,400
Year 2	3,000	2,268	26,000	19,656	40,000	30,240
Year 3	20,000	13,160	8,000	5,264	30,000	19,740
Year 4	40,000	22,880	2,000	1,144	10,000	5,720
Net flow	56,000	30,918	23,000	11,504	40,000	13,100

rates. You need to estimate where NPV is zero. Suppose:

NPV (discount factor L) = p

NPV (discount factor M) = –q

The values p and q must both be positive, so that NPV is positive at discount factor L and NPV is negative at discount factor M. Then IRR is given by this formula:

$$IRR = L + \frac{p}{(p + q)} \times (M - L)$$

Let's apply this method to project A. We have found, using a set of present value tables and trial and error, that project A has:

NPV (discount factor 70%) = £1,682.

NPV (discount factor 80%) = –£185

So, applying the formula, we get:

$$IRR \text{ (Project A)} = 70 + \frac{1682}{(1682 + 185)} \times (80 - 70)$$

$$= 70 + \frac{1682}{1867} \times 10$$

$$= 70 + (0.90 \times 10)$$

$$= 79.0\%$$

A similar process of trial and error and calculation gets an IRR for project B of 41.4 per cent and an IRR for project C of 26.1 per cent. So project A, with an IRR of 79 per cent, would be the best investment by this appraisal method. If the business invested in project A, it would get a return of 79 per cent.

The advantages of calculating internal rates of return are similar to those of discounted cash flows. It provides a means of comparing a variety of projects with completely different cash flows that takes account of the time value of money. The IRR result focuses on the return on the investment. So, if the business chooses between competing investments on the basis of the highest IRR then it should produce good returns on all of its investments.

The disadvantage of the IRR method is that it can oversimplify a business decision. There is a danger that investors will just rely on the calculation and not consider the underlying business proposition, including factors such as the inherent risk in the investment and the stability of the market. Some business people do not feel confident with the IRR calculation, and they may surrender the decision-making to financial professionals who are comfortable with this approach.

4 Return on capital employed

The return on capital employed (ROCE) is an investors' ratio that is usually found in the published accounts of public companies. The calculation is usually done annually, by dividing profits after interest and tax by the capital employed. This ROCE calculation can be simplified to compare fixed asset purchases and other investments. In practice, it does not matter how the calculation is simplified as long a consistent approach is adopted in all calculations so that it is possible to compare projects.

To illustrate the method using the projects introduced in Figure 11.22, we will take the capital employed to mean the money invested in the projects and the profits to mean the net cash inflows each year to the projects. ROCE can be calculated for each year of the project or for the whole project. In each case, the basic calculation is straightforward:

$$ROCE = \frac{profits}{capital\ employed} \times 100$$

So for year 1, Project A:

$$ROCE = \frac{£3000}{£10,000} \times 100 = 0.3 \times 100 = 30\%$$

Figure 11.25 (page 178) shows ROCE calculations for the three projects we have been considering in this topic. It produces a complex picture, and a business would need to consider these results in relation to its other investments. If it is looking for a quick return on investment, then project B looks like the best investment prospect. If it is looking for good returns in years 3 and 4, then project A would seem the better investment. Overall, project A is certainly the better investment, with ROCE of 660 per cent, but the big returns are not produced until years 3 and 4, by which time the business environment could have changed and these returns may never materialise.

Again, like the discounted cash flow and IRR methods, ROCE is widely used and understood by investment professionals, though some business people lack confidence in using ROCE and don't understand its limitations. However, the main advantages of the method are that:

■ it focuses on the returns that are attributable to the owners of the business and the investors

■ it can be calculated for individual years or for the overall project

■ a business can match ROCE to its product portfolio, and do further analysis to manage its future flows of profits.

Figure 11.25: ROCE for three projects

	Project A		Project B		Project C	
	£	ROCE	£	ROCE	£	ROCE
Capital employed	10,000		25,000		60,000	
Year 1 profits	3,000	30%	12,000	48%	20,000	33%
Year 2 profits	3,000	30%	26,000	104%	40,000	67%
Year 3 profits	20,000	200%	8,000	32%	30,000	50%
Year 4 profits	40,000	400%	2,000	8%	10,000	17%
Overall ROCE		660%		192%		167%

There are a many ways of calculating ROCE, therefore it is important to ensure that calculations are performed using the same underlying formula for all projects. Failure to follow this practice will mean that a business will not be comparing like for like. As well as this potential pitfall, there are some other disadvantages with the ROCE method:

■ it can be a complex task defining what is included in capital employed and profits for any project

■ it takes no account of the time value of money

■ results do not take into account non-quantifiable factors such as relative risks.

Financing decisions

If a business has decided in principle to make an investment, it needs to consider how it is going to finance that fixed asset. Most businesses acquire fixed assets through a mixture of financing methods. It needs to take several factors into account in making the financing decision.

Financial resources

One consideration is whether the business has the necessary funds to buy an asset outright from its cash reserves or retained profits. It then needs to see if there are other potential demands on these resources.

Loans and leasing

A business needs to consider whether it can finance fixed asset purchases through a loan, hire purchase or a leasing agreement. It needs to consider the relative interest rates as well as the availability of loans, leases and hire purchase. Many small businesses have to pay premium rates for any kind of borrowing.

Tax benefits

A business needs to consider the tax implications of the decision. Each option – buying fixed assets outright, or using a loan, or taking out a lease or hire purchase agreement – may have different impacts on a business's tax liability.

Tax legislation changes most years, so any decision needs to take account of current law and any new proposals announced in the government's budget statement. The decision depends on an individual business's circumstances. The tax regime for sole traders and partnerships is different to that for companies.

Any local tax office should be able to advise on how and when fixed asset purchases can be offset against tax due on profits. The HM Revenue and Customs Service website (www.hmrc.gov.uk) provides links to teams who are available to offer support and advice to businesses.

Type of asset

The decision may also depend on the type of asset that is being acquired. This can affect the availability of finance – car companies are very likely to provide different finance options for customers, an item of specialist machinery bought from Japan may be more difficult to finance. The type of asset will also influence the financing decision: some assets a business will want to buy outright, other assets might be more sensibly acquired by leasing arrangements.

The financing method will impact on the cash flows of the projects and will therefore also affect the calculations of any investment appraisal. Most banks and finance houses provide cash flow and cost schedules for their finance agreements when companies approach them for a quote.

assessment practice
Ferguson's Foods

Bob Ferguson is a sole trader who runs a shop selling organic foods. He wants to buy a freezer unit at the end of May so that he is able to sell premium, organic ice cream to his customers.

Bob has already undertaken some market research. Some research results are summarised in Figure 11.26. This shows sales forecasts (for each month) for the four varieties he plans to offer. Bob will price the goods as follows: single cone, £1.20; double cone; £1.80, tubs, £4.00; gateaux, £8.00. These retail prices represent a 45 per cent mark-up on the cost of buying the ice cream from Bob's supplier.

Bob estimates that half of the purchases of tubs and gateaux will be by new customers. He expects these new customers on average to also spend £30 on other products in the shop when they come in to buy ice cream each month. The mark-up on these sales is also at Bob's standard rate of 45 per cent.

Product research shows that Bob Ferguson has the choice of three models.

■ Freezer A, an upright freezer costing £950

■ Freezer B, a chest freezer costing £900

■ Freezer C, a storage freezer costing £400.

In order to accommodate the freezers, it will be necessary to incur some one-off costs to adjust the store's fixtures and décor.

■ Freezer A: £2,500 of adjustments

■ Freezer B: £4,000 of adjustments

■ Freezer C: no adjustments to the store.

Each freezer has some potential drawbacks. The chest freezer (option B) will make the shop too crowded and will reduce overall sales by £2,000 each month. An upright display cabinet (option A) could make serving difficult, Bob will need to employ an additional assistant in the summer months (June through September) to serve ice cream. This assistant will need to be paid the equivalent of £12,000 per annum.

Bob can raise £1,000 in cash to buy the new freezer unit. He wants his investment in the freezer to have a maximum payback period of two years. The shop's lease expires in five years' time, and so Bob is only interested in returns on investments in that period. He intends to use discount rate of 10 per cent to calculate net present value.

Figure 11.26: Bob Ferguson's sales forecasts

Month	Product			
	Single cones	Double cones	Tubs	Gateaux
June, July, August, September	900	800	200	150
October, November, December	0	0	80	30
January, February, March	0	0	70	30
April, May	200	175	150	140

A Assuming Bob buys the freezer outright, calculate the relevant cash flows for all three possible freezer options for the next five years.

B Calculate the impact each of the freezer options will have on profits.

C Calculate the payback period, the net present value, the internal rate of return, and the return on capital employed for each of the freezer options. (You will need to obtain a set of present value tables from your class teacher.)

D If the weather is bad throughout the summer, ice cream sales would remain at the levels for April and May. Bob is a pessimist and assumes that the weather this summer and next will be bad. Would this affect his investment decision?

E Write a report outlining your findings and recommending which freezer option to buy. Identify any non-numerical factors which are relevant and include an analysis of the suitability of appraisal methods you have used.

Investing in other companies

Setting the scene: Lush Cosmetics group structure

Lush is a cosmetics company, and its products are sold in many countries. As we saw in the case study at the beginning of Topic 2, Lush Cosmetics has developed and expanded its business through a network of companies.

This is a deliberate business strategy. It could have offered franchises, enabling independent businesses to offer Lush products. Instead, Lush Cosmetics Ltd has chosen to develop and distribute its products through subsidiary and associate companies in which it retains a strong financial interest.

With each subsidiary and associate, Lush Cosmetics works with the other shareholders to provide the Lush brand goods. This approach allows the company to maintain its brand integrity yet tolerate and exploit differences in the various countries in which it operates. All products are handmade, and local ingredients are often used to give a subtly different scent.

The notes to the Lush accounts for the period to June 2003 list 21 companies that are subsidiaries or associate companies of Lush Cosmetics Ltd. Normally subsidiary companies are those in which the holding company (Lush Cosmetics Ltd) has a controlling interest – that is, it owns over 50 per cent of the shares. At 30 June 2003, Lush subsidiaries included:

■ Lush Japan KK, in which Lush Cosmetics Ltd held 58.5 per cent of the ordinary shares

■ Lush BV Holland, in which Lush Cosmetics Ltd held 100 per cent of the ordinary shares

■ Lush USA Inc., in which Lush Cosmetics Ltd held 51 per cent of the ordinary shares.

Associate companies are those in which the company owns a significant but not controlling interest (defined as 20–50 per cent of the ordinary shares). In the 2003 accounts, Lush associates included:

■ Lush Sweden AB, in which Lush Cosmetics Ltd held 35 per cent of the ordinary shares

■ Lush Brazil Ltda, in which Lush Cosmetics Ltd held 35 per cent of the ordinary shares.

Note that Lush Retail, in which Lush Cosmetics only owns a 39.8 per cent holding, is listed in the accounts as a subsidiary. This is because Lush Cosmetics has "actual exercise of a dominant influence over the operating and financial policies of Lush Retail". This shows that associate or subsidiary status is not just determined by the percentage of shares owned by a holding, but it also reflects the degree of control the holding company has over the company in which it has invested.

The case for investment

Companies invest in other businesses for a variety of reasons. A company may invest in another business to secure its supply chain, or it may be looking to improve the quality and reliability of its supplies; it may see investment in another business as the best way of expanding into overseas markets or quickly establishing a presence in a new market; it may see the investment as the best way to boost profits and secure improved returns on its capital. In all cases, the investing company is looking to add value to its underlying business.

In assessing whether it is worth investing in another business, a company needs to evaluate the investment in much the same way it would consider any other investment decision. It needs to take a range of quantitative and qualitative factors into account. This means not only evaluating the likely financial return on the investment (usually a quantitative assessment) but reviewing qualitative factor issues such as:

■ the quality of the management running the business that is being targeted for investment

■ the quality of the target business's products and its current market position

■ intangible assets, such as any goodwill or brands built up by the target business, as well as the value of intellectual assets such as patents and copyrights.

Subsidiaries are companies which are controlled by other companies. The controlling company – called the holding company – usually owns at least 51 per cent of the shares in the subsidiary. The holding company has full control, and takes an active interest in the running of the subsidiary.

Associate companies are companies in which a holding company has a significant but not controlling interest. This is defined as owning 20–50 per cent of the ordinary shares. The holding company would usually take an active interest in the running of the associate business, but it would not control decision-making.

Investment companies are companies in which another company has made an investment of up to 20 per cent of the ordinary shares. There is no assumption that the holding company plays an active role in the investment company's management.

Debt investment is a means by which a company invests in another business by way of a loan.

Minority interests are shareholders in a company that is effectively controlled by another company or an individual through a majority shareholding. If, say, a company owns 80 per cent of the shares in a subsidiary, then there is a minority shareholding of 20 per cent in the subsidiary.

■ the potential for synergy – that is, would the two businesses be worth more together than as separate independent entities (will 2 + 2 = 5?).

It is important to identify clear objectives for an investment in another business, and to ensure that the investment case is evaluated in terms of those objectives. In large companies, the directors usually make investment proposals, but shareholders need to ensure that directors have their best interests at heart. This is particularly crucial when directors are proposing substantial investments such as the takeover of another business. Many takeovers add little value to the parent company, but they consume management time and they may be used to justify an increase in director and managerial salaries. Investment in other companies that only benefit the status of the managers is called "empire building".

Types of investment

Any business can invest in another company in a number of ways. One approach is to set up a new company from scratch. Another approach is to invest in an existing business, either through:

■ purchase of equity share capital

■ making that business a loan

■ active involvement in the business, including contributions of assets and expertise.

Equity investment

If a business chooses the equity share capital option, it needs to consider the level of its investment. The key question is what proportion of the shareholding of the target company should the business acquire. This will be largely determined by the purpose of the investment, and the level of the control that the business wishes to exert over the company in which it is investing. There are three broad options: subsidiaries, associates and investment companies.

Subsidiary companies

A business becomes a subsidiary if the holding company acquires more than 50 per cent of its shares, or if the holding company through its position as the dominant shareholder is able to exert decisive influence in the board room (this may not require a 50 per cent holding). A company will want to acquire majority shareholdings if it wishes to control the activities of the businesses in which it invests. Barclays Bank plc owns its worldwide network through a series of subsidiaries. The company operates an international banking network which needs to meet consistent standards worldwide, and this could not be achieved without a high level of control.

Associate companies

An associate company is one in which the holding company has an equity stake of 20–50 per cent of the shares. This is a significant stake, and with any equity holding over 20 per cent there is a presumption that the holding company has a participating interest in the company. This means that the holding company usually has a representative on the board of directors of the associate company, or that the associate company takes advice from the holding company.

business practice
Symbian Ltd

Symbian develops the systems that underpin many mobile phone networks. It is an associate company of Nokia, which has a 47.9 per cent holding, but other technology companies, such as Siemens and Panasonic, have significant stakes. According to Symbian's website, "each of the consortium members [has] contributed management resources, assets, intellectual property and know-how". Symbian is an associate company of Nokia, but it is also a vehicle for collaboration between companies in a project of mutual interest.

Investment companies

An investment company is one in which the holding company has any stake amounting to less than 20 per cent of the total shares. Some companies, for example, choose to invest in some of their suppliers. This enables the investing company to build a long-term relationships with the supplier, and to work with that business to develop high-quality standards.

Loans

Loans from one company to another are not unusual. A loan is a useful form of investment. The lender's liability and involvement is limited to the loan: there is no expectation that the lending company is under any obligation to do anything further to contribute to the management of the business in which it is investing. This may suit both parties.

A loan might be the chosen investment option if a company wants to develop a risky new project. The investing company may not want to be too closely connected with the development. In developing the project through a separate company, the investors can maintain an arms-length relationship through a loan rather than an equity interest.

Another case where a company may make an investment through a loan is in a situation where it sees that it is in its own commercial interest for the business requiring the loan to survive or develop. A company may make a loan to one of its suppliers, if that supplier is a vital part of its supply chain and it needs finance to see it through a tough period or to maintain continuity and quality of supply.

A company may support a new start-up through a loan rather than an equity interest. The Essex Pig Company was set up by Jimmy Doherty with finance from various sources including a loan from his old school friend Jamie Oliver. The Essex Pig Company clearly benefits: it gets both the finance and the goodwill that comes with being connected to Jamie Oliver, and it does not surrender control or decision-making to another business. The arrangement obviously suits Jamie Oliver too: he is in the restaurant and entertainment business, and while he wishes to support his friend's venture, he may not want his business to diversify into pig farming.

Equity versus loan capital

Figure 11.27 summarises the main differences between equity investment (buying shares) and debt investment (making loans). In this topic we have set out why businesses make these kind of investments, but it may be appropriate to end with a health warning. Any investment in another company is risky. A business should not invest in another company if it cannot afford to lose its investment.

It can be difficult to get any real security for the investment. It is not always easy to sell shares in business's in which a company has a stake. There may not be assets to use as security for a loan. More crucially, the survival of the business in which a company invests may be critical for that company's own future, particularly if it provides goods and services that are vital to the investing business. This might mean that the company maintains its investment longer than might seem prudent.

Figure 11.27: Equity versus loan finance

	Equity finance	Loan finance
Timing of repayment	A long-term capital investment. Usually repaid on selling or winding up the business in which the company invests.	Usually long-term, but a company may make a shorter-term loan. Typically repaid at a set date in the future.
Type of return	Dividends – typically a company makes an annual dividend payment if it is profitable. A company may choose to not distribute profits (subject to shareholder vote) and retain profits to grow the business.	Regular interest payments – at a fixed or floating rate as set out in the loan agreement.
Risk associated with investment	Equity capital is the lowest-ranking creditor. If the business has to be wound up, shareholders will be the last to be paid off. In these circumstances, a company will only get its money back if there are sufficient funds.	Loans can be secured against the assets of the business that receives the loan. The creditor has the right to seize the assets if loan repayments are not made when due. If the company goes into liquidation and the loan is not secured, then the loan is unlikely to be repaid in full.

For this exercise, you need to revisit LH Turtle Limited, the traditional DIY supplies and equipment store that first featured in Topic 1. In this exercise, you are to consider the potential for investing in the company.

First, we need to review some of the fundamentals. The business has plenty of potential and goodwill. It is a family business, that is very well known locally, but it is an old-fashioned store. The existing site is in the centre of town, and the only parking nearby is very expensive. It is difficult to collect any sizeable items from the store or to buy DIY supplies in bulk. However, the lease on the company's current premises is due to expire, and the site will be redeveloped for premium retail space.

There is potential to develop the business. The store has a website presence, but this could be greatly enhanced. The store does not run any seasonal promotions of goods which could be sold at a premium profit. For example, it could attractively package sets of tools in the run-up to Christmas, targeted perhaps at young people with instructions on how to build their own bird box, CD rack, etc. Although staff are really helpful to general enquirers, the store does not run basic DIY sessions for customers as some out-of-town competitor stores do.

LH Turtle Ltd is a private limited company. It has an authorised share capital of 80,000 authorised shares at £1. As at 31 January 2005 it had issued 50,000 £1 shares: this is the share capital of the company recorded in the accounts as "allotted, called up and fully paid".

There are three main directors, who are the principal shareholders. They are:

■ JC Turtle, who held 32,367 ordinary shares of £1 each at 31 January 2005

■ MR Turtle, who held 5,000 ordinary shares of £1 each at 31 January 2005

■ SJ Turtle, who held 5,000 ordinary shares of £1 each at 31 January 2005

Figures 11.1 and 11.2 (see page 145) show the company's profit and loss account and balance sheet for the period to 31 January 2005. Other details taken from the notes to these accounts include:

Directors' pay

Directors' emoluments for the year ended 31 January 2005	£62,400

Financial commitments

There were no outstanding loans

Non-cancellable operating leases, expiry date within one year	£98,100

Creditors

Amounts falling due was made up as follows:

Bank loans and overdrafts	£36,320
Trade creditors	£41,914
Taxation and social security	£37,437
Other creditors	£26,364
	£142,035

A Using the company website (www.turtlescroydon.co.uk), the information above and the accounts in Figures 11.1 and 11.2, analyse the strengths, weaknesses, opportunities and threats of LH Turtle Ltd.

B Suppose another company is considering investing in LH Turtle Ltd. Analyse the advantages and disadvantages of each of these options:

i   buying over 50 per cent of the authorised share capital

ii buying 37.5 per cent of the authorised share capital

iii buying a 15 per cent shareholding in LH Turtle Ltd

iv lending the company £500,000

v   providing business expertise and know-how in modern retailing methods.

C Assess the potential risks of investing in LH Turtle Ltd. Recommend whether another company should invest in LH Turtle.

Analysing accounts

Setting the scene: Symbian Ltd

symbian

Symbian (as we saw in Topic 7) was set up by some major technology companies to provide software for the mobile phone telecommunications industry. The company's financial accounts can be downloaded from its website (www.symbian.com).

The company's financial position according to its accounts to 31 December 2004 does not look good. Symbian made a gross profit of £47 million in 2004, on a turnover of £66 million. However, this gross profit was wiped out by operating expenses of £72 million. This meant that the company made a loss of £25 million on ordinary activities before taxation in 2004.

This loss is at least smaller than the previous year, when the accounts shows a £29 million loss to 31 December 2003. The company also has a reasonable asset base, with a net asset value of £44 million as at 31 December 2004.

To probe further into Symbian's financial health, we should undertake ratio analysis. This is

a valuable tool (introduced in Topic 3 and covered further in this topic) for assessing the worth of a business. Ratio analysis needs to be interpreted carefully, by drawing comparisons from past years' results or from similar businesses within the industry.

Ratio analysis also needs to be interpreted within the context of the underlying business. This applies particularly to a company like Symbian. It is working on software developments that should provide a benefit to the businesses of its principal shareholders. In effect, it is a cost centre shared by all its company investors, and traditional ratio analysis needs to be carried out with caution.

Financial analysis

Any business that is considering investing in another company is likely to undertake detailed financial analysis before committing to the investment. Financial accounts are the main source of data for this analysis, and in this topic we show how financial statements can be analysed using ratio analysis to assess a business's underlying financial health and performance.

However, before we start, it is worth noting two points. First, though important, financial accounts do not provide a full picture of any business, so it is always important to look for other supporting evidence when making an assessment of a business. Financial ratios are just one management tool. Second, when analysing accounts, always remember that they have limitations. This is because:

- accounts are out of date even when they are first published, as it takes time to prepare and audit a final set of accounts

- very small companies are allowed by law to produce abbreviated final accounts (which contain less financial information) and they are exempted from the requirement that accounts must be verified by an independent auditor

- larger companies, especially public limited companies, can treat the published accounts as a public relations exercise, and the figures are "spun" in the accompanying text and glossy pictures to paint a rosy picture of the business

KEY TERMS

Ratio analysis is a method of examining financial data. It provides a means of interpreting financial data by measuring aspects of a business's performance.

Liquidity is an assessment of a business's ability to meet its short-term debts. It is a measure of whether the business has enough cash (or assets which can be readily converted into cash) to pay bills and invoices as they come due for payment.

Profitability is a measure of a business's ability to generate more revenue from its activities than it costs to undertake those activities.

Going concerns are businesses that have the resources (current assets and estimated future income streams) to continue in operation for the foreseeable future – taken to mean the next year and a day.

- financial statements look backwards – they report what has happened, not what is going to happen.

Throughout this topic, we shall use the accounts of Ecological Sciences Ltd to illustrate financial analysis. Figures 11.3 and 11.4 (see Topic 1, pages 148–9) show the company's profit and loss account and balance sheet as at 31 December 2004 accounts. In this topic, these accounts are analysed from the point of view of a company considering investing in Ecological Sciences.

Profitability ratios

There are three main profitability ratios: return on net assets, profit margin and asset turnover.

Return on net assets

This is a basic investment measure that considers operating profit (ignoring taxes and loan interest) as a ratio of net assets in order to highlight how the fundamental business is faring.

$$\text{return on net assets} = \frac{\text{operating profit}}{\text{net assets}}$$

Ecological Sciences' return on net assets in 2004 was 47.4 per cent (£185,161/£390,328), up from 40 per cent (£106,903/£267,076) the previous year. It is encouraging that the company's return on its net assets is improving, and returns over 40 per cent and more look very reasonable compared with the interest rates you could get by investing money in a bank.

Profit margin

This is another basic performance measure. A strong profit margin will provide a company with the resources to help it meet its current liabilities, to reward shareholders with a dividend, and to invest further in the business.

$$\text{profit margin} = \frac{\text{operating profit}}{\text{turnover}}$$

Ecological Sciences' profit margin in 2004 was 16.4 per cent (£185,161/£1,127,618), up from 10.8 per cent (£106,903/£988,233). Again this is encouraging, and the company has paid £20,000 in dividends and retained profits to boost cash reserves to use for further investment in the business.

Asset turnover

Asset turnover is a measure of the productivity of the net assets. It shows how many times the net assets have generated their own value in one year.

$$\text{asset turnover} = \frac{\text{turnover}}{\text{net assets}}$$

Ecological Sciences had an asset turnover of 2.89 (£1,127,618/£390,328) in 2004. However, this has fallen: in 2003, asset turnover was 3.7 (£988,233/£267,076). This fall in asset turnover would cause a potential investor to ask further questions. The problem seems to lie with the increase in the net asset value: sales have increased by 14 per cent, but net assets have increased by 46 per cent.

To investigate further, you would look at – and seek to explain – the movements in individual net asset headings between the two years. For example, tangible fixed assets increased by £35,342. A potential investor would want to know when these assets were purchased during the year. What is their function and their expected internal rate of return, and what will be their contribution to profits when they work in the business for a whole year?

You could similarly investigate the changes in other elements of the accounts that comprise net assets:

- stock has increased by £2,022 (82 per cent) – what is the explanation for this?

- debtors has increased by £25,245 (13 per cent) – this does not seem too unreasonable given the 14 per cent increase in sales

- cash has increased by £81,237 (57 per cent) – what is the explanation for this?

- creditors has increased by 10 per cent – this seems reasonable given the increase in turnover.

Liquidity ratios

Liquidity ratios were introduced in Topic 3, where we showed how ratio analysis is a useful tool for assessing how well a business manages its working capital. The main ratios are:

$$\text{current ratio} = \frac{\text{current assets}}{\text{current liabilities}}$$

$$\text{acid test} = \frac{\text{current assets less stock}}{\text{current liabilities}}$$

$$\text{stock turnover} = \frac{\text{turnover}}{\text{stock}}$$

$$\text{debtors days} = \frac{\text{trade debtors}}{\text{turnover}} \times 365$$

Ecological Sciences' current ratio at 31 December 2004 is 1.58 (£451,806/£286,049), compared with

1.3 the previous year. Its acid test is broadly similar, 1.56 at 31 December 2004 and 1.3 the previous year. These results show that Ecological Sciences is a liquid company. It is able to pay its debts as they fall due. There is very little difference between the current ratio and the acid test, as the company holds little stock.

Ecological Sciences' stock turnover ratio was 251 in 2004. This figure is largely meaningless because of the nature of the company's business. It generates a significant proportion of turnover through consultancy services (which has no associated stock), and the stock that it does hold, such as compost, is very low-value and not core to the company's operation.

To calculate debtor days, you need to access the notes to the accounts so that you can find the figure for trade debtors. These are £197,942 at 31 December 2004, and £170,989 at 31 December 2003. Applying these figures in the formula gets debtor days of 64 days (£197,942/£1,127,618 x 365) in 2004, and 63 days in 2003. This means that Ecological Sciences' customers are paying their invoices after about two months on average. Given that many of the company's clients are public sector organisations that can be slow payers as they have bureaucratic procedures, this is not an unreasonable time for debt collection.

Gearing ratios

The main gearing ratio is a measure of a business's long-term financial stability. It is important to potential investors because it shows the extent to which the business is funded through loans, which must be financed through regular interest payments, rather than share capital.

$$\text{gearing ratio} = \frac{\text{long-term liabilities}}{\text{capital employed}}$$

where long-term liabilities = creditors falling due after a year + provisions

capital employed = shareholder funds + long-term liabilities

At 31 December 2004, Ecological Sciences has £38,096 (£20,642 + £17,454) long-term liabilities and £428,424 (£390,328 + £38,096) capital employed. This gives a gearing ratio of 8.9 per cent; the equivalent ratio for 2003 was 14.1 per cent. These figures show that Ecological Sciences Ltd has very low levels of long-term debt. The company could comfortably pay off or service the debt. Indeed, there is the scope for the business to raise further funds for development through long-term debt.

Another gearing ratio that is useful to investors is interest cover. This is a measure of a business's ability to service its debt from its operating profits. If a company has too high a debt burden, it is unlikely to be able to pay dividends to shareholders or retain profits for fuuture investment.

$$\text{interest cover} = \frac{\text{operating profits}}{\text{interest payable}}$$

Ecological Sciences' interest cover in 2004 is 17.2 (£185,161/£10,750); the 2003 figure is 9.7. These interest cover figures show that Ecological Sciences can easily pay its interest payments as they fall due. This reinforces the image of liquidity, and emphasises the fact that the company could manage a higher debt burden if it was needed.

Shareholder ratios

There are two shareholder ratios which would be of interest to any potential investor in Ecological Sciences. These are return on equity and dividend cover.

Return on equity is a measure of the rate of return that shareholders have obtained on the capital that they have invested in a business.

$$\text{return on equity} = \frac{\text{profit after tax}}{\text{shareholder funds}}$$

Ecological Sciences' return on equity was 36.7 per cent (£143,252/£390,328) in 2004, and 29.7 per cent in 2003. This shows that the company is generating good profits from the assets it employs, and isincreasing the margin of its returns.

Dividend cover shows whether a firm can meet its dividend payments out of its earnings. Note that some firms may choose to finance dividend payments from their reserves during times of low profitability to keep their shareholders happy.

$$\text{dividend cover} = \frac{\text{profit after tax}}{\text{dividends}}$$

Ecological Sciences' dividend cover was 7.2 times (£143,252/£20,000) in 2004, and 3.96 times in 2003. This means that the company could easily cover its dividend payments in both years.

Public limited companies

Ecological Sciences is a private limited company, which means that its shares are not traded on a stock exchange. However, if a company is considering investing in a public limited company (whose shares may be freely bought and sold), it would need to consider some other shareholder ratios. These ratios would be of potential interest.

$$\text{earnings per share} = \frac{\text{profit after tax}}{\text{number of issued shares}}$$

$$\text{dividends per share} = \frac{\text{dividends}}{\text{number of issued shares}}$$

$$\text{price earnings ratio} = \frac{\text{market price per share}}{\text{earnings per share}}$$

$$\text{dividend yield} = \frac{\text{dividend per share}}{\text{market price per share}}$$

These ratios are used by investors to judge the value of their shareholdings and to make comparisons between the performance of public companies. They are used by financial analysts to assess whether a company's shares are under- or over-priced.

Conclusions

The analysis shows that Ecological Sciences as at 31 December 2004 was a thriving business with a healthy profit margin (16.4 per cent). It could pay its debts as they fell due, it had very few long-term liabilities, and was established in the ecological waste management business. In short, it was a potentially attractive investment proposition.

It is interesting to note what happened next. On 31 January 2005 the entire issued share capital of the company was sold to Glendale Managed Services Ltd, a wholly-owned subsidiary of Parkwood Holdings plc. Ecological Sciences Ltd was purchased for £660,000 in cash plus £50,000 deferred consideration.

Glendale Managed Services deals mainly through long-term contracts with local authorities. The acquisition of Ecological Sciences was seen as a way of entering the "green waste recycling market", making Glendale's bids to local authorities more attractive. Glendale's management judged that while Ecological Sciences would generate profits as an independent company, it could produce an even better yield if combined with Glendale's expertise winning local government contracts. The 2005 interim report of Parkwood Holdings suggests that the acquisition was proving to be a shrewd investment.

assessment practice
Nutec Centre for Safety Ltd

After the Hemel Hempstead oil depot explosions and fires, Nutec Centre for Safety Ltd (www.nuteccentreforsafety.co.uk) is facing various opportunities. Imagine that you are working for a company that is interested in investing in Nutec to add to its portfolio of companies and business-to-business links.

You need to assess the company's potential using information from its financial accounts (see Figures 11.11 and 11.12, pages 161–2) and its website (www.nuteccentreforsafety.co.uk). You know that Nutec is owned by a holding company, Global Safety BV (formerly Nutec MTC Holdings BV), which has its registered office in the Netherlands.

The share capital of Nutec Centre for Safety Limited is:

■ authorised share capital 1,000,000 ordinary shares of £1 each

■ allotted, called up and fully paid ordinary shares of £1 each 950,245.

A Analyse the accounts of Nutec Centre for Safety Ltd using ratio analysis, drawing (in part) on any analysis you undertook in completing the data interpretation exercise at the end of Topic 3.

B Consider the scope to invest in Nutec as a subsidiary, an associate company, an investment company and through long-term loans.

C Consider any other non-numerical factors that might affect another company's interest in investing in Nutec Centre for Safety Ltd.

THIS UNIT EXAMINES WHY SOME BUSINESSES operate internationally. It features a range of different types of businesses that have an international presence and considers the impact of international trade on the businesses and economies of host countries.

It presents the context in which international business operates by examining institutions such as the European Union and World Trade Organization that control and regulate international trade. The European Union has policies and regulations on, for example, trade barriers and tariffs, subsidies for farmers, and taxes, and the unit considers the impact of this regulation on businesses and the cost implications of not meeting international agreements.

In working through this unit, you will investigate some businesses that have an international presence. This will involve gathering information about a business in terms of its legal format, target markets, sector and product range. You will define its aims and strategic objectives for having an international presence, and identify the competition it faces in domestic and overseas markets. You will consider the impact of the business's activities on customers, competitors, suppliers and the host countries.

International dimensions of business

Businesses with an international presence

Setting the scene: Paul Smith, fashion designer

Paul Smith started work when he was 16 in a clothing warehouse in his home town of Nottingham. He really wanted to be a professional racing cyclist. But when he was 17, he was involved in a serious accident which put him in hospital for six months and shattered his cycling ambitions.

Following his accident, Paul started studying tailoring at evening classes and designing menswear. His girlfriend Pauline – now his wife – was a graduate of the Royal College of Arts and helped Paul with his creations. Within two years, Paul was managing his first boutique. It was the beginning of an unparalleled success story in British fashion.

Today Paul Smith is the pre-eminent British designer, with 14 shops in England. Paul still designs in Nottingham and London, and his clothes are produced in Britain and Italy, mainly from British, Italian, and French fabrics. His collections include:

Paul Smith

Paul Smith Women

PS by Paul Smith

Paul Smith Jeans

Paul Smith London

R Newbold (Japan)

Paul Smith Accessories

Paul Smith Shoes

Paul Smith Fragrance

Paul Smith Watches

Paul Smith Pens.

When Paul Smith started in business in the 1970s, England was not the fashion capital of the world. To be noticed as a fashion designer, Paul knew he had to show his designs abroad. In 1976 he showed his first menswear collection in Paris under the Paul Smith label.

To conquer the fashion world and fulfil his potential, Paul continues to look beyond the UK. He has opened shops in Paris, Milan, New York, Hong Kong, Singapore, Taiwan, the Philippines, Korea, Kuwait, UAE and Japan. His collections are also wholesaled to 35 countries, where they are available through other fashion retail outlets.

Despite the growth and global nature of his business, Paul remains fully involved in the company as both designer and chairman. As a result, Paul Smith Limited retains a personal touch often absent in companies of a similar size and global reach.

Source: www.paulsmith.co.uk

Developing an international presence

Businesses develop an international presence for a variety of reasons. This means that there is no such entity as a typical international business. Consider these four examples of UK businesses with an international presence:

- BP plc is one of the world's largest energy companies

- Action Aid is a major children's charity, formed in the UK and now operating throughout the world

- Eddie Stobart Ltd is one of the UK's largest haulage and logistics businesses, with depots throughout the UK and Europe

- Anita Burghley is a jewellery designer, who has a workshop in London and works in partnership with a jeweller in Milan, Italy.

Obviously these businesses are very different in terms of size, type of ownership and aims. But they all share one aspect: they operate internationally in order to grow and become more successful.

In Topic 2, we look at some of the main reasons for developing an international presence. Here we consider some of the factors that influence whether or not a business develops an international presence (see Figure 12.1). We shall concentrate on four key aspects – legal format, target market, sector and product range – and show how they affect the ability of the business to develop internationally.

Legal format and size

Most businesses with an international presence tend to be large by their very nature. Indeed, the largest businesses in the world – such as the US car giant General Motors and the Japanese industrial group Mitsui – are international businesses. This has implications especially for control, management and finance. Larger businesses are more complex, with more staff and operations in different locations. They need a legal format that enables them to develop appropriate management systems and to get easier access to more substantial sources of funding.

A public limited company has access to more sources of finance, which it can use to drive growth through employing specialist staff and managers and to invest in technology and operating systems to help increase productivity. Public limited companies are therefore likely to find it easier to develop international operations.

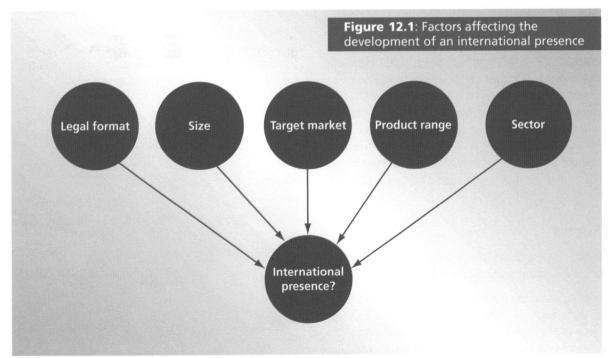

Figure 12.1: Factors affecting the development of an international presence

Legal format · Size · Target market · Product range · Sector

International presence?

However, this does not mean that businesses with other types of ownership – sole traders, partnerships, private limited companies, etc. – do not develop an international presence. Other forms of ownership have their own benefits. For example, by remaining a private limited company, Paul Smith has retained control of his business and yet he has been able to expand internationally through inspired marketing and by taking advantage of foreign demand for his products.

Smaller businesses can also develop an international presence by forming partnerships with businesses in other countries. This may involve a reciprocal selling arrangement, in which each business agrees to sell or distribute the products of the other partner in its domestic market. Each business retains its original form of ownership, although a more complex management structure might be needed if the arrangement leads to a big increase in production and sales. In time, this may also lead to a change in legal structure and type of ownership.

Target market

Any decision to develop an international presence must be based on research into the target market. Paul Smith decided to develop an international presence because the market – and demand – for his products is worldwide. By setting up his own shops in several countries, he has been able to supply international markets more efficiently and cost-effectively.

If the target market is purely local or national, then an international sales presence is obviously inappropriate. However, a business selling exclusively to its domestic market may still have an international operation. For example, a business may base some of its operation overseas if factors such as the availability of raw materials and parts, and the cost and availability of labour, are significant. A manufacturer of wooden pallets – a pallet is a base on which goods are stacked for transporting – may decide to acquire a forest and operate a timber mill in, say, Portugal in order to ensure that it has a steady supply of cheaper timber for its UK operation.

Sector

Businesses are classified as operating in one of three sectors: primary, secondary and tertiary.

Primary sector businesses are involved with growing or extracting raw materials. They tend to be located close to the sources of those raw materials. An international presence may therefore be appropriate if the materials are found in more than one country. The oil company Exxon, for example, has operations worldwide in the many countries and regions in which there are large oil deposits.

Secondary sector businesses take the products of the primary sector and refine them, or use them to manufacture finished products. They may locate close to sources of raw materials or their markets, depending on factors such as transport costs. For example, the Denby Pottery factory near Derby in the Midlands is located close to its source of raw materials. There is a china clay quarry at Denby. The car manufacturer Toyota also has a factory outside Derby. Toyota located its UK production site here because the excellent transport links enable the company to ship cars easily to its markets throughout UK and across Europe.

Tertiary sector businesses supply services, including retailing and distribution. Tertiary sector businesses are often the easiest to set up with an international presence. Many businesses in the tertiary sector establish an international presence. Barclays Bank, for example, operates internationally through offices linked by an extensive computer network.

Product range

Product range refers to the different products in a business's product portfolio. Some products have a purely local or regional appeal. A business which includes products that have a broader appeal in its portfolio is more likely to develop an international presence. Fashion is an increasingly global area of business, as styles of dress become more universal through media exposure on television and in magazines. Paul Smith's fashion designs are popular throughout the world and it therefore makes sense for him to have outlets internationally.

datainterpretation
BT Group plc

Before it was privatised, BT was the monopoly provider of telephone and telecommunications services in the United Kingdom. BT is now a global service provider, both in B2B (business to business) and B2C (business to consumer) markets. Although still based in the UK, the group has operations in 70 countries, spanning Asia and the Pacific, Europe and the United States. The group has some 100,000 employees, and its turnover was £18.6 billion in the financial year ending 31 March 2005.

In its B2B markets, BT specialises in helping multi-site organisations communicate and collaborate – any time, any place, through any device. The group is building the world's most advanced global IP (internet protocol) network, and it provides a wide range of options for transmitting voice, video and data.

Today, 10,000 major organisations worldwide trust BT with their communication requirements, including 3,400 multinational companies. Within the BT Group, there is a network of companies that provide services to the B2B market. These include:

- BT Albacom – the second-largest telecoms operator in the Italian business market, providing data transmission, voice and internet services to more than 240,000 Italian businesses and to international companies active in Italy

- BT Infonet – one of the world's leading providers of global managed voice and data network services for corporate customers

- Radianz – specialising in supplying secure, reliable and scalable connectivity to the global financial community.

There is more information about the BT Group on its corporate website www.btplc.com.

A What is the legal format of BT?

B How do you think the legal format of BT has helped the group to develop an international presence?

C Describe the target markets of BT.

D In what way have the target markets and product range of BT influenced the group's decision to develop an international presence?

Topic 1 Businesses with an international presence

Why businesses have an international presence

Setting the scene: Dyson becomes a world-beater

James Dyson's story shows how it is possible to build an international business from a good idea. It arose out of frustration with a standard household product: the vacuum cleaner. Vacuum cleaners work by sucking up dirt and depositing it in a bag. But as the bag fills, the efficiency of the vacuum reduces, and the cleaner's performance markedly suffers.

Dyson's idea was to overcome this problem by developing a bagless cleaner. Between 1979 and 1984, Dyson – an engineer by trade – built numerous prototypes. He knew the idea was good. The product worked and, he believed, it would have an international market: people all over the developed world want labour-saving devices to keep their homes clean.

Major multinational companies in both the UK and Europe were reluctant to invest in the idea. They had a considerable investment in the vacuum bag replacement market – worth some £100 million a year in the UK alone. So Dyson decided to produce his vacuum cleaner – now called the G-Force – himself. In 1986, he managed to break into the Japanese market, where the bagless vacuum proved a success.

Dyson knew that design as well as technical innovation was important if he was to take on the competition. He tested his ideas on an international stage. The G-Force was displayed at the British Design Exhibition in Vienna in 1987, and the New Traditions exhibition in Rotterdam, where it was featured on the poster. In 1991, Dyson's G-Force cleaner won the International Design Fair prize in Japan.

Success meant that Dyson could open his own research centre and factory in Chippenham, Wiltshire. Here he developed the Dyson DC01, which has become the best-selling vacuum cleaner ever, outselling its nearest competitor by a ratio of five to one. In August 1995 Dyson Appliances moved into a larger factory in Malmesbury.

Not every product developed by James Dyson comes off. In 2000, he launched a washing machine with two counter-rotating drums intended to mimic the action of hand washing. Selling at almost £1,000, the washing machine failed to establish itself, largely being seen as a gimmick.

However, the Dyson cleaners have found new markets. As well as selling in Japan and the UK, they have become popular in Europe and elsewhere. Sales and service subsidiaries have now been set up in Australia, Europe and the US.

In order to reduce manufacturing costs and be close to foreign suppliers and markets, Dyson has moved production to Malaysia, leaving only small production and research facilities in the UK. The washing machine has now been withdrawn from the UK domestic market, but Dyson's bagless vacuum cleaners continue to be world-beaters.

Source www.dyson.co.uk

Aims and objectives

Businesses develop an international presence for many reasons and, in this topic, we present the most common reasons for international expansion. At the outset, it is worth stressing that any decision by a business to develop an international presence must be based on its aims and objectives. It is important to focus the efforts towards the business's goals and not become distracted by other agendas.

Increasing sales

Many businesses develop an international presence in order to increase sales by accessing a larger, international market. The population of the United Kingdom is only around 60 million, while the population of the European Union as a whole is some 457 million, offering businesses the opportunity of selling to a much larger market. The population of the United States is 291 million.

Some markets are effectively international. For example, mobile telephones are now in everyday use throughout much of the world and it therefore makes sense for companies like Sony Ericsson and Nokia – the main manufacturers of mobiles – to have an international sales operation. This allows them to access a much wider market and reap the benefit from increased sales.

Profit maximisation

Profit is sales revenue minus expenditure. In order to maximise profit, a business must maximise sales revenue while minimising expenditure. Developing an international presence may help it achieve this: it might be able to increase sales in the larger market while containing or reducing expenditure through economies of scale.

Economies of scale are the cost benefits obtained from increased production and sales. For example, if larger quantities of raw materials are required to meet the needs of increased production, a business can negotiate higher discounts, thereby reducing the unit cost of production. This cost saving can be kept as increased profit or passed on to customers by reducing prices, which might of course generate further increases in sales.

Attracting new staff

Staff are integral to many business operations. Increasingly businesses are looking internationally both to obtain the right skills base and to deliver

efficiencies in staffing costs. Many large companies are transferring part of their operations abroad in order to take advantage of lower labour costs and to utilise specific skills found in other countries.

BT and Norwich Union, for example, have set up call centres in countries such as India to reduce their staff costs. Dyson has taken advantage of the mix of high-quality manufacturing skills and low wages found in a developing industrial economy like Malaysia to transfer production facilities abroad.

Improving customer service

Good customer service is an increasingly important aspect of business in today's world. This includes delivering a product where and when it is required by customers, and providing information and after-sales help. When a business's customers are in many countries, good customer service can often best be delivered by establishing a presence in those countries.

Many Japanese camera manufacturers, for example, have established sales and service facilities in other countries. They recognise that you are much less likely to buy a Japanese camera if you have to return it to the manufacturer in Japan in the event of it developing a fault. Sony, for example, has established a chain of dedicated sales outlets in major towns throughout the UK, and service and spare parts are available from its facility in Melton Mowbray, Leicestershire.

Cost cutting

We have noted that some businesses switch production and other facilities to other countries to take advantage of lower wage rates. However, an international presence can also cut costs in other ways. By servicing a larger market, companies can benefit from economies of scale and reduce their unit production costs (see above). By locating close to their sources of raw materials, or nearer to their customers, they can cut distribution costs.

Increasing efficiency

Efficiency is a measure of how well resources such as labour, raw materials and capital are used to produce and sell goods and services. The efficiency of a business has a direct impact on its average unit costs of production, and consequently on the profitability of the business.

The efficiency of a business can be measured by:

- profitability
- costs
- labour productivity
- capital productivity
- waste control.

We have seen that some businesses can lower costs and increase profitability through establishing an international presence. By organising international operations appropriately, a company can also benefit from other efficiency gains.

The British wine importer and distributor AJ Howling Ltd decided to relocate its buying operations to several of the major wine-producing regions, opening offices in Australia, Bulgaria, France and South America. By moving its buyers overseas, staff in the London-based part of the operation could focus on the warehousing, marketing and distribution side of the business. Overal,l Howling employs the same number of people worldwide, but the reorganisation produced a 20 per cent increase in labour productivity in its first year, partly due to the fact that each staff role had a greater degree of specialisation.

Appealing to a global market

A business may want to appeal to a global market for various reasons:

- some products, such as cars, fashion clothes and financial services, naturally appeal to a global market

- some products have a small domestic market, so that a larger market is needed to generate sufficient sales – an aircraft manufacturer like Boeing needs to operate on an international scale to generate significant sales volume

- some products may be declining in domestic markets, so a business may seek to sell in a global market as an extension policy – as sales of cigarettes decline in Western Europe, tobacco companies have switched focus to other markets.

Appealing to a global market, however, requires extensive market research and marketing. Consumers in different parts of the world have different tastes and requirements. Products may need to be altered in order to meet demand in other countries, and this may involve research and development. Market research, marketing, and research and development all cost money, and before taking a decision to establish an international presence to generate more sales, a business must weigh anticipated benefits against costs.

assessment practice
Tesco, grocer to the world

Tesco stores are a familiar sight in high streets and retail parks throughout the UK. In fact in 2005, £3 out of every £10 spent on groceries throughout the UK was spent in Tesco. And it's not just groceries. Tesco is now the largest clothing retailer in the UK as well.

The company has come a long way since its beginnings in a partnership between Jack Cohen and T E Stockwell in 1919 at the end of the First World War. Then it was no more than a few stalls in north London markets. But Tesco hasn't stopped growing since.

Tesco's long-term strategy for growth is based on four elements: to continue growth in the UK, to expand by growing internationally, to be as strong in non-food as in food markets, and to follow customers into new retailing services.

Today the group operates in 13 European and Asian markets (including the UK). Over 100,000 of Tesco's 367,000 employees work in the group's international operations, serving over 15 million customers and generating £370 million profit on sales of £7.6 billion.

In its 2005/06 financial year, Tesco planned to open 318 new stores, of which 207 were outside the UK. Even before this expansion, over half the store space is now outside the UK. A full breakdown of Tesco's international operations can be found on the company's corporate website, www.tescocorporate.com

Operating in international markets means adapting to the needs of customers.

■ In Thailand, stores open for the first time at 9.09 am precisely, as the Thai people believe that these numbers bring good fortune.

■ Tesco's expanding online E-Homeplus service in South Korea offers up to ten delivery slots every day so customers can get their groceries delivered when it suits them.

■ In Tokyo, many consumers like to shop daily for small amounts of extremely fresh food. Hypermarket formats don't meet the needs of these customers, so Tesco entered the Japanese market by acquiring a smaller-scale supermarket operator.

The company's stated aim is to create value for customers to earn their lifetime loyalty. It realises that success depends on people: customers and employees. If customers like what Tesco offers, they are more likely to return. If employees find their work rewarding, they are more likely to go that extra mile to help customers.

Source www.tesco.com

A What are the aims of Tesco as given in this mini case study? What other aims do you think that Tesco has?

B Suggest objectives that Tesco could adopt in trying to achieve its aims. Is there any evidence in the case study that Tesco has adopted these objectives?

C How is Tesco's international presence helping it to achieve its aims?

Competition at home and overseas

Setting the scene: battle of the giants

Coca-Cola is the world's leading manufacturer, marketer and distributor of non-alcoholic beverages. Coke is one of the most famous products in the world, but it is just one of nearly 400 beverage brands produced by Coca-Cola.

Coca-Cola's corporate headquarters are in the United States, but it has local operations in over 200 countries around the world. In 2004, total sales of Coca-Cola's products were almost $22 billion. More than 70 per cent of the company's income comes from outside the US. Coca-Cola's products meet the varied taste preferences of consumers everywhere.

Pepsi-Cola is a division of PepsiCo, Inc. PepsiCo's soft drinks include Pepsi, Diet Pepsi, Pepsi Twist, Mountain Dew, Mountain Dew Code Red, Sierra Mist and Mug Root Beer. These account for nearly one-third of total soft drink sales in the United States.

PepsiCo is one of the world's largest food and beverage companies. The company's principal businesses include Frito-Lay snacks, Pepsi-Cola beverages, Gatorade sports drinks, Tropicana juices and Quaker Foods.

PepsiCo brands are available in nearly 200 countries and territories, and they generate annual retail sales of around $78 billion. Many of PepsiCo's brand names are more than 100 years old. PepsiCo's mission is "to be the world's premier consumer products company focused on convenience foods and beverages".

Sources: www.cocacola.com and www.pepsi.com

KEY TERMS

Monopolistic competition is a market in which there is a range of suppliers each with a product that is differentiated from the products of its competitors: each product is therefore unique.

A **monopoly** exists where a major supplier is able – by virtue of its dominant market share – to control the market, setting prices and levels of quality and service provision. A major supplier is defined as a business that has 25 per cent or more of the market for its product. Situations where there is only a single supplier in a market are rare, and mainly exist for services such as defence and the police, provided by the government.

An **oligopoly** is a market comprising a few major suppliers. Products are broadly similar, and can be substitutes for each other, and competition is largely based on price.

Perfect competition exists in a market in which there are a large number of suppliers competing for the same business. Customers have a genuine choice of suppliers, and can make decisions about which product to buy based on a comparison of prices, quality and service provision.

Types of competition

Competition exists where two or more suppliers are trying to sell their products to the same customers. The degree of competition in a market depends on the number of suppliers of goods or services in the market, and is relative to the size of that market.

In a small market, even a few suppliers of the same or similar product can give rise to a high degree of competition. A new business may find it difficult to become established in this situation because of the high costs of marketing, and low prices and levels of sales.

It is very difficult to successfully launch a new national daily in the UK newspaper market, for example. Any prospective newspaper publisher faces high set-up costs and significant ongoing production costs, coupled with low levels of sales (at least initially) and keen pricing,

In a relatively large market, such as that for ringtones for mobile phones, a new business may find it easy to

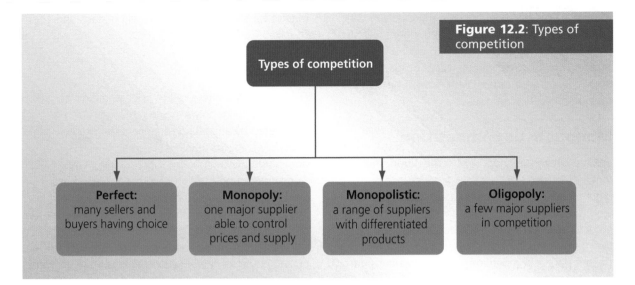

Figure 12.2: Types of competition

Types of competition

Perfect: many sellers and buyers having choice

Monopoly: one major supplier able to control prices and supply

Monopolistic: a range of suppliers with differentiated products

Oligopoly: a few major suppliers in competition

become established (if it has the technology) even if there are already many suppliers.

As the degree of competition in a market can significantly affect the ability of a business to achieve its aims, it is important to be able to assess market conditions and their effects. While it may not be possible to know the exact number of suppliers of a particular product in any market, it is possible to differentiate the degree of competition in different markets. This is done by dividing markets into four broad types.

Perfect competition

In a market in which there is perfect competition, there is a large number of suppliers providing goods and services to many customers. These customers have full knowledge of the goods and services provided by suppliers, including their prices. Customers can therefore choose freely between suppliers, and make informed decisions about which products to purchase. Competition to win customers from other suppliers is based on price, quality and service provision. Levels of marketing are high.

Any business can enter a market in which there is perfect competition. The business can freely compete with rival suppliers. However, in doing so, it must be aware of its competitors' products and prices. Unless it can at least match its rivals, by offering products that meet the needs of customers at competitive prices, customers will take their business to a competing supplier. In these markets, a USP (unique selling proposition) may help a business to win customers for its product.

An example of a market in which there is (almost) perfect competition is the fast food restaurant business. Gina's is a small pizza restaurant and

takeaway in Derby, one of many fast food restaurants ranging from fish and chip shops and small Indian and Chinese restaurants, to large multinational chains such as McDonald's and Kentucky Fried Chicken. Gina's competes very successfully on quality and service, and by offering a free delivery service in the local area. The restaurant is well known locally.

A restaurant chain like McDonald's, however, benefits from its strong brand and international presence. It operates throughout the world, and has access to the financial resources that enable it to market on a large scale and keep costs and prices to a minimum. Customers (and indeed non-customers) know the McDonald's name and brand, and will often seek out a McDonald's rather than a similar restaurant.

Monopoly

Monopoly is the opposite of perfect competition. A monopoly exists in a market in which products and prices can be unduly influenced by one major supplier. In this context, a major supplier is defined as any business that has at least 25 per cent of the market.

A new business will find it difficult to break into this type of market because of the difficulty of winning customers from the monopoly supplier. A monopoly supplier usually has the resources to compete with any threat to its position by reducing prices, improving quality, developing new products, mounting expensive marketing campaigns, and so on.

A monopoly is considered unfair competition and detrimental to consumers, who have to pay the prices and accept the product quality set by the monopoly supplier. Monopoly situations are therefore closely monitored and controlled, and if necessary broken up. In the UK, this is done by the Office of Fair Trading and the Competition Commission.

The Royal Mail still functions as a monopoly in the postal letter business in the UK, although it will be forced to allow other businesses to offer a letter service. The Royal Mail already faces competition in other areas of its business, with many other carriers offering parcel post services.

Monopolistic competition

In a market with monopolistic competition, there is a range of suppliers each with a product that is differentiated from the products of its competitors (and therefore unique). Consumers have a choice of product, and can select the product that most suits their needs. This contrasts with markets in which there is perfect competition, where consumers are likely to be faced with many suppliers offering similar products, and competition is likely to be on price.

In the UK, national daily newspapers operate in a market that is characterised by monopolistic competition. Each newspaper has its own features and characteristics and largely competes with other similar newspapers on the basis of price and, increasingly, free giveaways such as CDs and DVDs or special offers.

In monopolistic situations, suppliers must ensure that their products have sufficient features to make them attractive to customers. A business seeking to enter a global market in which there is monopolistic competition must ensure that its product is clearly differentiated, and it will need to undertake considerable promotion to make potential customers aware of the product. This situation exists in the market for cars – particularly family saloons and so-called executive cars.

Oligopoly

Oligopoly is often referred to as competition between the few. An oligopoly exists in a market which is dominated by a few large suppliers. An example of an oligopoly is the UK groceries market, which is dominated by the four big supermarket chains – Tesco, Sainsbury, Asda and Morrison. These have grown by buying up other chains and smaller outlets. The grocery market is closely monitored by the Office of Fair Trading, and in May 2006 it asked the Competition Commission to examine whether the buying power of the big supermarkets was distorting competition. This is will be the third investigation into the grocery market in seven years.

The strength of oligopolistic competition makes it difficult for a new business to enter the market. A business seeking to enter a global market which is controlled by an oligopoly is unlikely to succeed without considerable resources.

Sometimes suppliers in an oligopoly combine to protect their market from new entrants or to set prices, levels of production (and also therefore prices) or quality. These informal agreements or collusion between major suppliers in an oligopoly are known as cartels. Like monopolies, they are able to influence the market in a way that is detrimental to customers. Cartels are also therefore considered unfair competition and subject to the same control as monopolies.

assessment practice
British Airways vs Virgin Atlantic

British Airways and Virgin Atlantic are two of the largest airlines based in the UK. In 1999, Virgin Atlantic made a complaint to the European Commission that British Airways had abused its dominant position in the market.

Virgin alleged that British Airways was trying to influence travel agents unfairly by offering the agents large discounts for equalling or surpassing their previous years' sales of British Airways tickets. British Airways was able to do this because of its size and financial resources.

Virgin complained that the practice was unfair to competing airlines because travel agents, keen to obtain the higher discounts, tended to offer British Airways tickets rather than those of other airlines to clients.

A **What kind of competition exists in the airline market?**

B **Explain the statement that "British Airways had abused its dominant position".**

C **Do you agree with Virgin Atlantic's complaint? Justify your answer.**

D **What action do you think should have been taken if the complaint was upheld?**

Strategic objectives and the theory of comparative advantage

Setting the scene: Marks & Spencer fights back

For many years, Marks & Spencer was considered one of the UK's leading businesses. The government even suggested that public sector organisations such as schools and the National Health Service would benefit from adopting some of Marks & Spencer's management practicse.

But in the late 1990s things started going wrong for the company. It faced increasing competition, it had an outdated image, and Marks & Spencer's once-loyal customers started looking to other retail chains for clothing. Marks & Spencer's profits dropped dramatically and its share price fell, prompting the possibility of a takeover bid.

The paragon of British retailing was in serious trouble, and it needed to rethink its strategy. This involved a change in emphasis in both home and foreign operations. Some overseas retail outlets, notably in France, were closed in order to save costs. Other retail outlets in Europe, the United States and the Far East were sold off or cut back. Today, Marks & Spencer still operates abroad, and its overall strategy commits the company to expansion in overseas markets.

The slump in profits has also forced Marks & Spencer to rethink its production strategy. It had always been the company's policy to produce own-label goods sourced from UK suppliers wherever possible. This is an expensive strategy, and in a move to reduce costs Marks & Spencer decided to switch some production abroad to countries with cheaper labour. It is setting up fabric production in Turkey, for example. By reducing the amount of stock it holds, and by moving production to cheaper suppliers, Marks & Spencer hopes to save around £260 million and increase its operating margins by over 2 per cent.

Marks & Spencer's managers have also realised that the market is changing, and that it needs to be more responsive to market trends to retain customers. In response, the company is introducing cheaper, fast-fashion lines to compete with retailers such as Primark.

The strength of Marks & Spencer remains its name, experience and reputation. These still give the company a competitive edge and a comparative advantage over many of its rivals. Coupled with its new strategies, this should see the company regaining its position as a leading retailer over the next few years.

Strategic objectives

The strategic objectives of a business are its long-term targets. These targets set out what the business is trying to achieve in order to fulfil its overall corporate aims. Typical corporate aims include:

- maximising profit
- increasing profitability (that is, raising profit margins)
- maximising sales revenue
- growth
- increasing market share
- meeting the needs of stakeholders.

A business must identify the strategic objectives that will help it realise its corporate aims. For example, a business that has an aim of maximising profitability may set a strategic objective of reducing costs. This was the approach that Marks & Spencer adopted (see introduction) – the company looked to cut its production costs to improve its profit margins.

The strategy of the business is its plan of action, which sets out how its strategic objectives will be accomplished. For example, a business that aims to increase market share may set a strategic objective of becoming more price competitive in order to win customers from other businesses. It may therefore develop a strategy which involves improving its efficiency, so that it matches or betters its competitors' prices, and it may seek to achieve efficiency and productivity gains by introducing new technology.

Many businesses can achieve their aims in local (or domestic) markets; however, some businesses adopt a strategy of developing or expanding their international presence to achieve their goals. This could be for several reason.

- By looking for sales in larger international markets, a business may be able to increase its sales.

- By increasing sales through overseas expansion, a business may be able to reduce its unit costs through economies of scale in production.

- By establishing a local presence in countries in which it has significant sales, a business may be able to provide better customer service.

- By locating closer to its international markets or its sources of raw materials, a business may be able to reduce transport costs and improve distribution.

- By relocating some operations to other countries, a business may be able to take advantage of lower wage rates and reduce other costs.

In all cases, any move to develop an international presence should be designed to achieve strategic objectives derived from corporate aims, such as increasing sales by being more competitive or finding new markets.

For example, Marks & Spencer's decisions to close some of its overseas stores, to look for suppliers outside the UK and to set up production facilities in countries where costs are lower were taken to achieve its strategic objective of reducing costs. In other words, decisions on its international presence were taken once it had established its strategic objectives, which in turn were set to achieve its overall corporate aim of increasing profitability.

When identifying strategic objectives and strategies that will help it achieve its corporate aims, a business must take into account its own strengths and weaknesses, and the opportunities and threats that will arise from following a particular course of action. This should, of course, involve a SWOT analysis. It should also any comparative advantage it has over its competitors.

Absolute and comparative advantage

The theory of comparative advantage was originally applied to the economies of countries, and it is used to explain international trade. It is based on the concept of opportunity cost. The opportunity cost of producing a particular good or service is the alternative goods or services that could be produced using the same resources.

It is perhaps easier to explain the concept of opportunity cost through some examples. If, for example, a country decided to use its timber resources to build new houses, the opportunity cost of the new houses would be the furniture, paper and other products that could have been produced using the same timber. Similarly, if a country decides to allocate labour to producing coal, the opportunity cost of the coal is the alternative goods or services that could have been produced using the same labour.

So how do countries decide how to use their resources? Some countries are better suited to producing particular goods and services than others. There are many reasons for this: for example, France is better at producing wine than the UK because its soil and climate are better suited to growing vines; Japan is better at producing cars than Nigeria because it has the appropriate technology and a skilled workforce.

The climate, traditions and soil give France a natural advantage in producing good wine

Variations in the availability of raw materials and in access to other factors of production (such as technology and skilled labour) mean that particular goods and services can be produced more cost-effectively or to a higher standard in some countries than in others. A country that can produce a product more cost-effectively – or at a lower opportunity cost – than other countries is said to have an absolute advantage in that type of product.

Countries therefore tend to specialise in producing those goods and services in which they have an absolute advantage. Note that, in market economies, actual decisions on the use of resources are not taken by central governments but by businesses. However, these general principles of absolute advantage and opportunity cost still apply.

Again it is perhaps easier to understand these principles by considering an example. Figure 12.3 shows the amount of labour typically required to produce two different goods in two countries. It shows that Malaysia has an absolute advantage in producing food, while the UK has an absolute advantage in producing clothes.

If each country in Figure 12.3 now channels its labour resources into producing those goods in which it has an absolute advantage, so Malaysia produces only food and the UK produces only clothes (see Figure 12.4), the maximum advantage is taken of the labour costs in each country. So with lower labour costs for each unit of each product, the combined total production would show a production increase in each type of good.

Figure 12.3: Labour requirements of producing food and clothes, UK and Malaysia

Unit labour requirement (hours per unit of production)	Malaysia	UK
Food	5	6
Clothes	60	30
Total for one unit of each product	65	36

Figure 12.4: Labour requirements of producing food and clothes, UK and Malaysia, using absolute advantage

Unit labour requirement (hours per unit of production)	Malaysia	UK
Food	5	0
Clothes	0	30
Total for one unit of each product	5	30

Any surplus production of clothes in the UK could then be traded for surplus production of food in Malaysia. This benefits both countries in two ways.

- More units of each type of product are available for consumers in both countries.

- Average production costs of each of type product are lower, which should result in lower prices for customers.

If the increased production also gives rise to economies of scale, further cost savings will be generated for both consumers and suppliers.

Of course, the real situation is more complicated because labour is not the only factor of production. Other factors must be taken into consideration, including the cost and availability of raw materials, the level of capital used in production, the efficiency of producers in each country, and exchange rates.

This complexity doesn't alter the key point that the principles of absolute advantage and opportunity cost underpin international trade. Countries – and businesses – specialise in particular goods and services because they have:

- they have easy and relatively cheap access to the raw materials

- an appropriately skilled workforce needed for a particular type of product

- knowledge of production methods

- the technology to produce the product efficiently and cost-effectively.

Note that these factors aren't fixed in time. Technology and expertise can quickly be passed from country to country; new sources of raw materials (such as oil deposits) are discovered; investment in education and training allows a country to raise the skills base of its workforce. As circumstances change, international businesses are increasingly looking to switch their operations between countries in order to take advantage of the availability of lower cost factors of production.

Comparative advantage

Even where a country does not have an absolute advantage in producing any type of goods or services, it may benefit from specialising in producing those goods and services in which it has a relative or comparative advantage.

Figure 12.5 shows the typical costs of producing sweatshirts and DVDs in the US and the UK. It shows that the US has an absolute advantage in producing

both types of goods. US producers make both sweatshirts and DVDs more cheaply than UK firms.

Figure 12.5: Costs of producing DVDs and sweatshirts (in 100s) in the US and UK

Cost	US	UK
DVDs	£72	£120
Sweatshirts	£10	£12

However, if we look at the comparative costs in each country we can see that the opportunity cost of producing a DVD in the US is 7.2 sweatshirts. This means that for every DVD, the US could have produced 7.2 sweatshirts (£72 divided by £10). While the opportunity cost of producing a DVD in the UK is 10 sweatshirts; for every DVD the UK could have produced 10 sweatshirts (£120 divided by £12).

The US can therefore be said to have a *comparative advantage* in producing DVDs, while the UK has a *comparative advantage* in producing sweatshirts. The greatest number of DVDs and sweatshirts would be produced if the US channelled its resources into producing DVDs while the UK channelled its resources into producing sweatshirts.

Specialisation

Specialisation occurs at various levels: by country, by industry, by business, and by operation within a business. Where a country has a comparative advantage in producing a type of good or service, this is usually reflected in the industries that develop in that country. A country such as Canada, for example, has vast forests of timber suitable for making paper. It has therefore developed an industry to exploit this sustainable natural resource. There are many Canadian businesses specialising in growing timber, forest management and operating timber and paper mills.

In the UK, where there are few suitable forests for paper producers, any business that uses a large amount of paper in its operation must import its supplies from paper-producing countries. Given that paper is a significant production cost in newspapers and books, it is not surprising that some UK publishers have taken action to secure low-cost paper supplies. For example, DMGT plc, which publishes the Daily Mail and other national and regional newspaper titles, has established its own forests, timber mills and paper mills in Canada to minimise its paper costs and to ensure continuity of supply.

assessment practice
Argon Hair Care

John Hay is a well-known hair stylist. His main salon, *Argon Hair*, is in London's West End, with other salons in Birmingham, Cardiff, Manchester and Oxford.

John has built up a reputation as a stylist to the "stars", and travels extensively in the UK and throughout the European Union and parts of Eastern Europe, concentrating on work for clients before they appear at high-profile events such as awards ceremonies and fashion shows. During regular trips around the UK and Europe, he demonstrates his techniques, takes master classes for other stylists, and promotes his hair products to trade buyers. Every year he "invents" a signature style that he promotes through these events and through his celebrity clients.

He is keen to get media coverage – on television and in fashion and hairdressing magazines. He has developed a website where customers can view his salons and get to meet his staff, examine different hairstyles and colours, and see some of his celebrity clients, but John finds it hard to keep it up to date.

The UK salons, with similar fittings and furnishings, all operate with a manager and a tightly run system of procedures, prices, products, uniforms and customer service. The stylists are fully trained and spend two weeks' induction in the London salon under John's head stylist. John himself tries to meet each new stylist, and his wife Lara maintains a tight check on the personnel side of the business. Even junior staff are required to be trained to a high standard.

John has a range of hair products – shampoo, conditioner, colourings, etc. They are manufactured in relatively small quantities in a factory in Wales in partnership with a local cosmetics firm. They are currently used in his own salons and sold directly to other hairdressers, although he has hopes of making them available directly to individual customers. He thinks this side of the business has a lot of potential if supported by the salon business and his reputation.

John still runs Argon Hair Care Ltd, which includes the salons and the products, with his wife Lara, but last year he appointed two other directors – a marketing director, Jane Freeman, and a commercial director, Bryan Colston – to help with the business side.

At the first meeting of the new board, John said that he wanted to concentrate on the creative side of the business. He wanted the new directors to develop and implement his strategic plan for the next five years, which he called "the way forward". His vision is for:

- revenue growth of 5–6 per cent per annum
- increased operating profit margins
- an established international presence.

A Suggest three strategic objectives that Argon Hair Care might set.

B How would a strategy of developing an international presence help Argon to achieve progress towards these objectives?

C Identify and describe Argon Hair Care's comparative advantage.

D How might developing an international presence increase Argon's comparative advantage?

Impacts and incentives

Setting the scene: Olga Knight

Olga Knight is an artist from East Harling near Norwich. She specialises in animal designs, but also has a wide collection of flowers and birds in her portfolio. Her core business is designing greeting cards, which are printed in Hunstanton and sold in the UK and overseas, but she is also having success selling the copyright to some of her designs.

Now thanks to help from UK Trade & Investment, a government organisation that supports companies in the UK to trade internationally as well as helping overseas companies do business in the UK, Olga Knight is building up her business in the United States.

UK Trade & Investment helped fund exhibitions of her work at two stationery shows in the USA, from which Olga has secured a distributor based in Tennessee for her greeting cards and a contract with one of the largest licensing agents in the country, Applejack Art Partners. As a result, Olga's work can be found on a range of merchandise – from purses and spectacle cases to greeting cards and prints – in US stores.

"Without the help and advice of the International Trade and Business Link team I would have been unable to make the two visits to the National Stationery Show in New York." said Olga Knight. "Every member of the team, as well as the British Consulate staff in New York, had our best interests at heart at all times. Without this backing and advice, it is unlikely that I would have made such progress in establishing my presence in the United States."

UK Trade & Investment international trade adviser, Leszek Wysocki, has been helping Olga at every step of the exporting process: "Sometimes smaller companies shy away from selling abroad: this is certainly not the case with Olga Knight, and

she is reaping the rewards. She has made informed judgements and has not allowed international boundaries to hamper her entrepreneurial flair."

Leszek Wysocki has been able to assist Olga through the government's Passport to Export scheme, helping her with market research into the US market and putting her in touch with UK Trade & Investment's commercial staff in the United States. "The Passport to Export programme is there to offer practical support to companies wishing to take a proactive approach to trading internationally. Olga Knight is a shining example of this approach," he said.

For information on UK Trade & Investment, visit **www.uktradeinvest.gov.uk.**

Adapted from a case study on the DTI website (www.dti.gov.uk). For more information on Olga Knight, visit www.olgaknightdesigns.com

Impacts

A decision to start trading internationally can have a major impact on a business and its customers, competitors and suppliers. Figure 12.6 summarises the main impacts of trading internationally. The most obvious impacts of trading internationally are, perhaps, on the business itself. International markets offer businesses opportunities to increase sales, to expand their customer base, and to grow revenues

and profits. In some industries, an expansion into international markets is a natural move as competition intensifies at home or as domestic markets become saturated. Many mobile phone companies have looked for opportunities in the emerging markets of south and east Asia, as it has become increasingly difficult to gain new customers in European markets – in part, because most people now have a mobile phone. (See the Vodafone case study, Unit 14 Topic 8, pages 310–13.)

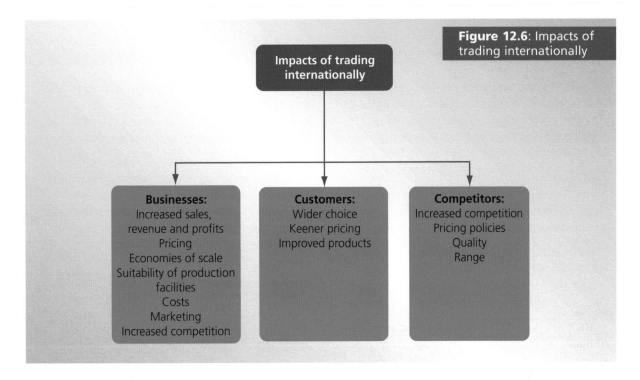

Impacts of trading internationally

Businesses:
Increased sales, revenue and profits
Pricing
Economies of scale
Suitability of production facilities
Costs
Marketing
Increased competition

Customers:
Wider choice
Keener pricing
Improved products

Competitors:
Increased competition
Pricing policies
Quality
Range

Any move into international trade requires a business to think how it might need to adapt its product and its marketing for each new market. Few businesses can simply transfer products from one overseas market to another without making modifications to their marketing mix. A business needs to consider how each element of its marketing mix – product, promotion, price and place – might need to be tweaked to meet the needs of local customers.

Pricing, in particular, may be a tricky issue. A business needs to take into account the competitive pressures and market situations in each territory. It needs to set a price in line with what its research suggests will succeed in winning trade in each international market rather than simply converting its UK prices into the equivalent price in the local currency. It may need to reconsider its pricing strategy. For example, a policy of penetration pricing may be necessary to break into an overseas market if the business is competing against already established companies in the same market. This can have an impact on profits, offsetting some of the profit growth it hopes to achieve through increased sales.

A business also needs to consider the impact on its costs of developing an international presence. It may be able to reduce its production costs if it is able to benefit from economies of scale as output is increased to meet the needs of the wider market. On the other hand, it may also be necessary to invest in new production facilities to meet the increased demand for its products. Promotion is another area where increased costs may be incurred in order to establish a

presence in new markets. Indeed, some businesses invest considerable sums in trying to establish their products into instantly recognisable global brands.

The impact on customers in the new market will – at least in the short term – be beneficial. They will be offered a wider choice of products. If there are already established companies in the market, the resulting competition can lead to keener pricing, improvements in product design and quality, and a wider range of goods and services – all of which benefit consumers.

By moving into a new market, a business will force the established companies in that market to become more competitive. In this way, even a company that operates only in a local or national market is not immune to the impact of increasing international trade – it will have to respond if an overseas business attempts to enter its markets and win market share. This increased competition could force businesses to respond in several ways. They might cut prices and start a price war, or they may try to retain customers by improving quality or by developing new products. This will affect their profits, at least in the short term.

Finally, note that a decision by a business to move into international markets will also have an impact on its suppliers. The business's existing suppliers may not have the capacity or capability to meet its international requirements. Some suppliers may lose out if the business can find alternative suppliers that can offer a service in all territories in which it operates. Some suppliers may win new business by acting as a local source of goods and services for an

Tiscali is an internet service provider, offering customers high-speed broadband connectivity. In the UK, the company has nearly one million broadband customers and had revenues of around £220 million in 2005.

Although the UK accounted for around 44 per cent of Tiscali's revenues in 2005, the Tiscali group is not a UK company. With headquarters in Italy, the group is listed on the Italian Stock Exchange.

Tiscali has tried to establish itself as a European-wide internet service provider. However, it has found the competition in many national markets intense, particularly from the broadband services offered by some of the major telecommunications companies. The company was unable to generate sufficient revenue growth to service the debt it incurred in financing its European expansion.

In its 2004 annual report, Tiscali's directors announced that the company would change its strategic focus. It would sell its subsidiaries in what it described as "non-core" countries, and concentrate "the group's activities in markets offering the most potential for value creation".

As a result, Tiscali has sold its subsidiaries in Austria, South Africa, France, Norway, Denmark, Sweden, Switzerland and Belgium. By the beginning of 2006, Tiscali had retrenched to focus on four key markets: Italy, the UK, Germany and the Netherlands.

international company. The opportunities for local companies to act as suppliers to an international business are one of the reasons that most governments are keen to attract multinationals to set up operations in their territories.

Incentives

International trade doesn't just benefit the businesses involved; it has a wider positive impact on the economy in terms of jobs, tax revenue and overall wealth. For this reason most governments provide encouragement for businesses based in their country to trade internationally. This support can take various forms. Many governments organise overseas trade missions to help companies based in their countries to export goods and services. Many also offer incentives to businesses that want to trade internationally.

In the UK, government support for export businesses is organised through UK Trade & Investment. Bringing together staff from the Department of Trade and Industry and the Foreign and Commonwealth Office, UK Trade & Investment has offices in the UK as well as a presence overseas in UK embassies, high commissions, consulates and trade offices. Its website is www.uktradeinvest.gov.uk.

UK Trade & Investment staff can provide research into potential markets and opportunities, information on cultural and communication requirements, and help in arranging marketing and promotional material. For example, the agency's website claims that "we can help to create a buzz about your products in the overseas trade press by producing professionally translated press releases for new and innovative products". Not all services are free, but companies with fewer than 250 employees may be eligible for a grant of up to 50 per cent of the agreed cost of market research projects.

UK Trade & Investment also helps groups of UK companies attend major international trade shows and take part in British overseas trade missions. Through the Tradeshow Access Programme, eligible companies can receive three grants of £1800 to help them acquire knowledge and experience of exhibiting effectively overseas, as part of their longer-term export strategy

Passport to Export

Passport to Export is UK Trade & Investment's flagship scheme for new exporters. It provides advice and support to new and inexperienced exporters. An assessment and skills-based programme, it provides the training, planning and ongoing support exporters need to compete successfully in overseas markets. The programme offers up to £3,000 worth of support, including up to six days of advice and support from an expert in the international trade team. A business can get help in:

■ developing an export strategy and action plan

■ undertaking preparatory work before visits to an overseas market

■ evaluating visits and reviewing strategy

■ determining and fulfilling any training needs in, for example, export marketing, administration, documentation, language and cultural awareness.

Companies in the scheme can also access the full range of services offered by UK Trade & Investment.

Export Credits Guarantee Department

The Export Credits Guarantee Department (www.ecgd.gov.uk) is a separate UK government department that provides finance and insurance to UK exporters of capital goods and services to assist them in winning overseas orders.

The department mainly supports exports to developing countries in the Far East and South Asia, the Middle East, Latin America and South Africa. It mainly offers insurance services, thereby offering a safety net for UK exporters in case their customers default on payments.

assessment practice
Pink Soda

Pink Soda is a high-quality fashion company based in London, with concessions at Selfridges and Top Shop's store at Oxford Circus. Following a recent export drive, exports have risen to 60 per cent of total sales, boosting profits by 55 per cent.

The company decided to explore international markets in 2002, and it joined the Passport to Export programme to take advantage of the advice and services available to novice exporters. At an initial review, several potential markets were identified. These included Japan, Europe and the United States. Pink Soda received UK Trade & Investment funding to exhibit at European fashion trade shows, including *White* in Milan and *Atmosphere* in Paris. As a result, the company was able to meet agents across Europe, significantly increasing its profile in Italy, France and Spain.

To develop the Japanese market, Pink Soda commissioned an Overseas Market Introduction Service report from the British Embassy in Tokyo. David Solomon, managing director of Pink Soda, met with Etsuko Muto, commercial officer from the embassy at UK Trade & Investment's offices in London. Ms Muto recommended that Mr Solomon join a trade mission to Osaka and Tokyo. The team at the British Embassy prepared meetings and market information for Pink Soda and distributed details of the company's product range to potential distributors in the market. During the mission, David Solomon visited a dozen companies and attended a briefing at the embassy, providing further advice on conducting business in Japan. With Etsuko Muto's assistance Pink Soda was able to select a distributor with confidence and business continues to grow in Japan.

David Solomon said: "Having the opportunity to visit Japan as part of a subsidised UK Trade & Investment trade mission was extremely useful. The assistance we received through the embassy in Tokyo was superb. The quality of the information and its strategic value was first-rate; it would have been very difficult to find a distributor without the guidance of Etsuko Muto."

Source: adapted from www.businesslink4london.com

A **Explain how incentives provided by the UK government have helped Pink Soda.**

B **Suggest the main impacts that trading internationally would have on (i) Pink Soda, (ii) Pink Soda's customers, (iii) Pink Soda's suppliers.**

C **Discuss whether penetration pricing might be a sensible approach for Pink Soda in expanding into new markets.**

D **Evaluate Pink Soda's decision to trade internationally.**

The European Union

Setting the scene: EU trade rows with China

Trade disputes between the European Union and China have been hitting the headlines. There has been "an underwear war" and "a shoe dumping crisis". Behind the headlines lies the challenge that the emergence of China as a manufacturing power poses to European businesses.

In 2005, millions of Chinese textile products were blocked in European ports as officials claimed that textile imports from China had exceeded their quota for the year. The quotas were imposed to protect European jobs and European businesses against a huge increase in Chinese textiles coming into European markets.

The dispute over shoes began in March 2006. China exports around 1.2 billion pairs of shoes to Europe, and the European Commission has said that it had "identified clear evidence of disguised subsidies and unfair state intervention to the leather footwear sector in China".

China strongly disputes these claims, but the European Union has imposed duties on shoes from China, and taken a similar measure against Vietnam.

Speaking to the BBC, European Union trade commissioner, Peter Mandelson said: "It is important that we act against unfair trade while encouraging legitimate and competitive trade from emerging countries. We do not target China

and Vietnam's natural competitive advantages, only unfair distortions of trade."

These disputes highlight some of the competing pressures within the European Union. Retailers want to buy goods from the cheapest supplier, consumers want less expensive products, but member states with sizeable clothing and footwear sectors want to protect their industries and save jobs.

Source: adapted from reports on the BBC News website, 5 September 2005 and 23 March 2006

Facts and figures

The European Union's origins are in the European Economic Community, which was established by the Treaty of Rome in 1957. The founding member states were France, Germany, Italy, Belgium, the Netherlands and Luxembourg.

In 1973, the original members were joined by the United Kingdom, Denmark and Ireland. Greece joined in 1981, Portugal and Spain in 1986, Austria, Finland and Sweden in 1995. The European Union then saw a major enlargement in 2004, when ten more countries joined: Cyprus (the Greek part), the Czech Republic, Estonia, Hungary, Latvia, Lithuania, Malta, Poland, Slovakia and Slovenia.

The enlarged European Union (as of 2006) has 25 members, and has a total population of around

457 million. It is set to grow further. Bulgaria and Romania are due to join in 2007, and other candidates for entry in the future include Croatia and Turkey.

The main aim of the European Union (EU) is to "bring about lasting peace and prosperity for all its citizens". In 2006, the EU budget was €121 billion (around £84 billion), equivalent to around €232 per head of population. The budget was allocated as follows:

■ competitiveness and cohesion – 39%

■ agriculture – 36%

■ rural development and the environment – 11%

■ international affairs including aid – 7%

■ other spending including administration – 6%

Figure 12.7: The European Union (as at 2006)

EU member before 2004

EU member since 2004

Countries applying for EU membership

Countries not applying for EU membership

B.-H.	BOSNIA-HERZEGOVINA
L.	LIECHTENSTEIN
MAC.	MACEDONIA
MOL.	MOLDOVA
R.F.	RUSSIAN FEDERATION
S.M.	SERBIA AND MONTENEGRO
SWITZ.	SWITZERLAND

The single European market

The European Union is both a customs union and a free trade area, designed to encourage economic growth and employment. The single European market allows the free movement of goods, services, capital and labour between EU member states, and sets common external tariffs on goods coming into the European Union.

The market is regulated, to some extent, to maintain a competitive European environment. For example, the European Commission was instrumental in shaping the media business in Europe. It would only allow the merger between the US organisations AOL and Time Warner in 2000 to proceed under certain conditions so as preserve European competition.

The single market rivals the US in terms of numbers of consumers, and it has encouraged the development of large pan-European multinationals that can benefit from economies of scale. Large US and Japanese companies have also set up production and distribution facilities in the EU – many of them in the UK – in order to have a foothold in the single European market.

By reducing the formalities for goods crossing frontiers between member states, the single European market has resulted in lower costs and increased competition. This has brought about benefits to consumers in terms of lower prices and increased efficiency. The European Commission claims that the single market has helped to create 2.5 million new jobs and €800 billion in additional wealth since 1993.

Opening up borders to allow the free movement of labour between member states has shown less obvious benefits. The mobility of labour, especially between countries, is limited, and the formation of pan-European companies has led to some job losses. As the workers are allowed to bring their families, there are implications for an individual country's immigration policies, and potential pressures on services such as education and social security. However, the European Union is keen to promote flexible labour markets, and 2006 is European Year of Workers' Mobility.

There were concerns that there would be a large influx of workers to Western Europe from the countries of the former Soviet bloc that joined the EU in 2004. Some member states introduced transitional arrangements to place restrictions on workers coming from countries like Poland and Hungary to look for jobs. The UK government took a more relaxed approach, and initial studies suggest that the UK economy has benefited from being able to draw on this additional pool of skilled labour. The implications on education and universities, for example, are less clear, as many students now have access to UK education at UK rates rather than overseas student rates.

The single market is not a finished project. It is still developing, both in regard to enlargement and in respect to European Monetary Union (see below), which is an essential and integral part of harmonisation of the market.

Tax policy

The European Union has limited powers to shape tax policy. It has no authority to set direct taxes, such as income tax – these remain primarily a matter for national governments. The EU does have some responsibility for indirect taxation, such as value added tax. The case for a degree of tax harmonisation across the EU on indirect taxes is that if individual member states impose widely different tax tariffs on goods, it will affect the free movement of goods and services between countries – a fundamental principle of the single market.

Any EU tax proposal must be agreed unanimously by all member states, which effectively gives each government the right of veto to any proposal. The position of UK governments has generally been to resist demands for greater tax harmonisation within the European Union. They have strongly opposed any proposals that would harm UK interests, and argued that tax policy should remain the responsibility of national governments.

Structural and cohesion funds

The European Union has set up a number of structural funds designed to reduce differences in prosperity and living standards across Europe. These funds account for approaching 40 per cent of the EU's budget. The aim has been to use the funds to promote economic and social cohesion, and to create opportunities for all EU citizens in the single market.

Some funds have helped finance regional development projects, environmental improvements and major transport infrastructure projects. The European Social Fund, one of the four structural funds, supports projects to help people improve their skills and job prospects.

In the past, the poorer areas of the UK – including regions with high unemployment – have benefited significantly from EU funding in a range of small and large projects including education and training, building construction in regeneration zones, development of the labour market, and promotion of enterprise and entrepreneurship. Many projects were run in conjunction with regional development agencies and other government bodies.

In June 2005 Advantage West Midlands, a regional development agency, launched a fresh initiative to improve access to loan finance of up to £50,000 to existing small businesses, social enterprises and individuals looking to start up new firms. The £3.7 million Advantage Small Loan Programme, which is supported by funding from the European Regional Development Fund, offers grants to community development finance institutions (CDFIs) and other non-profit distributing lenders to enable them to increase their lending in the period. The scheme is due to run to December 2008.

In the future, the new member states are likely have a stronger claim for financial support to develop their economies.

The Social Chapter

European social policy is an increasing area of EU activity, although it is one that UK governments have traditionally viewed with suspicion. The Social Chapter of the 1992 Maastricht Treaty sets out some of the key elements of EU social policy. The Social Chapter covers:

■ the rights of workers within the EU

■ equal rights for employees, including fair pay

■ improvements to working conditions, including hours

- the right to training

- the provision of social security for those on low incomes or unemployed

- freedom of association, with the right to collective bargaining

- health and safety at work

- the provision of employment opportunities for the young, disabled and those over compulsory retirement age

The UK government negotiated an opt-out to the Social Chapter when it was first introduced. The then Conservative government felt that it would compromise the flexibility of the UK labour market, increase the power of trade unions, and lead to higher costs for business, which would in turn lead to increased unemployment. In 1997, the incoming Labour government signed up to the Social Chapter, with the proviso that no new EU laws should damage the competitiveness of British firms.

European monetary union

European monetary union (EMU) is designed to harmonise the economies of EU member states through the adoption of a single currency (the euro) and one interest rate set by the European Central Bank. Other measures, such as common rates of tax, have also been proposed although they remain politically controversial. EMU is part of a move towards greater political integration in the EU.

The euro was launched as a single European currency on 1 January 1999, when it was adopted by 11 of the then 15 EU member states. Greece adopted the euro in 2001, leaving Denmark, Sweden and the UK (of the 15 member states at the time of adoption) outside the euro zone. The citizens of Denmark and Sweden voted against joining the euro zone in national referenda. The new member states – the ten countries that joined the EU in 2004 – are required by the terms of their accession treaties to join the euro eventually. The actual date of joining the euro will vary from country to country, depending on the progress of their economies.

The European Central Bank is an essential ingredient of European monetary union. Based in Frankfurt, its main aim is price stability throughout the area covered by the euro. It has set a target of a 2 per cent year-on-year increase in the "harmonised index of consumer prices" – the EU equivalent of the retail prices index. Like the Monetary Policy Committee of the Bank of England, the Council of the European Central Bank meets monthly to set interest rates.

Council votes are split between the countries that have adopted the euro on the basis of a simple majority vote. Unlike the Bank of England, the European Central Bank does not publish the minutes of its meetings, or its inflation forecasts. The national central banks of euro countries are now agencies of the European Central Bank.

Perhaps as a tourist you have been to Europe and experienced how easy it is to use euros in each country you visit. You don't have to worry about different exchange rates, or changing your money every time you cross a national border. You don't "lose" money each time you exchange money. Take a look at the different prices for buying or selling currency at your local bank. There are hidden charges here, as well as a commission charge that might be imposed. By adopting the same currency, it is easy to compare prices in different countries, whether it's for a cup of coffee in a local café, a can of Coca-Cola or a McDonald's hamburger.

Imagine businesses operating in similar ways. There are no exchange problems and charges, and prices – for supplies, for products, for services or for labour – can be instantly compared. This has forced European car manufacturers to standardise their pricing across different countries. As a result car prices have come down in Europe, as consumers could simply cross the border to get a better deal on a similar model.

UK position on the euro

The UK government's position (as of 2006) is broadly in favour of adopting the euro. However, it has set a number of conditions to entry. It has announced that no decision would be taken without a referendum on the issue – and before any referendum is held, it should first be established that the UK economy would benefit from adopting the euro. The government has set five economic tests that need to be passed.

- Britain should achieve sustainable economic convergence with other countries that have adopted the euro.

- Britain's economy should show a sufficient level of flexibility to cope should any problems emerge.

- It must be established that adopting the euro will lead to better conditions for firms making long-term decisions to invest in Britain.

- There must be no adverse effects on the UK's financial services industry.

- Adopting the euro must benefit employment, economic growth and stability.

The euro debate is politically controversial. Those in favour of joining argue that the removal of exchange rate uncertainties must benefit UK firms. With a single currency for Europe, there will be no currency transaction costs for exporters. This may lead to an increase of trade within the euro area for British business. Advocates for joining the currency also argue that there is a danger that unless it adopts the euro, Britain could lose out on some benefits to be obtained from EU membership.

Those who oppose the euro point out that currency unions have collapsed in the past, and argue that the UK should not take part in a risky experiment. There are fears that some of the stronger EU economies and larger countries, such as France and Germany, will dominate EU economic policy. There are concerns about interest rates: the European Central bank may set a rate which reduces inflation in one or two member states but which damages the economy of other countries.

There is also the issue of sovereignty. Critics argue that by joining the euro, the UK would lose the right to undertake some economic decisions, such as devaluing sterling in order to restore international competitiveness.

In or out, however, the euro has important implications for the UK.

- British firms trading with the EU have to deal in euros.

- Movement in the exchange rates of the pound against the euro can adversely affect Britain's trade in Europe.

- Greater transparency of prices throughout Europe may force some British firms to change their pricing strategies.

A policy success?

It is difficult, after such a relatively short time (in economic terms), to assess whether the euro has been a success. Ultimately, its success will be judged on whether it has:

- led to lower long-term inflation and interest rates

- encouraged sustainable economic growth throughout the area of its adoption

- helped to reduce unemployment and improve living standards in member states

- led to closer economic, political and social integration.

Common Agricultural Policy

When the European Economic Community (the forerunner to the EU) was formed in 1957, over 20 per cent of its working population was employed in agriculture, and each of the six founding member states had some form of agricultural protective policy. The Common Agricultural Policy (CAP), which began operating in 1962, sought to establish fair trade in agriculture through a single policy that operated throughout the community.

In its early years, CAP was set up to ensure fair living standards for farmers and to increase agricultural productivity by paying farmers a subsidy if the market price for particular agricultural products fell below agreed target prices. In effect, the policy linked subsidies to production – the more farmers produced, regardless of any market demand, the more they got paid – and the CAP consumed a huge proportion of the overall EU budget.

Over the years, this policy has come in for considerable criticism. It has been open to abuse, and because it rewards production, it became synonymous with butter mountains and wine lakes. The guaranteed prices were high enough to result in surplus production that had to be stored – a notoriously expensive process – and eventually sold, usually overseas, at low prices. Critics argued that:

- the excess production implied a waste of economic resources

- prices were artificially high – in effect, consumers and taxpayers subsidised farmers

- the overseas sale of surplus output means that the EU subsidised foreign governments and consumers.

The old-style CAP highlighted one of the general effects of the single European market – and indeed of tariffs in general: that of trade creation and trade diversion. Trade is "created" behind the tariff barrier as consumers are encouraged to buy home-produced goods. At the same time, trade is diverted from its normal channels as overseas producers lose their traditional markets.

In recent years, the CAP has undergone significant reform. There has been a gradual erosion of the link between agricultural support and production. The latest CAP reforms, which were implemented in 2005, provide a single farm payment to EU farmers, independent of production, and linked payments to food safety, animal welfare and the maintenance of environmental standards.

The Common Agricultural Policy budget has been falling as a proportion of the total EU budget in recent years. The terms offered to farmers in the new member states – those joining the European Union in 2004 – are far less generous than those available to those in the original 15 member states.

There will be pressures for further CAP reform, both from farmers in the developing world, from bodies such as the World Trade Organization, and from those EU member states that have relatively small farming sectors. Any move in this direction will be fiercely contested by countries with strong agricultural lobbies such as France and Poland, which has 2.5 million farmers. It remains to be seen whether the new system, with its much clearer emphasis on animal welfare and environmental management issues, will receive wider public support as well as the backing of European farmers.

assessment practice
MB Precision Tools

MB Precision Tools plc is based in the West Midlands. The company has two main product lines: cutting tools and cutting machines. Key competitors are located in Germany, Spain and Italy. The company also has three major domestic competitors, each roughly the same size, two of which are also located in the West Midlands. Although the number of competitors is small, price competition is extremely high.

The company's main customers are firms in the automobile manufacturing and automobile components industries. These are demanding customers, seeking quality improvement and price reduction. As a result, the company has focused recently on improving its product quality in order to obtain quality certifications from main customers and to become ISO-certified.

MB Precision Tools uses many small and medium-sized suppliers, the majority of which are located in the European Union, to source its raw materials (steel) and electronic components. Dependence on a specific supplier is low.

The company has four commercial departments (sales, purchasing, finance and IT) and two technical departments (engineering and construction, and production). It uses stand-alone IT applications for accounting, invoicing and CAD. There is no IT-based inventory control or production planning and control system. There are no interfaces between accounting and invoicing applications. Only Microsoft Office-based PC applications are used. The company currently employs 190 employees.

Since the creation of the single market and introduction of the euro, MB Precision Tools has faced increased competition from companies in other EU member states. It needs to cut costs and adopt a keener pricing policy. At the same time, the company believes that the European Union offers scope for widening its market, and increasing both sales and profits.

It prime objectives are revenue growth and becoming the market leader in its field. In order to achieve these objectives, and take advantage of the opportunities offered by the European Union, the company knows that it must rethink its corporate strategy and plan carefully.

A Why do you think that MB Precision Tools "must rethink its corporate strategy and plan carefully" if it is to achieve its corporate objectives?

B What are the benefits of UK membership of the European Union for MB Precision Tools?

C What are the threats of UK membership of the European Union for MB Precision Tools?

International trade agreements

Setting the scene: regulating world trade

International trade is governed by a number of agreements between countries to ensure a freer and more open system. These agreements are renegotiated regularly to remove import tariffs and other barriers to trade and, as this article shows, the business organisations are often involved in lobbying to further their interests.

Whisky group toasts WTO progress

The Scotsman, 20 December 2005,
© The Scotsman Publications Ltd

Representatives of the Scotch Whisky Association (SWA) have returned from the World Trade Organization (WTO) meeting in Hong Kong expressing "relief" over significant gains towards facilitating trade in Scotland's most valuable export.

The SWA had joined forces with the international trade body the World Spirits Alliance to lobby the Doha round meeting for a range of measures, including the reduction of tariff and non-tariff barriers, improved protection against counterfeiting, and simplification of customs and certification procedures.

"Given that there had been fears that there would be no progress in Hong Kong we are relieved that the whole process is moving forward," said David Williamson, the public affairs spokesman for the SWA. "We are pleased that the ministerial meeting has resulted in an agreement between WTO members, with the opportunity to go further next year. The EU's decision to end export subsidies by 2013 is particularly welcome as we have long advocated the elimination of trade-distorting measures."

But he warned that limited progress at Hong Kong, even if better than expected, was not sufficient to allow a let-up in the SWA's lobbying efforts: "Clearly, the first quarter of 2006 is going to be crucial to advancing the Scotch whisky industry's priorities. Our key objective remains improved market access through the reduction of high import tariffs on spirit drinks, for example in India and Thailand, and while much work remains before agreement on a tariff-reduction formula is likely, the signs in Hong Kong were that agreement is possible.

"It is encouraging there also appears to have been progress towards an agreement on trade facilitation. It would be good news for an export-oriented business like Scotch whisky if excessive document requirements and onerous customs procedures were simplified."

The worldwide spirits industry, including the SWA, is hoping to build on the success of its "zero for zero" agreement in the Uruguay round of the WTO, which secured tariff-free access into major markets such as Japan and Canada.

Negotiations during the Doha round comprise part of the SWA's agenda to boost sales in key growth markets such as India and Thailand, where domestic producers of molasses-based spirits are believed to be instrumental in lobbying governments to maintain national and state-level barriers of up to 150 per cent.

Non-tariff measures under discussion at Hong Kong included import quotas, licensing requirements and "inappropriate" product standards and labelling requirements.

Also under discussion was the EU proposal of a register of geographical indications (GI), an extension of the trade-related intellectual property rights agreement during the Uruguay round. EU food and drink producers have advocated a legally binding register of GIs, a move opposed by countries including the United States, New Zealand and Canada.

The World Trade Organization

The World Trade Organization is the leading agency involved in the regulation of international trade. It develops ground rules for international commerce and mediates trade disputes between countries and trading blocs. This material has been adapted (with permission) from the WTO website (www.wto.org).

Established in 1995, the World Trade Organization (WTO) is the successor body to the General Agreement on Tariffs and Trade (GATT). These two bodies – first GATT which was set up in the wake of the Second World War and now the WTO – have overseen an exceptional growth in world trade. Total trade in 2000 was 22 times the level of 1950.

The world's current international trade system has been developed through a series of trade negotiations, or rounds, held under GATT. The first rounds dealt mainly with tariff reductions, but later negotiations included areas such as anti-dumping and non-tariff measures. Now, through the WTO, the overriding objective is to help international trade flow

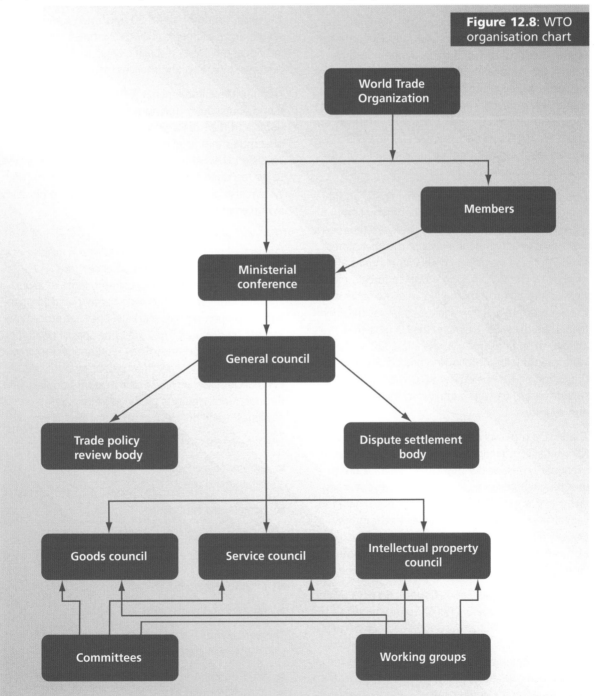

Figure 12.8: WTO organisation chart

smoothly, freely, fairly and predictably. The WTO does this by:

- administering trade agreements

- acting as a forum for trade negotiations

- settling trade disputes

- reviewing national trade policies

- assisting developing countries in trade policy issues, through technical assistance and training programmes

- cooperating with other international organisations.

As at December 2005, 149 countries were members of the WTO. These countries currently account for over 97 per cent of world trade. Around 30 other nations are negotiating WTO membership. Decisions are made by the entire membership, typically by consensus. A majority vote is also possible but it has never been used in the WTO, and was extremely rare under the WTO's predecessor, GATT. The WTO's agreements have been ratified in all member countries' parliaments.

Over 100 developing nations are members, and their approaches to trade may be rather different from those of the developed nations. There are tensions as WTO tries to act in the interests of member states, although these may have conflicting priorities and objectives. The WTO has no power to force a member to take any action, although it can allow other nations to take retaliatory action against countries that don't follow the rules. For example, the US restricted imports of shrimps from Malaysia in 2000 as they were caught without following procedures for the protection of sea turtles; the WTO eventually supported this ban although it discriminated against one country.

The WTO's top-level decision-making body is the Ministerial Conference which meets at least once every two years. Below this is the General Council (normally ambassadors and heads of delegation in Geneva, but sometimes officials sent from members' capitals) which meets several times a year in the Geneva headquarters. The General Council also meets as the Trade Policy Review Body and the Dispute Settlement Body.

At the next level, the Goods Council, Services Council and Intellectual Property (TRIPS) Council report to the General Council. Numerous specialised committees, working groups and working parties deal with the individual agreements and other areas such as the environment, development, membership applications and regional trade agreements.

WTO agreements

The WTO's agreements are the result of negotiations between the members. The current trade rules (as at March 2006) were the outcome of the 1986–94 Uruguay Round negotiations which included a major revision of the original General Agreement on Tariffs and Trade (GATT).

GATT is now the WTO's principal rule book for trade in goods. The Uruguay Round also created new rules for dealing with trade in services, relevant aspects of intellectual property, dispute settlement, and trade policy reviews. The complete set runs to some 30,000 pages consisting of about 30 agreements and separate commitments (called schedules) made by individual members in specific areas such as lower customs duty rates and services market opening.

Through these agreements, WTO members operate a non-discriminatory trading system that spells out their rights and their obligations. Each country receives guarantees that its exports will be treated fairly and consistently in other countries' markets. Each promises to do the same for imports into its own market. The system also gives developing countries some flexibility in implementing their commitments.

The WTO agreements cover goods, services and intellectual property. They spell out the principles of liberalisation, and the permitted exceptions. They include individual countries' commitments to lower customs tariffs and other trade barriers, and to open and keep open services markets. They set procedures for settling disputes. They prescribe special treatment for developing countries. They require governments to make their trade policies transparent by notifying the WTO about laws in force and measures adopted, and through regular reports by the secretariat on countries' trade policies.

The agreements fall into six main categories:

- an umbrella agreement (the agreement establishing the WTO)

- agreements for goods

- agreements for services

- agreements for intellectual property

- dispute settlement

- reviews of governments' trade policies.

The agreements for the two largest areas, goods and services, which start with broad principles, are:

- the General Agreement on Tariffs and Trade (GATT) (for goods)

- the General Agreement on Trade in Services (GATS).

These are followed by extra agreements and annexes dealing with the special requirements of specific sectors or issues. These are the detailed and lengthy lists of commitments made by individual countries allowing specific foreign products or service-providers access to their markets. For GATT, these take the form of binding commitments on tariffs for goods in general, and combinations of tariffs and quotas for some agricultural goods. For GATS, the commitments state how much access foreign service providers are allowed for specific sectors, and they include lists of types of services where individual countries say they are not applying the "most-favoured-nation" principle of non-discrimination.

Note that these agreements are not static; they are renegotiated from time to time and new agreements can be added to the package.

The G8 and WTO

The G8 group is an unofficial forum of the heads of leading industrialised democracies, and includes the US, the UK, Russia, Japan, Germany, France, Canada and Italy. It is not a full international organisation and doesn't have the same kinds of formal rules and regulations as the WTO. However, it does have influence and holds regular summits, with member countries holding the presidency in rotating six-month terms.

The Make Poverty History campaign in 2005 has lobbied both the WTO and the G8 in its attempt to get a better deal for the poorer parts of the world. It called upon the WTO to deliver trade justice – not free trade – in world trade talks in Hong Kong in December 2005. Some 250,000 campaigners marched in Edinburgh before the G8 summit in 2005 calling for more aid, debt cancellation and "trade justice".

Many campaigners feel that many developed nations are taking advantage of developing nations by forcing them to liberalise through trade agreements. This tends to take place – they claim – despite rather than because of the WTO.

Other campaigners, particularly human rights activists and environmentalists, feel that the WTO should take a stronger line with countries where child labour is used, or which permit hazardous working conditions and poor environmental practices. In developed nations these issues are usually covered by legislation, but this is not the case in developing nations. There are tensions if individual countries ban imports of some products in protest, say, at child labour practices, and it is contrary to the WTO rules of free trade.

Other international agreements

Besides the European Union and the World Trade Organization, there are many other international trade agreements and alliances. Some cover particular regions, some cover particular sectors, and some are bilateral agreements between two countries.

These are some of the most significant regional and sectoral alliances.

- The **Association of South East Asian Nations (ASEAN)** organises political, economic and social co-operation between nations in South East Asia in order to ensure regional peace and stability.

- The **European Free Trade Association (EFTA)** was founded in 1960 with the purpose of removing trade barriers between its member nations (currently Iceland, Liechtenstein, Norway and Switzerland).

- The **Organisation of the Petroleum Exporting Countries (OPEC)** was originally established in 1968 to promote co-operation among the Arab nations in economic activities related to oil. Membership has now expanded to include oil-producing countries in Africa, Asia and Latin America.

- The **North American Free Trade Agreement (NAFTA)** covers environmental and labour issues as well as trade and investment. The United States hopes to expand the area to the rest of Latin America creating a Free Trade Area of the Americas (FTAA), but key countries like Brazil are sceptical of its benefit.

- The **Central American Free Trade Agreement (CAFTA)** was sanctioned by the US Congress in 2005. By March 2006, the US government had reached a free trade agreements with El Salvador but it was still negotiating with Costa Rica, Guatemala, Honduras, Nicaragua and the Dominican Republic.

- The **Asia-Pacific Economic Co-operation forum (APEC)** is a loose grouping of the countries bordering the Pacific Ocean that have pledged to facilitate free trade. It has 21 members including China, Russia, the United States, Japan and Australia, and accounts for 45 per cent of world trade.

International trade issues

As well as being an economic issue for countries, international trade is also a political issue. Governments can and do intervene regularly with a whole array of rules and regulations concerning tariffs, import quotas, voluntary export restraints, local content requirements, administrative policies and anti-dumping duties. There are also – as we have set out in this topic and Topic 6 – innumerable trade agreements that should be followed by governments and businesses.

The government view

There are many effects of international trade, both direct impacts from international competition itself and indirect impacts as a result of trade legislation. For example, in 2002 the US put an import tax on steel imports to help its domestic steelmakers that were suffering from intense global competition and were laying off workers. This bought in tax revenue for the US government, decreased competition from foreign imports, but increased the cost of steel in the United States.

In general, it is not easy to predict the impact of this kind of government intervention in trade. The final impact depends on the industry, the level of the tariff, and the effects on domestic producers and consumers, and how the global marketplace responds. Many economists argue that tariffs simply reduce the overall efficiency of the world economy, as domestic producers have little incentive to produce efficiently.

Governments also protect their domestic producers through subsidies – either as cash, or tax breaks for

example. Import quotas are another way of protecting domestic producers from competition. They are usually imposed by import licences issued to foreign companies. A voluntary export restraint is a quota agreed by the exporting country following a request from the importing country.

Government protection is often found in agricultural markets. Many rich developed countries subsidise their farmers so that they are protected from low commodity prices elsewhere in the world. However, this can result in over-production – and surplus crops are sold on world markets, depressing prices and making it more difficult for farmers in developing nations to compete. According to Oxfam, the US government spends about three times as much on cotton subsidies as it does on aid to Africa. It is estimated that the aid given by developed nations to developing nations is matched by the reduction in income forced by these developed nations paying subsidies to their farmers. Some take the view that not paying subsidies would result in fairer competition and expanded markets: farmers in developing nations would get higher prices for their produce, and consumers in developed nations would benefit from lower taxes and lower prices.

As well as economic arguments for government intervention in international trade – to protect domestic producers, jobs and industries – there are other political reasons for governments to act. The are concerns about:

- national security in sensitive areas

- protecting health – for example, by banning the import of hormone-treated meat into the EU

- foreign policy – many countries place trade embargos on states which they feel support terrorism

- protecting human rights – some countries halt trade because of a country's internal human rights policy, such as the sanctions placed on South Africa during apartheid.

A final reason for governments intervening in trade is retaliation. Put simply, if a country imposes a restriction on your imports then you can block its exports to your markets. A country might also retaliate if it feels that its businesses are being treated harshly in some way. China has been forced to introduce copyright legislation by the US threatening to impose high tariffs on its imports, following years in which US companies lost revenue to piracy (of software, films, books and other intellectual property) by Chinese firms.

Society's view

The development of international trade is viewed rather differently today than it was 20 years ago. Previously, the consumer's desire for ever-cheaper products took precedence over many other issues. Today, as you can see from a whole array of advertising, promotional materials, websites, mission and vision statements, and actual products, the key business messages seem to be "green", "fairtrade", "ethical", "sustainable", and made without any child labour.

Marks & Spencer, for example, maintains: "One of the best ways to tackle poverty in developing countries is to build trade links with farmers and their communities. That's why we are selling more and more products that carry the Fairtrade label."

Ali Hewson, wife of U2 rock star Bono, has just started her own fashion label called Edun. She has visited every factory in Africa that is making her clothes to check they are running under safe conditions, with a fair wage and no child labour. This is very much how Anita Roddick started out when she was sourcing her products for The Body Shop. "Our trade with these communities is not just about creating another product or market for The Body Shop. It is about exchange and value, trade and respect, friendship and trust," she has said. Anita Roddick has subsequently sold The Body Shop to L'Oreal, and it will be interesting to see if it continues her philosophy.

Some might argue that this kind of approach is just marketing – it is people in developed nations "do-gooding", and it is only scratching the surface of poverty and inequality. Should we be telling the developing world how to do things anyway? Some would argue for and some against.

The environment

On a slightly bigger scale, and with more focus on the environment, Unilever, a vast food and consumer goods manufacturer, with Groupe Danone and Nestlé has established the Food Industry Platform for Sustainable Agriculture (SAI Platform) with other companies such as McDonald's, Kraft Foods and Findus Foods. These companies hope to develop a sustainable agriculture programme – "a productive, competitive and efficient way to produce agricultural raw materials, while at the same time protecting and improving the natural environment and the social and economic conditions of local communities."

With the current emphasis on global warming, many people have concerns about a country's or a business's approach to CO_2 emissions. These may be controlled in some countries, but not in others. In the UK, for example, the government has introduced the climate change levy, a business tax on energy use. Companies that reduce energy use in line with government targets are eligible for 80 per cent tax discount. There are also strong views about destroying rainforests, overfishing, contaminating water supplies: there's an endless list of environmental issues. At the moment the focus is on businesses in the developed world, but increasingly developing countries will come under pressure to introduce stronger environmental legislation. They might argue: why should they put a brake on economic development when they lag so far behind the living standards in the developed world?

Copyright and consumer protection

Finally, international trade also raise some consumer protection issues. Opening up of global markets raises awareness of the marketability of different brands, and sometimes there is little regard for intellectual property. So many items are simply copied and sold as fakes. These obviously destroy the manufacturer's sales but also they may harm the consumer. Fake designer beauty products have not been tested properly and they might contain harmful ingredients that could cause burning, corrosion and allergic reactions. They commonly contain urine as a stabiliser and colour corrector. Fake sunglasses don't have UV filters and could damage your eyes. So beware of bargains at car boot sales, on market stalls or on eBay.

Opening up trade in services

Rich and poor countries are heading for a clash at the World Trade talks over deregulating the international services sector. Some developing countries want to limit the scope of the draft proposals, which are designed to open up international markets in services. Businesses involved in providing services, however, are pressing the WTO to go much further.

A new proposal put forward by Collins Magalasi from Malawi, the state which chairs the services sector group of the ACP (African, Caribbean and Pacific countries), would eliminate all target dates for implementing individual plans to open up service sector markets, and stop countries working together to demand service sector openings. The ASEAN countries tabled a similar amendment.

Guy Ryder, general secretary of the International Congress of Free Trade Unions (ICFTU) said: "It is hypocritical that the world's richest countries, some of whom have protected their own public services from unregulated liberalisation and intend to do so in the future as well, are now pushing developing countries into opening up their services markets."

But any proposed changes will be strongly opposed by the international business community and the European Union, both of whom feel that the existing plan on services is already too weak. International businesses say developing countries have everything to gain by opening up their markets – from more efficient services such as banking and insurance to better infrastructure such as faster delivery and shipping and more reliable telecommunications. But they are worried that the tertiary sector does not seem to be getting the priority it deserves.

The Global Services Coalition, which represents leading service industries in the EU, United States, Japan, India and Australia, said that the current WTO plans are "an important starting point, but only a starting point" for negotiations on deregulating international services markets. In a background briefing, EU officials said that opening up the services sector was a key negotiating objective, and the EU could not possibly accept any amendments which would weaken it. But they remained non-committal, saying only that they wanted to ensure that developing countries made real and substantial offers within a strict deadline.

Source: adapted from the BBC News website, 15 December 2005

A **Why do the Global Services Coalition and the European Union want the international services market opened up to free competition?**

B **Why do ACP and ASEAN countries and the International Congress of Free Trade Unions want the international services market regulated?**

C **What opportunities and threats would deregulation of the international services markets provide for UK businesses?**

The growth and influence of multinational operations

Setting the scene: Monsanto takes farmer to court

A Canadian Federal Court has found against a 70-year-old Canadian farmer and in favour of Monsanto, the multinational seed giant. The case arose after Monsanto had accused the farmer of infringing its patent on a genetically modified crop.

Percy Schmeiser, the farmer, accepted that Monsanto's patented gene was present in his crop but claimed that it had got there by accident after being blown in from neighbouring fields where farmers had legally planted the crop. Mr Schmeiser said that Monsanto had originally accused him of illegally obtaining the seeds. But, it eventually withdrew these allegations and the company admitted that the seeds had just spread.

But then the judge ruled that it doesn't matter how Monsanto seeds get on to a farm, whether they cross-pollinate or are blown in by the wind. The judge said it was up to the farmer, who ought to know that once it appears there he must stop growing that crop.

Mr Schmeiser believes this is impractical. "How would a farmer know when he has a genetically altered plant? It looks exactly the same as another plant." He added that the unusual thing about this ruling is that the judge said if a seed blows on to a farmer's land, he has the right to use the seed from those plants the following year – as long as it is not one of Monsanto's genetically altered seeds.

Mr Schmeiser believes this gives the big companies complete control over farmers, because if some of their seed blown on to a farmer's land contaminates the seed and cross-pollinates, it then becomes the property of the big company.

Mr Schmeiser says that local farmers have always thought that if you contaminate and destroy your neighbour's crop, you are responsible for what has happened. If you were spraying and the spray drifted into your neighbour's crop, you were responsible. This case has challenged that belief.

Source: BBC World Business Archive
First broadcast 4 April 2001

KEY TERMS

Coincidence of interests is a situation in which the interests of a business match the interests of the country (or countries) in which it operates. For example, the business may want to make a profit, a government may want to generate tax income from business profits and protect jobs. This means that it is in the interests of both the business and the government for the business to be successful.

Host countries are countries in which a business operates but in which it is not registered or headquartered.

Parent country is the country in which a business is formally registered and where it usually bases its headquarters. Most businesses also operate within their parent countries. Some businesses, however, are registered in a country for tax reasons alone and conduct all their operations outside the parent country.

Economic impacts

Multinational companies have considerable influence in the countries in which they operate, and in developing countries the operation of a multinational cause more problems than it solves. The operations of a multinational in any particular country have an impact on the economies of both the host country and the multinational's parent country. These impacts are often positive, though not all the economic consequences are beneficial.

Rather than simply exporting its products or licensing its products to a local manufacturer, a multinational can invest directly in the country to market and/or produce its goods through building a new operation or by acquiring or merging with an existing operation. This is called foreign direct investment (FDI).

Historically, FDI has been directed at developed nations as multinationals invested in other countries in Europe and North America. The US has been the largest recipient of FDI. More recently, developing nations are now attracting investment. China, for example, is offering tax incentives for foreign companies to open up in particular regions, and has been upgrading the skills of its labour force to meet demand, and improving the transport infrastructure.

Countries can choose to encourage or discourage foreign investment, and may do so from an ideological standpoint. Up until the 1980s multinationals were rather seen as a "wicked" instrument of capitalism and imperialism, that merely benefited the home country and exploited the host country. However, with the failure of communism in Eastern Europe, a consensus has emerged that FDI is important for technology transfer and economic growth. Many argue that FDI accounts for the strong economic performance of developing capitalist countries such as Singapore and Taiwan.

Many nations attract investment as multinationals seek to increase global market share and produce goods closer to their markets. Developing nations in South and South East Asia have attracted significant investment. They have benefited from being close to China, which has now opened up to foreign investment and is seen as a huge marketplace. Latin America is also seen as a developing region, but with great potential. However, Africa, with political unrest, armed conflict and frequent changes in regional economic policy, continues to attract very little investment.

Figure 12.9: Economic impacts of multinational organisations

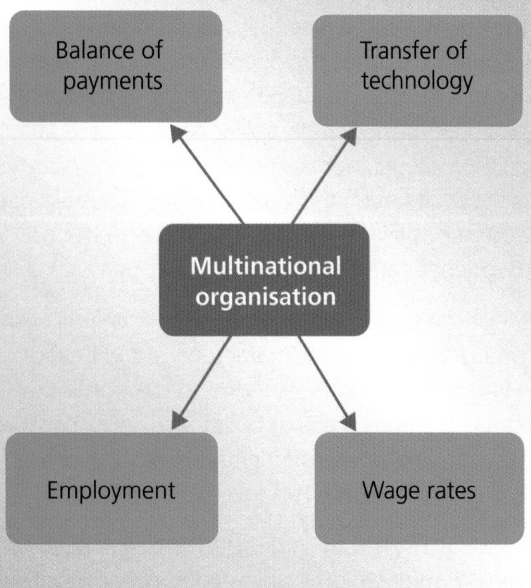

One of the direct economic effects of multinationals is that employment *should* increase in the host country. A multinational will often use local labour to build any new plant and facilities it requires, and then employ local staff for its operations in the host country. There are also jobs created in associated companies in the supply chain. If multinationals buy or merge with a local company, they may initially cut jobs through restructuring, for example, but then build up the manufacturing base. All these jobs, however, come at the expense of employment or potential employment in the multinational's home country. Multinationals don't just bring jobs: they may bring capital finance that would not normally be available for, say, the initial plant costs, and they also may bring management resources and technology

These benefits can have a long-term impact and be a spur to economic development, but they don't necessarily last. Jobs are not guaranteed in the host country if the company decides to relocate. In 2006, Peugeot announced that it would be closing the manufacturing plant in Coventry and taking production to another of its European factories, with the loss of many UK jobs directly and in the supply chain. Note one developed nation investing in another, and affecting the employment situation.

Multinational companies are involved in international transactions, and these will affect the balance of payments of both the parent and the host country to some extent. Initially capital will be transferred from the home country to the host country. This will be harmful to the balance of payments of the former, and helpful to the balance of payments of the latter. Later, when profits are made on the investment and returned to the home country, the balance of payments gains and losses are reversed.

There may be further balance of payments effects. Exports from the home country to the host may be reduced since the goods can now be produced in the host country. Since its imports are reduced, the host country benefits, and that benefit will be increased if the new factory itself begins exporting to other countries.

The effects on a country's GDP are complex. Think about the US company Starbucks. It started as a single store in Seattle 30 years ago, and by 2005 it had over 6,000 stores worldwide. It has grown through buying up chains – for example, in 1998 it bought Seattle Coffee, a British coffee chain with 60 stores – through licensing to foreign stores and chains, and through joint ventures with foreign companies. In each case, there is a slightly different flow of money and goods depending on the contractual agreements, how the

Starbucks stores are run in each country and how they respond to the prevalent local conditions and economic growth.

The position is even more complex when considering an industry. Take the coffee shop market again. Starbucks is operating in the UK with a mix of US and UK staff and local suppliers, but Pret a Manger, a UK company, has branches in New York, also with US and UK staff and local suppliers. This is again developed nation to developed nation; the situation may be more complicated where a developing nation is involved.

During the 1990s and early 2000s, Ireland increased its GDP significantly through a massive increase in exports. This came about because of the inward foreign direct investment, especially from large multinationals. They saw Ireland as a good base for the rest of Europe, and accounted for 80 per cent of the country's exports. Microsoft, Intel and Dell all have substantial Irish operations. Ireland encouraged this investment through tax breaks and grants organised through an investment and development agency. It offered companies a stable, skilled workforce, and a good infrastructure.

More indirect economic benefits occur through technology transfer. Multinationals can sometimes be credited with the transfer of technology from one country to another, especially from developed to developing nations. This, in time, facilitates economic progress in the host country. Other businesses benefit from access to the technology – and to the increased skill levels in the workforce – and the level of economic activity in the host country would be expected to increase.

Venezuela invited foreign oil companies to join the state-owned PDVSA to develop the oil industry in the 1980s and 1990s. Venezuela wanted foreign capital investment for exploration; it needed technological resources and skills in exploration, oil field development and sophisticated refining; and it wanted to be able to use the management expertise developed in the joint ventures in its own operations. All the major oil companies, such as Total, Conocco, Shell, Exxon and Mitsubishi, became involved. Venezuela has continued to depend on foreign investment and will do so until at least 2010 when its current 10-year plan ends. However, in May 2006, the Venezuelan government doubled the tax rate for foreign oil companies extracting oil to 33 per cent. This will have a big impact on the major oil companies operating in the country, and force up oil prices to developed and developing nations without oil reserves.

Negative economic impacts

If a company is located solely in the United Kingdom, for example, developments that benefit the company also benefit the whole economy. If the company increases its exports, this helps both the company's profits and the UK's balance of payments. If the company makes higher profits, it contributes more through taxation, thereby benefiting the wider economy and society.

This kind of coincidence of interests does not always exist in the case of multinational firms. For example, a multinational is often able to fulfil extra export orders from one of several plants worldwide. Managers will organise production according to what is best for the company, not for a particular economy. An increase in the multinational's overseas orders will not necessarily result in a benefit to the parent country's balance of payments.

Similarly, multinationals can also take advantage of their situation to minimise their tax liability. Suppose a multinational has factories in two countries, A and B, and that the factory in country A supplies components to the factory in country B. If profits are taxed at 50 per cent in country A and 10 per cent in country B, it is beneficial for the multinational to ensure its profits arise in country B rather than country A. The company can arrange for the factory in country A to sell goods cheaply to the plant in country B, so that profits on its operations in country A are kept to a minimum while profits in country B are increased. Governments are often constrained in what they can do to tackle this practice: a reversal of tax rates would simply lead to the multinational reversing its pricing policy.

The taxation example is just one illustration of the way in which large firms are able to get round government policies. Many multinationals are able to relocate to countries which they regard as more business-friendly, countries which perhaps have lower tax rates or a less regulated business environment. Multinationals have even more power in countries where they play a central role in economic development. In some developing countries, for example, multinationals may even be in a position to dictate to governments anxious not to jeopardise valuable overseas investment.

Costs and benefits of foreign direct investment

At this stage, it is worth summarising the costs and benefits of foreign direct investment to the home country and the host country, respectively.

The host country benefits from:

- employment
- balance of payments – inward flow of capital investment
- technology and management skills transfer.

The host country is likely to have several concerns. It will be concerned about the possible adverse effects on competition – a multinational may have access to funding that will enable it to reduce selling prices and adversely affect local businesses, or to buy up competitors and create monopoly power.

A host country will also be concerned about the adverse effects on the balance of payments – outflows of money to the home country show as a debit on the capital account; imports of supplies can also show as a debit on the capital account.

Some host governments are worried that a multinational can hold the country to ransom as it has no loyalty to the country. During the 1980s and 1990s, the US viewed European and Japanese FDIs in this way.

The home country benefits from:

- balance of payments, as there is an inflow of foreign funds
- employment, as the foreign subsidiary wants supplies of home components
- learning about new production and management techniques in the foreign country.

Volvo moved into manufacturing in South Korea by buying up part of Samsung. Although it made a massive capital investment and brought in management expertise, Volvo benefited and learned from the self-managing work teams that existed in Samsung's plant.

The home country is likely to be concerned about:

- balance of payments through the initial outflow to set up operations, potential replacement of direct exports, reimporting low production cost products
- replacement of home production.

The dynamics of these issues depend on the home and host countries, and whether they are developing

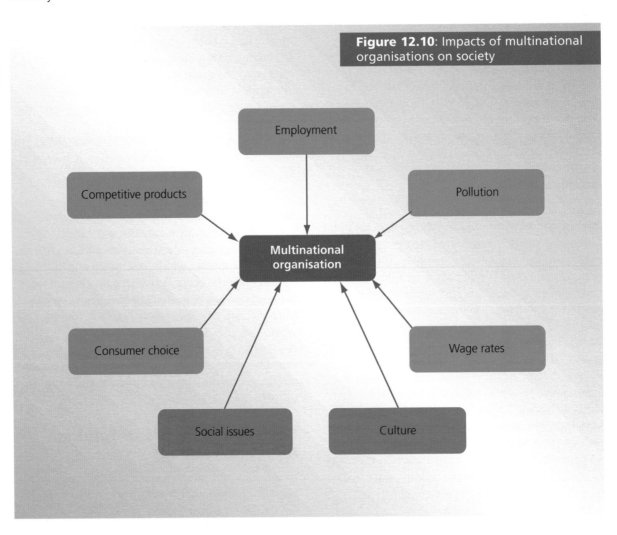

Figure 12.10: Impacts of multinational organisations on society

or developed economies. It is also influenced by the state of the countries' respective economies, industries, products and markets. Home and host countries can choose policies that encourage or restrict outward FDI, and encourage and restrict inward FDI respectively.

Toyota has developed a large plant in France manufacturing the Yaris exclusively for the European market. France offered a skilled workforce and government subsidies, including tax breaks that may have amounted to about 10 per cent of the value of the investment. The plant has created thousands of direct jobs as well as indirect jobs in the supply chain. It provides exports to other European countries, helping the balance of payments, and has helped Toyota greatly increase its market share. Toyota chose to develop the French factory rather than increase its UK production base because France was in the euro zone.

Impacts on society

Multinational companies' influence reaches beyond the pure economic sphere, and through their operations they can impact on society in many ways. There are some very specific benefits for the consumer.

- You can buy clothes from Zara, the Spanish chain, in London's Oxford Street.

- You can get cheaper phone calls on your mobile as Vodafone and O_2 reduce their tariffs.

- You can drink Starbucks coffee on many high street corners.

- You can drive any make of car you want.

The list is endless, and not just in the UK but throughout the world the consumer has access to an amazing array of goods and services.

Labour markets

Multinational companies can have a major impact on local labour markets. If a multinational is a major employer in a host country, it may be able to influence wage rates throughout the economy. In developing countries, where there are high unemployment rates, a company may be able to pay extremely low wages. Governments may be reluctant to take action for fear of discouraging employment.

Some multinational companies have even been accused of using child labour in order to keep labour

costs low. These cases are rare, fortunately, but high-profile. Child labour can increase family incomes in some developing countries, and so parents may encourage it (in a rather similar way to the use of child labour in the UK during and before the industrial revolution). While generally deplored and legislated against in developed countries, child labour is nevertheless common in others.

BA operates in the US with a flourishing business. Many flights are full, and it offers US travellers more choice and better service. It is an example of a business based in one developed nation operating in another developed country. In May 2006 BA announced that it would cut salaries of the 60 US sales force by 10 per cent, reducing their basic pay, but top up the difference with performance-related bonuses. BA obviously believes that this action will reduce costs overall, and that staff will not suffer as they will achieve their targets. Individuals may not feel so happy about the plan. In the future, if BA decides to merge with American Airlines in the US, then more cost savings might be made as more US staff would be hired, and US employee contracts have fewer company benefits than UK ones.

Multinationals don't always have a negative impact on the labour market. They can bring competition into the labour market, causing wage levels to rise and so increasing standards of living.

Environmental practice

Pollution and environmental degradation is an escalating problem in today's industrial world. Large multinational organisations can add to the pollution problems when setting up operations in other countries. They may be able to adopt practices that would be outlawed in more developed economies where there are often stringent health and environmental regulations, although there is a lot more pressure on multinationals to apply the rules and regulations in their own developed country to the developing country. However, multinationals from a developing nation, such as China, are a different matter, and function according to their own rules.

Multinational organisations can also contribute to other environmental problems such as deforestation and the depletion of non-renewable natural resources (such as oil). This exploitation of natural resources may benefit a host country in the short term, but it can leave the country's economy very vulnerable in the long term.

More positively, multinationals often have the financial resources to undertake research and exploration. As well as locating new resources, this process can increase the sustainability of existing resources.

Culture

One obvious impact of multinationals is the global spread of consumer culture. Global companies can increase competition, benefiting consumers by driving down prices and increasing choice in host countries throughout the world.

Perhaps more detrimentally, some critics argue that the presence of multinational companies throughout the world tends to spread a uniform – predominantly US and Western European – culture, threatening the survival of host countries' local cultures, lifestyles and traditions.

Impacts on other firms and communities

The growth of multinational organisations also has impacts for other businesses, providing both opportunities and threats.

Increased competition may be an opportunity and a threat. Smaller businesses are more flexible and able to respond more quickly to the requirements of consumers, putting large multinationals at a competitive disadvantage. However, most multinationals have large financial reserves and can, for example, cut prices, starting a price war that will drive smaller businesses out of the market.

There is a strand of public opinion opposed to the idea of multinationals and globalisation. This is an opportunity for smaller businesses, and some companies seek to exploit this public sentiment by emphasising their small size and local roots. However, giant multinational businesses such as Coca-Cola and McDonald's are so well known – and have such large marketing budgets – that their reputation to a large extent can withstand such public opinion.

Many governments encourage multinational companies to locate operations in their country, by offering incentives such as trade subsidies, tax concessions and grants for job creation. These incentives for multinationals can pose threats to smaller businesses.

The Make Poverty History campaign in 2005 has highlighted the role that developed nations can play in aiding the poorer developing nations. Enterprise Solutions to Poverty, from the multinational Shell, shows how the "value-creating financial assets such as Shell can be harnessed to provide greater social returns on investment". It calls for a partnership between "government, civil society and big business to be recast so that business thinking can be applied to the poverty challenge by ensuring the enabling environment can deliver the jobs and economic growth that the poor desperately want".

We shall see if the current business climate in developed nations does ultimately have an effect on poorer countries. It is unlikely to do so without government intervention and support from both sides of the equation.

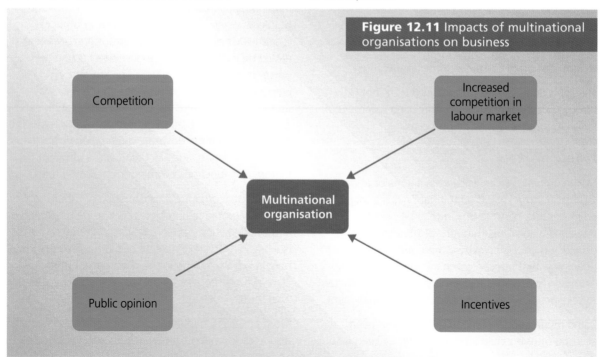

Figure 12.11 Impacts of multinational organisations on business

Nike's heritage

Twenty years ago, Bill Bowerman said "If you have a body, you are an athlete". Then, it defined how he viewed the world. Today, it defines how Nike pursues its destiny. Bowerman was the University of Oregon athletics coach who taught his athletes to seek competitive advantage everywhere – in their bodies, their gear and their passion.

In 1962 Phil Knight, a University of Oregon accounting student and middle-distance runner under Bowerman, had an idea. He wanted to bring low-priced, high-tech athletic shoes from Japan to dislodge German domination of the US athletic footwear industry.

The same year, Bowerman and Knight formed a partnership. Reportedly they each put in $500, shook hands and started importing. Soon, shoes from Onitsuka Tiger started showing up on American feet, brought into the US by a company nobody had heard of called Blue Ribbon Sports (BRS).

Bowerman was always seeking ways to improve Tiger designs, and Knight wanted them to work for themselves, creating new designs. They set up a new company. The company was called Nike. They started by selling shoes out of the back of a van at high school track meets in 1965, and in 1966 opened their first retail outlet in Santa Monica, California. Now Nike is the largest sports and fitness company in the world.

A lot has happened at Nike in the years since. The world headquarters is in Beaverton, Oregon, the hub of a business empire that reaches to every corner of the world. Nike employs approximately 24,300 people. Nike has also acquired companies to extend its reach within and beyond sports.

■ Converse, based in Massachusetts, designs and distributes athletic and casual footwear, apparel and accessories.

■ Cole Haan, based in Maine, sells dress and casual footwear and accessories for men and women under the brand names of Cole Haan, g Series and Bragano.

■ Bauer Nike Hockey, based in New Hampshire, manufactures and distributes hockey ice skates, apparel and equipment, as well as equipment for skating, and street and roller hockey.

■ Hurley International, based in California, designs and distributes a line of action sports apparel for surfing, skateboarding and snowboarding, and youth lifestyle apparel and footwear.

■ Exeter Brands Group, based in New York, includes the Starter, Team Starter and Asphalt brand names and is the master licensee of the Shaq and Dunkman brands. The Exeter Brands Group is devoted to designing and marketing athletic footwear and apparel for the retail channel.

Nike operates on six continents. Its suppliers, shippers, retailers and service providers employ close to one million people. The diversity inherent in such size is helping Nike evolve its role as a global company.

Today, Nike sees a bigger picture than when it started, one that includes building sustainable business with sound employee practices. The company wants to act on its responsibilities as a global corporate citizen.

Adapted from www.nikebiz.com

A **Discuss the advantages and disadvantages for Nike of being a multinational company.**

B **Evaluate the likely impacts of Nike on:**
   i **employment in a developing host country**
   ii **other businesses in the US and Europe (one of the reasons Nike was first set up was to offer an alternative to German athletic footwear)**
   iii **global culture**
   iv **wage rates in Thailand.**

Business in practice: Bravis Disinfectants

Bravis Disinfectants Ltd was set up eight years ago by Bill Bravis and his sister Kate to develop and distribute animal disinfectants. They still run the business as a family concern, but in the last five years Bravis has transformed itself from a supplier of disinfectants to a total biosecurity provider with specific experience in emergency disease control. Its website has been crucial in achieving this expansion, and Bravis now exports to Europe, Africa, Japan, Asia and the United States.

Product background

Biosecurity encompasses measures taken to prevent the spread of lethal or harmful organisms and diseases. It is especially important in agriculture where both crops and livestock may need protecting.

The most recent bio-threats in the UK have been the outbreak of foot and mouth disease in 2001 and the threat of avian flu in 2006.

Biosecurity is essential for the protection of animals and crops from disease, and also for the protection of neighbouring farms and the countryside. There is also a need for rapid response, both from the government and biosecurity companies, during outbreaks of certain diseases that are known to spread rapidly.

In the UK, the Department for Environment, Food and Rural Affairs (DEFRA) issues guidance for livestock keepers and poultry keepers on the protection of birds from avian flu (www.defra.gov.uk). Many other countries have their own government departments with authority to monitor, protect from and control diseases in crops and animals.

Commercial companies like Bravis sell products such as disinfectants and other chemicals that help to prevent or control outbreaks of disease.

Bravis's website

Operating out of a unit on an industrial estate in Warrington, Bravis's website sits right at the centre of its business – it's a vital resource for customers and allows Bravis to respond quickly to the needs of its customers and suppliers at home and internationally. The site provides information about all the products

Bravis distributes, how they work and why they're needed. And, because Bravis is dealing with customers around the world, the pages are available in ten languages, including Japanese and Mandarin Chinese.

John Marston, Bravis's marketing and international sales director, explains how the company uses the website: "All enquiries from the site are automatically added to our database. The system logs which country the e-mail is from and sends an e-mail to the nearest distributor." The site includes PowerPoint presentations, video clips and the Product Calculator, which suggests appropriate products for customers according to the user's country and biosecurity procedures.

Bravis's account customers have taken the electronic ordering and invoicing route, which can all be done online. There are also secure areas specifically designed for partner distributors.

As a marketing tool the site is invaluable, says John: "The cost of delivering the same amount of information to the same people by other means would be enormous. The cost of a one-page ad in *Pig International* is $4,000, and that buys us a lot of web pages. Since we implemented the new model we've increased our export of animal health products by 80 per cent from £4.7 million in 2001/02 to an expected £8 million in the year ending March 2007."

The next challenge

The speed with which Bravis has developed its export market has taken Bill and Kate by surprise. Kate wants to build on their success and develop a stronger international presence by opening production and sales operations abroad. Bill, however, is more cautious. He is impressed by the website and thinks that the company should continue to develop it as a marketing tool before going further.

activities

Eager to put her ideas about developing the international presence of Bravis Disinfectants Ltd to the board at the next meeting, Kate has asked you for advice. Write a report to Kate making your recommendations on the best course of action for Bravis. Your report should cover:

- the implications of legal format and type of business

- typical objectives for developing an international presence and their importance

- impacts on the business, its customers and suppliers

- the roles of international organisations such as the WTO

- the advantages and costs of developing an international presence for Bravis

- the sources of support available to help Bravis develop its export business.

THIS UNIT EXAMINES THE KEY ELEMENTS THAT GO INTO PLANNING, organising, running and evaluating a large-scale event such as a conference, a meeting or staff outing. It gives you the framework to plan, manage and administer to completion a one-off event.

This is a practical unit. You are required to organise an actual event, and in doing so you will need to draw on some of the practical knowledge, understanding and skills that are needed in the business world.

To help you organise your own event and produce your presentation and final report, the unit is organised into four broad sections:
- feasibility of the event
- planning the event
- staging the event
- review and evaluation of the event.

Organising
an event

Intro

Event management: an overview

Setting the scene: charity events

When disaster strikes, Oxfam needs all the support that people can give to help it relieve the suffering of those affected.

By organising an event for Oxfam, the organisers can:

- raise funds to make sure that Oxfam can respond quickly and save more lives

- raise awareness of emergencies and how Oxfam works

- provide a way for people to get involved and make a real, positive difference.

Oxfam is obviously keen to support and encourage anybody who wishes to raise money in this way. Oxfam publishes advice for event organisers on its website (www.oxfam.org.uk) and also produces a fundraising kit.

One group of students responded to media coverage of the major earthquake in Pakistan in 2005 by deciding to hold a fundraising event. They realised that they would have to stage a large event in order to raise a substantial sum of money. They eventually decided on running a disco on the grounds that they could organise it quickly, and they should be able to make a large profit as many college staff were willing to help the students for no charge.

The students believed that they could sell tickets for £8, a premium price, as the disco was being held to raise money for charity. They planned to sell soft drinks at a £1 each, and the college catering department agreed to provide the drinks on a sale-or-return basis at cost price (£0.25 each). They had to pay £200 for the DJ, and decorations for the hall cost a further £30.

The disco sold out – the hall had a maximum capacity of 300 people under the terms of its insurance for entertainment purposes – and 580 drinks were sold during the evening. The event made a profit of £2,605.

When the students reflected on the event they were very pleased with how it had gone, but they were able to identify several ways in which they could have raised more money and worked more efficiently.

Event management in business

Businesses organise events for a wide variety of reasons. Events can be a showcase for customers, a chance to raise team morale, an opportunity to build investor relations. Consider these four scenarios, all different, yet all requiring you to organise an event of some sort.

- You have just started your first office job, and your boss informs you in November that, as the newest employee, it is your job to organise the office Christmas party.

- After leaving school, you open a small shop. You want to stage an event to publicise the business and to encourage people to visit the shop.

- Your company has a new product that it wishes to show to investors. You have been asked to organise a one-day event for potential investors. The day must be relaxed amd entertaining, and give people a chance to try out the new product.

- You are a newly appointed business studies teacher. Your head of department has asked you to organise an information evening for parents and students about the subject.

Most people have to organise an event of a significant size during their working lives, and some people even make a career of event management. Organising an event can be a career opportunity, giving individuals the chance to show that they can organise a medium-sized project and manage a budget before moving on to larger-scale management responsibilities.

Event organisation exposes individuals to high risks in their careers – nobody benefits when events go wrong. It is also a high-risk moment for a business, as it is likely to have invested considerable time and energy into a major event. This investment is clearly designed to help the business to achieve its wider objectives, but if the event goes horribly wrong, it can have the opposite effect.

It is vital, therefore, to practise the skills of event organisation in a "safe" environment, without putting the future of a business at risk. This is the principle that underpins this unit. This is the dress rehearsal for some key career moments in your lives. Make sure that you make the most of the opportunities to learn and reflect. The assessment at the end of the unit is designed to help you maximise your learning. As you work through the unit, keep records and notes that will help you build up a portfolio for the assessment.

What this unit covers

This unit will guide you through the running of a substantial one-off event. It covers the key steps in setting up and running a large event. It doesn't just suggest what you have to do to organise a successful event, but by presenting some case studies of poorly organised events (at the start of most topics) it is also designed to help you learn from other students' errors.

Research and feasibility

Before starting to organise any event, it is important to ensure that the event will fit in with the overall aims of the sponsoring organisation. You need to know (or determine) the budget for the event. You need to set the event's aims, objectives and expected outcomes. And you need to identify any constraints that could prevent you achieving your objectives.

To do this, it is often necessary to carry out market research. This will help you know if the event is appropriate or achievable, and the research findings may be used to decide between several possible events. For any large-scale event, it is essential to carry out a risk assessment.

Planning the event

Once the overall aims, objectives and general shape of the event have been decided, the real planning work begins. This means ensuring that the appropriate resources are available at the right time for the event. It requires communicating with all stakeholders so that everyone understands their expected contribution or role in the event. It also requires drawing up contingency plans for the day of the event itself.

During the planning stage, the team organising the event should allocate responsibility for different aspects of the event to individuals. It is a good idea to give everyone in the team responsibility for some aspect of the event, on the clear understanding that everyone is responsible for taking leadership and team roles throughout the event. This planning stage should include regular opportunities for both individuals and the organising group as a whole to reflect on, and find strategies to improve, their performance.

Staging the event

On the actual day, if everything has been well planned, the event should run smoothly. However, there is always likely to be some unexpected problem, so you should have contingency plans in place and the flexibility to cope with last-minute changes. There are a variety of tasks that need to be undertaken on the day, from monitoring access and fire exits to ensure that they are clear, to maintaining the security of cash and other assets. At the end of the day, when it is over, take time to consider what you did to contribute to the success of the event.

Evaluation

If SMART targets are set at the start of the project and there is regular review, reflection and evaluation throughout the exercise, then the final event evaluation should be a straightforward exercise. This might involve asking stakeholders to fill in an event assessment, which should include room to make recommendations for improvement. From this feedback, it is possible to produce an analytical report on the staging of the event.

Topic 1 Selecting the event

Setting the scene: coming up with ideas

There are many events that you could reasonably choose to organise. Before you decide on an event, think about the some of the different reasons for staging events. Brainstorm some ideas with other students.

You might, for example, decide to hold an event to raise money for charity or to promote a local business by, say, organising a product sampling event. You might organise an event such as a "battle of the bands" as part of a Young Enterprise company programme.

Another option is to focus on your school or college. You might hold an event to promote your college to future students, perhaps through a Year 11 problem-solving day held in conjunction with the Armed Forces, your local

Chamber of Commerce or the Construction Industry Trade Board.

Other college-based ideas might be to hold a business studies evening, inviting in local business people and university speakers to talk about various aspects of business, or to organise and run the annual college dance.

The event you choose must be "substantial", but it must also be manageable given the number of students involved and the time your teacher has to supervise your activities.

KEY TERMS

An event is **viable** if it is capable of working successfully. It is **feasible** if it can be organised relatively easily.

Primary source data is information gathered at first hand through methods such as questionnaires and interviews.

Secondary source data is information obtained second-hand, such as data collected by another group for another purpose, or data in publications.

Making choices

Your group needs to understand why it is holding the event that you are going to organise. The primary purpose for holding the event should not be simply to fulfil your exam specification requirements. The event should have some other primary purpose. This might be:

- to raise funds for a charity or cause

- to boost sales at a store or improve the public relations of a local business

- to maximise your profits, if you are running a mini-enterprise company

- to boost recruitment to your school's or college's Key Stage 5 programmes

- to help you with your studies

- to provide entertainment and a sense of community to your peer group.

Clearly defining the reason for holding the event is critical to enable you to progress further and define your aims, objectives and the research that you need to carry out.

Your event needs to be "substantial" in order to fulfil the assessment specification. Some events suggested by the exam specification could take many months to organise. Certainly, you should be thinking in terms of an event which could be organised and run over a period of perhaps two or three months. This would give you time to arrange venues, organise the publicity, book leading personalities you might want at the event, and so on.

The logistics and timings should be a key factor in choosing an event. Generally, events are better managed if they are contained in one term. It makes most sense to stage the event in the winter or spring term so that it does not clash with the externally assessed examinations in the summer.

Another consideration is the scope for teamwork and full participation by the group. Will organising and running the event provide enough roles for all individuals in the class to play a significant part? Is it too ambitious, so that it becomes too burdensome and seems like full-time employment?

What sources of support might be available? For example, if you decide to organise a business studies trip to Belgium for three days, can you get assistance from a travel agent with booking hotels, company visits and coaches? If so, the group's role in the exercise may be more manageable.

Through class discussion, and by developing ideas in smaller groups, try to produce a short list of your best ideas for an event. Ideally you want a short list of two or three possible events at this stage. This will allow you to move to the next key stage: assessing the viability and feasibility of each event on the short list. Here you will be expected to show high-quality analysis and evaluation in your final report.

Viability and feasibility

The purpose of assessing the viability and feasibility of your short-listed events is to enable the group to make a reasoned choice between the options. A viability and feasibility study requires some research. All organisations should do some research before they commit to a potentially expensive event. This enables them to identify ways in which to minimise the cost of the event and to maximise the benefits to the stakeholders. Furthermore, it is important to identify very early on whether there is any interest for the proposed events. This should take into account any cost – the three-day trip to Belgium might not look so attractive once the event has been costed.

Primary research that could be undertaken could include:

■ surveys – ask potential participants to identify which events, if any, they would like to attend and (if appropriate) to state what they might be willing (or prepared) to pay

■ interviews – for example, ask students which business studies topics they feel most insecure about and which they would like to be covered in an one-day conference

■ supplier prices – if, for example, you are organising a leavers' ball, get quotes from halls, DJs and caterers.

Secondary research could also be invaluable. If you are staging an event to promote a local business, obtain local authority data on the socioeconomic mix and type of housing in a neighbourhood. Whatever your event, it might be useful to read reports from other groups of students that have worked on similar problems. These may give you access to costings for a similar event to yours, they may highlight unexpected problems, and they may contain customer feedback surveys done by former students.

Make a list of research that it might be useful to do to assess the viability and feasibility of each of your short-listed events. Then prioritise the research you can do within the time available. Allocate responsibility to individuals within the group for carrying out different elements of this research, and set yourselves clear deadlines to collect the data.

When the data is collected, you should first look at the data on your own. Analyse all the data collected by your group and arrive at your recommendation for which event to undertake. This ensures that you are practising research and analysis skills, and you start to build up a body of your own work which can be credited in your final report.

It is good practice in business to arrive at meetings well briefed, and that includes preparatory analysis of data. It is very difficult to analyse data at the same time as following discussions in a meeting. Making your own analysis and recommendations is also a useful check on the decision-making process, although it doesn't follow that your decision will be the one that the group ultimately pursues.

Aims, objectives and outcomes

The business aims of your event need to be stated succinctly, so that it provides your team with the long-term vision for the whole event. Think of a sentence that sums up your vision for your event. Work with your organising group to agree on a vision that everyone can agree on. Once everyone is committed to a vision, keep the vision clearly in front of all stakeholders by displaying it on notice boards, letter headings and any publicity materials for the event.

The objectives for the event need to be SMART. This means that they should be:

- **specific** – explain exactly what is to be achieved

- **measurable** – a form of measurement is essential to establish what has been achieved

- **achievable** – should provide a challenge (to motivate) but should be capable of being delivered

- **realistic** – it should be reasonable to expect that the objective can be met by those responsible for doing so

- **time-bound** – it should have a defined timescale, setting out when objectives should be achieved.

If an agreed vision and SMART objectives are in place from the start, there is a strong framework for monitoring the progress of the event management and evaluating the outcomes of the event.

For example, if a group of students organised a subject evening for business studies, their vision might be "to cover all the syllabus content for Unit 8 such that by the end of the evening all attendees have a sound understanding of the structure and content of a business plan".

The group's SMART objective might be "to run a business studies conference from 5–7 pm on 20 November and to achieve evaluation feedback which lies between satisfactory and good". To achieve this objective, it might set a number of targets:

- to have secured (by 15 October) three speakers from local companies to talk about their experience of business planning

- to invite a bank manager to reflect on the bank's experience of receiving business plans and to identify what makes a good plan from a bank's perspective

- to publicise the evening, produce a programme and sell tickets by 25 October

- to have a suitable venue booked by 25 September

- to have printed all speaker materials and evaluation sheets for attendees three days before the conference.

Allocating roles

From the start of any enterprise, it is important that all the participants are allocated clear responsibilities for various aspects of the operation. These roles do not have to be set in stone for the whole life of the project, but can be changed around so that everyone gets experience of more than one area of responsibility.

There needs to be someone who is clearly in charge, someone who chairs meetings, has the final say on decisions and to whom all the other members involved in the event report to. Someone must also be allocated responsibility for the role of secretary – the really important role of keeping a record of all meetings, setting agendas and communicating between all members of the enterprise. Finance is also an important area of responsibility that must be clearly allocated and managed meticulously from the outset.

Other areas of responsibility might include market research, sales, publicity, logistics (booking the venue, checking electricity supplies, checking the availability of equipment and organising the post-event clear-up), catering and any other areas that are key to the event's success. If a role is particularly large or an area of high risk such as finance then more than one person may wish to take on the role so that the area is always covered even if one member is unable to make a key team meeting or take care of an activity.

Within each role, there ought to be a clear set of responsibilities. The team member carrying out that role should be set objectives and targets. There should also be regular opportunities for team members to reflect on how well they are meeting their individual targets and how they can improve their performance.

The event team also needs to set aside time to reflect on how the team is working together to meet its team goals and objectives, and how the team could adjust its working practices to perform at a higher level. It is essential that this continuous review and reflection takes place, and is well documented.

assessment practice
A multiculturel evening

Suppose you have decided to hold a multicultural evening to reflect the diverse cultures and beliefs at your college.

The event can only be held on 20 November in the college hall, though you will also have access to the college canteen. In your planning, you have decided that you want the event to comprise:

- dance displays

- musical pieces

- an international food buffet

- displays from the languages and geography departments

- a contribution from the college's equal opportunities officer

- talks about working and trading internationally from businesses linked to the college.

The hall has a legal capacity of 300 people and the canteen's capacity is 200 people. The college has 2000 students. It is now 20 September.

Your task is to draft some SMART objectives for this event. These objectives should create a structure for all the elements of the event to come together on time. Success criteria should be based on numbers of participants and displays, and the size of the audience.

Setting the scene: careless with cash

A team of Year 12 students decided to run an evening to raise money for charity. They had booked a celebrity chef for the evening to display some of her recipes. They were also going to produce a CD with favourite recipes from several well-known personalities.

The planning and management of the event seemed fine. The CD production was excellent. They had raised working capital through running a disco. Unfortunately, the group started to have cash flow problems.

On investigation, it was shown that there were several flaws in the team's financial planning. The financial records were not really up to date, so it was difficult to see what was happening. The team had decided not to open a bank account, but to make all payments in cash.

They did not realise that they had left around £300 in cash on top of their lockers in an old plastic bag. Fortunately, the cash had been handed to the school's deputy head, who was just waiting for the group to notice that this money was missing.

KEY TERMS

Financial constraints are the limitations imposed on event managers by the event's budget. Any event must be organised within a budget.

Risk assessment is the formal process of considering all the risks associated with the event and ensuring that they can be managed. If the risks cannot be managed, the event should not go ahead.

Risk management is the process of managing risks associated with the event.

Financial systems

Any event will incur some costs, as well as possibly generating some revenue. It is essential that you plan and budget for all expenses and income. It is only too easy to lose control of cash, income and expenses. From the start every group organising an event needs to have strict rules and procedures for all aspects of financial management. These need to be in place to protect team members from going over budget and to ensure that all money is properly accounted for, preventing any accusations of theft.

It is important that you select the key accounting and costing tools that you need to do the job. You need to have the tools and skills to prepare budgets and to undertake some basic financial analysis. These tasks can be made easier with appropriate software. Some free financial software can help you here – this can be preferable to using complex (and often expensive)

professional accounting packages or to trying to reinvent the wheel. You should be able to get some useful free software from Young Enterprise (www.young-enterprise.org.uk) and Shell LiveWIRE (www.shell-livewire.org).

Budgets

Budgets are statements of the expected costs and revenues associated with the event. You have already encountered budgets as part of your AS studies, see Unit 2 pages 82–7 of your AS textbook. You should also use the next Stop and Think activity to reinforce your knowledge and understanding.

Laying out budgets

Many people may need to check and use an event budget. It is important, therefore, that this financial information is laid out clearly. Figure 13.1 shows how the budget for the remembrance event (see "stop and think" opposite) could be laid out.

Checking budgets

It is very easy to forget to include some major expense in the draft budget. It is also easy to include items that will not result in actual expenditure. Minimise these risks by doing checks for full and no false inclusion. For example, before anyone drafts a budget, the whole group could discuss and agree what should be included in the budget. When the budget is complete, ask a friend or someone with

Figure 13.1: Budget income and expenditure account for multi-faith remembrance event

Income	£	£
Donations from college and religious groups	xx	
Collection on the night	xx	xxx
Expenditure		
Travel, board and lodgings for historian	xx	
Refreshments	xx	
Hire of hall and caretaker	xx	
Floral decorations	xx	
Printing and publicity	xx	xxx
Net surplus/loss		xxx

stopandthink

A group of students is organising a multi-faith act of remembrance for victims of terrorism. The organisers want to show terrorism in its historical context, and have asked a leading university historian to make a presentation at the event.

The students must pay the historian's travel, accommodation and meal costs (£200); the hall and the caretaker for the night will cost £150; the printing of posters and other publicity material will cost £70. Around 500 people are expected to attend the remembrance service, and they will be offered a drink and a biscuit which will cost 15 pence per head.

The students' college and some of the participating religious groups have contributed £600 towards the cost of the event. A flower shop is donating floral decorations. A collection will be taken at the end of the event, which it is hoped will generate an average £1 donation per person.

Any surplus funds will be donated to a relevant charity. How much do the students expect to be able to donate to charity?

business experience to check it over. Ask them whether it includes everything that they would expect to be in the budget.

Financial analysis

One way to understand the expenses associated with an event is to divide all expenditure items into fixed and variable costs. This type of financial analysis was covered in Unit 2 (see pages 92–5 of the AS textbook). Fixed costs are expenses that have to be incurred regardless of the number of people attending the event. Variable costs are expenses that will increase in direct proportion to the number of people attending the event.

Suppose that you planning a dinner dance. The fixed costs include the hire of the venue and the fees for a DJ and/or a band. These expenses have to be paid regardless of the numbers attending the dance. The catering cost, however, will depend on the numbers that attend, so this is a variable cost. Figure 13.2 sets out a typical cost structure for the dinner dance.

Figure 13.2: Cost structure for a dinner dance

Fixed costs	£
Hire of hall	200
Hire of DJ	200
Cost of band	300
Total	700
Variable costs (per person)	
Helium balloon and small memento	5
Food	12
First drink	1
Total variable cost per person	18

By organising event expenditure into fixed and variable costs, you can easily work out the contribution of each paying guest and the breakeven point of the event. These are given by the formulae:

$$\text{contribution} = \text{ticket price} - \text{variable costs}$$

$$\text{breakeven} = \frac{\text{fixed costs}}{\text{contribution}}$$

You can use these formulas to work out the number of people you would need to attract to an event to make it break even for any given ticket price. For example, suppose the dinner dance is priced at £30 per person. Then, from the data in Figure 13.2, the contribution per person is £12 (30 – 18); and the breakeven point is 58.3 (700/12), which means that 59 tickets need to be sold for the event to break even. Note that if the ticket price for the dinner dance is less than £18 per person, then it would be impossible for the event to break even because each person would be paying less than the variable cost and would therefore be making no contribution towards the fixed costs of the event.

This type of breakeven analysis allows event organisers to make a decision about ticket prices. Obviously, this decision is not made by simply considering costs alone, but it needs to take into account any capacity constraints – say the number of people the hall can accommodate – and any market research that is undertaken prior to the event, such as prices the target audience are willing to pay.

Figure 13.3 shows the breakeven calculations for three suggested ticket prices for the dinner dance. Clearly, the organisers need to sell fewer tickets to break even if they charge higher prices. However, they need to take into account the fact that a high price may deter most of the target audience, and they would need to do some market research to see what people might consider a reasonable ticket price. A lower ticket price might attract a larger audience, and it could lead to a more successful event with a better atmosphere.

Figure 13.3: Breakeven analysis for the dinner dance

Ticket price	Contribution	Breakeven
£25	£7	100
£35	£17	42
£45	£27	26

stop and think

Suggest ways in which the organisers of the dinner dance could reduce their costs so that they could run a successful event at a lower ticket price.

Assume it is possible to reduce variable costs to £13, with fixed costs still at £700. If the organisers decide to charge £16 a ticket, how many tickets would they need to sell to break even?

Event finance

Ticket sales are not the only way of generating the revenue to pay for an event. Funding can come from a variety of grants and donations, and you will need to explore the options for raising the money to stage your event. For example, your school or college may have a budget for social events or for promoting extracurricular subject development. Often local businesses are willing to donate small sums – up to, say, £100 – towards mini-enterprise projects.

In order to get sponsorship from local businesses, you need to make contact in person or by telephone. It is highly unlikely that any business or individual will give sponsorship if they just receive a letter. If you wish to send a letter in advance, then follow it up within days with a phone call and try to arrange a meeting. The sort of businesses that are most likely to support your event are:

- those which supply the school with goods and services
- those whose owners have children at the school or college, or are governors
- those businesses that wish to sell goods or publicise their services to students or their parents.

Obvious businesses to approach include banks, building societies, sports clubs, garden centres, printers, restaurants, childrens' activity organisers and car hire companies. Many students simply dress formally and go door to door to local businesses asking for sponsorship. Other organisations that might consider sponsoring a student event include the chamber of commerce, the local branch of the Chartered Institute of Directors, the local Rotarians and other business network organisations.

You will need to consider how to raise some working capital for the event. (See Unit 11, page 156, for information on the concept of working capital.) Most events will require some expenditure in advance, so you will need some resources even if you intend to cover all your expenses through the money you raise at the event itself. Some student groups agree to donate £10 each towards the working capital for setting up an event. Some groups organise money-raising ventures to generate the funds to support the actual event that they are holding. A well-run Key Stage Three disco, for example, ought to be able to yield £1,000, providing sufficient capital to plan a substantial event.

In reality, however, most student groups have relatively few resources to stage events. Therefore, it is important to learn the skills of managing within a very tight budget and making the most of resources that are donated free. This is a good discipline for life.

A small budget should not dampen your enthusiasm. Your group may well be able to stage an excellent publicity event for a local small business just by donating your time and energy. Just think what you could do with relatively little expense:

- analyse the socioeconomic profile of the local population

- design publicity materials pitched at this population

- deliver leaflets to, say, 1000 homes in three different areas

- set up and run a publicity event while the owner concentrates on the customer relations

- carry out customer surveys before, during or after the event.

Risk assessment

Risk assessment is a process of identifying and assessing all possible risks that could affect the organisation and running of the event. Once all risks have been identified, each needs to be assessed for how big a threat it poses to the event. This is usually done using a 1–5 scale, with 1 being a low risk and 5 being a very high risk. For example, if insufficient funds would mean that the event could not take place, it would be ranked as a risk of 5.

Many organisations use risk assessment forms to formalise the process. This is often organised under headings to break the task down into manageable units. Figure 13.4 shows a risk assessment form that could be used in the planning of your event. Obviously, the nature of your event will determine the specific risks you might include on the form.

Once all possible risks have been assessed, it is important to think of strategies to manage risks. For example, in the scenario presented in the Stop and Think exercise, the group may want to manage the risk of a member of staff not turning up by offering a meal out at a restaurant to members of staff that turn up on the night. A strong teacher presence at the event may well also reduce several other risks, such as tackling underage drinking, dealing with boisterous behaviour, and coping with security behind the stage.

Figure 13.4: Risk assessment form

Type and description	Rating of risk (1 to 5)
Financial	
Insufficient funds are raised to finance the event.	☐
Cash is not properly accounted for.	☐
Proper accounting records are not kept.	☐
Personnel	
A key member of the team is removed from the course.	☐
Members of the team get drawn into conflict.	☐
There is a high level of absence by some team members.	☐
Meetings are chaotic.	☐
Asset management	
Hired assets get damaged during the event.	☐
The stock of materials for the event is damaged.	☐
Assets are stolen.	☐
Legal and insurance	
Your insurance does not cover events held off the college premises.	☐
People are dissatisfied with the event and demand their money back.	☐
Health and safety legislation is breached.	☐
Sales and marketing	
The posters are not ready on time from the printers.	☐
Nobody comes to the event.	☐

s t o p a n d t h i n k

Your team decides to run a battle of the bands event at a local theatre. You will be working with Youth FM, a local radio station. The radio station insists that a member of staff from your college is present all evening. List all the risks that might be associated with this event. Assess each risk on a scale of 1 to 5.

Birkbeck College, at the University of London, is a popular conference venue in central London. It is a convenient location for Euston and Kings Cross stations, and it can accommodate a reasonable number of delegates.

Suppose you are organising a one-day conference and you are thinking of using Birkbeck College to hold your event. Search Birkbeck's website (www.bbk.ac.uk) to find the cost of hiring a lecture theatre to accommodate 120 delegates, the cost of catering (with a room for 120 delegates, standing) and the cost of hiring equipment (one flip chart and a television).

You have estimated that printing and posting publicity for the conference will cost £1,500. The administration for handling conference bookings will cost £2,500. Travel and accommodation for speakers will cost approximately £1,000.

A Draft a budget for the conference.

B If the conference price is set at £120, calculate how many delegates need to attend in order to break even.

C What is the lowest price at which you could offer this conference and still break even? Note that you can only accommodate 120 delegates.

D In which ways could you trim your costs if only 50 people book places at the conference?

E Draft a risk assessment for the day. Are there any risks that would cause you to cancel the conference?

Planning the event

Setting the scene: a training event for Year 12 mini-enterprise students

A Young Enterprise area board asked a group of Year 13 students to run a training event for new young enterprise achievers who are just setting up their companies.

The Year 13 students had a long list of tasks to achieve to ensure this event was a success:

- a venue needed to be booked immediately at a local company

- catering needed to be arranged, with final numbers to be given 48 hours before the event

- invitations to the event had to be e-mailed out to all YE companies and link teachers

- speeches and activities for the training event needed to be planned, written and rehearsed

- audiovisual equipment needed to be booked with the host company

- handouts and evaluation forms needed to be photocopied (the company was willing to do this if the students e-mailed the material 24 hours before the event).

The students held an initial planning event in which they set deadlines for all these tasks. They also exchanged e-mail addresses in order to establish regular communication between themselves, the host company manager and the YE fieldworker.

The event turned out to be highly successful. An evaluation showed that key factors in this success was that the students had controlled the resources from the start and set up effective communication links.

KEY TERMS

Resource requirements are the inputs, such as time, money, equipment and manpower, that are needed in order to stage an event.

Resource constraints are the factors that limit access to resources, such as time constraints, lack of money, lack of workers, lack of equipment, and also legislation.

Contingency plans are the plans that have been made in advance to provide a fallback position or alternative arrangements in case something goes wrong.

Managing resources

All events will require a variety of resources. In planning and running an event, it is important that the necessary resources are available as and when they are needed. Given the limitations on budgets, it is also important that organisers make the best possible use of any resources available. Without disciplined planning, it is really easy to miss opportunities or waste time.

In business, there are various tools that help managers to plan and make effective use of the available resources. Managers' future pay and promotion often hangs on being able to manage resources well, so these are vital skills to learn.

Wall planners

Wall planners are simple visual tools, usually A1 size calendars, used by managers to monitor resource movements, staff holidays and key events at which all staff should be present. They cover a set period of time, typically a 12-month period. Colour-coded stickers are used to represent different people and/or resources.

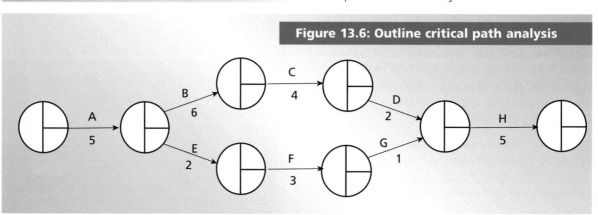

stop and think

Your group could set up a planner on the classroom wall and use it in planning your event. As you work through the planning and management of your event, reflect on the uses and limitations of a wall planner.

Gantt charts

Gantt charts are not very different from wall planners, but rather than being a general calendar, they are set up for each project. The project weeks/days are given along the top (rather than actual dates), and project activities are listed down the side. Figure 13.5 shows a Gantt chart used by a group of students to plan, organise and control a Valentine's Day Fair in the school hall.

Figure 13.5: Gantt chart for a student event

Task	week 1	week 2	week 3	week 4	week 5
Briefing meetings	XXXXX				
Workshop sessions		XXX	XXX	XXX	
Cookery room			XXX	XXX	X
Purchase wrappings			X		
Advertise			XXX	XXX	
Book rooms	X				
Run event					XX
Evaluate event					X

Gantt charts can be easily set up using an Excel (or similar) spreadsheet program. The advantage of using a software package as opposed to a wall display is that it is easier to share your planning with the group by e-mail. Everyone in the group can have access to the plans as long as they can access a computer. It is also easier to modify and adapt the plans.

stop and think

Use a Gantt chart as part of the monitoring and review of your event. (Setting up a Gantt chart for your event is relatively simple if you use a spreadsheet program.) At the end of the event, evaluate the usefulness of the Gantt chart and suggest how you might improve your use of this tool for future event management.

Critical path analysis

Critical path analysis is a development of the Gantt chart concept. Instead of displaying a project's activities in a time chart, they are displayed in a diagram where:

- arrows represent activities
- nodes (a small circle, with a half and two quarters) represent the start and finish of activities.

Figure 13.6 shows an outline critical path analysis diagram. As you can see, there is a letter above, and a number below, each arrow. The letter represents the name of that activity. The number represents the time that activity will take – so, for example, activity A will take five days. The diagram is arranged in the order activities must be undertaken. So, in this case activity A must be completed before activities B and E can commence. Activities B, C and D can be undertaken at the same time as activities E, F and G, but all must be completed before activity H can commence.

Figure 13.6: Outline critical path analysis

In a completed critical path analysis, there are three data items given at the nodes. First, each node has a number – 1, 2, 3 and so on – which is written in the left-hand side of the circle. Nodes are numbered from left to right. Second, the top right-hand quarter of the node contains the earliest start time (EST) for the next activity (or activities). Third, the bottom right-hand corner of the node contains the latest finish time (LFT) of the previous activity (or activities).

In Figure 13.6, activity A is at the start of the project, so the node at the start of activity A will be node 1, and the earliest start time for the activity will be day 0. (You assume that the first activity starts on day 0.) The node at the end of activity A will be node 2, and the earliest start time of the next activities will be immediately after the end of activity A, that is day 5.

To complete a critical path analysis, you need to fill in the data at each node. This requires a calculation of earliest start times and latest finish times of each activity. To show how this is done, we will use Figure 13.6 as an example. Start, by numbering and defining each node, as in Figure 13.7.

Figure 13.7: Defining the nodes

Node	Activity before	Activity after
1	n/a	A
2	A	B and E
3	B	C
4	C	D
5	E	F
6	F	G
7	G and D	H
8	H	n/a

Earliest start times

The earliest start time (EST) is calculated by adding the EST of the previous activity to the duration of the previous activity. So, the EST of activity B (node 2) is found by adding EST of activity A to the duration of A, which is day 5 (0 + 5); the EST of activity C is found by adding the EST of activity B to the duration of B, which is day 11 (5 + 6); and so on.

If you do all the calculations, you will find that the earliest time that activity H can start is on day 17. As activity H takes 5 days, the minimum time the whole project can be completed in is 22 days.

Latest finishing times

The latest finishing times (LFT) of activities are calculated by working from right to left, that is by working back from the end of the project. The project can be completed in 22 days, so we give the LFT for activity H (node) as 22 days, otherwise we would be delaying the whole project unnecessarily. The LFT for node 7 (activities G and D) is day 17; that is, all the activities prior to activity H must be finished in 17 days in order for activity H to start on time; the LFT for node 6 (activity F) is day 16, and so on.

Figure 13.8: ESTs and LFTs

Activity	Duration of activity (days)	Earliest start time	Latest finish time
A	5	0	5
B	6	5	11
C	4	11	15
D	2	15	17
E	2	5	13
F	3	7	16
G	1	10	17
H	5	17	22

Figure 13.8 shows the ESTs and LFTs for all nodes in the diagram in Figure 13.6, and you can now complete this diagram by filling in the three data items in each node (the node number in the left of the circle, the EST in the top right-hand corner, and the LFT in the bottom right-hand quarter). You should see that on the path ABCDH, the ESTs are the same as the LFTs. This means that on this path each new activity must commence once the previous activity has been completed. There is no spare time, and any delay would result in the whole project running late. This is known as the critical path, and it is marked on the diagram by putting two lines through each activity arrow that is on the path, like so:

In our example, there are three activities – activities E, F and G – that are not on the critical path. These activities could be delayed for up to six days without causing the project to overrun. This time is called the float. It is useful to know where the float is in a project. If your resources are limited, you should focus on the critical activities and be able to delay (float) some of the non-critical activities without jeopardising the whole project.

Other constraints

The planning tools we have considered in this topic enable event teams to manage time in relation to their physical resources. For example, they are useful in terms of booking equipment, rooms and contractors on time, in ensuring that the right personnel are available at the right times, and in thinking through some basics of contingency planning if things do not run smoothly.

There are however other constraints that need to be considered and built into your planning. Principally,

you will need to consider the legal obligations placed on event organisers. Does your event comply with health and safety legislation, for example? You can find summaries of current health and safety regulations on the DTI website (ww.dti.gov.uk).

You will need to consider the legal constraints and obligations imposed by any contracts that you enter into for the event. If you book a venue such as a hall, the contract is likely to have sections covering behaviour at your event, paying for any damages, drinks licences, the legal capacity of the venue for different types of events, the limits of the venue's insurance cover, and so on.

Professional event organisers will have insurance cover to minimise their risks. Does your college's insurance cover your activities adequately? If you are organising this under the umbrella of the Young Enterprise Company Programme, your registration fee will ensure that you have some cover for your event, but it specifically excludes certain items such as food preparation and explosives. You need to ensure that your event is well within those activities covered by your insurance.

assessment practice
Football training

Suppose you have decided to run a football coaching day for Year 5 and 6 pupils from some primary schools. You will charge a fee for the training day – to be paid by the parents of each pupil attending – to cover your costs. In order to run the day, you need to compete these tasks.

- Book the football pitches at a local sports facility.

- Pay for the football pitches.

- Design and print publicity materials.

- Organise insurance for the event.

- Open a bank account to handle the money.

- Draft a letter for the Year 5 and 6 students to take home to their parents.

- Photocopy the letter to parents so that each school has 120 copies to give out.

- Visit schools to collect booking forms and fees.

- Organise some teachers from the primary schools to be present on the day in case of emergencies.

- Book a first aider for the day.

- Collate a list of all those students taking part, with their parents' names and contact numbers.

- Design a programme of activities for the day.

- Invite a representative of a local football club to hand out prizes and certificates.

A Organise the list of tasks that need to be undertaken into some sort of order.

B Scan the list and think around the event. Have you forgotten any obvious preparation that needs doing?

C Try to use a management tool (a wall planner, a Gantt chart or critical path analysis) to represent the planning of this event visually.

D How might the event be affected by other constraints, such as health and safety regulations, child protection legislation and contracts with the owners of the sports facility?

Communication, communication, communication

Setting the scene: Matt the hat loses his cool

Angela, the managing director of the mini-enterprise company, found a note on her desk one morning. It was from one of her colleagues in the company.

I am fed up, I don't know what is going on, all I seem to do is make hats with bells on day and night, I don't know if they are sold, I don't know if we are making a profit, I haven't seen any adverts about for our product, nobody tells me if there are any problems with the hats, we never seem to have any meetings, and when we do everyone screams at each other or just talks to their friends. No one else is making any hats. What happened at the sales event on Saturday? I quit! **Matt**

Angela did not know what to do. Matt was right, he was the only one in the team making hats; the rest of them were busy selling, but everything was a bit chaotic. She phoned her business adviser, Bill Jones, to let him know the bad news and to ask for help. Bill was not totally sympathetic, but he had some ideas that Angela had heard before and he kept repeating that Angela needed to communicate more formally and more effectively.

Bill agreed to help Angela with the business's communications, starting with an e-mail to all members of the company thanking them for their work at and before the sales event on Saturday. The e-mail noted that they had sold 24 hats, at a total value of £192.

Bill drafted an agenda to circulate in advance of that week's meeting. He made Angela talk to Matt and agree to his requests to be kept better informed. He encouraged Angela to chair the company meeting effectively, by keeping to the agenda and persuading the secretary to produce clear minutes straight after the meeting. Bill then asked Angela to work with her finance team to improve the quality and timeliness of the financial reports.

KEY TERMS

Communication management is the process of ensuring that all members of a project team are informed of key events and decisions without overwhelming them with too much information.

Financial reporting is the process of communicating financial information to stakeholders using financial summaries such as cash flow forecasts, budget profit and loss accounts, and balance sheets.

The importance of communication

The importance of communication is highlighted in the opening case study. Failure to communicate with stakeholders can result in frustration, demotivation and dissatisfaction for all parties.

■ Poor communication with team members can result in demotivation, failure to work as a team, bitterness between individuals and a loss of business opportunities.

- Poor communication with suppliers can lead to failure to receive the right products at the right time, and the business might be charged for goods returned.

- Poor communication with customers can result in disappointing sales of goods and services.

Formal written communication

Business correspondence is often read by more than one individual, and therefore care must be taken to communicate as clearly as possible.

Formal business communication follows a set style and pattern. To simplify your event operation, it is good practice to agree an in-house style for all communications. This sets a standard for everyone in the team to follow and creates a good basic image for your operation. Correspondence tends to follow basic rules. The notes that follow should give you some ideas for how to set up pro forma documents for your event team to use.

Letters

If you do not know the name of the person you are writing to, begin a letter "Dear Sir/Madam" and end it "Yours faithfully". If you do know the person's name. begin "Dear (insert the name)" and end with "Yours sincerely".

Put a sentence at the start of the letter stating the subject of your correspondence and referring to the recipient's reference (if there is one), such as an order number. Keep to short paragraphs that outline why you are writing, what action you wish to be taken and thanking the recipient (in advance) for their promptness in dealing with the matter.

Reports

Make sure that all reports start by clearly stating who the report is being sent to, who the report is from, the date of the report, and the subject of the report. The front page should contain a brief executive summary of the report, which picks out its key points. The detailed report should then follow. The pages of reports should be numbered, and lengthy reports should have a contents list.

E-mails

E-mails should follow the same basic rules as letters. At the end of e-mails it is courteous to include the name of your business, contact phone numbers, your e-mail address and any website address.

General documents

Documents are often generated and circulated within a business anonymously. It is good practice to put a footer on all documents that gives the initials of the person producing the material and the date it was produced. This makes it easier for everyone to put documentation into context.

Standard documentation

Businesses often have their own standard documentation to record transactions, give receipts, authorise payments, and so on. This makes sense because:

- it ensures people record key information needed for transactions

- it stops people using scraps of paper to record communications, with the risk of losing vital information

- it makes the business look professional.

Formal spoken communication

Much business communication takes place in meetings or in working groups. Following a meeting, it is important that:

- minutes of the meeting are written – these should be concise and to the point

- any decisions taken are notified to a wider audience

- minutes are circulated to stakeholders.

In the meeting, discussions should focus on the task in hand. Meetings therefore need to be managed, which requires some advance planning. Time spent in business meetings that do not produce clear outcomes is both wasted and expensive. Before a meeting is held, an agenda should be drafted (usually by the chair) that outlines the broad topics for discussion. This should be circulated in advance to the people attending the meeting so that they can plan their contribution.

Meetings should be timetabled, with clear start and end times. It is up to the chair to keep participants to the agenda and to move the meeting along so that it finishes on time. It is the duty of the other people attending the meeting to listen to each other, contribute only constructive comments, and make it possible for the chair to manage the meeting.

Figure 13.9: Pro forma for an event meeting

Date of meeting:

Location:

List of attendees:

Agenda
    Apologies
    Minutes of the last meeting and matters arising
    Chair's report on progress of the event
    Report from:
    Report from:
    Any other business
    Date of next meeting

stop and think

Draft an agenda for your next meeting using the pro forma in Figure 13.9

The decisions and discussions arising from a meeting should be recorded in a manageable format. To avoid information overload, many organisations limit minutes of meetings to a summary of key discussion points, decisions taken and action to be undertaken (and by whom). Minutes should be circulated as soon as possible after the meeting. They should be sent to all those entitled to attend, including anyone absent from the meeting, and to any stakeholders (people that need to act on decisions or need to know the outcomes).

Keeping meetings formal makes it easier for decisions to be made, leaders to lead and for all team members to contribute constructively. If meetings are not working, you can invite a third party (a teacher or a business person) to attend and to work with the team to improve its meeting skills.

Communicating financial information

Financial information needs to be communicated to stakeholders both inside and outside of the business. It is important that financial documents are clear and concise because many people feel intimidated by numbers. Do not let yourself be daunted by finance, keep going back to the simple questions.

- How much cash is coming into the business, and where is it coming from?

- How much cash is going out of the business, and where is it going to?

- Is the business making a profit or a loss?

- Does the business need more funding (capital)?

- Can the business ever make enough profit to repay the capital?

Financial reports should be laid out in a neat and clear manner. Spreadsheet programs can help you here, but if you are writing your accounts by hand, stick to some basic rules: keep all figures neatly in columns, provide clearly labelled descriptions, and use appropriate sub-headings and headings. See Unit 11 for examples of how real businesses present their accounts.

stop and think

List all the income and expenses connected with your event (perhaps working with others in your group).

From this list, work on your own to draft a cash flow forecast for your event. Make a note of all assumptions you make about when expenses will have to be paid for and when any money or receipts are likely to be collected.

Working with your team, negotiate a cash flow forecast for your event. Identify how much capital you will need to raise in order to manage the event, then add 10 per cent for contingencies.

Consider how your team is going to raise this capital, or suggest ways in which you could reduce costs if you think you would be unable to raise the money for all your capital needs. What is the minimum capital that you need to run the event?

For your event management, you will need to use cash flow forecasts. These allow you to analyse your sources of cash, and to estimate your expected outgoings and your cash balance at the end of each week or month. These forecasts are the key tool for predicting your cash needs throughout the project, allowing you to arrange sufficient funding to cover your financial needs in advance.

General Podbury, the chair of the governors, had always run the school fair with military precision. There were clear lines of communications, regular briefings, concise minutes of meetings, and the plans for the final operation were always executed well in advance. Everybody had known precisely what they were supposed to be doing on the day.

Though well organised, the fair had not been popular with the staff or the students because they did not feel that it was their event. But now that General Podbury has retired as a governor, the head teacher and the school council have decided that the event should be organised by Year 13 students studying Applied Business.

A Produce a report for the head teacher and the school council outlining how you intend to use your communication skills to involve all stakeholders while at the same time retaining a professional approach to event management.

B As the chair of the event management team, send a memo to the team reminding them of the most important elements of managing meetings. Note that the school fair meetings will involve stakeholders outside the Applied Business group.

C List the key elements that you would expect to see in the cash flow forecast for a school fair. Where do you think you might get the capital from to run the event?

Staging the event

Setting the scene: the Spring Ball

Ravi and his friends had organised a mini-enterprise business to stage a Spring Ball for students at the college. Ravi had been responsible for booking the venue, so he had signed the contract with Hotel Le Grande. The booking had required a payment of £1,000 to be paid on or before the date of the event. The contract stated that bookings could not be cancelled within two weeks of the event.

The rest of the planning for the event had not gone so well: the tickets and the posters had been printed too late, and few people wanted to go at such short notice. Fewer people still were prepared to pay the £40 ticket price. It turned out that the market research had actually been invented by two of the organisers at home one night, so nobody was sure whether there was ever any demand for the event at any price.

The team had been unable to book a really good band or DJ for the night, as they had planned to do, but at least that was one expense spared. The marketing manager for the team had claimed to have a long list of people waiting to buy tickets. This was not true. The whole event looked like it was going to be one very big loss-maker.

Ravi had not cancelled the hotel booking in time and was now personally liable to pay £1,000 for the hire of the venue without any hope of being able to recoup his outlay. He was not sure that the rest of the team would help him pay this debt.

Ravi was desperately anxious. He went to see the college principal. The principal was not very sympathetic, but she telephoned the hotel management and pointed out that the hotel should not have taken a booking from underage students without a countersignature from a responsible adult. She stated that the contract was unenforceable as Ravi was still a minor (that is, he was under 18 years of age). The hotel agreed to cancel the booking with no charge.

In Ravi's evaluation of the project he realised that although the event had been an utter shambles, he had learnt lessons that he would never forget. He just wished that learning from your own mistakes wasn't quite so painful.

KEY TERMS

Contracts are agreements which are enforceable in a court of law. The key elements of a contract are an offer (say of goods and services) from one party to another, an acceptance of the offer, and a consideration (that is, details of payment).

Marketing, in this context, covers activities which promote an event, such as advertising, sponsorship, publicity, invitations to special guests, etc.

Operations management is the process of managing an event on the day.

Contracts

As part of organising an event you will probably have to sign several contracts. Unless you are representing a company (with limited liability) or your school or college, by signing the contract you become personally liable. This is a serious undertaking. It is quite normal for the other party to the contract to ask for a parent or a teacher to countersign your signature – this has the effect of making the parent or the teacher ultimately liable for the contract.

Contracts are not always set out in writing. They can also be made and amended verbally. Take great care in recognising precisely what you are agreeing to. Do not be afraid to state that your team's rules require all deals to be confirmed in writing. This keeps things clear and prevents misunderstandings on the day. For example, if the DJ arrives claiming that someone on the team has agreed to a higher fee than you have arranged, it is useful to have the signed written agreement to hand to resolve the problem.

To be enforceable, contracts need to have three basic elements:

- an offer – a business or an individual offers to supply goods and services to another party

- an acceptance – the other party (again, a business or an individual) accepts this offer to supply goods and services

- the consideration – a payment for the supply of goods and services.

Note that the value of the payment does not affect the enforceability of the contract. The contract is still enforceable even if the specified payment is not in cash or is only for a notional peppercorn sum.

Many organisations keep a log of significant contracts, so that they can keep track of all their major commitments. It would be useful for your event management to keep a log of all contracts, listing:

- supplier name and contact details (phone number, e-mail, address, etc.)

- key details of the contract

- the individual in the event management team who agreed and signed the contract

- details of any persons who were required to countersign the contract.

Disagreements can arise between the parties to a contract. However, it is highly unlikely that you will sue or be sued. It is more normal for any disagreements to be settled out of court. The larger the value of the contract, though, the more worthwhile it is for the injured party to pursue the claim. Many businesses clear their outstanding debtors once a year through the small claims court, so do not think that you are in the clear just because you have not heard for some time from a business to which you owe money. Further, remember that there are long-term consequences of failing to pay debts: it can affect your personal credit rating for a long time.

A simple guide to breaches of contract, and to the mechanics of taking cases through the courts, is on this website: www.bcentral.co.uk/finance/law/litigation-and-insurance.mspx.

Marketing

All aspects of communicating with prospective customers and participants are part of the marketing of the event. In the early stages, you will have already communicated with a section of your potential audience through your market research. To ensure the success of the event on the night, it is critical that your team promotes the event in many ways to all potential participants during the operations stage.

Every event is going to need a different portfolio of marketing activities. These need to be targeted at the stakeholders who are likely to attend your event. You may also wish to promote your event to a wider audience of stakeholders who might not attend, such as providing publicity material for your sponsors or looking at other ways to promote yourselves.

So, first, consider all the stakeholder groups that you want to reach. Then make a list, like Figure 13.10, of the ways in which you think it would be most appropriate to promote your event to each group. Then allocate the responsibility for the promotional activity directed to each stakeholder group to one or more team members.

Figure 13.10: Marketing to different stakeholders

Stakeholder group	Type of marketing
Customers	Tickets, posters, leaflets, etc.
College staff	Posters, direct mail, etc.
Other students	A poster of who's who in the organisation and a display of objectives
Sponsors	Display for a sponsor's offices, emphasising the value of the sponsorship
Visitors to your school	A display of business in action at reception

The team member responsible for marketing should not be allocated any other tasks on the day of the event. Marketing continues on the day of the event, and the marketing person must check that everything is going to plan and any problems are solved as quickly as possible. The marketing role will be supported by excellent customer service with programmes, guest lists, etc.

Operations management

Operations management covers all aspects of preparing for and running the event on the day. It covers a diverse range of activities, from providing timetables for guests and participants, allocating duties to each person, training people to offer a certain style of customer service, solving problems as they arise, contingency planning, monitoring the event throughout the day, and organising the evaluation and feedback on the event.

Before an event takes place, it makes sense to carry out a rehearsal or walk-through to check that you have thought of, and are prepared for, every eventuality. Before the walk-through starts, event managers should equip themselves with a clipboard, paper and a pen to make notes of any small details that need to be sorted out to make the event a real success and to minimise the chances of failure. The walk-through should help you produce timings for each part of the event.

Suppose, for example, that you are organising the school prize-giving. You will need to schedule the day carefully, and the walk-through can help you produce a practical programme. You will require a set of realistic timings for the special guests: the time of their arrival, the time they are taken to meet the head teacher and staff, when lunch is served and consumed, and when the guests are assembled to parade through the school hall. Then the official programme takes over with timings for speeches and the handing out of prizes. Finally your special guests are allocated time to have tea with the prizewinners (and their parents) before they take their leave. Setting event timings out on a Gantt chart, see Figure 13.11, will help all team members visualise and clarify their understanding of the event timings.

There will be another set of timings for the students and parents to assemble for the prize-giving. The site managers will have a set of timings to lay out chairs, collect and display flowers, etc. all the way through to the stacking away of the chairs at the end of the day.

stop and think

For the main stakeholders involved in your event, work out roughly what routes they are going to take through the event and at what times. Physically trace the routes the different stakeholders will have to take throughout your event and produce some rough timings. Your group should draft and agree a final timings schedule for everyone to use on the day.

Figure 13.11: Gantt chart for school prize-giving

Activity\Time	12:00	12:15	12:30	12:45	1:00	1:15	1:30	1:35	3:30	3:45	4:00	4:15	4:30
Arrival of guests	▓												
Meeting head teacher and staff	▓	▓											
Lunch served			▓										
After-lunch coffee				▓									
Seating of students and staff				▓									
Arrival and seating of parents				▓									
Guests gather themselves						▓							
Students stand							▓						
Platform party (guests and head) process through the hall							▓						
Platform party sits								▓					
Students sit								▓					
Formal programme													
Everyone stands									▓				
Platform party leaves the hall										▓			
Head and guests afternoon tea											▓		
Students and parents leave the hall											▓		
Students and parents leave the school premises												▓	
Staff join head and guests for tea												▓	
Guests depart													▓

On the day of a big event, everyone needs to know what job they are doing – and how they are going to do it. It is important that everyone sticks to their allocated tasks. One person needs to be in overall charge. This person should not be allocated specific tasks, but should be ready to tackle emergencies or problems as they arise.

Well before the event starts, the person in charge of the event and some of the team who are free should walk the site and check that everything is in place. This will allow you to check that:

■ everyone in the team has turned up and is at their post in good time

■ the event is clearly signposted from all entrances that are being used

■ furniture is laid out in the correct formation

■ the site is clean and litter-free

■ all fire exits are properly marked, clear of obstructions and can be opened in an emergency

■ there is adequate access to the site for disabled people

■ toilets (including a toilet with access for the disabled) are properly signposted and useable.

Make sure that the reception for your event looks smart and is staffed from early in the event. The team members staffing the reception point should have access to key event details. They should know where to send early arrivals and whether bands, DJs or other key personnel have arrived or are on their way.

Pay attention to security. During an event, it is easy for thieves to help themselves to unsecured valuables. Check that rooms that should be locked are locked. It makes sense to lock every room that does not need to be open. If you have hired a security firm, walk round the site with them. Talk through how they are going to handle difficult situations and in which situations they would call in the police. Introduce them to the member of staff who is responsible for the event.

stop and think

Produce a key list of things that need to be checked on the day of your event. Compare your list with others in your group, and produce a definitive list of everything that has to be checked on the day of the event.

assessment practice
Celebrating student achievement

You have been asked to help organise a prize-giving event for Year 13 students to mark their achievements in exams and extracurricular activities in Year 12. The event is being planned and run by a representative from each tutor group.

Rather than the usual formal event, it has been decided that the event will be an informal celebration with performances of music, dance and theatre. There will still be a prize-giving element, but awards will be made in small batches throughout the evening by a representative from the Chartered Institute of Management. This will include awarding the institute's CHAMPS certificates to students who have displayed management skills in Year 12 activities.

It is planned to invite parents and teachers to the event. The aim is to create a relaxed environment. Guests will be seated at candle-lit tables, and served small snacks and soft drinks throughout the event.

A Draft a memo for the first meeting of the tutor group representatives giving advice about entering into contracts with suppliers of public address systems.

B Identify the key information that you should put on the event invitations to parents, teachers and external agencies.

C Prepare a list of the key issues the organisers need to check before the event starts.

D Suggest how the organisers could plan to manage any unexpected events.

Controlling cash and meeting legal responsibilities

Setting the scene: school disco

The organisation of the KS3 disco had involved so little hassle. The publicity had been organised by asking KS3 students to text their friends. No posters were put up, no tickets were issued. The disco was booked for a local hall on a Friday night starting at 7 pm. By 8 pm, it had attracted around 700 students, each paying the £3 entrance fee.

The organisers had kept everything simple. Guests' hands were stamped as the arrived, and the entrance money was thrown into a bucket. The DJ was a friend, and they agreed to pay him £200 out of the bucket. It seemed the organisers had achieved a spectacular success.

Unfortunately, things quickly turned sour. The problems started when some boys set fire to the toilets. Then the fire brigade and the school principal turned up at the same time. (The principal had been alerted when she was phoned in by Miss Jones, the teacher who was supposed to be present throughout the event. Miss Jones had been given the wrong directions to the hall.)

A quick assessment by the fire brigade was enough to end the evening. The small fire in the boys' toilets was no problem, but one of the fire exits was jammed and the other one was blocked with kit. The hall only had a licence for 200 people, and was dangerously overcrowded. The school's insurance was invalid because there wasn't a member of staff present. The fire officers turned off the music, and ordered everybody to leave.

The principal insisted on taking charge of the cash, just in case anybody demanded a refund. The organisers had to stay on to count and sign for the cash. With 700 students paying £3 each, less £200 for the DJ, there should have been around £1,900 in the bucket. There was only £232.43. The principal threatened to call the police, and the organisers admitted that the bucket was left unattended while they went to sort out a fight between two boys.

Cash controls

Cash is the easiest asset to steal. Even if people are not dishonest, it is easy to be too casual in handling cash. Individuals can easily mix their own money with the money due to an event. Problems arise when money goes missing, or is not properly accounted for, and people start blaming everyone else. Cash must therefore be managed with respect – weak individuals must not be drawn into temptation and honest individuals should not be subjected to false accusations of theft.

When running an event, it is important that cash is properly controlled. Procedures need to be in place from the start. You should find out if your school or college has written procedures for handling cash. If not, this check list of basic rules applies in any situation.

Cash-handling procedures

Takings

- All cash takings must have a record of a receipt. For example, this could be the stubs of tickets issued to paying guests at your event.

- All cash takings should be reconciled to receipts. The total value for receipts should be the same value as the total cash takings.

- All cash takings should be banked intact. No cash payments should be made out of takings. A separate petty cash fund should be held for these purposes.

- All takings should be checked against the bank statement, as part of the bank reconciliation.

Payments

- Most payments should be made by cheque.

- All cash payments should be supported by third-party documentation such as a till receipt or an invoice.

- Cash payments should be made from the petty cash account.

- The petty cash account should be run on an imprest system. If, say, the float starts out at £100, at any time there could be a spot check on the petty cash box, and the payment vouchers plus the cash will always equal £100.

Security

- There should always be two people present, if at all possible, when handling cash.

- Every day that cash transactions are made, the cash should be counted, a cash count sheet filled in (see Figure 13.12), and the cash count checked by a second person.

- All cash should be kept in the school or college safe until it is banked. There should be procedures for signing the cash in and out of the school safe.

- As a further check to protect students from false accusations, a teacher should regularly check cash-handling procedures.

Figure 13.12: Cash count sheet

Date		
Cash counted by	Checked by	
Denomination	**Number**	**Total value**
£20 notes		
£10 notes		
£5 notes		
£2 coins		
£1 coins		
50p coins		
20p coins		
10p coins		
5p coins		
2p coins		
1p coins		
Total cash counted		

stop and think

The student event organisers are running a petty cash system with a cash imprest of £200. During the year they have experienced several problems.

- One week, the cash left was £60, and the till receipts and invoices for purchases came to £150.

- Another week, the cash left in the till was nil, and the till receipts and invoices for purchases equalled £230.

- In the last very busy week, the cash in the till was £45, and the till receipts and invoices for purchases only came to £130.

Give explanations for why the imprest system did not always add up to £200.

Explain what money-handling procedures could be implemented to prevent these problems arising.

Basic legal responsibilities

When running an event, particularly one which may involve members of the public, there are several basic legal responsibilities placed on the organisers. Event organisers must be aware of:

- insurance requirements
- health and safety regulations
- equality issues.

Public liability insurance

All organisations that come into contact with the public have a statutory duty to take reasonable care in their activities so that people don't get injured or otherwise harmed. Public liability insurance covers an organisation against any claims for damages by a member of the public who suffers injury or damage while on the organisation's premises or when interacting with the organisation's staff. All venues that stage public events (including schools and colleges) will have public liability insurance.

It is not unusual for insurers to insist that a specified number of adults over 21 years of age are present at enterprise events organised by Year 12 and 13 students, and that at least one of these must be one of the students' teachers. It is important, therefore, to check insurance requirements early on to ensure that the date of the event is acceptable to any responsible adults who have to attend.

If your event is due to be held at your school or college, check the details of your institution's public liability insurance. If the event is being held at another location, get the owners of the venue to check their insurance cover.

Health and safety legislation

Health and safety legislation covers a wide range of activities and situations, from the specifics of food handling to the provision and location of fire exits. Your school or college should have a health and safety committee that can help you to meet your obligations under current legislation.

The key areas that you should consider are:

- safe access and movement around the site – make sure that there are no trailing flexes that may trip people over, that no heavy objects are obstructing walkways, that paths are well lit and free from ice or anything else that might cause an injury, etc.

- fire procedures – fire exits should be well signposted, clear of any obstructions and working (the doors aren't locked, for example) and fire evacuation procedures should be explained to both staff and the event audience

- food handling – if nobody in the team has a valid food handling certificate, you may be limited in the type of food you can prepare and serve, and you will also need to clearly indicate if any food is home-made

- first aid – ensure that there is a first aid kit available and, if there isn't a qualified first aider on the site, it might be a good idea to ask the St John Ambulance to provide a volunteer for the evening.

Make sure you are prepared for any eventuality. Ensure, for example, that there is a telephone available to contact the emergency services. Keep the contact numbers of the duty site manager and the college principal or a senior member of staff.

The important point here is to take all reasonable steps to ensure the safety of everyone involved in your event. In UK law, you can defend any charge of negligence if you are able to show that you acted "reasonably" and displayed a "reasonable duty of care".

> **stop and think**
>
> Go around your college or school and identify five potential health and safety risks. If you are responsible for health and safety, what action would you take to reduce or remove these risks?

Equality issues

Ensuring equality of opportunity is a legal and moral duty. Any event that is open to an audience must ensure equality of access. The event must be open to anyone to attend regardless of disability, sex, race and religion. This is not always as straightforward as it seems – as the following examples show, it is easy to forget basic aspects of other people's culture, religion and physique that can exclude them from full involvement in the event.

- A choral event is being organised in the sixth form common room. It is open to all, but the common room is on the third floor and there is no lift.

- The year group dance is open to all, but both the band and the DJ only play one genre of music that is favoured by one ethnic group of students.

- A debating event is organised for all Year 12 students in the city. The event is held in a very exclusive private school in an upmarket area. Poorer students from the other side of the city felt socially insecure throughout the event.

- A make-up and beauty event is organised for a lunch time in college. The only cosmetics companies invited to the event produced products that are mainly designed for white-skinned people, yet around 70 per cent of the college student population do not have fair skin.

- The mayor is hosting a Young Enterprise competition. Refreshments are provided for the participating students, but there is no vegetarian option and an abundance of savoury items such as pork pies, sausage rolls, scotch eggs, liver pate and beef sausages. The town prides itself on its ethnic and religious diversity.

Think carefully and sensitively when you organise your event. Everyone wants to feel a fully involved, empowered and respected member of the community. Try to make that happen at your event.

assessmentpractice
Another multicultural evening

The annual multicultural event is one of the highlights of the school year. The principal tries to choose an organising team that represents all aspects of the school's cultural diversity. She wants everyone to feel included in the final event.

This year's multicultural evening arrived. The team organising the event had left a legion of parents organising a huge buffet of foods from around the world in the canteen. On stage in the hall, wires and electrical equipment trailed everywhere across the stage. Huge banners showing different countries' flags had been plastered all around the hall by the Year 7 students, covering up all the regular signs. As many chairs as possible had been packed into the main hall, and the main entrance was crowded with display stands showing the school's international links.

Outside, students delivering resources for the evening had parked their cars right up close to the building, and visitors were going to have to squeeze between the cars to get in. An enthusiastic group of Year 9 students were already positioning themselves at the school gates, at least one hour early, to collect money for disaster relief.

A Make a quick list of all the issues that would concern you about the organisation of this event.

B Suggest how each of the issues that you have identified could be rectified.

C What steps could the principal take to ensure that next year's event is more accessible and safer?

Evaluation and feedback

Setting the scene: the annual student management conference

The annual student management conference was held over two days. Throughout the event, students from two different schools had worked together in competing teams handling a wide variety of management challenges. At the start, most participants had not known each other, but over the two days they had worked with their industry coaches to develop problem-solving and interpersonal skills. By the end of the event, the students from the two schools considered themselves firm friends and they planned to meet up for a post-course celebration.

Though the event had ended, the event organisers – the head of careers and a student committee – still had work to do. Once the students had left, the organising committee had arranged tea for themselves, the industry coaches and the teachers involved in the event. This allowed an opportunity for an informal group discussion on what had gone well and what could be better organised next year.

On the Monday morning following the conference, the organising committee began examining the feedback they had received. All the student teams, and their industry coaches, had completed an evaluation of the event before they left. Individuals in each group had to evaluate their own and their team's performance over the two days. These evaluation forms were designed to help the committee to identify how well the event had gone and what could be done better next year.

The Monday session concluded with a self-evaluation exercise. Each member of the committee evaluated their own and the group's work over the last three months in setting up and running the conference. Some of the team were very self-critical, while others thought that they were perfect. The team tried to structure their individual and group evaluation in a manner that would enable everyone to keep things in perspective, be honest with themselves and be realistic about their achievements.

KEY TERMS

Evaluation is an ongoing process throughout a project, through which a team and individuals reflect on how effectively they are achieving their objectives.

Monitoring is the process of comparing the actual outcomes of a project against its targets and objectives.

Feedback is the process whereby stakeholders provide information to the event's organisers on how well they think the event went and how far it met their objectives.

Fitness for purpose is an assessment to ensure resources are used efficiently and effectively to deliver a project's objectives.

Self-evaluation is the process of assessing one's own strengths and weaknesses in relation to the production of a certain event, and identifying strategies to improve one's performance.

Team evaluation is an assessment of the way a team works together, identifying the team's strengths and weaknesses and how the members can develop as a team to work more efficiently.

Gathering evaluation evidence

Evaluation is not an activity that should be left until an event is completed. From your first meetings, your team should have been building in regular reviews and evaluations to assess whether the event that you are organising is likely to achieve its objectives and targets.

Evaluation is also not an activity that is the sole preserve of the event organisers. As part of the event management process, you need to set up opportunities for all stakeholders to provide feedback on the event in general and their specific role in the event.

This feedback can come in several ways. It could be through the completion of a written evaluation form or through comments in a visitors' book; clients could be questioned as they leave an event; the audience could be photographed or videoed during the event;

some participants might be willing to take part in a discussion group after the event. The choice of feedback mechanism depends on the event and how it is managed.

Feedback documentation

Any documentation that is to be used to collect feedback needs to be planned well in advance. It needs to be tied into the objectives of the event. and there should always be room for respondents to suggest ways in which the event could be developed in future. The documentation should not lead stakeholders to give biased replies. It should be easy to fill in, quick to complete, and be collected in promptly. Figure 13.13 shows a typical template for an event feedback form. You should think how you could adapt it to design feedback forms for the participants and stakeholders at your event.

Focus groups

Focus groups are small groups of up to 10 participants that are organised to discuss various aspects of a product or service. These sessions are usually well structured, with a member of the team chairing the group and working through a number of pre-set questions. The objective of focus groups tends to be to identify good aspects of the current goods or services under discussion, and to suggest ways in which they could be developed to meet the customers' needs more closely.

Focus groups can be used to gather feedback at the end of an event. It is difficult to take a detailed note of all contributions to a focus group as participants often become quite animated and talk over each other. You may therefore wish to video (or record) the discussions, allowing you to analyse the comments

Figure 13.13: A feedback form

Name of event: ………………….......……………………… Date of event: ……………………………

Objective of event: …………………….......…………………………….......………………………………

………………………………………………………….......……………………………………………………

Do you think that this event met these objectives?

Please rank it on a scale of 1 to 6 (1 being high, 6 being low):   1 2 3 4 5 6

What aspects of the event did you most enjoy and find most useful?

…………………………………….......………………………….......………………………………………

………………………………….......………………………….......……………………………………………

Which aspects of the event did you find least helpful and enjoyable?

………………………………………………………….......………………………………….......……………

………………………………………………….......…………………………………………………………

In what ways could this event be developed in future years?

…………………………………………….......…………………………………….......……………………

………………………………………………………….......………………………………………………

In what capacity did you attend the event (circle as appropriate):

                    student   teacher   industry   visitor   speaker

other (specify) …………………………………………….......………………………………….......………

Any other comments ………………………………….......…………………………………………………

………………………………………………………….......……………………………………………………

………………………………………………………….......……………………………………………………

Thank you for completing this evaluation sheet. Pease hand it in as you leave.

later. This approach also allows you to review the tone and manner of each contribution, and so pick up further feedback from the body language of the focus group members. The disadvantages of recording a group discussion is that it can be played many times, and a small criticism can grow out of proportion because it is aired so many times.

Note that without sophisticated equipment you are unlikely to capture the contributions of the whole group – both visual and verbal – but it is worth attempting this technique to gain important feedback and to develop understanding of the challenges of running a focus group.

Photographic records

Another approach is to take a record of the event. A video recording and still photographs of the event can be a useful form of feedback. You can use them to get a feel for the audience reaction, for example.

However, you need to exercise a degree of caution here, because the visual record is likely to reflect the best of the event. A photographer is unlikely to take many pictures of people who are not enjoying themselves. A photographer will always try to focus on the most dramatic and visually arresting moments of the event.

Fit for purpose check list

Budgets and finance

- Was the revenue target met?
- Were expenses budgets stuck to?
- Was cash controlled and accounted for properly?

Resource management

- Were there any areas where resources could have been used more efficiently?
- Was there any duplication of effort?
- Was the preparation for the event within the abilities and resources of the team ?

On the day

- Were the rooms used adequate?
- Was there sufficient ICT equipment available?
- Were there enough members of the team available at all times during the event?
- Was signage adequate? Could clients easily navigate the event?

Health and safety

- Were there any incidents related to health and safety during the event?

Equality issues

- Were there any issues arising during the event related to equality of access?

Communications and marketing

- Did any issues arise during the event planning and operation as a result of poor communication?
- Was all marketing effective?

Evaluation

The purpose of any evaluation exercise is to learn lessons for the future, to build on successes and approaches that worked, and to took for ways to rectify mistakes. In evaluating the event, you need to assess all the feedback you received, to review the event itself – did it work, did it meet its objectives, etc. – and to reflect on your own contribution (and that of the group as a whole) to the planning and event management process.

Assessing feedback

Feedback from customers and other stakeholders needs to be handled carefully. People can be very sensitive to any perceived criticism, and feedback can be open to bias or distortion. For example, a feedback form might have been completed by one of your friends who thinks that it is funny to give hugely negative feedback and suggest outrageous things should be done next year. These responses should be set to one side.

Feedback from other participants may also be skewed in a way that makes it difficult to use. If an industry speaker produces a particularly bad presentation, and feels that they have let themselves down, their feedback on the whole event may be affected, and you might get a very negative set of responses.

You need to collate feedback to establish an average view from those who attended. This should give confirmation of what went well and provide ideas about what could be developed. Any criticism should not be seen as a personal attack on you as a group, or on individuals. Your objective is to become competent at managing events, so any ideas and constructive advice are useful tools for your later development.

Fit for purpose

If a product does not meet the needs of the target customers, then it is not fit for purpose. A surprisingly large number of products and services that reach the market fail this test. The same criterion of fit for purpose can be applied to projects and events. Every project ought to be assessed in terms of its fitness for purpose so that the organisers can ensure that the next project is better. Fitness for purpose is therefore a useful method of assessing a project.

Fitness for purpose is still a new concept for many managers. It is used in assessing whether housing projects meet the needs of residents, resulting in dramatic improvements in the quality of public sector housing. It is also used by companies to assess what

sort of IT equipment and software they need to support their operations. Nursing is using this concept when assessing what treatment is appropriate for patients. Accountancy firms are using fitness of purpose to define their services and to provide value for money to clients.

The idea is to focus on the use of resources, and to assess whether these were used in the most effective manner to secure the project's objectives. Assessing whether an event is fit for purpose requires consideration of a range of factors, including whether:

- it has met its budge, and the other resource constraints

- it has been carried out in a safe and legal manner, with due respect for equality of access

- all funds have been properly accounted for

- advertising and communication was appropriate to the needs of the event.

An event would be fit for purpose if it met these tests and achieved its objectives. This is quite a difficult check to carry out and will benefit from support from teachers. However, you may find it useful to use or adapt the check list (see page 263).

Team evaluation and self-evaluation

The final task for the event management team is to evaluate their own performance and to identify how they could do better next time. This evaluation process is very important. It is essential that you learn to review your own performance, so that you can develop your management skills and are able to make the most of career opportunities. Good evaluation also usually involves working with a mentor or teacher to help you put your strengths and weaknesses into perspective and to set realistic future goals.

Evaluation takes time: make sure that you set aside enough time to do it. This is the time when most students will really internalise their learning, so do not rush this opportunity. We would suggest you set aside a day for the evaluation. Have a timetable for the day. Here is one suggestion for how the evaluation could be structured.

The start

The evaluation event should be a positive, constructive occasion. Start with an informal session looking at any photographs and videos of the event. Have a final team photograph.

Figure 13.14: Key skills usage

Key skill	Feasibility	Planning	Staging event	Evaluation
Application of number				
Communication				
Improving own learning and performance				
Information and communications technology				
Problem-solving				
Working with others				

Session one

Start the formal part of the day with a session that involves listing all the things that have gone well with the event and that worked in the planning and operations that led up to the event. This should be a long list. Make a habit of thanking individuals for the contribution that they made to creating these successes. Ensure that all successes are acknowledged, including the work put in on the dull and unglamorous tasks as well as the front-of-house high-profile jobs. Find evidence to support as many of the successes as possible. In compiling this evidence, use feedback forms, any videos of focus groups, photographs or videos of the event, marketing materials (posters, programmes, etc.) and the documentation associated with the event, including minutes of meetings.

Session two

Remind yourselves what a great job you have done. Look back at all the aspects of the event that went well, and ask yourselves how could things have been even better. Now list ideas of how the event, the teamworking, the planning and so on could have been done better. Be constructive, try to avoid making overly personal or negative comments, and thank people for any ideas and strategies that are relevant and appropriate. Again try to find evidence to support any suggested areas for development.

A useful framework for evaluating a team's performance in any management activity is to consider key skills. The Qualifications and Curriculum Authority defines key skills as application of number, communication, improving own learning and performance, information and communications technology, problem-solving, and working with others. Using the framework in Figure 13.14, analyse your team's performance by mapping its use of key skills against the four stages in event management. This will help you when you write up your evaluation.

Session three

The first two sessions focused on the work and performance of the group. Now, you should consider your individual contribution to the management and running of the event. You should work alone to evaluate your contribution to the success of the project. To do this, list your successes and generate ideas for how you could have developed and improved your contribution to the project. Many of these ideas should come out naturally from the work with the team in the earlier sessions. Again you can use the framework in Figure 13.14 to structure your self-analysis.

Session four

Individuals should go through their self-evaluation with their tutor in private in one-on-one sessions, while others begin writing up their evaluation. Do not include every small detail of the evaluation for the write up: select the best ideas, the ones most supported by the feedback evidence. End the day with everyone taking turns to say what was the best moment for them.

However the evaluation is structured, it needs to be a positive experience that acknowledges the efforts of all the individuals in the team and the achievements of the team as a whole. Businesses are not about producing perfection, they are about the best efforts of individuals on the day, working hard with limited resources. No business can afford to fund absolute excellence. One of the most important skills that you can learn in business is to manage failure: recover from mistakes, keep going and revise your strategies.

assessmentpractice
Evaluating the KS3 learner event

Year 13 students had organised an event for Year 7, 8 and 9 pupils on "how to become a more effective learner". A theatre group was used to deliver a varied programme of activities designed to get pupils to reflect on how they learn most effectively.

The Year 13 students had run three sessions themselves: the introduction to the day, the wrap-up at the end during which pupils were asked to fill in the evaluation forms, and a "learn from our mistakes" session where they explained how they'd got into messes with their learning and the strategies that they'd used to sort out the mess.

The organising team collated the feedback sheets. Figure 13.15 summarises the responses on how the event had gone. The team had also taken photographs and videos of the day, and had asked for staff feedback. The feedback from staff was very positive, and this backed up the photographic evidence which showed the participants fully involved throughout the day and producing useful action plans for how they were going to improve their study skills.

Figure 13.15: Event feedback

	Year 7	Year 8	Year 9
Did you enjoy the day?	Yes 97%	Yes 84%	Yes 56%
	No 3%	No 15%	No 22%
What did you most enjoy?			
Theatre group	60%	55%	10%
Year 13 student presentation	40%	40%	5%
Lunch	0%	5%	60%
What could be done to improve the day?			
Nothing, it was great	92%	85%	35%
Use teachers instead of Year 13 students	2%	5%	15%
Use the theatre group only	2%	5%	12%
Do not use the theatre group	4%	5%	10%

A **Study the data in Figure 13.15. Comment on the usefulness of asking students to provide written feedback on their experiences of the event.**

B **In what ways might the video and photographic evidence be biased?**

C **How might the feedback from teachers to the Year 13 students be biased, and why?**

D **Does this feedback tell the team anything that they could use to develop the event next year?**

E **How could the team structure their feedback to focus it further on the development of the event for next year?**

The big event

A business studies conference

The Applied Business A level students wanted to run an event that would support their studies and help people at other schools who were studying the same course. They knew that the assessment evidence for Unit 13 Organising an Event required a report and a presentation which documented:

- research into the feasibility of the event
- the planning of the event
- the staging of the event and evaluating their own contribution
- an evaluation of the success of the event, making recommendations for improvement.

The set-up

As a first step, each member of the group set up their own files to make sure that they collected the necessary evidence for the assessment. Their teacher had told them that if they kept well organised files, documenting and writing up what they did as they went along, the final report and evaluation would not be too onerous. They used file dividers to divide files into the four main assessment areas. At the front of every section, each student wrote a list of the things that should be included. They matched their check lists against the syllabus specification.

The students set up a wall planner and identified some possible dates for their event. They worked back to identify deadlines for each stage of the project. The aim was to complete the project within a 13-week term. At their first lesson, they produced an outline plan (see Figure 13.16).

To complete the project, the group used their textbooks and the internet to determine and source the key documentation that they would have to have in place at each stage. In some cases, they set up (in some cases by downloading from business support websites) documentation templates that they filed under the appropriate headings in their lever arch files. This documentation covered:

- **feasibility**
  spreadsheets for budgeting
  a risk assessment form

Figure 13.16: Outline project plan

Week	Activity
1	Set-up
2	Research and feasibility
3	Research and feasibility
4	Research and feasibility
5	Planning the event
6	Planning the event
7	*Half term*
8	Planning the event
9	Planning the event
10	Planning the event
11	**Staging the event**
12	Evaluation and write-up
13	Evaluation and write-up

- **planning the event**
  Gantt charts
  health and safety guidance
  cash flow forecast spreadsheets
  details of the college's insurance cover for student events
  standard formats for all correspondence
  basic guidelines for running meetings

- **staging the event**
  the college's equal opportunities policy
  sheets for recording cash takings

- **review and evaluation**
  documentation to evaluate individual and team performance.

For each form, the students looked at a range of different sources, assessed the quality of the documentation, and evaluated which would be most appropriate for their needs.

At the end of the event, in the light of experience, the students identified ways of improving the documentation so that it was more appropriate. All the students wanted to keep a file of well-designed documents that they could use later in tasks for university and future employers.

Roles and responsibilities

The students felt that it was important to allocate roles and responsibilities, so that everyone in the group was involved and had clearly designated tasks. There were 15 students in the group, and they allocated these roles amongst themselves:

- managing director
- secretary
- assistant managing director
- finance director, in charge of producing financial records (profit and loss, etc.)
- management accountant, in charge of budgets and costings for the event
- cashier, in charge of cash controls and banking
- marketing manager
- sales manager
- production manager
- logistics manager
- legal officer
- human resources manager
- administration manager
- assistant administration manager
- quality control manager

The students defined the tasks associated with each role to avoid overlap between roles and minimise the risk of clashes between individuals in the team.

Feasibility

The team held a brainstorming session to come up with ideas for an event that would support their fellow students in getting higher grades in their studies. They narrowed the choice to three main ideas:

- an exhibition by business of work experience opportunities and available support for business students
- a breakfast networking event for students, teachers and local businesses
- a conference on a particular aspect of the A level specification.

After carrying out some market research the team was able to rule out the first two options. These didn't seem feasible as:

- local businesses did not want to invest time in promoting work experience placements – they thought that students had a responsibility to research opportunities for themselves
- very few business people wanted to attend a breakfast meeting and no students were willing to get up that early
- other schools and colleges were not keen on an event that would make their students late for lessons.

However, most students and teachers welcomed the idea of a one-day conference on an aspect of applied business studies. Over 80 per cent of students said that they would find a conference based around business development (Unit 8) useful.

The team held a meeting to research and consider what a conference on business development might involve. From the syllabus specification, they picked out three elements that they thought needed covering:

- drafting a business plan
- requesting finance for a business venture
- sole traders and partnerships.

Planning

They team wanted a hands-on conference: the day would not be a series of lectures but consist of a range of practical activities that would help participants develop their understanding about business development.

Their next task was to identify speakers and agencies that might come into college to help run some sessions during the day. Their teacher guided them, and helped them through contacts with the Business Links organisation, the chamber of commerce, a branch of the Institute of Directors, and people who had helped the college previously in local banks, accountants and law firms. They also approached the Prince's Trust and the Chartered Institute of Management, and drew on information on the Shell LiveWIRE website.

It took the students longer than they expected to find speakers and presenters for this conference. Many people just would not speak to them, or they were overseas on business or they had no free time for the next three weeks. The team found that they had to send two representatives to a business networking meeting at 7 am one morning to explain to a group of 30 business people what it was that they were trying to set up.

The people at the breakfast meeting liked the students' pitch. They made contact with a man who acted as a broker between small businesses and potential investors, an accountant who specialised in start-up businesses, a representative from the local economic development board, an entrepreneur who now had a very successful business but had experienced many problems in raising start-up capital, and a local banker who ran training programmes for small businesses in how to write business plans and raise finance.

In the week that followed, the students redrafted their conference programme. They negotiated with speakers, and worked on strategies for delivering interactive sessions that would support the exam specification. Once the programme was finalised at the end of week 8, the students focused on booking a conference venue and promoting the event to other schools and colleges. That was when things started to go wrong. They needed a large lecture theatre or hall, with a suite of smaller seminar rooms, but all appropriate venues seemed to have been booked up months ago.

Other schools and colleges were reluctant to free their students up for a whole day at such short notice. The business people that had agreed to speak were expecting an audience of 80 to 100 students, but two weeks before the event only the organisers – that is, 15 students – were definitely booked for the day

The students became desperate, and started to blame each other. At this stage an adviser for Young Enterprise came into the room and overheard the team arguing. He was able to make some useful suggestions.

The university often had lecture theatres available, that it let out for about £400. This event would be after the end of the university term so these facilities might be free. Young Enterprise could e-mail all its Year 12 and 13 students in the local area and invite them and their teachers to the conference. The adviser suggested that a lunch needed to be organised for the speakers, which would cost £100.

The outcome

The event went ahead and was a big success. The students took lots of photographs and summarised the speeches, which they put on the college website. The evaluation day was finished off with a meal at a curry house to which the students invited their speakers, the Young Enterprise adviser and teachers.

activities

1 Identify the five best things the event management team did in organising their event.

2 What were the root causes of the team panicking in week 8?

3 If the lecture theatre held 150 people and it was 70 per cent full, how much would the students have had to charge for the conference to be sure of covering all their costs?

4 What should the students do in the future to make sure that they avoid the problems that arose in planning this event?

EVERY BUSINESS IS AFFECTED BY A VARIETY OF EXTERNAL influences or factors. It is difficult for businesses to control these factors, but it is vital to the success of any business that it has contingency plans to deal with any significant developments in its external environment, from changes in economic factors to the introduction of laws and the development of new technologies.

This unit will focus on the four major areas of a business's external environment, looking specifically at:

■ legal influences

■ economic influences

■ environmental influences

■ technological influences.

It is important that a business is aware of the environment in which it operates and the specific external influences it faces. This allows it to respond to changes in its external environment and to turn potential threats into business opportunities.

In studying this unit, you will learn to analyse how a business has reacted to external influences through the actions that it has taken and the changes it has made to its practices and activities.

External influences on business

Introducing external influences

Setting the scene: Thames Water

Thames Water provides water and sewage services to the whole of London. Its key external stakeholders are its customers. These customers have no choice but to use Thames Water, as the company is in a monopoly position.

Customers pay for the service through their water bills, and prices are fixed by the water industry regulator. Thames Water can only therefore increase profits by cutting costs. It contracts out much of its work to independent plumbers, who respond to emergency calls, and to subcontractors.

This approach allows Thames Water to manage an important external factor: the labour market and the potential threat of labour skills shortages. By using independent operators, the company is rarely faced with the recruitment, training and retention issues involved in employing large numbers of plumbing engineers. The potential downside for the consumer is the risk of poorer service: some private contractors may have little incentive to provide an excellent service for Thames Water.

Although residents in Thames Water's area have to use the company's services, they are not powerless. The government has established two agencies to monitor and regulate the services of the water industry on behalf of the consumer:

- the Water Services Regulation Authority sets prices in the water industry, with reference to efficiency and value for money

- the Consumer Council for Water represents consumer interests to the water industry and the individual water companies.

Thames Water needs to manage its relationships with its customers, the regulatory and consumer agencies, and other pressure groups such as MPs that represent water users. It also has to monitor and respond to a wide range of other external factors. These include:

- legal factors – the company must comply with all laws relating to the water industry specifically and to employers generally

- technology factors – new technology may enable Thames Water to offer a better service and to cut its costs by working more efficiently

- environmental factors – the company must meet public expectations for good environmental management as well as comply with current environmental regulations

- economic factors – the state of the economy impacts on the company's business – for example an increase in interest rates will make it more expensive to finance its investment programme.

What are external factors?

A business's external factors are anything outside the business which affects its operations, its commercial activity and, ultimately, its profits. All businesses, however small, are subject to different external factors which affect their income and impact on the costs of their operation. For example, a corner shop is affected by:

- the socioeconomic mix of its neighbourhood

- the availability of parking

- the presence of other businesses in the locality, and whether these are direct competitors or complementary businesses that might attract more customers to the area

- the state of the local economy, including the level of employment and local wage rates

- changes in the global economy – for example, it may be easier and cheaper to stock some Polish goods rather than relatively more expensive UK goods now that Poland is a member of the European Union

- legislation relating to employers, including health and safety regulations, income tax and national insurance

- legislation relating to retail businesses, including regulations relating to the storage and handling of fresh food, and value added tax

- environmental regulations, covering, for example, disposal of waste and visual pollution from the shop's neon signs

- technological changes – for example, the shop might consider using software packages to automate sales, stock and VAT records.

A business could choose to ignore external factors and adopt a "head-in-the-sand" approach. More far-sighted and proactive businesses will monitor their external environment on a continual basis, and research, anticipate and plan for any changes in relevant external factors.

Not all factors can be foreseen in detail. Businesses in London, Madrid and New York could not know precisely the ways in which these cities would be severely disrupted by major terrorist attacks. However, it is possible to reflect and consider what plans are in place in the event of a terrorist attack or a natural disaster. Even something simple such as keeping emergency contact numbers on mobile phones and

KEY TERMS

Pressure groups are organisations, such as Friends of the Earth, Amnesty International and Greenpeace, that work to influence governments and/or companies to change their policies and practices.

External contractors are individuals or businesses that manage work on behalf of a company but are not employed or owned by that business. For example, a school might use an external contractor (a catering company) to operate the school canteen on behalf of the institution.

External stakeholders are groups or individuals with an interest (but not a direct involvement) in a business. These include the business's suppliers, customers and competitors, residents who live near the business's premises, and the local authority.

Internal stakeholders are a business's owners and employees – that is, people who have a direct involvement in the business.

Legislation comprises the laws and regulations introduced by governments and passed by Parliament. Acts of Parliament are formal legal documents which set out and define legislation.

Case law is the law as established through the interpretation of legislation in the courts. Lawyers often use test cases to clarify what is meant by an Act of Parliament. The results of test cases set precedents which can be used in future legal actions.

Risk analysis is the process of identifying all risks that a business faces, the probability of their occurring and their relative importance. Through risk analysis, it is possible for a business to devise an action plan to minimise its exposure to risk.

PEST analysis is the process of analysing a company's external environment under the headings: political, economic, social and technological.

SWOT analysis is the process of analysing a business under the headings: strengths, weaknesses, opportunities and threats.

backing up computer records at another site can help a business respond and recover from these extraordinary events. Planning for external shocks should be part of a business's normal risk assessment procedures.

Many companies also undertake regular strategic planning to ensure that they are able to respond positively to any changes in their external factors. This planning typically involves using tools such as SWOT and PEST analysis. These tools enable a business to identify and maximise its benefit from opportunities in its external environment and minimise the impact of any perceived or actual threats.

What this unit covers

This unit examines critically how businesses manage their external factors to ensure that they have strategies in place to overcome external constraints. The unit focuses on four aspects of a business's external environment that can produce constraints: these are, respectively, legal, economic, environmental and technological factors.

Legal influences

Any business needs to operate within the law, and must be aware of the potential impact of new or impending legislation. The focus in this unit is on the impact of relatively new legislation, so we look at the key Acts of Parliament introduced since 2000 covering:

- consumer legislation relating to the sale of goods and services

- employment legislation.

There is also a more wide-ranging review of data protection legislation, covering developments over the last ten years.

Economic influences

No business is immune from changes in the economy in which it operates. If the economy is buoyant and growing, customers are likely to feel more confident about spending money, and businesses benefit. Conversely, if the economy is weakening, most businesses will find it harder to generate sales growth. This unit examines trends in both the UK national economy and the global economy.

Environmental influences

There is growing concern about the impact that business has on the environment. This is an area which is subject to increasing regulation. This unit examines:

- UK legislation and regulation for control of pollution

- methods and benefits of waste reduction

- underlying concepts in environmental legislation.

Technological changes

New technologies have transformed the way that many businesses operate. Many processes have been automated, and technologies like the internet have opened up new ways of communicating with customers and distributing products. This unit looks at the impact of:

- cheaper, more powerful computer hardware

- human-computer interface technologies

- integration packages

- software applications such as desktop publishing, word processing and spreadsheets

- new communications technology including broadband, e-mail and mobile phones.

Assessment

The assessment of this area of study requires you to produce a document in the style of a chairman's report to shareholders which analyses the impact of legal, economic, environmental and technological influences on a business. This report should include analysis and evaluation, and the exercises at the end of each topic are designed to help you develop these skills.

A quick footnote on terminology: the head of the board of directors in most large companies is called the "chairman" regardless of whether the postholder is a man or a woman.

Consumer legislation

Setting the scene: tackling underage drinking

The Licensing (Young Persons) Act 2000 and the Criminal Justice and Police Act 2001 tightened the law on the sale of alcoholic drinks to underage persons. This legislation even allows the police to make test purchases on licensed premises by sending in persons under 18 years of age to test whether controls are within place.

All licensed premises must take note of this legislation. They need to take active steps to prevent underage drinking on their premises: they cannot just plead ignorance. If a licensed premises is caught selling to an underage person, it risks incurring fines and possibly even being closed down.

In effect, the law allows the courts to put a licensee out of business for a period of time. This is a high cost to pay for the individual licensee and for the company that owns the premises. It is one example of how an external factor – in this case, consumer legislation – can affect the very survival of a business.

KEY TERMS

Criminal legislation is that body of law dealing with crime. It comes under the jurisdiction of the police and the criminal courts. Anyone convicted of a criminal offence faces a criminal penalty, usually fines and/or imprisonment.

Civil legislation relates to the law between two civil parties. These parties can be companies or individuals. Civil legislation covers contract and property law. It also covers tort, a civil wrong or injury arising from actions such as negligence or libel.

European legislation is law established by the institutions of the European Union. This legislation is integrated into UK law through treaties, specific Acts of Parliament and government directives. Only in very rare circumstances does the UK not adopt European legislation.

Case law is the law as established through the interpretation of legislation in the courts. The results of test cases set precedents which can be used in future legal actions.

Complying with consumer law

There is a considerable body of consumer legislation. This covers all aspects of the sale of goods and services and, as such, provides protection to consumers and regulates the operations and activities of business.

Much consumer legislation has been in place for several years and governs any business involved in trading. For example, the various Sale of Goods Acts passed in 1979, 1994 and 1995 are likely to apply to all businesses. But businesses must also be alert to legislation which impacts on their specific industry. As the introduction to this topic shows, public houses must comply with the Licensing Acts. but these will not concern (or be of any interest to) the vast majority of businesses.

A full summary of consumer legislation that applies in the UK can be downloaded from the Trading Standards website (www.tradingstandards.gov.uk). You need to navigate through the site to the appropriate page by first clicking on "For business" and then "Legislation".

In this topic, we focus on consumer legislation introduced since 2000. From the full listing on the Trading Standards website, it is possible to identify the two key pieces of recent consumer legislation:

■ Licensing Acts relating to underaged consumption of alcoholic drinks

■ The Copyright, etc. and Trademark (Offences and Enforcement) Act 2002

Two pieces of consumer legislation in five years does not seem to place too great a burden on businesses. (We discussed some of the implications of the Licensing Acts in the introduction to this topic, and we consider the copyright legislation below.) However, this is not the full story, for businesses also have to consider changes in European legislation and regulations. These changes are more difficult to follow, as this legislation is not so widely reported.

In order to keep track of changes to European legislation that relates to their industries, many businesses subscribe to specialist magazines or information websites, and are members of trade associations. In the hospitality industry, for example, a business might subscribe to Caterer and Hotelkeeper magazine or use the Caterer Search website (www.caterersearch.com), both published by Reed Business Information. In January 2006, you could use the magazine and website to find advice on:

■ European Regulation EC 852, concerning the hygiene of foodstuffs, which tightened up the current law on food handling, cleaning of food areas, and thawing and chilling of food

■ a new order to the Price Marking (Food and Drinks on Premises) Order 1979, which covers the pricing of soft drinks including the visibility of those prices

■ the 2004 deadline for implementing The Disability Discrimination Act 1995 requirement to make reasonable adjustment to premises to accommodate disabled consumers

■ the proposed ban on smoking in public places and how it will affect consumers' rights and businesses obligations

■ the Regulatory Reform (Fire Safety) Order 2004, which changes the duty of businesses towards consumers and the public in relation to fire safety.

This list shows the challenge of keeping up to date with consumer legislation. A business needs to monitor not just the new legislation passed by the UK parliament, but the European regulations and directives, and amendments or new orders issued to existing laws.

Implications for business

Consider what a business in the hotel and catering industry needs to do if it wants to be in compliance with current consumer legislation. This involves action in three areas:

■ planning

■ training

■ implementation.

Planning

In order to manage any response to legislative changes, a business needs to plan ahead. Note that there is often a considerable gap between an Act being passed and its regulations coming into force. This gives businesses time to adapt to new regulations. So managers need to think through the implications for their business of the legislation. They need to assess the costs of compliance, and the potential consequences if they are found to be in breach of the law.

For example, J D Wetherspoon, the public house chain, has responded to proposed legislation for a ban on smoking in public places by establishing in advance non-smoking pubs. This gives the company the chance to test out how to adapt its business, so that when anti-smoking legislation comes into force it knows what are the most cost-effective strategies for implementing this change.

Training

Staff often need to be trained to ensure that a business is able to implement new legislation. If the legislation is far-reaching, all employees may need to receive training. This imposes a cost, impacting on the profitability of the business, but failure to undertake training and risking breaking the law might be far more expensive in terms of penalties and bad publicity. Local authorities and professional associations often run courses to update employees on their legal responsibilities.

Implementation

Changing business operations to comply with new legislation is not always straightforward. For example, all businesses should have modified their premises to comply with the Disability Discrimination Act by 2004, but because of the vague terms of the legislation some businesses have hung back from making changes. They are waiting to have the situation clarified by test cases through the courts.

Implementing extensive changes which are in keeping with the spirit of the Disability Discrimination Act may be beyond the means of some marginal businesses. Other businesses will have the financial means to comply with the Act, and organisations such as hospitals, schools, colleges and leisure facilities will see implementation as an important part of their ethos and values. Most businesses will fall somewhere in the middle.

Copyright legislation

The Copyright, etc. and Trade Mark (Offences and Enforcement) Act 2002 was passed by Parliament after the pressure group Alliance Against IP Theft lobbied the government to tighten legislation on intellectual property theft in the UK.

The main types of businesses affected by intellectual property theft are companies that distribute films, music, software, jewellery, branded goods and published materials. These businesses are particularly concerned about illegal trading from market stalls and car boot sales. The new Act makes it much easier for the authorities to seize computers which are suspected to have been used in the illegal duplication of copyright material. It also provides for much heavier penalties for counterfeiting and piracy.

The Alliance Against IP Theft lists its members on its website (www.allianceagainstiptheft.co.uk). These members are trade associations, representing the

interests of legitimate businesses, and they play an important role in monitoring that the new legislation is being enforced and in reporting examples of action under the new regulations. For example, the Entertainment and Leisure Software Publishers Association has reported that seven people were arrested in Cannock for the production and distribution of counterfeit goods.

Copyright legislation supports legitimate business activities and it enables them to protect their intellectual property rights: it is therefore seen by business as a benefit rather than a burden. By enforcing legislation to protect legitimate producers' rights, the government is seeking to help businesses in the content industries:

■ protect their return on investments

■ ensure their long-term viability

■ protect their intangible fixed assets.

Although businesses clearly benefit from the copyright legislation, the Act also arguably serves the long-term interests of consumers. Of course, not all consumers appreciate the value of paying a fair price for intangible goods, which they can easily steal with new technology. But, by protecting the return on their investments, businesses like software houses, games developers and film companies will have both the confidence and the incentive to develop new and better products. In the long term, this mean that businesses should produce a wider range of good quality goods for consumers. More immediately, by clamping down on illegal counterfeit and pirated goods, consumers should have more confidence that they are buying products that are protected under consumer legislation.

This legislation came about as a result of lobbying by the industries affected by piracy and counterfeiting. The Alliance Against IP Theft has said that it took three years of lobbying to realise its aim, and various member associations of the Alliance are lobbying for more inspectors to enforce the legislation. It is instructive to ask why businesses have been lobbying so hard for tougher legislation. For the answer, you have to look at another area of these businesses' external environment: it is technological changes – another key external factor – which have exacerbated the counterfeiting problem. The advent of new digital, networking and computer technologies makes it much easier to copy films, software, music and other goods without the makers' consent. This is why businesses have lobbied long and hard for a change in the law.

The Unfair Commercial Practices (UCP) Directive (2005/29/EC) places a general duty on all businesses not to trade unfairly with consumers. In particular, businesses are not to mislead consumers through acts or omissions or subject them to aggressive commercial practices such as high-pressure selling techniques.

The Direct Selling Association (www.dsa.org.uk) represents the interests of businesses that are involved in selling to consumers by door-to-door selling, or by telephone, post and e-mail. The DSA already has a voluntary code of practice for its members in relation to how they should conduct themselves and to the selling techniques they should adopt.

Over recent years direct selling has boomed in the UK, and this method of trading is now used extensively by loan companies, insurance firms, double-glazing businesses and many other industries. Some of the businesses that support direct selling operations, such as the Royal Mail and call centres, have grown on the back of this boom.

There have been many complaints about direct selling techniques, however. Industries which have been subject to the most criticism include:

- timeshare holiday businesses

- home damp-proofing

- lottery and share schemes, particularly e-mail scams

- double-glazing companies

- financial services, particularly through the mis-selling of endowment mortgages.

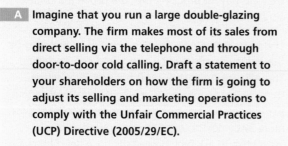

A Imagine that you run a large double-glazing company. The firm makes most of its sales from direct selling via the telephone and through door-to-door cold calling. Draft a statement to your shareholders on how the firm is going to adjust its selling and marketing operations to comply with the Unfair Commercial Practices (UCP) Directive (2005/29/EC).

Ensure that your statement covers:

- **the main provisions of the directive**

- **the threats that the directive will present to the business**

- **the opportunities that the directive offers the business**

- **suggestions for how the business can maximise its sales within the constraints posed by the new directive.**

Employment law and data protection

Setting the scene: the cost of employment legislation

In June 2005, Management-Issues (an independent online resource on leadership and business) reported that small and medium-sized enterprises (SMEs) were being damaged by the excessive cost of employment legislation.

Management-Issues presented the findings of a survey of 500 SMEs by Tenon Forum, a think tank of leading entrepreneurs, which found that:

- the costs of running a business have been increased by the obligations imposed by legislation granting maternity, paternity and disability rights

- employment legislation deters employers from taking on extra staff.

Richard Kennett, chairman of the Tenon Forum, stated that: "On the whole, the businesses we deal with think that employment law is probably the most complex and far-reaching area of all the legislation and regulation that applies to them... It is arguably more complex than tax, health and safety, and the regulations of the Financial Services Authority."

Both the Federation of Small Businesses (FSB) and the British Chambers of Commerce have been actively lobbying against the burden of employment legislation for several years. In a 2002 report, the British Chamber of Commerce estimated that the average business spent £8,906 a year on complying with employment legislation and 11.8 hours per week dealing with employment issues.

Alan Tyrell, chairman of FSB Employment Affairs, commented in 2004 that: "Small businesses employ over 50 per cent of the private sector's employees, that is some 12 million workers. But the typical UK small business owner is a one-person HR department, and heavy increases in the administrative burden can have a direct influence on their productivity and ability to create jobs."

Sources: Management-Issues (www.management-issues.com), British Chambers of Commerce (www.chamberonline.co.uk).

Employment legislation

Employment is the process of engaging people to perform specified jobs. Employers can be businesses (of all kinds), individuals, voluntary bodies and government organisations. All employers have statutory (that is, legal) responsibilities. They have a duty to collect an employee's tax and national insurance contributions and to make any other agreed deductions from pay, such as for a pension. From recruitment onwards, employers must comply with equal opportunities and employment legislation.

Businesses need to stay abreast not only of current UK legislation but also of changes to UK and EC regulations and to interpretations of employment law by the courts. A good resource on British employment law is the website www.emplaw.co.uk. The free area of this site has a complete listing of current employment legislation, and provides a brief explanation of each relevant Act of Parliament and any recent case law.

KEY TERMS

Disability covers any physical or mental special need. Within reason, disabilities should not be a barrier to employment, and employers are expected to make adjustments to accommodate people with a disability.

Maternity leave is the period a woman is allowed off work both before and after the birth of a child without losing the right to take up her job again. This includes periods of paid and unpaid leave.

Statutory maternity pay is a legal entitlement for women taking maternity leave. The law sets out the eligibility criteria, the minimum rates of maternity pay and the period for which it must be paid. Employers can claim back some maternity pay from the government.

The emplaw website lists 76 current pieces of legislation that relate to employment. This is an area of law which changes frequently, demonstrated by the fact that 53 Acts have been introduced since 1999.

Some of the most significant of the recent regulations and Acts are:

- the Employment Act 2002
- the Income Tax (Earnings and Pensions) Act 2003
- the Minimum Wage Regulation 1999
- Part Time Workers Regulations 2000
- Social Security Contributions (Share Options) Act 2001
- Tax Credits Acts 1999 and 2002

Most employment legislation impacts on all employers. However, some legislation only applies to particular groups of employees or specific types of businesses. There is a series of regulations covering the armed forces, including the Armed Forces Act 2001, the Armed Forces Discipline Act 2000 and the Armed Forces Pensions and Compensation Act 2004, and legislation covering the activities of gangmasters, the Gangmasters Licensing Act 2004.

Employment Act 2002

The legislation that has probably caused the most concern to employers in the last five years has been the Employment Act 2002. This is wide-ranging legislation that covers many areas in the workplace.

One major area of the Employment Act 2002 is a series of provisions to require employers to offer more family-friendly terms to employees. Specific provisions provide for entitlements for:

- six months' paid maternity leave and six months' unpaid maternity leave for working mothers
- six months paid leave and six months unpaid leave for adoptive parents
- two weeks' paid paternity leave for working fathers
- statutory maternity pay to be increased from £62 per week to £100 per week.
- parents of young children (usually under 6 years old) to request flexible working arrangements.

The government recognised that these provisions place additional burdens on employers, and it did build some help for businesses into the Act. In particular, employers can get some maternity, paternity and adoptive parent leave payments reimbursed by the government. Small businesses get full reimbursement of these leave payments plus an additional bonus payment.

The provisions of the Employment Act 2002 do not just deal with maternity and childcare issues. They concern many other areas of employment. For example, the Act sets out:

- a right for trade union learning representatives to paid time off work
- a requirement that all employers, however small, must operate minimum standard compulsory disciplinary and grievance procedures
- new rules for the written terms of employment to which all employees are entitled
- new rules for fixed-term workers, bringing them in line with other employees.

Employers' organisations are worried about the impact of the Employment Act 2002. Some have claimed that it is causing businesses to spend more time at tribunals to settle disputes with employees. The website www.startinbusiness.co.uk has warned that although compensation claims against employers for unreasonably refusing flexible working arrangements are capped at £2,600, there is a further risk to employers in relation to claims for sexual discrimination in the case of female employees, which carry the risk of unlimited damages.

Small and medium-sized firms are complaining that they are finding it difficult to bear the burden of carrying key employees for up to 12 months' absence on maternity leave. They claim that many workers are difficult to replace in the short term. There is much discussion in employer forums about employing women of a child-bearing age or those that have very young children, with the implication that it may be less risky not to employ them in the first place.

There is evidence that some companies have yet to comply with the Act in particular areas. Many businesses have failed to keep their contracts of employment up to date so that they comply with the legislation. Others have not yet complied with the requirement to operate minimum standard compulsory disciplinary and grievance procedures.

Assessing the impact on a business

In the assessment of the unit, you are required to consider the impact of new employment legislation on a chosen business. In analysing the impact of employment legislation on your business, and its readiness to meet forthcoming regulations, it is important to identify the make-up of the business's workforce in terms of:

- sex
- age

- types of contract of employment

- types of work

- hours of employment and the need for overtime

- rates of pay (particularly if minimum wage legislation might apply).

New employment regulations usually come into effect some time after an Act is passed by Parliament, to give businesses time to plan. All businesses should be planning for changes announced in new employment legislation. In assessing the performance of a business in managing its response to employment legislation, you should therefore consider not simply whether a business is compliant with current legislation but any planning it undertakes to cope with change. Large companies appear to be organised in this respect. Unfortunately, few small and medium-sized businesses are keeping up with the pace of change, never mind preparing for forthcoming regulations.

stop and think

Suppose you have arranged a visit to a company to study the impact of employment legislation on its operation. Draft a list of questions to ask key staff. (If you are doing this for real, you should ideally e-mail this list to the company in advance so that staff can consider the questions before your visit.)

Data protection

In the last ten years there have been significant changes to the rights of individuals and organisations to have access to information about themselves held by others. This is partly a response the huge increase in the use of information technology, which makes it much easier to store, collate and exchange data on individuals.

The changes in the law also reflect the increasing liberalisation of society. There is increasing recognition that people should have a right to know what information is collected about them, that they should be able to correct inaccuracies in the personal data that any organisation holds, and that there should be some legal protection to prevent that data being used without the individual's consent.

The Information Commissioner's Office was set up by the government to protect personal information and to promote access to official information. This agency monitors and enforces the main pieces of legislation in this area.

- Data Protection Act 1998 – places a legal requirement on any organisation holding information on people to ensure that the data is accurate, securely stored and not misused.

- Freedom of Information Act 2000 – gives people a general right of access to information held by or on behalf of public authorities.

- Piracy and Electronic Communications (EC Directive) Regulations 2003 – establishes new rules for e-mail marketing, to reduce the amount of unsolicited e-mail.

- Environmental Information Regulations 2004 – establishes the right for individuals to request environmental information from public authorities and any other bodies carrying out public functions.

The Information Commissioner's Office can provide advice to individuals, businesses and public bodies on their rights and responsibilities under the legislation. It provides information on the detailed regulations arising from the primary legislation, and on the implications of how any rulings established through case law affect them. Further information can be found on the agency's website www.ico.gov.uk.

The Data Protection Act 1998 places responsibilities on any business that holds information on its customers, suppliers and other stakeholders. Companies need to take care that they comply with the current legislation. The broad responsibilities were discussed in the AS textbook (see pages 100–1 and 182), but it is worth reiterating the main principles that must be applied in handling customer data. These are that it should be:

- fairly and lawfully processed

- processed for limited purposes

- adequate, relevant and not excessive

- accurate

- not kept for longer than necessary

- processed in line with an individual's rights

- secure

- not transferred to countries that do not have adequate data protection legislation.

The Act only applies to personal data, which is defined as:

> data which relate to a living individual who can be identified
>
> (a) from those data, or
>
> (b) from those data and other information which is in the possession of, or is likely to come into the possession of, the data controller, and includes any expression of opinion about the individual and any indication of the data controller or any other person in respect of the individual.

The scope of the Data Protection Act has been clarified by case law. The judgement in the *Durant vs. Financial Services Authority 2003* ruled that CCTV footage should be classified as data within the terms of the Act.

The Durant case also held that data needed to be held in "a relevant filing system" and that the Act was only intended to cover manual systems "if they are of sufficient sophistication to provide the same or similar ready accessibility as a computerised filing system". The Durant judgement defined "a relevant filing system" for the purposes of the Act as being limited to a system:

> 1 in which the files forming part of it are structured or referenced in such a way as to clearly indicate at the outset of the search whether specific information capable of amounting to personal data of an individual requesting it under section 7 is held within the system and if so in which file or files it is held; and
>
> 2 which has, as part of its own structure or referencing mechanism, a sufficiently sophisticated and detailed means of readily indicating whether and where in an individual file or files specific criteria or information about the applicant can be readily located.

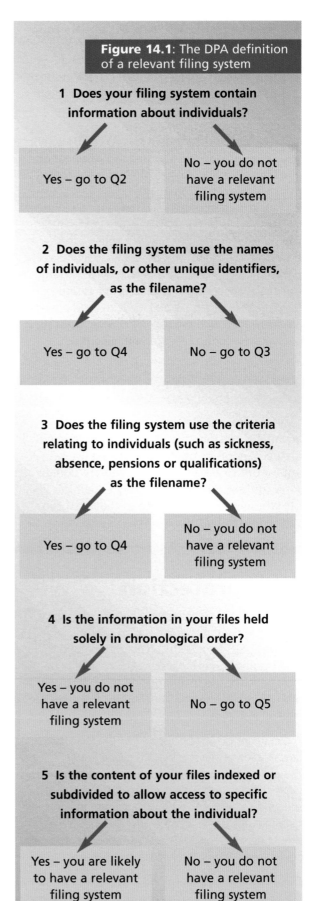

Figure 14.1: The DPA definition of a relevant filing system

1 Does your filing system contain information about individuals?

Yes – go to Q2

No – you do not have a relevant filing system

2 Does the filing system use the names of individuals, or other unique identifiers, as the filename?

Yes – go to Q4

No – go to Q3

3 Does the filing system use the criteria relating to individuals (such as sickness, absence, pensions or qualifications) as the filename?

Yes – go to Q4

No – you do not have a relevant filing system

4 Is the information in your files held solely in chronological order?

Yes – you do not have a relevant filing system

No – go to Q5

5 Is the content of your files indexed or subdivided to allow access to specific information about the individual?

Yes – you are likely to have a relevant filing system

No – you do not have a relevant filing system

The legal extracts from the Act and related case law (set out opposite) show the challenge for any business in trying to ensure that it is compliant with the Act. In practice, no business needs to refer directly to the legal documents as there is readily available guidance which sets out the legal responsibilities in plain language. Figure 14.1 shows the guidance produced by the Information Commissioner's Office to help any organisation determine whether it has a relevant filing system under the terms of Data Protection Act (DPA).

assessment practice
A new travel business

You were appointed chairman of a new travel company 12 months ago. You are now drafting your first chairman's statement.

Your business has seen tremendous growth in terms of sales. As a result, the company which began the year with three employees now has 125 staff. The profile of the workforce is as follows:

- 70 per cent are women between 25 and 35 years of age

- two staff members are registered disabled, and one is in a wheelchair

- 30 per cent are from ethnic minorities.

The business has been established through effective use of internet selling. The company purchased lists of potential customers from businesses that sell non-travel products to the same target group – in other words, people with the economic and social profile that your travel company is trying to reach.

A **Draft the relevant sections of the Chairman's report that explain how the business might have managed to deal with the constraints imposed by:**

- **The Disability Discrimination Act 1995**

- **The Employment Act 2002**

- **The Data Protection Act 1998 as clarified by the Durant case.**

For each Act, write one paragraph on the implications of the legislation for your business and one paragraph on the measures you could have adopted to ensure the business complies with the law.

National economic influences

Setting the scene: Harrington the builders

John Harrington is a builder in the south of England. He is willing to work on any small to medium-sized project, from shopfitting to renovating Victorian residential properties.

John often works alone, but he brings in friends and co-workers to get a big job done. On some projects he needs to work with electricians, plumbers and other specialist contractors. Some work, such as painting and decorating, does not pay well, so John subcontracts that to other workers if he can get better-paying work.

When there is strong demand in the building industry, there are occasional skills shortages. John minimises the impact of these skills shortages on his business by being able to call on the same group of building contractors that he has worked with for years. He has developed close ties, and his co-workers tend to prefer working within their own social network rather than for large companies.

John manages to maximise his income not just by contracting work out when he can get higher-paying work but by taking on different types of work. Being able to move from work in the retail sector to commercial office work and then to residential work means that John is not tied to the success of one business sector and is less affected by fluctuations in its business cycle.

Wider economic factors impact on John's business. Demand for his services is influenced by general consumer confidence, and by the effect of interest rates, inflation and tax rates on levels of disposable income. However, it is only in a general economic slump that John finds himself short of work or taking on work that has very poor margins. In general, his ability to move from work in one economic sector to another has served him well. In this way, he manages his external economic environment.

Economic factors

All businesses are affected by a wide range of economic factors. No business can completely isolate itself from the economy in which it operates. In Topic 4 we shall consider the impact of the wider global economy. However, in this topic, we look specifically at how trends in the UK national economy impact on business by considering:

- the business cycle

- inflation

- the labour market

- consumer debt

- interest rates.

Before looking at each of these factors in turn, it is important to emphasise that although the general

trends in the economy impact on the overall business climate, they do not explain the circumstances of individual businesses. To monitor and plan for the impact of economic factors on its own business, a company needs to be aware of price changes, labour supply, stage of the business cycle and the consumer profile of its own industry.

Businesses need to look at how general economic trends will impact on their customers and suppliers. They must understand the impact on their industry. The impact can be quite different even for companies apparently in the same industry. For example, the tour operators Saga and Club 18–30 both operate in the package holiday industry but, as the case study opposite illustrates, recent economic trends have impacted on the two companies quite differently because of the distinctive nature of their respective target customer groups.

Economic cycle is the pattern of economic output by the whole economy. Historically, the cycle has tended to follow a pattern (over several years) of growth, boom, recession, depression and recovery.

The **unemployment rate** is the number of people looking for work expressed as a percentage of the total labour force. To be counted as unemployed, a person has to be actively searching for a job and available for work. Students and retired people are not counted in the unemployed figures.

Inflation is the increase in general price levels in the economy over a period of time, or the fall in the purchasing power of the pound.

Interest rates are the price paid for borrowing money, or the price charged for lending money. Lenders set interest rates partly on the basis of the market – borrowers will chose lenders that offer the lowest interest rates – and partly on their assessment of the level of risk attached to the loan.

The business cycle

The general business cycle is an average of all the different cycles in the industrial sectors that comprise the economy. As Figure 14.2 shows, the business cycle moves in a regular pattern from boom to recession, to slump, to recovery and back to boom.

In the boom period of the business cycle, there is full employment and there are often shortages of other resources as the economy makes full use of all factors of production: materials, labour and capital. Consequently, booms are often accompanied by inflation, as companies try to outbid each other for the limited resources.

Booms are not sustainable. Lack of confidence in some aspect of the economy triggers a fall in general demand, which leads to unemployment as companies reduce their workforces. Unemployment, in turn, can lead to a further fall in demand: not only do those workers that have been made redundant reduce their spending, but rising unemployment can dent general

business practice
Saga and Club 18–30

Saga Holidays specialises in holidays for people over 50 years of age, while Club 18–30, as the name implies, caters in holidays for young, mainly single people. Although both companies largely sell holidays to UK residents, their customer profiles are very different: they cater for people at different stages in their lives and subject to different sets of economic influences.

Saga Holidays grew massively during the 1980s and 1990s, when the number of people entering retirement was growing rapidly. Saga's customers are in the later half of their lives, they tend to have substantial savings, and many live on their savings rather than earned income. During the 1980s when interest rates were high, Saga's customers had considerable disposable income from the high returns on their savings.

When interest rates fell in the early 1990s, there was a direct impact on Saga's business. Saga's response was to expand its customer base by dropping the original age profile from 60 plus to 50 plus. This picked up higher-earning individuals who had professional salaries and were probably at the top of their earning potential. Saga also diversified its product range, bringing in many new services to provide for people as they planned their retirement and inheritance. The result has been

that Saga has been able to grow its turnover despite significant cuts to the income of its original target market.

In the last 10 years, Club 18–30 holidays has also seen the potential spending power of its consumers reduced. Although the overall economy is stable, with low inflation and low interest rates, the housing market has been very volatile with high levels of inflation, a result in part of a housing shortage in many areas of the UK. Consequently the real income of young people has been squeezed by the need to pay high housing costs. This, in turn, has restricted Club 18–30's potential for growth. Unlike Saga, Club 18–30 has less room to manoeuvre: its market is fairly well defined – if it sought to relax its customer age profile, it would move into the family holiday market and risk diluting its unique selling proposition – and the economic pressures on young people are unlikely to be short term.

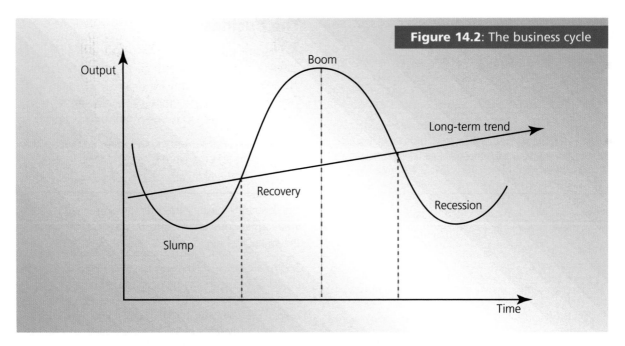

Figure 14.2: The business cycle

consumer confidence so people spend less and demand is depressed. This can cause a spiral of rising unemployment and falling demand, leading to a recession.

When the fall in demand slows down, an economy can settle at a lower level of general output with sustained unemployment. This state is known as an economic depression or slump. Many Eastern European economies were in depression during the late 1990s and early 2000s, where over a long period there were high levels of unemployment and low levels of general output.

In order for an economy to emerge from depression, many economists have argued that it requires a catalyst to "pump-prime" demand, such as an increase in government spending or considerable overseas investment. This can increase employment, which in turn further increases demand in the economy, which in turn triggers an upward spiral of demand and rising employment – this is the economic recovery.

Many governments have tried to reduce the severity of the business cycle. In the 2000s, the UK government sought to introduce greater economic stability and bring an end to "boom and bust". This has many benefits, if it can be achieved. A long-term stable economy encourages businesses to invest and take risks, which should increase the wealth of the country in the long term. An economy that is growing steadily also attracts further investment and resources from overseas. The influx of workers to the UK from Poland and other countries that have recently joined the enlarged European Union has been seen as a positive factor in supporting the UK economy and encouraging wealth creation.

As well as the general business cycle, most businesses are affected by their own trade cycle in their own industry. This may follow the general pattern of the general business cycle or may exhibit a different pattern, perhaps more or less extreme than the general cycle or with periods of growth and decline out of synch with the general cycle. In late 2005, for example, most UK retailers were reporting tough trading conditions, with falling demand. But this wasn't a uniform trend – some sectors were doing well: in particular manufacturers and retailers of electronic and computer equipment were experiencing high sales as consumers upgraded their phones, computers and games consoles.

Some industries can benefit from a downturn in another sector. The restaurant industry, for example, is likely to follow the general business cycle quite closely: people tend to eat out more when the economy is doing well, and tend to cut out some luxuries and eat at home when the economy is in recession. However, people may buy more takeaways or ready-prepared meals as a substitute for eating out, so producers of these products may see an increase in demand in a recession when the restaurant industry is experiencing a downturn.

The business cycle describes overall economic trends, but the impact of any particular set of economic circumstances on businesses in the same industry with the same customer base will not be identical. Some business will fail during a recession; others will survive. There are several factors which affect a business's ability to survive an economic downturn. Three key factors are:

- the closeness of a business its customers – clothes retailers who understood the needs of the consumers did well in the winter of 2005/6, while those that didn't issued profit warnings

- the efficiency of a business – a business that has greater efficiency and hence higher profit margins than its competitors is better placed to survive a slump in demand

- insulation from business and consumer markets – a company that does considerable business with the public sector may be relatively protected from the business cycle as government spending is less prone to short-term fluctuations.

Inflation

The inflation rate is the change in the relative purchasing power of the pound. If it cost a company £100 to buy one tonne of sproggets in 2005 but the price rises to £110 per tonne in 2006, then the purchasing power of each of the company's pounds has fallen. It costs 10 per cent more to buy exactly the same amount of sproggets one year later.

In the UK, inflation is measured by the retail price index (RPI). This is a weighted average of the prices of a "basket" of goods and services. The basket reflects the goods and services bought by typical consumers. The inflation rate is usually expressed as the percentage change in the retail price index in a 12-month period. In early 2006, the annual UK inflation rate was a little over 2 per cent.

Note that the RPI is just represents the prices of goods and services bought by a "typical" family. It does not give an inflation rate for particular goods or for individual industries. Cheap imports from China have kept price increases of mass-manufactured goods such as toys and garments well below the general inflation rate. In contrast, the housing shortage in the UK resulted in house price inflation well above 10 per cent in the early 2000s, and although the housing market has "cooled", the Halifax House Price Index – a measure of inflation in the housing market – was 5 per cent in February 2006, which is still three points above the RPI.

To understand how inflation affects individual businesses, it is important to identify any changes in price in the business's main expenses, such as rent, wages and raw materials, and compared these to changes in the price of goods that the business sells. If a business can pass on price changes to customers,

then the impact of inflation on the business is not too significant. If, however, a business cannot pass on price changes in inputs to its customers, then the impact of inflation will be to squeeze profits unless the business can find ways of increasing efficiency.

In general, businesses prefer price stability. This is because steady rates of low inflation allow a business to plan ahead with greater certainty, and therefore to take more investment risks. Price stability also benefits companies in other ways.

- Customer behaviour is more predictable, and consumer confidence is likely to be higher if people are not subject to constantly changing prices.

- Demand is likely to be higher as inflation cuts into the real spending power of people with fixed incomes, such as senior citizens who do not have index-linked pensions.

- A business cannot hide inefficiency behind price rises, therefore managers have to face up to the need to make real efficiency improvements to the underlying business.

- Interest rates are likely to be low and stable, so it is cheaper to borrow money and easier to predict the return on investments.

The labour market

The labour market works like any other market: there is an interaction between demand and supply in order to arrive at the market price for labour. However, unlike other markets, the general price for labour does not change daily; it usually only changes when people change jobs.

If there is low demand for labour, then the market price for labour tends to fall. This is true even for professional staff – computer staff who changed jobs immediately after the dotcom bubble burst in 2000 often could only find jobs by accepting lower pay. Some businesses even have senior staff on lower pay rates than more recent junior arrivals, because changing market conditions forced them to offer higher pay rates to attract new employees. (These firms obviously take a decision not to bring the pay of all employees in line with market rates, a policy which may work in the short term but could cause resentment and increase staff turnover.)

The other consequence of low labour demand is unemployment. Conversely, when demand is high, and the economy approaches full or high levels of employment, employers compete for workers and labour shortages arise. In this situation, employers may compete for new recruits by offering higher pay, resulting in wage inflation.

In the 2000s, the UK economy has been quite successful in avoiding wage inflation despite high levels of employment. This is because of several current features of the UK labour market:

■ an influx of workers from other parts of the European Union, in effect increasing the pool of labour available to UK businesses

■ the trend for outsourcing or subcontracting work to other countries with lower wage rates, such as India and Malaysia

■ regulations which allow employers more flexibility to hire and fire than in many other European countries and to bring in workers on seasonal and short-term contracts

■ a higher proportion of women in the workplace than most European countries – and despite the Equal Pay Act being law since 1970, women still tend to be paid less than men on average

■ the trend for more flexible labour contracts, providing jobs for people such as students and those with dependents who want to work for, say, four hours a day.

In the long term, these solutions may not be so effective in keeping wage inflation low if the economy continues to exhibit high employment levels. For example, if the economies of Poland and India grow and create their own demand for skilled workers, this will reduce the pool of people who might be attracted to migrate to the UK for jobs and/or reduce the capacity in these countries to take outsourced work from the UK.

Again, overall employment levels in an economy don't provide an indication of the situation of the labour market – and the potential for skills shortages – in particular industries. For example, many traditional graphic artists have found themselves superseded by computerisation, while those working in IT are in high demand. There are some skills shortages in the construction industry as the UK undergoes a building boom. In general, skills shortages are more likely in highly skilled occupations.

To assess the impact of the labour market on individual businesses, it is useful to interview managers in charge of recruitment to find out whether they are experiencing any difficulties in recruiting employees or finding staff prepared to work for the wages on offer.

stop and think

Prepare a list of questions that you could use as the basis for an interview with a manager responsible for recruitment in a business of your choice.

Consumer debt

Consumers in the UK have access to considerable levels of credit through credit cards, store cards, loans from banks, car financing companies, suppliers of utilities such as mobile phones, and so on. The media bombards consumers with images of desirable products, encouraging an appetite for spending that is partly fuelled by a surfeit of "buy now and pay later" offers. In early 2006, it was estimated that total UK personal debt (including the money owed on mortgages) was £1.1 trillion compared with £440 billion in 1995.

Businesses benefit when consumers spend freely, but excessive borrowing and high levels of consumer debt also pose several threats.

First, if debt levels reach such a point that consumers stop spending in order to take control of their finances and pay off their loans, then demand could fall sharply – which could hit retail businesses particularly hard.

Second, if consumers adopt a more responsible spending pattern, then the businesses that service excessive consumer borrowing such as the credit card companies will see a drop in their earnings as consumers migrate to cheaper solutions to their financial problems.

Third, if consumers do not stop spending beyond their means, then there is the risk that some debts will just not be paid. Some consumers could be forced into bankruptcy, which will mean that businesses will not get paid all that they are owed and there will be a general reduction in consumer demand in the economy.

The long-term consequences are perhaps most serious for individual consumers. Some may end up with such a bad credit rating that they are unable later in life to buy a house or start their own business as they will be unable to borrow money, or will only be offered loans at punitive interest rates.

Interest rates

Interest rates in the UK have been set by the Bank of England since 1997. The government has no direct control over rates. The decision to move control of interest rates from central government control was taken following the success of the German economy in the latter part of the twentieth century. The independence of the German central bank to set interest rates bought considerable stability to the German economy and was credited with encouraging long-term business growth.

Interest rates are set by the Bank of England to ensure that price rises within the UK economy are within the government's inflation targets. In this way, moving interest rates is a general economic tool for controlling inflation. Movements in interest rates can also have other economic effects. Let's consider the impact of raising interest rates (reducing interest rates will have the opposite effects).

■ Higher interest rates attract investment in sterling in its own right. So changing interest rates can influence exchange rates, which impact on businesses that are involved in import and export markets.

■ Higher interest rates can deter businesses from investing in new projects as they may not be able to make a high enough return to pay the cost of the loan and make a profit.

■ Higher interest rates can deter consumers from borrowing for immediate consumption or from taking out mortgages to buy property. Not all individuals are affected in the same way by high interest rates – the annual interest rates of up to 30 per cent charged on some loans and by some credit card companies suggest that many consumers are oblivious to interest rates. This cannot be sustained for ever, and the long-term effect is that consumers may have to cut spending in other areas to afford their loan repayments.

■ Higher interest rates boost the spending power of people who are dependent on their savings for their income, such as senior citizens with little or no employment income but often with a high level of savings.

As we have previously discussed in this topic, any assessment of the impact of general movements in economic factors on individual businesses needs to take their particular circumstances into account. This applies equally to interest rate movements, although most businesses like stable interest rates, whatever the rate, so that they can plan ahead and take investment risks.

Note also that individual businesses face different rates of interest on their loans. The Bank of England only sets the base rate, and individual lenders are free to set any interest rate that they think the market (that is, potential borrowers) will bear. As a general rule, the smaller and riskier the business, the higher the rate of return that financial institutions demand before they will lend to the business. Large businesses, which have a significant asset base, are a more attractive proposition to lenders. As there is more probability that loans will be repaid in full – and there are other assets that can be offered as security against the loan – larger businesses tend to be offered lower interest rates on any loan finance.

The Firs Rest Home Ltd

Running a home for senior citizens who wanted to live in a pleasant environment with 24-hour care on call seemed like a stable business when Geoff and Margot set up the Firs Rest Home Ltd in 1985. They envisaged housing up to 30 residents, who would still be mobile and would not require intensive nursing care. Their market research suggested that residents would stay on average for eight years, and that they would have a waiting list.

Twenty years later the business still broke even, but it had not yielded the returns that the couple had expected. The business did not operate in a bubble, but was subject to a wide variety of economic factors just like any other business.

Interest rates

The fall in interest rates in the mid-1990s had reduced the average income of the residents and potential residents of the Firs Rest Home. The residents no longer earned high levels of interest on their savings. This had reduced demand for the services of the Firs Rest Home and made it difficult for Geoff and Margot to increase prices.

Residents were becoming increasingly dependent on their relatives to pay their fees. These relatives all seemed to be employed in well-paying jobs and to be benefiting from the UK's long-term economic stability, but it was apparent that their spending power as far as the Firs was concerned was affected by two main factors.

■ House prices had risen faster than wages, and the very high cost of housing was reducing their real net income.

■ High levels of personal debt, combined with near compulsive shopping for consumer goods, meant that they could not increase their overheads even further.

The positive side of the fall in interest rates was that the interest being paid on the outstanding mortgage was now much lower. The high interest rates of the late 1980s and early 1990s nearly finished the business off.

Unemployment and skills shortages

The Firs was located just outside the M25, about 30 miles from central London. Unemployment was very low in the area, and it was very hard to recruit ancillary staff at rates below £8 per hour. It was also difficult to attract young workers from overseas as they all wanted to be in the centre of big cities and with groups of their own compatriots.

Skills shortages also meant that it was very difficult to register new residents with an NHS dentist. This meant that residents needed to be taken 15 miles to the nearest NHS dentist that was willing to take on new patients.

Gas price shocks

The Firs' heating and cooking were run on gas. This had seemed a good strategy in 1985, but in 2006 with threats of 25 per cent and then 50 per cent increases in gas prices, the implications of being dependent on gas were frightening and could affect the survival of the business.

A **Imagine you are the chairman of Firs Rest Home Ltd. Write a critical report on the impact of the external economic factors affecting the business. Explain how Firs Rest Home Ltd could attempt to maximise income within these constraints.**

The global economy

Setting the scene: the rise of China

China is an exciting young economy. The Chinese economy is growing rapidly, with an annual growth rate of 9 per cent (as at February 2006).

Cheap manufactured goods from China, including toys, garments, plastics and electrical products, are beginning to dominate world markets. For example, it is estimated that 70 per cent of shoes produced in the world are manufactured in China. The European Union is China's largest export market, and in addition to direct exports the country is also drawing in contract work from European companies.

Incomes are growing quickly. In the last 25 years, 300 million Chinese have come out of poverty, and it is expected that by 2050 nobody will be living below the poverty line. By then, researchers estimate that half of the Chinese population will enjoy a middle-class lifestyle with their own cars, and the transition from a rural to an urban, industrialised economy will have been completed.

China can be seen as an opportunity or a threat. As the largest consumer market in the world, China offers countless business opportunities; however, it also poses a threat in terms of being a low-cost base for manufacturing. There is also huge potential for China to develop its technological base. It is building up a huge stock of intellectual capital – in 2003, 817,000 students graduated from Chinese universities with science and engineering degrees, eight times as many as in the United States.

KEY TERMS

Globalisation is the trend for businesses to operate in global rather than national markets.

Migration is the permanent movement of people from one area to another.

Multinational corporations are companies that have operations in more than one country. Increasingly, multinationals operate on a global basis, manufacturing in several locations and offering services and products in many countries.

Geopolitical trends

Improvements in transport and communications have made it much easier for businesses to work on a truly international scale. In Unit 12, we looked at some of the international dimensions of business, discussing the impact of international trade and reviewing the institutions and agreements that underpin the global market. (See, for example, Unit 12, Topic 7 for an outline of the main world trade agreements, and the role and activities of the World Trade Organization.)

In this topic, we consider some of the recent geopolitical trends which are impacting on businesses. We focus on four specific features of the geopolitical landscape which are both shaping international trade and impacting on businesses in a variety of ways:

■ the expansion of the European Union

■ the impact of war

■ the threat of terrorism

■ the movement of jobs to developing countries.

Note that the impact of these global trends can be felt by any business, not just those that operate internationally. For example, the expansion of the European Union means greater competition in UK domestic markets; the ability to outsource jobs overseas may enable competitors to cut costs; a terrorist attack can affect any business unlucky enough to be in the wrong place at the wrong time.

This means that all UK businesses need to be aware of trends in the global economy, just as they need to monitor UK national economic trends (as we discussed in the previous topic). A business obviously needs to make an assessment of the threat that each trend poses to its operation, but it also needs to be aware that greater access to international markets offers opportunities. This is starkly illustrated by the emergence of China as an economic power: this poses both a threat to some UK businesses as they may be undercut by more efficient Chinese competitors, but also an opportunity to sell into the booming Chinese consumer market.

Expansion of the European Union

The European Union is an association of European countries that operate a free trade zone. Through the harmonisation of trade laws and economic policies, and the removal of trade barriers, the European Union functions as one large economic market. This makes it much easier for any business based in a member state to provide goods and services throughout the European Union.

In 2004, there was a major expansion of the European Union when ten new countries were admitted. These new member states are Cyprus (the Greek part), the Czech Republic, Estonia, Hungary, Latvia, Lithuania, Malta, Poland, Slovakia and Slovenia. As a condition of entry, these countries have made economic and political reforms to bring their systems into line with the existing member states. Several other countries from Eastern Europe have expressed interest in joining the European Union, and Bulgaria and Romania are due to join in 2007.

The most obvious impact of opening up the membership of the European Union is that the size of the market has grown dramatically. As of February 2006, the European Union covers 25 countries, with a combined population of 457 million people (see Figure 12.7, page 211). Some of the first companies to take advantage of this development have been the supermarket chains. Tesco, for example, has branches in Hungary, the Czech Republic, Slovakia and Poland, and it now claims to be the leading retailer in Central Europe.

The production capacity of the European Union has also grown significantly. This has manifested itself in several ways.

■ Many UK companies (and other Western European businesses) are contracting work out to businesses in the new member states of Eastern Europe, where there is a high standard of education but unemployment is high and business overheads are low.

■ Employees are migrating from areas of unemployment in the new member states to countries in Western Europe that have skills shortages – it is estimated that in 2005 some 30,000 people came from Poland to the UK looking for work.

■ Food production is increasing across the European Union, and with the new countries able to produce cheaper food, particularly fruit-based products such as jams and juices, this is posing a threat to UK food producers as they find it incresingly difficult to compete on price.

Enlargement has also provided opportunities. There is scope to help with the continuing transformation of the new member states from centralised to market-driven economies, as part of the process of harmonisation with the more advanced economies of Western Europe. These opportunities are as diverse as providing services such as training and consultancy to building key infrastructure such as roads and telecommunications networks. More generally, the rapidly changing and growing economies in the new member states offer many investment opportunities for banks and finance houses.

The expansion of the European Union has had a widespread impact on the general UK economy. However, like any economic factor, the impact on individual businesses is very variable. An employment agency which specialises in recruiting labour from Poland to meet UK skill shortages may be overwhelmed by work, a pub in the highlands of Scotland may barely notice the impact.

War and UK foreign policy

The UK takes a prominent role in international affairs. It plays an active part in conflict resolution in arenas throughout the world. The UK is a member of the North Atlantic Treaty Alliance (NATO), a grouping of US and European armed forces originally established to keep peace in Europe. It is a permanent member of the security council of the United Nations, and provides troops to support UN peacekeeping activities throughout the world.

More contentiously, the UK's armed forces have recently been engaged in military intervention in several countries. The UK was the most high-profile supporter of the United States in the 2003 war to bring regime change to Iraq. In March 2006, the UK has considerable numbers of troops committed overseas – not only in Iraq, but also on peacekeeping operations in Afghanistan, Macedonia and Serbia, and providing support to suppress drug barons in Central and South America.

Some of these interventions are politically controversial but, right or wrong, the UK's foreign policy – and its wider international role – has implications for UK businesses. Some are positive.

■ Many businesses in the UK benefit directly from government contracts to supply armaments and general supplies to the armed forces.

■ The commitment of British troops to conflicts, and the strong diplomatic support given to the United States, may advantage UK suppliers when contracts are being awarded for reconstruction projects after the fighting stops.

■ More generally, the threat of war also benefits the UK's defence industries – the UK is a significant manufacturer and exporter of armaments.

However, there are potential downsides to business from the UK's commitment to intervention in international disputes.

■ The large mobilisation of armed forces potentially diverts government resources that might have gone into health, transport or education.

■ International disapproval of UK foreign policy – with regard to Iraq, for example – may result in the loss of business to UK firms or the refusal of some countries to do business with UK nationals.

■ The role of the UK and the USA as "international policemen" may sour relationships with other governments – international trade thrives on trust and certainty; distrust and uncertainty inhibit the growth of trade.

The threat of terrorism

Terrorism is a form of low-level warfare carried out by a group of people, usually against a nation state. By making random and unexpected attacks on key targets or the general public, terrorists can create a disproportionate impact on society. The terrorist attacks on the World Trade Centre in New York and the Pentagon in Washington in 2001 still reverberate today.

One consequence of the 11 September attacks, and the subsequent bombings in Bali, Madrid and London, is that the threat of terrorism seems to be far greater today. This may be fuelled by the immediacy and reach of press reporting – the world seems a smaller place – but although it is difficult to assess the level of the threat, there is no doubt that UK interests are at risk of attack from radicalised groups who are dissatisfied with the role the UK, Western Europe and the USA are playing in the world.

For some businesses, even terrorism is an opportunity. Any business producing security equipment or supplying services to the police and the intelligence services can expect to benefit from the current emphasis on counterterrorism. For all businesses, however, terrorism is a direct threat. Any business needs to consider ways of:

■ improving security

■ contingency planning

■ maintaining customer confidence

■ planning its sphere of operations.

Security

Any business needs to consider whether it has adequate security measures in place to protect its buildings, personnel and customers from attack. Clearly, the potential threat varies from business to business. Some businesses need go no further than members of the general public in taking precautions such as looking out for abandoned bags. Other businesses may need a wide range of procedures and measures to ensure adequate security.

British Airports Authority (BAA), for example, manages an infrastructure that is an obvious potential terrorist target. BAA security measures are likely to include screening all employees, including cleaners and baggage handlers, installing security cameras, hiring additional security guards and deploying the latest technology for scanning luggage for weapons and explosives – all of which adds to the cost of running an airport.

Contingency planning

No level of security can completely remove the risk of attack. If the worst happens, businesses need to have plans in place to ensure that the disruption to their operations is minimised and that they can continue operating after a terrorist attack.

All major banks and many companies maintain a complete back-up – of both data and operational capability – so that they can continue to function and serve their customers in the event of one of the facilities being destroyed. However, a significant number of small and medium-sized companies have no contingency plans – in the event of an attack they could easily lose vital information, plans and records that could threaten the survival of their businesses.

Customer confidence

Terrorist attacks and the threat of attacks – with the false alarms and heightened public anxiety – disrupt the smooth flow of business. The London bombings in July 2005 brought the transport system to a halt, caused meetings to be cancelled and forced many business premises to close. This costs businesses time and money, but it also created a potential legacy in that some customers may have been deterred from visiting London for fear of further attacks.

The impact on demand – at least in the short term – can be far more costly in terms of lost revenue. Following any terrorist incident, businesses need to reassure customers and their staff wherever possible that they can operate normally and safely. In some cases, all that may be required is more visible security measures; in more dangerous situations, a business may need to relocate or change its operating methods.

Sphere of operations

In some parts of the world, the threat of terrorism is so great that many individuals and companies feel that it is simply not viable to conduct business. It is difficult to work normally if there is a real danger of being kidnapped or attacked. In Iraq, for example, British companies that might wish to be involved in the reconstruction of the country have to balance the potential benefit of valuable contracts against the difficulties of working in a dangerous and politically volatile region. As a minimum, a business needs to factor in the cost of providing sufficient security for its employees and customers. Most UK businesses will go further, and take a strategic decision to limit their sphere of operations to regions where there is an acceptable level of political stability.

Relocating jobs to developing countries

With electronic communication it is possible for business to be effectively operational 24 hours a day. The business day starts in Tokyo, moves in turn to Hong Kong, Singapore, India, Europe (Frankfurt and London), then to the east coast of the USA (New York and Washington), then to the close of the business day in Los Angeles, San Francisco and Seattle, before handing on for the start of a new day in Tokyo. The world is now global.

Most factors of production can now be traded in an international marketplace, and that includes labour. Given that labour is a major cost of production for many businesses, it is not surprising that companies are looking to drive down costs by relocating work to regions with lower labour costs. Tasks can be delegated to the area in the world that can offer the lowest costs for the best (or most appropriate) quality. Jeans manufacturers, for example, have used low-skilled workers in newly developing countries for many years for the bulk work of cutting and long seam sewing. The partly finished garments may be sent on to another country for more complex work, such as fitting the zips or adding any decorative work.

It is important to note that it is not simply low-skilled manufacturing jobs that are being moved to developing countries. Increasingly, many relatively high-skilled jobs are also being relocated in this way, and service industries are taking advantage of the lower wages in the developing economies as much as manufacturing. In recent years, many UK companies have moved their call centres, back office functions and parts of their operations overseas to developing countries. Although the main driver for this move is access to cheaper labour – allowing a business to minimise its costs, to price its goods and services more competitively and to deliver good returns for its shareholders – there are other advantages.

First, relocating work overseas can provide access to skilled labour. The UK has skills shortages in IT, and many companies have outsourced computer jobs to the Indian cities of Hyderabad and Bangalore. Here there is a network of IT businesses – some subsidiaries of Western companies, others Indian-owned firms – which specialise in work for multinationals. These businesses produce high-quality work, benchmark to international quality standards and operate at a fraction of the costs of IT businesses based in the UK.

Second, in an increasingly 24/7 world, by having customer service centres around the world it is easier for a business to offer 24-hour support to customers.

Many customer helplines now run continuously, because parts of the operation are running out of countries around the globe.

Third, many UK companies are moving jobs overseas because many new business opportunities lie in developing countries. Global businesses are shifting their centre of operations away from the developed world. There is strong interest in the fast-developing economies of south and east Asia, especially China and India which between them account for half the world's population. Many UK businesses are already heavily involved with infrastructure development in China's new cities.

Other global trends

Globalisation has opened up many opportunities for UK businesses. However, the global economy is arguably subject to more volatility than the UK economy. So, in addition to monitoring the impact of the trends discussed so far in this topic, businesses also need to consider many other factors in their planning and long-term forecasts.

Two areas of particular concern are the availability (and depletion) of natural resources and the impact of natural disasters – both the short-term impacts of, say, earthquakes or volcanic eruptions and the long-term effect of climate change. For example, UK businesses might consider:

- their exposure to oil prices – with the depletion of North Sea reserves, the UK is now a net oil importer, and it has not been so exposed to the world oil markets since 1979, so companies need to consider the security and price stability of supplies from oil-exporting countries like Russia

- the potential use of alternative fuel sources (other than oil, gas and nuclear power) – the raw sugar market has boomed on the back of expectations that it can be an efficient source of raw material in the production of ethanol, an alternative fuel to power motor vehicles

- the impact of global warming – companies need to consider how this might affect their operations, for example the growing strategic importance of water supplies could either drive up costs or make it difficult to operate in some regions.

assessment practice
British Airways

In recent years, British Airways has struggled to live up to its self-awarded accolade of the "world's favourite airline". A succession of economic events have impacted on the company, and produced tough trading conditions.

The deregulation of international air travel and the opening up of low-cost routes has transformed the airline industry. In the past, British Airways was relatively insulated from competition from low-cost carriers, but today British Airways finds that it is losing businesses on some routes to "no-frills" airlines that fly to small airports on short-hop flights throughout Europe.

The threat of terrorism has impacted on the entire industry. British Airways has had to introduce a range of additional security procedures, and its operations have been disrupted by many false alerts, forcing flights to be redirected, delayed or cancelled. Immediately after 9/11, there was a dramatic fall in business travel. This hit British Airways particularly hard as it specialises in the premium end of the market.

Oil price inflation also impacts on airlines as this increases the cost of aviation fuel. British Airways has been subject to high rises in fuel prices, and it has found it difficult to pass the full cost of these increases on to consumers in the very competitive air travel market.

However, the growth of globalisation and the trend for UK businesses to move jobs to developing countries has favoured the airline. British Airways benefits from this globalisation of the labour market as more business customers travel the world to manage overseas operations.

A Research the current economic situation in the airline industry by looking out for recent news reports and visiting the corporate websites of some leading airlines.

B Write an extract from the chairman's report for British Airways, analysing the impact of external factors on the business.

Regulation and control of pollution

Setting the scene: from bottles to fleeces

Fleece jackets are a popular garment with many age groups. They serve as functional sporting and casual wear. Many schools now have them as part of their uniform.

Fleeces are made from fibre-based materials. They are ideal fabrics for outerwear, as they are lightweight, repel water and dry quickly. The fabrics can be made, in part, from material recycled from plastic drinks bottles.

The manufacture of fleeces therefore provides a way of recycling soft drink bottles. Companies like Coca-Cola can use this example to argue that its operations do not have a substantial impact on the environment, demonstrating its "green" credentials. Environmental campaigners, however, argue that far too many plastic drinks bottles are still discarded as litter and end up in landfill sites.

In the UK, companies are now required to pay for some of their waste. They are charged for every tonne of waste sent to a landfill site. It is now in a company's interest to find less costly ways of disposing of or recycling their waste.

The charge on business waste is made through a landfill tax. Note, however, that this tax only applies to direct waste produced by a business not the packaging on products supplied to consumers.

Environmental responsibilities

All businesses need to be concerned about the impact of their operations on the environment. To some extent, this responsibility is forced on a business by its stakeholders. Any company that shows wilful disregard for the environment risks alienating its customer base, inciting the unwelcome attention of environmental pressure groups, and ultimately losing business.

However, in addition to societal pressure, any business has various legal obligations. There is a comprehensive system of regulation for the control of pollution and the protection of the environment established through UK legislation and European Union directives. This legislation establishes a duty upon all businesses to minimise the environmental impact of their activities.

In this topic, we examine some of the main environmental issues that impact on businesses.

Regulation of pollution in the UK

Control of pollution in the UK is not a new phenomenon. In the early to mid twentieth century, there was a growing awareness of the dangers of damaging the environment which resulted in laws to make it compulsory to use smokeless fuels in cities (to eradicate smog), laws to outlaw the pollution of waterways, and laws to outlaw or control dangerous substances such as chemicals and asbestos.

More recently, many pollution laws have now been amended and updated in the light of experience, in response to growing public concern and lobbying from pressure groups, and to bring UK legislation in line with European Union directives. This has extended the scope of the legislation, so that it covers:

- visual pollution, including restrictions on intrusive sources of light from business operations

- sound and noise, including limits both on overall volume and restrictions on noise-generating activity at antisocial times

KEY TERMS

Externalities are costs incurred through the operations of a business that are paid for by society. For example, the costs of cleaning up litter generated from a fast food outlet are met by the local authority.

Pollution is the process of contaminating the environment. It includes the discharge of any contaminant into the environment, from noise to chemicals to litter.

Waste is the by-product of any process. In manufacturing, for example, it is the material used in the production process that does not become part of the finished goods. Waste has the potential to be reused, recycled or scrapped.

Duty of care is the legal requirement in UK law to behave in a responsible way to those around you. It is a defence in a negligence case that a reasonable duty of care had been exercised.

- air quality, including controls on emissions from factories and from products such as aerosol sprays

- water quality, including controls to prevent the contamination of drinking water supplies

- land quality, including regulations to prevent land being heavily polluted by chemical leakages from farms or from industrial use

- the safe disposal of waste, including regulations to minimise non-biodegradable waste

- traffic, including limits on vehicle emissions and some controls on congestion.

This legislation affects all businesses, impacting on the disposal of waste products, limiting the activities they can carry out on any particular premises, restricting emissions from vehicles, placing controls on the level of noise and light coming from a business, and so on. Firms are monitored by the Environment Agency, local authorities and factory inspectors. Inspectors have the right to go into a business and monitor its emissions. Local authorities can provide advice on how to manage and comply with environmental legislation.

Some industrial operations by their very nature pose a particular threat to the environment, and as such are the subject of specific regulations. There are separate regulations controlling the activities of companies engaged, respectively, in oil refinery, the supply of water, nuclear power generation, and the manufacture and distribution of chemicals.

An oil refinery is required to appoint a team of staff to take responsibility for auditing all emissions from the plant and taking any necessary action to minimise environmental damage. Any leaks must be reported to the authorities so that any necessary clean-up action can be taken by all relevant parties. The company operating the oil refinery will be charged for the cost of any clean-up and may be taken to court if there is any suspicion of negligence. It must take full responsibility for the whole cost of any pollution from the plant, and it can face punitive fines if it cannot demonstrate that every reasonable step was taken to prevent pollution.

Any business dealing with substances which pose a substantial risk if they escape into the environment is advised to take these precautions.

- Keep written records of how it handles and monitors the use of the dangerous substances.

- Use experts, either employees or consultants, to keep up to date with recent legislation, case law and technical developments in pollution control.

- Work with local environmental agencies and the emergency services so that all parties know the risks on the premises and are informed about any shipments of dangerous substances.

- Carry out regular crisis management exercises, including fire practices and mock evacuation procedures, and practices for tackling spillages of dangerous substances.

Waste reduction

The amount of waste generated in the UK has grown substantially since the Second World War. The consumer society produces, uses and discards material at an alarming rate, producing a mountain of unwanted plastics, household durables such as refrigerators and motor vehicles, and disposable products such as babies' nappies, compact discs (which are designed to be very robust) and electrical batteries.

This creates a problem. There is a finite amount of space to dispose of non-biodegradable waste. The UK has a high population density, particularly in the South East, and outside the main conurbations the rural environment is highly valued for farming, for leisure and for its beauty. It is not possible to go on generating waste at current rates and burying it in landfill facilities – there is simply a shortage of suitable sites.

Businesses are coming under increasing political and social pressure to minimise the waste generated by the production, consumption and ultimate disposal of their products. There are various strategies that can be used to minimise waste.

■ Selecting input materials that create fewer disposal problems. Biodegradable inputs allow a product to be composted when it has finished its useful life – for example, some burger bars now produce their cartons for takeaway food from cardboard (a biodegradable material) rather than polystyrene. Alternatively, choose inputs that can be recycled and reused, metals that can be melted down, glass that can be crushed and reused, and so on.

■ Re-engineering a product so that it requires less input material or it makes more efficient use of resources during its consumption. This can be as simple as reducing the amount of unnecessary packaging at the point of sale. However, some companies are using relatively sophisticated computer-aided design (CAD) and computer-aided manufacture (CAM) techniques to redesign products with improved functionality from fewer resources.

■ Identifying ways to recycle by-products of the production process or non-biodegradable resources that remain once goods have been consumed. For example, the Body Shop recycles plastics into combs and other novelty goods. The construction industry can use discarded compact discs, by crushing them up and mixing with Tarmac to make extremely robust road surfaces.

■ Finding a second use for unwanted or discarded products. Some recycling and poverty action campaigns collect products discarded by Western consumers, such as mobile phones, spectacles and clothing, which can be productively reused by the developing world.

The benefits of minimising waste

Although there is strong pressure on businesses to minimise the waste generated by their production processes and products, it can also be in a company's own interest to reduce waste and limit the impact of its operations on the environment.

Waste, by definition, involves discarding resources that could perhaps be used profitably. Through more efficient use of inputs, a business can reduce the costs of production, helping it to maximise profits or to maintain more competitive prices. This approach has been successfully implemented by many Japanese companies. They have been highly successful in minimising waste – and creating world-leading brands – through a combination of re-engineering products, just-in-time stock controls and implementing quality circles. The idea behind quality circles is that, by continuously reviewing production, it is possible to deliver improvements in processes through a series of small incremental changes.

Products which are more efficient, and have lower environmental costs than competing goods, can be very attractive to consumers. The labelling on electrical goods must display the product's ranking in terms of its efficient use of energy – this can be a key factor when consumers make a purchase decision. A product's environmental credentials – and its energy efficiency – can become part of its unique selling proposition. For example, many consumers are very interested in fuel consumption rates when they purchase a car, and there has been increasing demand for fuel-efficient vehicles.

There is also a potential business benefit for companies that have good environmental practices. Games theory would suggest that a business that appears more virtuous than its competitors will be more attractive to consumers. For example, the Body Shop parades its credentials to consumers through its "recycle, reuse" slogans. There is a potential risk to this approach: if a business takes the moral high ground, it may pay a high price if its operations fall below best practice or if it doesn't live up to its claims. The Body Shop's claims and business practices have come under considerable scrutiny from environmental campaigners.

Good environmental practices can impress other stakeholders. Employees of companies that adopt environmentally friendly policies are often more highly motivated – many people do not like to be associated with wasteful companies that pollute the planet. Working for a business that people feel proud of and involved in contributes to greater motivation and higher self-esteem, and can result in improved productivity and commitment to the business's goals.

A final benefit of good waste management practices is that it reduces the regulatory burden. It is generally more expensive to merely comply with current legislation than to voluntarily impose high standards of waste management. Companies that handle waste well are far less likely to breach legislation and regulations on waste management. They are less likely to attract fines or incur charges for waste disposal. They also contribute to a political climate in which more restrictive legislation is less likely to be introduced covering their industry because they manage waste efficiently without regulatory control.

Underlying concepts in environmental legislation

In the past, companies did not have to pay the cost of cleaning up the pollution caused by their operations. They could deliver waste to landfill sites, and the local council would accept the rubbish and manage the site without charge. Smoke could belch out of factories, contributing to health problems and blackening buildings, and society would suffer in silence or pay for the costs of clean-up. Vehicles could drive into central London, creating congestion and generating pollution from their emissions, without having to pay a contribution towards the environmental costs.

These environmental costs generated by business activities but incurred by society are called externalities. Pollution is created by a business – and, often, the individual consumer – during the production, distribution and consumption of a product, but the environmental costs are not borne by the company or the consumer, but by society.

More recently, new legislation has attempted to shift these costs from society to the producers and consumers of products. This is the idea behind taxes such as the landfill tax, the central London congestion charge and airport taxes. By applying these charges, the government aims to increase the cost of the products to something nearer their true economic cost.

The process of applying this concept of requiring businesses and individuals to internalise these external costs is not straightforward. It is difficult to attribute costs between the consumer and the producer. Should, for example, the cost of disposing of an out-of-date computer be met by the current owner of the machine or the original producer? If congestion charges are introduced more widely on road traffic, effectively taxing drivers more heavily, what incentives does that give to the car industry to produce more efficient cars with cleaner emissions?

Some products arguably serve the wider public interest, so society should perhaps meet some of the cost. For example, you could have a system in which rail travellers pay the full costs associated with each journey, including the fuel costs, a contribution to the cost of pollution generated by the railway and to the maintenance and investment in new tracks and rolling stock. But it could be argued that it is in the national interest to have a comprehensive rail network, so some costs should be meet by society.

Another complicating factor is that some lobby groups can exert a strong influence on government policy. Environmental campaigners have long argued that car users – and car manufacturers – do not pay the full cost of motoring, when the true environmental and public health costs are taken into account. This, they claim, is because of power of the road transport lobby, which includes bodies such as the RAC and the Road Haulage Association. In this case, it could also be claimed that there might be some resistance from the public – at least initially – if any government tried to introduce road charging throughout the UK or increased duty on petrol to reflect the true cost of motoring.

Despite these difficulties, the direction of both UK and European environmental legislation is to place more of the cost of tackling pollution on producers and consumers. New legislation also allows for punitive damages to be charged against companies and individuals that breach environmental legislation. The rationale for punitive damages is that it can act as a deterrent: ideally it should be more expensive for businesses to breach than comply with legislation.

It has been much more difficult in the last few years for companies to get planning permission to develop out-of-town shopping centres. This has been because many people have expressed concerns about the impact of out-of-town shopping centres on the environment.

One obvious concern is that they lead to greater car use. These centres are designed around the car. Many journeys to out-of-town shopping centres involve considerable queuing on congested roads, and consequently increase car pollution for the local environment. They arguably cause further social exclusion, as people on low incomes who do not have access to their own transport can find it very difficult to access these shopping facilities.

There is also anxiety about the impact on the traditional town centre environment. As many retail businesses relocate to out-of-town sites, the old commercial centres become deserted. These areas dominated by closed shops develop a threatening atmosphere. The death of town centres makes towns less attractive places in which to live. This increases demand for more housing in the country, putting more pressure on the green spaces in the UK, and leads to greater car use as the car is often the only option given the state of the rural public transport system.

Yet businesses, and many consumers, like out-of-town shopping centres: they are convenient, they have lower operating costs for business, and turnover is higher. Given that it is hard to get permission to open in new locations, there is strong competition to maximise a retail presence in existing centres. One of the reasons why the fight to take over Safeway in 2004 was so keenly contested between retailers was because the winner stood to gain more out-of-town store locations. The battle for Safeway was eventually won by WM Morrisons Supermarket plc.

A **Imagine that you are the chairman of Morrisons. Analyse the impact of the government's change in policy for out-of-town shopping centres on your business. Explain how the takeover of Safeway stores has mitigated the situation.**

Technological influences

Setting the scene: the pace of change

In 1990, less than twenty years ago, the technology available to business was very different from today. Much of the technology we now take for granted was in its infancy. It was another world, in which communication was much slower and much less connected.

Mobile phones were the new executive toy in 1990. They were bulky, the network coverage was very patchy, and they could not be used for international calls. Text messages were unheard of – the first commercial text message was sent in December 1992. Even on landlines, it had only recently been possible to make many international calls by direct dialling. Previously, if you wanted to call, say, China from the UK, it had been necessary to book the call via an operator. Video conferencing was in its early days and required a significant investment in hardware.

Personal computers had been introduced, but their memories were relatively small and their functions were not integrated. In 1990, Microsoft introduced version 3.0 of its Windows software, and Apple launched the first Macintosh Classic model.

The internet was still relatively new, and used by very few private individuals. There was no online banking or shopping. In 1991, it was estimated that 4 million people had access to the internet worldwide. By 2005, the number of worldwide internet uses topped one billion – a 250-fold increase – and current projections suggest the two billion user milestone will be reached in 2011.

Word processing and desktop publishing were fairly well established, although interfaces tended not to be user-friendly. Databases were also in widespread use, but again they were not very

user-friendly. Newspapers were just starting to sell their archive material on compact disc, which, if you had a computer that could read CDs, made it very much easier to do business and economic research. Films were still being cut and pasted by hand, and there was no software to generate cartoons or edit film footage.

Spreadsheets had been in widespread use for about 8–10 years, and were gradually making an impact in business. Banks and other financial organisations were replacing large numbers of staff who organised financial records and accounts manually with relatively fewer computer-literate staff who could produce and manipulate spreadsheets by computer.

Impact of technology

New technology has fundamentally changed the way business is carried out. The technology available to any business today is completely different from that available 15 years ago. Businesses have access to:

- cheaper, more powerful computers, with vastly improved human-computer interface technologies and with integration packages that allow data to be easily transferred between applications

- sophisticated and relatively inexpensive software, including graphics packages, desktop publishing, word processing, spreadsheets and databases

- advanced communications technology, including websites, e-mail, mobile phone technology, video conferencing, broadband technologies and networking.

The technological transformation of business began with the computerisation of existing applications. It

Human-computer interfaces are the systems by which people respond to and interact with computers. By designing interfaces with simple procedures, clear icons, help buttons and on-screen pop-up advice, software engineers have made computers much more accessible.

Integration packages enable two or more computer software programs to communicate with each other and process the same data.

Synchronised data is the process of ensuring that all data on a network of computerised devices is updated at the same time.

Management information is the key data used to analyse and evaluate the performance of a business. It is used by managers to set realistic new goals and measure how far the business has achieved those goals.

was possible to relate the impact of each development to specific business applications. Modern applications, however, are much more complex – they bring together a wide range of technologies which enable companies to make significant jumps in the way they do business. This means that to understand how technology has impacted on business it is necessary to analyse how it is shaping key areas of business practice. In this unit, we focus on six areas:

- sales and distribution

- information storage and retrieval

- management information

- working practices and procedures

- business communications

- collaboration with other businesses.

Sales and distribution

Technology has influenced the way in which businesses sell and distribute goods and services. One obvious development in the last 15 years is the introduction and growth of electronic business (or e-business). This subject is covered comprehensively in one of the optional units of the AS course, see Unit 4 of the AS textbook (pages 152–95).

Niche businesses that might not have succeeded in the pre-internet days are now highly viable. Look, for example, at www.xaphoon.com – this website uses a vast array of technological applications to promote and sell bamboo saxophone and complementary products and to engage with fans and customers. Even for businesses that do not use the internet to sell directly to customers, the web is an important

communication tool. Small businesses have been able to reach a much wider audience through establishing an internet presence.

The other side of this technological revolution is that businesses that do not engage find themselves marginalised. Many people expect to be able to find information about businesses on the internet – indeed if a business does not have a website, some might begin to doubt its existence. There is an expectation that it should be possible to reach a business by phone or by e-mail.

It is not just the internet that is transforming the sales and distribution functions. As the Tesco case study opposite illustrates, many companies are using new technologies throughout the retail environment to achieve operational efficiencies and higher sales.

Information storage and retrieval

Database software applications allow businesses to manage, retrieve and utilise large amounts of data extremely efficiently. Tesco, for example, uses many database applications to enhance its stock control systems, its customer relationship management and its financial monitoring. By storing all its records electronically in a series of well-designed databases, any business benefits in a number of ways:

- cost savings – it is expensive to store large volumes of paper-based records, and digital data is not only cheaper to store but, with appropriate back-up systems, is more secure

- accessibility – information is easily available to any member of staff in the business through a computer network

- market research – because it is much easier to analyse data held on a computer database, a business's own records become a much more valuable source of information.

The growing trend for all organisations to hold records electronically also means that businesses not only have better access to their own information but can access some of the vast amount of data that is now held online. The internet is a rich mine of useful information – much of it free of charge, some requiring subscription or a fee. For example, businesses can easily and quickly access government reports and statistics, information on the law including the actual text of legal instruments and advice on their implications, and company accounts and reports.

A massive data resource, in itself, is of little use if you cannot quickly find the information you require or the

Tesco owes its success in part to the fact that it makes better use of technology than its competitors. The company's computerised tills work faster, allowing greater throughput of customers, fewer queues and increased productivity of staff.

The tills in each Tesco store are linked to their stock control systems. This means that automatic alerts are sent to Tesco's central distribution depots so that new stock can be delivered before a store runs out of any item. Tesco also uses information technology throughout its national and international supply chain to improve communications with its producers and suppliers, and to ensure that there are no delays or bottlenecks in the supply of goods to its depots and stores.

Sales are tagged to loyalty cards, wherever possible, enabling Tesco to identify the socioeconomic breakdown of customers at each store and to analyse the shopping habits of individual customers. This enables managers to target special offers at particular shopper groups

and adjust the stock in each store to reflect the needs of the local community.

For those customers who prefer online shopping, Tesco has an internet store and delivery service. Tesco also uses e-mail to keep in touch with its customers, sending regular mails to customers on its e-mail database as well as mailshots to customers on its postal database.

Technology is being used to improve security. Wireless technology is used to monitor high-value stock imported from overseas, so that it is very much harder for items to be pilfered while they are in transit. Electronic tags are placed on high-value products when they are displayed in stores, so that it is difficult for items to be removed undetected. Video cameras are also used to deter theft and to provide evidence against shoplifters.

Financial management is also made much easier by technology. Managers no longer have to wait weeks to receive reports on the performance of each store; instead, up-to-date financial information is readily available online. It is easy to pick out and praise top-performing stores, and perhaps more importantly to quickly identify low-performing stores and work to find strategies to overcome problems.

The overall impact of the varied application of technology in its operations is that:

- it reduces the cost of running each retail outlet

- it simplifies the task of managing stores throughout the country and internationally

- it has enabled the company to increase profits

- it has allowed Tesco to gain a dominant share of the UK retail market.

document that might be of help in the task in which you are engaged. The internet has been transformed into a valuable resource because of the considerable investment by many different organisations in storage, searching and retrieval systems. Efficient search engines such as Google now offer businesses the ability to retrieve the information that is needed quickly. (Note that companies that design and manage search engines are not doing it for the greater good; however, it is in their own interest to design better and more effective engines because that

attracts more users, and a higher volume of users attracts more advertising, and that generates more revenue for the search engine provider.)

The ability to make fast, accurate internet searches has many benefits for business. Two specific impacts are worth highlighting.

The cost of secondary market research

The internet has reduced the cost of secondary market research. Market research can easily be carried out from a desktop computer. There is no need these days to go to the main business libraries, queue at Companies House for copies of company reports and filed accounts, or contact HM Stationery Office for key government publications. Most electronic reports can also be downloaded free of charge – many organisations used to charge for paper-based documents to cover the cost of printing and postage.

A boost for globalisation

The internet doesn't recognise national borders. Broadly speaking, access to the online knowledge resource is available anywhere in the world. (Note this principle isn't universal – some internet service providers and search engines have agreed to Chinese government demands to censor some of the content and search results available to internet users in China.)

Universal access allows knowledge-based industries to operate anywhere in the world. Some market research organisations already outsource some work to countries like India which have lower staff costs. The internet also makes it easier for developing countries to keep up to date with economic, technological and business developments, and thereby makes a contribution to economic development.

Management information

As the Tesco case study illustrates, the capacity for a business to store, access and analyse its records digitally has significant implications for the way a business is managed. In particular, it changes the way a company uses its financial information.

In the past, a company would have to wait until it was able to close off the month-end accounts or other records before it could assess its own performance or the financial returns from subsidiaries and branches throughout the world. Often financial records would have to be sent to head office by fax or courier, which built another delay into the system. This meant that managers were often working with data that was weeks out of date, and this made it very difficult to respond quickly to difficult or fast-changing trading situations.

Today, most corporations are able to monitor their operations online. This makes it easy for head office to have a clear, up-to-date picture of operations in all branches and subsidiaries of the company. This is an immensely powerful tool to control cash holdings worldwide, stock and supply chains, product development and other operations.

Manual records were limiting in other ways. Managers often avoided complex calculations, as it involved so much time collecting, entering and checking data to calculate ratios and variance analysis. The automation of accountancy systems allows these calculations to be produced accurately and effortlessly, so managers can spend their time interpreting data rather than collecting and processing the information.

This has encouraged a greater use of benchmarking: managers assess the relative performance of their business against that of its immediate competitors or its industry as a whole. This is done by buying comparative data on the financial performance of similar businesses and industry averages from business research organisations such as Dun and Bradstreet. Although these exercises have always been possible, the immediacy of the data – and the fact that it is available online – makes benchmarking a much more valuable tool to managers today than it was in the past.

Another growth area in management information is the use of exception reports. Systems can be set up to monitor the efficiency of any aspect of a business's operation – production, quality control, level of complaints, the effectiveness of workers in, say, call centres, and so on – by collecting data on key performance indicators. Exception reports flag any performance indicator that varies either positively or negatively from the expected normal range. This gives managers far more control on their business operations, and allows them to take action more promptly to correct any adverse trends.

Working practices and procedures

The application of information technology to businesses has revolutionised working practices. Information technology is now embedded in many products – including washing machines, televisions, mobile phones, cameras and so on – adding a layer of interactivity and changing usage patterns. This trend is increasing as IT components become smaller, more reliable and more powerful.

Consider the BlackBerry. This small hand-held computer is a powerful piece of technology because it allows business people who are working at clients' premises or are travelling to other offices to stay abreast of their business commitments. They can use their BlackBerry to communicate with their office computers, receive and send text messages and e-mails, check their diaries and stay in touch with their colleagues. The unique selling proposition is that the office and the BlackBerry systems update themselves simultaneously – all data is synchronised.

Devices like the BlackBerry contribute to changing working practices. They allow business people to spend less time in their offices, because their work is not disrupted when they are visiting clients, meeting suppliers or working at home. Some of the main impacts of IT on the way business is conducted are:

- greater flexibility and more remote working
- efficiencies in administration
- better presentations and documentation
- increased automation.

Remote working

Information technology is changing the way people work – both in terms of their work location and their working hours. The improvements in communications and connectivity means that it is possible for many people to work from home or work flexible hours. There is less need to have employees in the same physical environment as documents, images, communications can easily be read, shared and edited by e-mail and over the a company intranet.

Administrative efficiencies

Businesses that previously employed large numbers of administrative staff have experienced big changes. As business records are no longer kept manually, there is no need to have large numbers of administrative staff to do clerical duties like copy typing and filing. There are fewer basic administrative jobs, but those that remain involve more complex tasks and require a wider range of IT skills.

Presentations

New technology makes it much easier to produce high-quality presentations for customers, staff, senior managers, potential investors, etc. In the past, the best business presentations tended to be typed and presented on acetate sheets – the worst were badly hand-written. Today, presentations are far slicker, often incorporating graphics and film clips. As a result, there has been an improvement in the quality of communication and in the frequency of presentations, which are used to complement (or as a substitute for) written reports. The presentation has become an important business communication tool, and many staff have had to learn the art of compiling and delivering presentations to different audiences, a not always welcome experience for people who are not comfortable speaking in public.

Automation

Production and design processes have been revolutionised by computer-aided design (CAD) and computer-aided manufacture (CAM). In the past, manufacturing used to be very labour intensive – many people were needed to laboriously draw out and revise plans by hand, and were fully involved at each stage of the production process. Today even the most complex tasks can be automated. Machinery can be programmed to copy human movements, and to repeat tasks accurately 24 hours a day without needing breaks or affecting quality. Not only that, machinery can be monitored remotely and, in many situations, maintained and repaired online, reducing the travel demands on maintenance engineers.

Business communications

As we have discussed, the speed, quality and variety of information available to all levels of management has increased dramatically with the widespread use of information technology. Staff devote less time to collecting and processing information and more time to analysing, evaluating and decision-making – and they take more responsibility for communicating decisions and results.

Business communications have been transformed by the automation of information gathering, storage and retrieval, and greatly enhanced by the widespread availability of the internet, e-mail, mobile phones, video conferencing and broadband technologies. This has changed the way businesses communicate with their customers and other stakeholders, and it has reshaped internal business communications.

Communication between a business and its customers is a two-way process. Businesses can exploit new channels – e-mails, text messaging, the internet, etc. – to communicate with customers. There are clear promotional advantages if customers can access detailed product descriptions and see trailers and product reviews before they purchase. Customers (potential or existing) can also use these channels to communicate with businesses, providing feedback on products and a valuable source of market information on customer needs, desires and preferences.

Modern technologies also benefit internal business communications. Colleagues can build up better relations by using e-mails, mobile phone calls and video conferencing to maintain close contact with each other even if they work on opposite sides of the globe. Personnel management can be enhanced by conducting staff surveys and 360-degree appraisal online. This can be carried out by the company itself or by companies that specialise in this work.

Easier access to communication does bring some disadvantages. Businesses need to prevent:

- e-mails getting accidentally sent to the wrong recipient and causing embarrassment

- e-mails being written in too informal or inappropriate language

- staff becoming overwhelmed by information – they need to select relevant information from the mass of material that might pass across the desk

- staff spending most of their time sending each other pointless e-mails or surfing the internet

- staff becoming demotivated by the way their work is constantly monitored by management

- staff being constantly interrupted by phone calls and e-mails, so that they find it difficult to complete their core tasks

- too great a reliance on electronic communication, so that colleagues do not get the chance to build relationships through face-to-face meetings.

Business collaboration

Technological development has been the spur for greater collaboration between businesses. This is because the cost and complexity of information technology is such that it makes economic sense for businesses to work together so that new software packages and products with a high IT component have a high level of integration.

Businesses often work together to develop a suite of new products. There is little point in a games developer producing a fantastic new game if it cannot be played on some of the most popular platforms. Similarly, there is little value in investing millions in a new games console if there are few games that operate on the platform. It makes sense, therefore, for the companies that develop games and those that develop game consoles to collaborate.

Compatibility is crucial for many products. Mobile phone operators realise that they all stand to benefit if customers can use their mobiles to contact people who have phones with other network providers. The major mobile phone companies have collaborated to ensure that there is a robust system that enables users to communicate between mobile phone networks.

Another area of collaboration is in the general area of technology convergence. The technologies that underpin mobile phones and personal computers are gradually being brought together, with many companies working on different features of hardware and software. Mobile phones are being developed to offer "wallet" services, such as the facility to pay for groceries, book tickets, and carry out online banking.

Collaboration does not necessarily involve high-tech products. The Nectar card is an example of a product that embodies relatively simple technology, but yields considerable benefits for a group of businesses working together. The Nectar card brings together several retailers – each could, in theory, operate their own loyalty card systems, but by collaborating they gain economies of scale in promotion and advertising.

assessment practice
Film on phones

The next generation of mobile phones will have the facility to download films. These films might not be feature-length films, but could be shorter films which will be cheaper to produce and might have commercial applications.

Imagine that you are working for a major retail chain that sells a range of electronic goods, and you have been asked to produce a report on the commercial possibilities of film downloads to mobile phones.

A Search the internet to discover when the new film-compatible phones will be on the market and find out their expected cost.

B Research the business-to-business links that are taking place between mobile phone companies, film companies and any other potential stakeholders to make sure that all the systems are fully integrated.

C Develop ideas for how this technology might be exploited by retail businesses. Evaluate the opportunities it brings and threats it might pose. Consider, for example, ways in which films might be stored and retrieved on demand.

D Bring your research and ideas together in the form of a short report that you could present to senior managers in the company.

Reporting to shareholders

Setting the scene: accessing annual reports

The assessment of this area of study requires you to produce a document in the style of chairman's report to shareholders, which analyses the impact of legal, economic, environmental and technological influences on a chosen business.

It makes sense, therefore, to look at how actual companies report on the impact of external influences on their operations and discuss changes to their external environment. The internet is a considerable help here, because the vast majority of public companies make their annual reports available for download on their websites.

There are a couple of important points to note when searching for company reports on the internet. First, many companies have several websites. Often they have separate sites for customers – which provide information on their products and, sometimes, act as e-commerce sites – and for investors. The annual reports are usually found on a company's corporate website.

Second, the corporate website of any company can contain a considerable amount of information, both for investors, potential employees and other stakeholders. A good place to look for annual reports is to follow links to "investor relations" and "documents". Annual reports tend to be lengthy documents, and although some can be viewed online, most will need to be downloaded in pdf format.

References to external factors can be in several possible locations within an annual report. They may be found at the start of the annual report to shareholders, and not just in the section entitled "Chairman's report". In your chairman's report for the examination keep to one simple report that covers the key areas required by the specification.

Chairman's statements

In this section, we are going to look at the reports of three companies. This will provide a brief overview of the ways companies report to shareholders on external factors.

You should notice the differences in style and presentation between the reports. Each report is unique to the company, and reflects the issues that are of most importance to that company's strategic survival. The same basic headings are covered by each company, but the amount of depth devoted to one topic depends on its strategic importance to the business.

BT Group plc

BT Group's annual report and summary financial statement 2005 can be downloaded from the investor centre section of the company's corporate website (www.btplc.com)

The chairman's message on page 3 of this report covers areas such as long-term finance (in this case a share buy-back programme), acquisitions of other

companies, and regulation by Ofcom. It sets out the company's wider responsibilities to the environment and to the national and international communities, and provides a general statement on the outlook for the coming financial year.

BT Group plc used the chief executive statement (pages 4 and 5) to give an in-depth analysis of how the business is dealing with the changing external factors which are core to its operations. This sets out the current developments in IT and the telecommunications industry which are impacting on the BT Group.

Cadbury Schweppes plc

Cadbury Schweppes' annual reviews can be viewed online or downloaded from the company's corporate website (www.cadburyschweppes.com). Go to the investor centre, and click on "reports and accounts". It is worth comparing the 2004 and 2005 annual reviews to see how the presentation can change from year to year.

The 2004 annual review has a two-page chairman's statement (pages 5 and 6) covering:

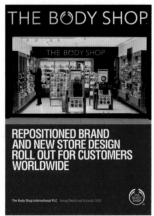

- a review of the year's performance, including a comment on the impact of the US dollar on profits

- acquisitions – the purchase of another company, Adams

- management issues, including being voted "Britain's most admired company"

- governance, including a section on the treatment of people

- corporate and social responsibility, including efforts to improve the lives of all employees around the world such as its workers in Ghana where the company buys most of its cocoa

- the board of directors, dividend payments and the company's future outlook.

This statement is then followed by a further piece by the chairman John Sunderland entitled: "from hero to villain, the challenge for the food industry". This article takes a detailed look at the public health concerns being raised about some manufactured food products, particularly with regard to obesity. It considers the impact of these concerns on the company's business.

The format of the 2005 Cadbury Schweppes annual review has been completely revised to incorporate the requirements of US legislation and new international reporting standards. Instead of a two-to-three page chairman's report followed by reports from other directors, the revised format of Cadbury Schweppes' financial statements offers a detailed 26-page analysis (on pages 2–27) of the business, under

the title of "description of business". Note that the "directors report" which follows only gives details about the directors.

The more comprehensive, detailed nature of these 2005 statements provides a useful format to copy in drawing up a report on your chosen business. It will help you ensure that your report meets the requirement to be analytical and evaluative. However, you would not be expected to produce something approaching the length of the Cadbury Schweppes report: you should be selective about which areas of your company's business you comment on to meet the exam requirements.

The Body Shop International plc

The Body Shop's annual report and accounts 2005 can be downloaded from the company's corporate website (www.thebodyshopinternational.com). You need to follow the links to investor relations and financial releases.

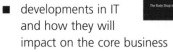

This report comments on external influences through a letter to shareholders signed jointly by the executive chairman and the chief executive officer. This letter covers a wide range of issues, including:

- developments in IT and how they will impact on the core business

- the growth of emerging markets

- competitors and The Body Shop's brand positioning

- sources of finance

- product and store development

- franchising and acquisitions

- Body Shop values

- the current and future trading outlook.

Researching your company

To analyse the legal, economic, environmental and technological influences on your chosen business, you will need to carry out secondary research to find out how your company operates and to map the legal, economic, environmental and technological aspects of its external environment. You may even need to do some primary research if information is not easily available from secondary sources such as the internet.

You might begin by collecting data on two or three companies to gauge how easy it is to find the necessary information, before making your final choice about which company to focus on. Clearly, it makes sense to select a company that is relatively easy to research.

Steps in researching companies

1 Obtain a copy of the company's financial statements and any recent announcements on the company's interim performance. These should be on the company's main website under the headings "investor relations" or "financial reporting".

2 Obtain recent copies of financial statements for close competitors. These may contain clues and ideas about how a company's external factors are changing.

3 Search online news websites for recent news about the company. Sites such as *The Guardian* (www.guardian.co.uk) and BBC news (www.news.bbc.co.uk) are free to access. Other useful sites such as the *Economist* magazine (www.economist.co.uk) are subscription sites, but your school or local library may have access.

4 Search the Competition Commission website (www.competition-commission.org.uk) for any recent in-depth analysis of your company's market or industrial sector.

5 Some management consultant websites have analyses of the factors affecting particular industry sectors. See, for example, PricewaterhouseCoopers (www.pwcglobal.com). These sites can provide useful basic information which you can refine during your investigations.

6 Visit any outlets the company has locally to get a feel for the business.

7 E-mail any specific queries you have to the company, but be aware that most companies can take a long time to answer student queries, so this must be done in good time.

assessment practice
The Body Shop International plc

Produce a chairman's report for The Body Shop International plc as at the end of the most recent quarterly result period. Use the company's most recent set of quarterly financial results as the data upon which to base your report.

Ensure that your report covers:

■ legal issues

■ economic issues

■ environmental issues

■ technological issues.

Remember that in your actual assessment you will be judged on your knowledge and understanding, the application of knowledge and understanding, research and analysis, and evaluation. Try to ensure that your report demonstrates these key assessment areas.

Topic 8 | Business in practice: Vodaphone Group plc

Vodafone Group plc is a leading mobile communications company. This case study draws on articles, press releases and reports on Vodafone's corporate website. It shows the range of external influences that impact on a large multinational company. The material that is directly reproduced from Vodafone's website is presented in the boxes. Further information is available at www.vodafone.com.

The company

Vodafone Group plc provides an extensive range of mobile telecommunications services, including voice and data communications. It is the world's largest mobile telecommunications company, with a presence in Europe, the United States and the Far East through the company's subsidiary and associated undertakings. Around 25 per cent of the world's mobile phone users are connected to Vodafone.

Vodafone has equity interests in 26 countries and partner networks in a further 13 countries. The group's mobile subsidiaries operate under the brand name "Vodafone". In the United States the group's associated undertaking operates as Verizon Wireless.

At 31 December 2005, based on the registered customers of mobile telecommunications ventures in

which it had ownership interests at that date, the group had 179.3 million customers, excluding paging customers, calculated on a proportionate basis in accordance with the company's percentage interest in these ventures.

The company's ordinary shares are listed on the London Stock Exchange and the company's American Depositary Shares (ADSs) are listed on the New York Stock Exchange. The company had a total market capitalisation of approximately £80 billion at 15 November 2005.

Legal and political influences

Legal considerations are central to the evolution of the mobile communications industry. Vodafone – as one of the biggest players – has to be extremely alert and responsive to any changes in the law that might affect the way it runs its business.

The telecommunications industry is heavily regulated. The UK telecommunications regulator is Ofcom, which operates to protect the interests of consumers and to ensure competition within the phone market. Ofcom can place restrictions on the operations and expansion of companies such as Vodafone. Health and safety legislation and data protection laws also impact on

---

German mobile communications providers sign ethics code to protect the children

Mobile communications providers are fully aware of the special responsibility that they have towards their young customers. In Germany, an ethics code has been signed with the objective of protecting children and young persons from content that could impair their development or endanger them.

The code sets clear rules governing the responsible handling of content, advertising and chat rooms, as well as videos and games for mobile phones. In the future, parents will be able to block development-impairing content on their children's mobile phones.

The ethics code came into force in summer 2005 when it was signed by representatives of debitel,

E-Plus, mobilcom, O_2 Germany, Phone House Telecom, Talkline, T-Mobile Deutschland and Vodafone D2. It will be regularly amended to reflect technical developments in the field of mobile communications.

The Commission for Youth Media Protection, as the central supervisory authority for national media establishments, expressly welcomed the ethics code.

This measure demonstrates that German mobile communications providers are willing and able to join forces in developing efficient solutions relating to consumer protection issues at their own initiative.

Having a mobile phone in your car makes it easier to contact emergency services when necessary and assists breakdown recovery. However, using a mobile phone while driving can distract drivers and increase the risk of accidents. Using a handheld mobile while driving is illegal in some countries.

Vodafone requires operating companies to advise customers never to use a handheld mobile while driving, and only to use hands-free when it is safe to do so.

Vodafone Ireland has distributed 100,000 copies of its Safe Driving consumer guide. The guide was written in conjunction with Ireland's National Safety Council following a nationwide survey commissioned by Vodafone Ireland. The survey showed 23 per cent of Irish drivers admit to using their mobile phone while driving without using a hands-free kit, headset or earpiece. The guide urges drivers to limit the use of mobile phones while driving to hands-free use in brief, exceptional or emergency circumstances.

The leaflet contains a number of key recommendations, including:

- never use a handheld mobile phone while driving

- stop in a safe place to take or make a call

- ask a passenger to take care of dialling or answering the phone

- avoid stressful calls – call back when the car is safely parked

- if in doubt, switch off the phone altogether.

Vodafone supports national legislation to promote safe use of mobile phones to drivers. In the UK, it launched an awareness campaign for customers, to help communicate new UK legislation making it illegal to use handheld phones when driving.

---

the way that Vodafone's products are used. The two articles (below and opposite) on an ethics code and driver safety demonstrate how seriously Vodafone takes its responsibilities in this area.

At a more political level, Vodafone can be affected by major incidents. When London was hit by bombings on 7 July 2005, the authorities disabled the mobile network for a brief period of time, largely over fears that mobile devices might be used to set off bombs, as had happened the year before in Madrid.

Economic influences

The telecommunications industry is perhaps less affected by trends in the general economy than other industries. As telephones and mobiles are increasingly regarded as "must-have" products, customers don't stop spending during economic downturns. However, a more buoyant economic outlook does help Vodafone, and other telecommunications companies, persuade customers to migrate to higher tariff 3G and next-generation services.

Interest rates are important for a company like Vodafone. Like its competitors, it has borrowed significantly to invest in acquiring licences from national governments to allow it to operate, and in building up its transmission network. A low interest rate environment makes it much easier for Vodafone to service its debt.

Competition from other telecommunications companies is a key economic influence on Vodafone. Increasingly strong competition is driving down the cost of calls, giving consumers increasing bargaining power. Vodafone has to work hard to maintain its market share by producing the right combination of price and services that will enable it to retain its existing customers and win new business.

Vodafone has achieved a high growth rate in recent years, in terms of both revenue and numbers of customers. However, like other major players in the industry, it is finding it increasingly difficult to maintain previous levels of growth as the markets in economically developed countries near saturation point. In the future, telecommunications companies might have to rely on emerging markets such as China and less economically developed communities as engines of growth.

Environmental factors

Vodafone must adhere to general environmental legislation as well regulations for control of pollution specific to telecommunications. Electronic waste is one of the biggest environmental issues facing

All our operations generate waste. We are committed to reduce, reuse and recycle where possible. Typical wastes from our network include equipment (such as redundant switches), cables, metal (from antennae and ironwork supports), construction waste, wood and batteries. Our hazardous waste consists mainly of lead acid batteries, used as a back-up power supply for network equipment.

Waste data are notoriously difficult to capture accurately, but we believe our data provide a reasonable indication of the total waste stream. We generated 3,480 tonnes of equipment waste in our network in 2004/05.

This includes 2,445 tonnes of non-hazardous waste (such as radio equipment, metal and cables) and 1,035 tonnes of hazardous waste (mostly lead acid batteries). Of this, 3,340 tonnes (96 per cent) were sent for reuse or recycling [see Figure 14.3]. Other waste streams where we do not have reliable data include wood, concrete and some plastics.

The EU Waste Electronic and Electrical Equipment (WEEE) Directive will come into force in 2006. There is some variation in the implementation of the directive between countries, and we are taking care to adapt our efforts to reflect local variances. We do not generally import handsets into the countries where we operate. However, the handset

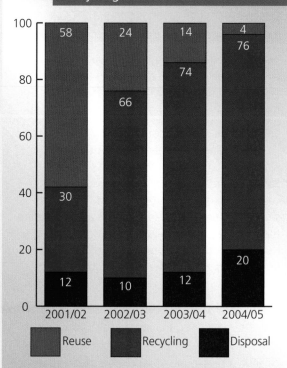

Figure 14.3: Vodafone network equipment waste sent for reuse or recycling

recycling schemes that we have set up in all of our operating companies provide an easily accessible return mechanism for all handsets.

Vodafone 3G customers can now watch a live streamed television news bulletin on their 3G mobile just like they'd see on the box at home.

In a New Zealand first announced today, Vodafone in partnership with Prime News will deliver 3G customers "Prime News: First at 5.30" daily as part of the Sky News streamed channel.

Tim Nichols, head of Vodafone live! says this marks the first evolution of the service since its launch. "For the first time we can now offer a whole show to watch on your mobile at the same time it screens on the TV network. The fact that it's a news show is particularly relevant in today's fast-paced world as many of us need to keep up to date but don't often make it home for the news."

Vodafone has been closely monitoring viewing trends since launching 3G to deliver a service tailored to customer habits. Since launch, figures show the Sky News made-for-mobile channel is the most popular amongst customers, with viewing times spiking around lunchtime, the early evening and late at night.

"As a result of these trends, Vodafone has partnered with Prime to deliver customers a streamed bulletin service during a time when they demand news most – the early evening," says Tim. "Vodafone live! Mobile TV with 3G means you can get news in a way that suits your lifestyle. Whether you're waiting on the bus in traffic or working late, the news is right at your fingertips."

telecommunications companies. Vodafone is aware that it must meet statutory requirements and public expectations that major companies take a responsible attitude to the environment (see box opposite).

Technological influences

As well as the impact of technology on the way Vodafone operates its business, the reliance on new technology to underpin the next generation of products is incredibly important. This requires massive research and development costs. The press release at the bottom of the opposite page is from Vodafone New Zealand. It highlights the rapid evolution of products through technological innovation.

Exploring the future

Businesses rarely have any control over external influences. Therefore it is important that they look to the future to anticipate potential trends and changes to the business environment in which they operate. This is how Vodafone describes its future vision.

Vodafone takes the future very seriously. The mobile communications industry operates at the forefront of technology, and the services it provides are essential tools for people from all walks of life. It offers mainstream mobile services alongside the pioneering new products that will become the indispensable services of tomorrow.

New developments in science and technology, along with shifting socioeconomic trends and increased globalisation, are all having an impact on the way we live and work. Vodafone plans to anticipate and meet the changing needs of all our customers in this constantly evolving environment.

Smarter, smaller devices with faster, "fatter" wireless connectivity are coming. We will soon expect all of these devices, from handheld to household, to "talk" to each other and for all the embedded services to become an invisible feature of our extended, enabled environment. This could challenge existing industry and infrastructure boundaries and charging models, and encourage new alliances and standards to deliver seamless solutions across a multitude of networks and devices.

For this, Vodafone depends on the expertise of its research and development (R&D) and future products specialists worldwide, and their internal and external networks. Both are core to strategic future planning and new product development activity. Vodafone constantly monitors developments and maps trends in areas such as technology and social change. This helps it to think about how emerging technologies could be used to meet people's needs now and in the future.

Research and innovation is not about rashly reacting to exploit every new development: it is evaluating which developments will enable new services or operational improvements to meet real needs, reliably.

Sources

All material adapted from www.vodafone.com, © 2001–2006 Vodafone Group

activities

Looking at the articles and press releases from Vodafone, try to identify where Vodafone has reacted to external influences. These could be legal, economic, environmental or technological influences. You should also consider the influences on the mobile communications industry as a whole.

1. What do you think might happen to Vodafone if the government decided to bring in legislation that banned the use of mobile phones in schools and colleges?

2. What economic effects does intense competition in the telecommunications market have on Vodafone?

3. Do some research into the latest features available on the Vodafone network. What prompted Vodafone to introduce hi-tech features?

4. Take a look at Vodafone's corporate responsibility statement (available on its website) about its impact on society and the environment. Looking at the various issues listed, identify which have been put into practice due to the various external influences that you have covered in this unit. Organise these issues and their influences into legal/political, economic, environmental and technological. Some may fit under more than one category.

Index

Applied Business A2 for Edexcel